You're Reading in the Wrong Direction!!

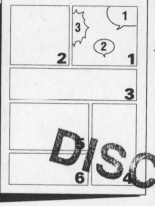

Whoops! Guess what? You're starting at the wrong end of the comic!

...It's true! In keeping with the original Japanese format, **Assassination Classroom** is meant to be read from right to left, starting in the upper-right corner.

Unlike English, which is read from left to right, Japanese is read from right to left, meaning that action, sound effects and word-balloon order are completely reversed... something which can make readers unfamiliar with Japanese feel pretty backwards themselves. For this reason, manga or Japanese comics published in the U.S. in English have sometimes been published "flopped"—that is, printed in exact reverse order, as though seen from the other side of a mirror.

By flopping pages, U.S. publishers can avoid confusing readers, but the compromise is not without its downside. For one thing, a character in a flopped manga series who once wore in the original Japanese version a T-shirt emblazoned with "M A Y" (as in "the merry month of") now wears one which reads "Y A M"! Additionally, many manga creators in Japan are themselves unhappy with the process, as some feel the mirror-imaging of their art skews their original intentions.

We are proud to bring you Yusei Matsui's **Assassination Classroom** in the original unflopped format.
For now, though, turn to the other side of the book and let the adventure begin...!

—Editor

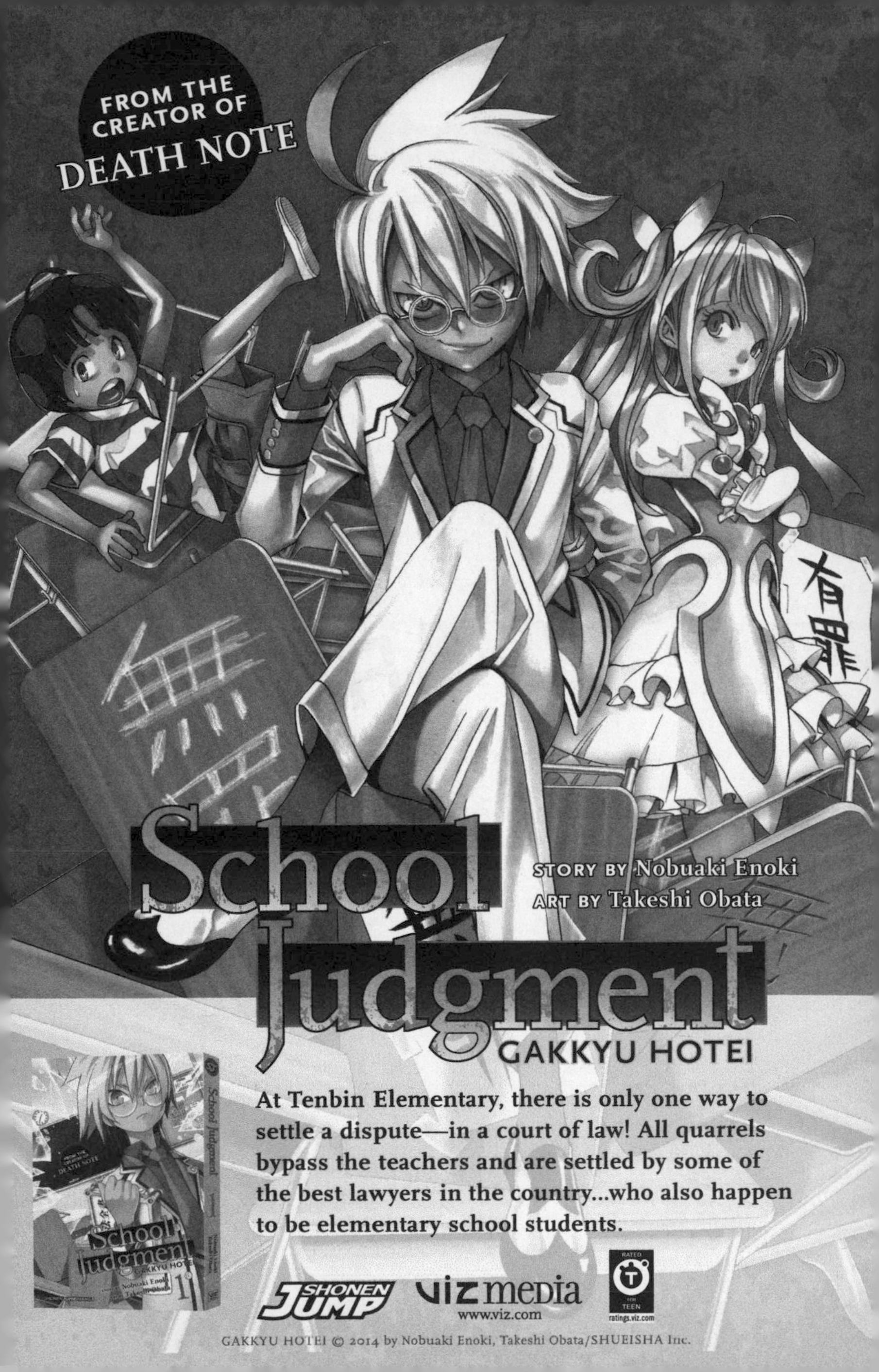
FROM THE CREATOR OF
DEATH NOTE
無罪
有罪
School Judgment
STORY BY Nobuaki Enoki
ART BY Takeshi Obata
GAKKYU HOTEI
At Tenbin Elementary, there is only one way to settle a dispute—in a court of law! All quarrels bypass the teachers and are settled by some of the best lawyers in the country...who also happen to be elementary school students.
SHONEN JUMP
viz media
www.viz.com
RATED T FOR TEEN
ratings.viz.com
GAKKYU HOTEI © 2014 by Nobuaki Enoki, Takeshi Obata/SHUEISHA Inc.

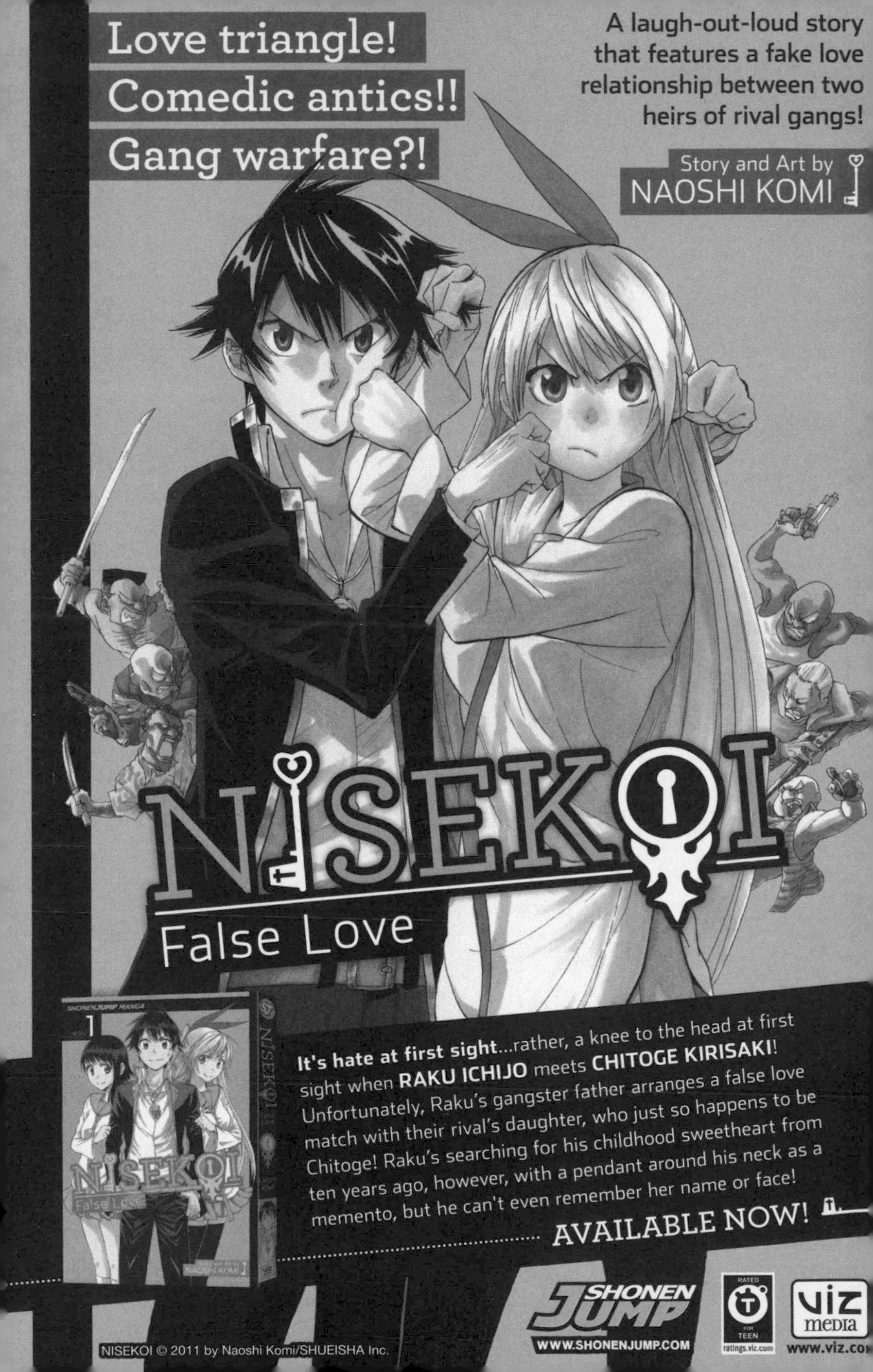
Love triangle!
Comedic antics!!
Gang warfare?!
A laugh-out-loud story that features a fake love relationship between two heirs of rival gangs!
Story and Art by NAOSHI KOMI
NISEKOI
False Love
SHONEN JUMP MANGA
VOL. 1
NISEKOI False Love
Story and Art by NAOSHI KOMI
It's hate at first sight...rather, a knee to the head at first sight when RAKU ICHIJO meets CHITOGE KIRISAKI! Unfortunately, Raku's gangster father arranges a false love match with their rival's daughter, who just so happens to be Chitoge! Raku's searching for his childhood sweetheart from ten years ago, however, with a pendant around his neck as a memento, but he can't even remember her name or face!
AVAILABLE NOW!
SHONEN JUMP
WWW.SHONENJUMP.COM
RATED T FOR TEEN
ratings.viz.com
VIZ media
www.viz.com
NISEKOI © 2011 by Naoshi Komi/SHUEISHA Inc.

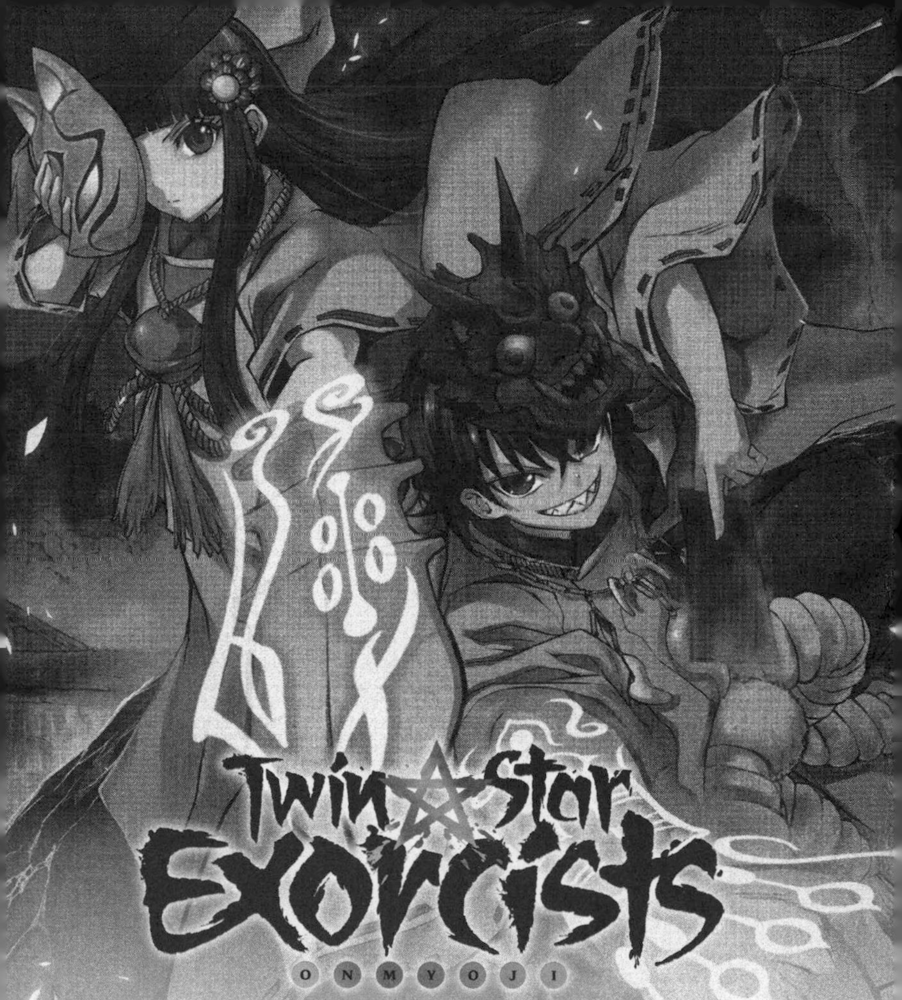
Twin Star Exorcists
O N M Y O J I

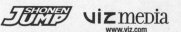

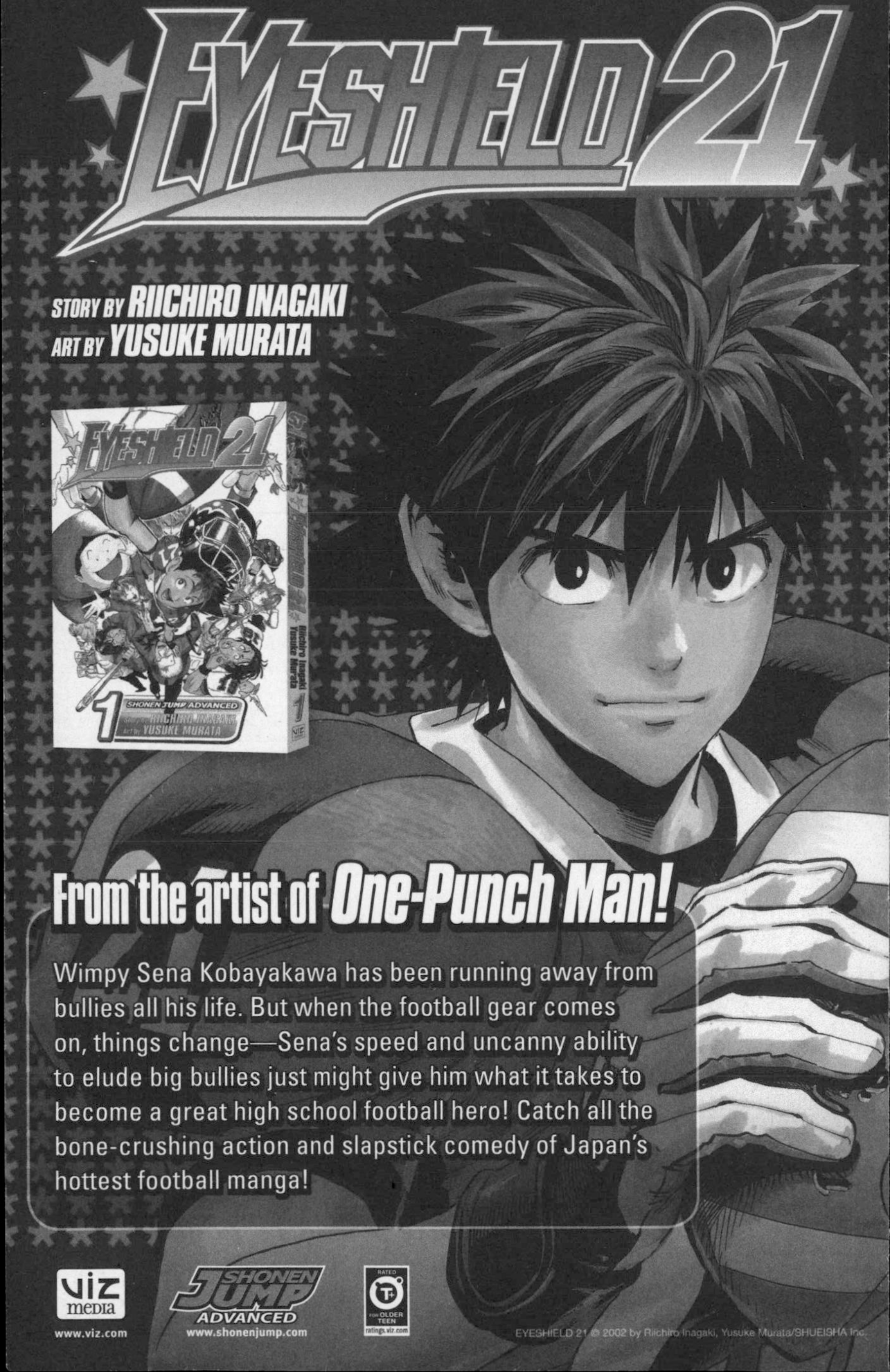
EYESHIELD 21
STORY BY RIICHIRO INAGAKI
ART BY YUSUKE MURATA
From the artist of One-Punch Man!
Wimpy Sena Kobayakawa has been running away from bullies all his life. But when the football gear comes on, things change—Sena's speed and uncanny ability to elude big bullies just might give him what it takes to become a great high school football hero! Catch all the bone-crushing action and slapstick comedy of Japan's hottest football manga!
viz media
www.viz.com
SHONEN JUMP ADVANCED
www.shonenjump.com
RATED T+ FOR OLDER TEEN
ratings.viz.com
EYESHIELD 21 © 2002 by Riichiro Inagaki, Yusuke Murata/SHUEISHA Inc.

ASSASSINATION CLASSROOM

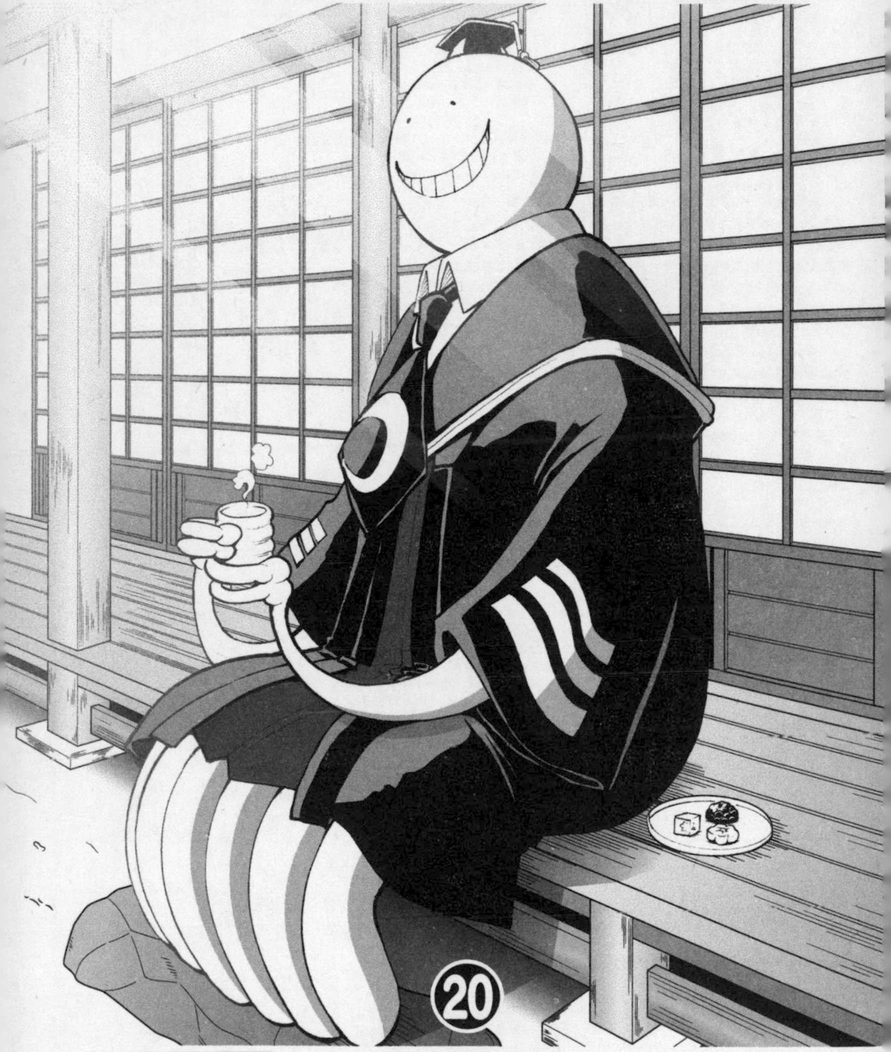
20

TIME TO GRADUATE

YUSEI MATSUI

SHONEN JUMP ADVANCED

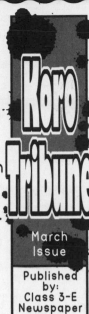

Koro Tribune

March Issue

Published by: Class 3-E Newspaper Staff

Our everyday life has suddenly come to a screeching halt... The countdown to Koro Sensei's assassination has begun!

Story Thus Far

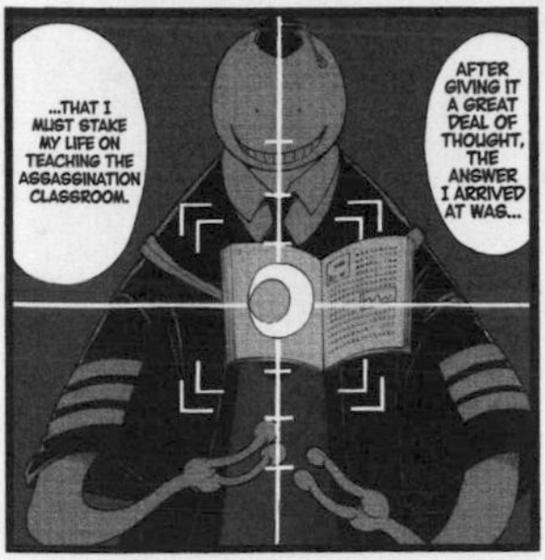
AFTER GIVING IT A GREAT DEAL OF THOUGHT, THE ANSWER I ARRIVED AT WAS...
...THAT I MUST STAKE MY LIFE ON TEACHING THE ASSASSINATION CLASSROOM.

Kunugigaoka Junior High Class 3-E is taught by a monster who even the armies of the world with all their state-of-the-art technology can't kill. That monster, Koro Sensei, is fated to self-destruct and take the planet Earth with him, so...

...a bounty has been placed on his head. It comes down to his students in 3-E, the so-called "End Class." Once looked down upon by the rest of the school, this class of misfits is now respected for the athleticism and powers of concentration they have developed thanks to the dedicated instruction of Koro Sensei and Mr. Karasuma of the Ministry of Defense. A strong bond has formed between the students and Koro Sensei, transcending their relationship as assassins and targets. Then a multinational assassination operation is set in motion, putting Koro Sensei in serious jeopardy. The students manage to get through the firewall of formidable enemies to reach their beloved teacher... but now what?!

Koro Sensei

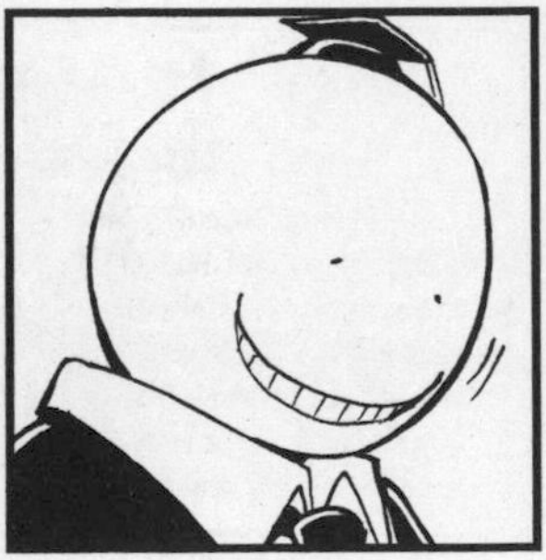

A mysterious, man-made, octopus-like creature whose name is a play on the words "koro senai," which means "can't kill." He is capable of flying at Mach 20 and his versatile tentacles protect him from attacks and aid him in everyday activities. He followed in the footsteps of Aguri, the woman who saved his humanity, by becoming the teacher of Class 3-E.

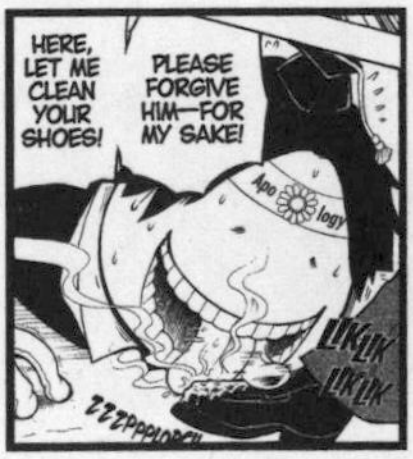
PLEASE FORGIVE HIM—FOR MY SAKE!
HERE, LET ME CLEAN YOUR SHOES!
Apo logy
LIKLIK LIKLIK

Nagisa Shiota

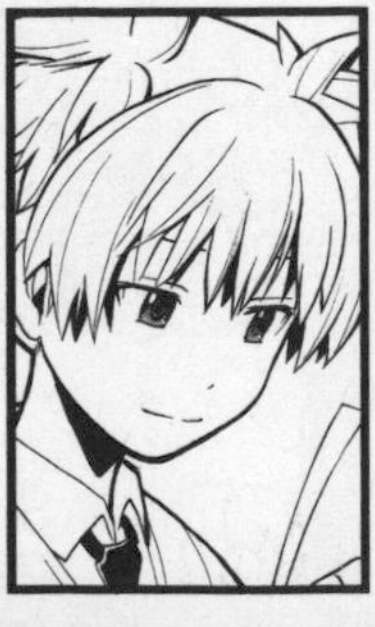

Class E student. He has a hidden talent for assassinations and decides to hone those skills to help others.

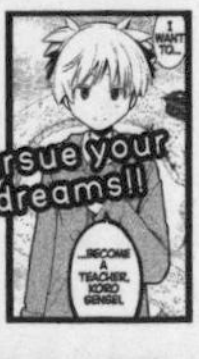
I WANT TO...
Pursue your dreams!!
...BECOME A TEACHER, KORO SENSEI.

He's a good kisser too.

Kaede Kayano

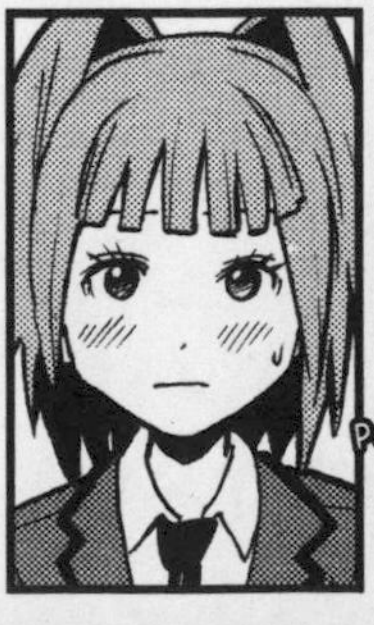

Class E student. She enrolled in Class E to avenge her sister's death by killing Koro Sensei. Her tentacles have since been removed. Does she have special feelings for Nagisa now...?!

Yuma Isogai

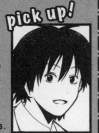

pick up!

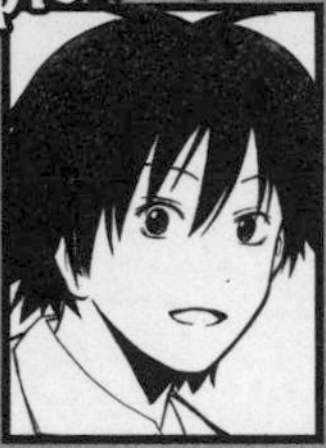

Class E student. When he takes the initiative, he considers the needs of the entire class. That's why his classmates always trust his leadership when it comes to important decisions.

Karma Akabane

Class E student. He learned to take his studies a bit more seriously after some initial failures and earned first place in the overall school scores on the second semester midterm.

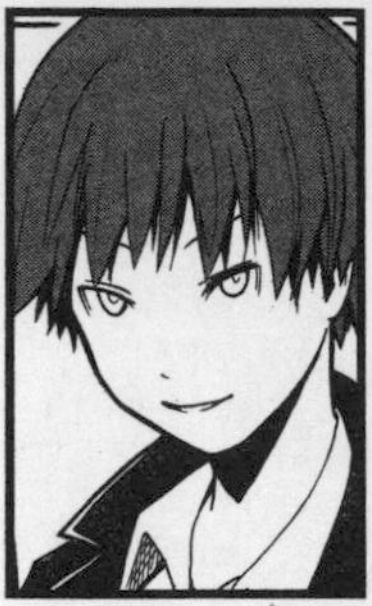

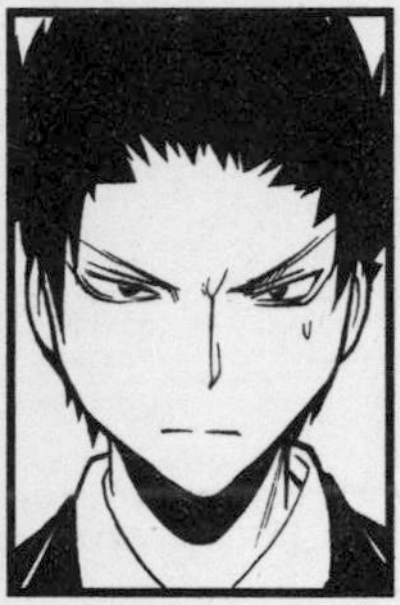

Tadaomi Karasuma

Member of the Ministry of Defense and the Class E students' P.E. teacher. Though serious about his duties, he has successfully built good relationships with his students.

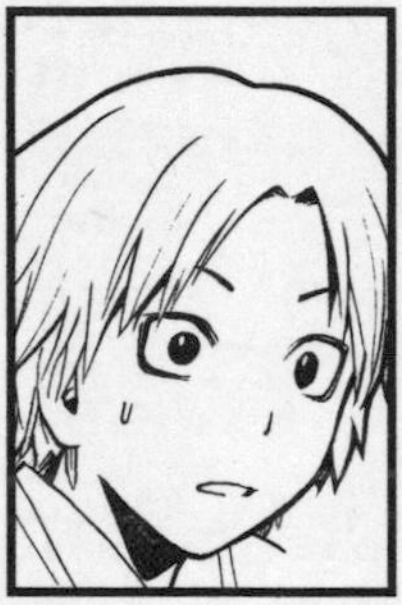

Hiroto Maehara

Class E student. Skilled at both academics and assassinations, he is also the biggest gigolo in Class E. He has been hitting on girls from other schools, but now his heart is finally set on Okano... probably.

Waves of Escapes and Infiltrations!

No frontal assaults! Attack from the shadows! Make full use of all the assassination skills you've learned for a fun-filled rout of even the most experienced mercenaries!!

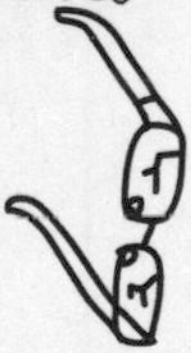

Irina Jelavich

A sexy assassin hired as an English teacher. She's known for using her "womanly charms" to get close to a target. Karasuma has finally admitted that he reciprocates her feelings for him and they have moved in together.

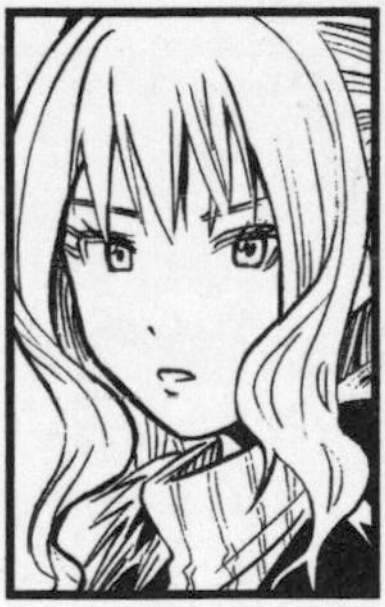

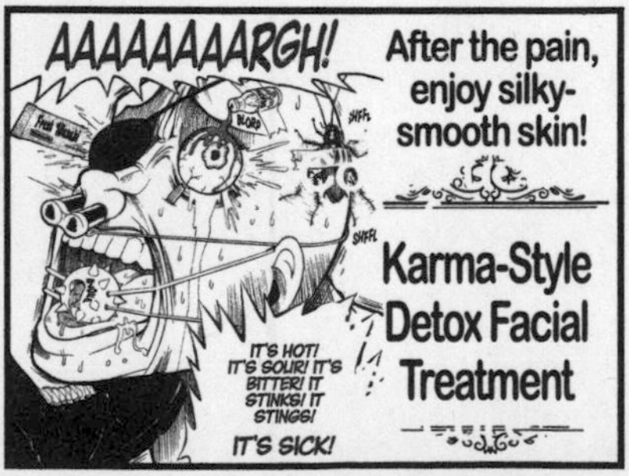
AAAAAAAARGH!
After the pain, enjoy silky-smooth skin!
Karma-Style Detox Facial Treatment
IT'S HOT! IT'S SOUR! IT'S BITTER! IT STINKS! IT STINGS!
IT'S SICK!

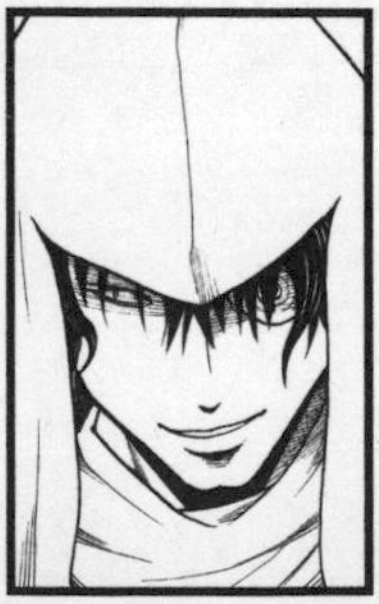

Kotaro Yanagisawa

This scientific genius who created Koro Sensei hates his experimental subject for ruining his reputation and has vowed revenge.

ASSASSINATION CLASSROOM 20 CONTENTS

(ANSWER SHEET)

Grade	3	Class	E	Name	CONTENTS	Score	

...ment, which Japan's climate
...motions and burgeoning
...aristocratic culture
...spread of a writing system
...d development.
...and strong samurai culture
...bination of these cultures
...of war depicting the
...esses of the samurai
...profound work of
...his.
...lt the Golden Pavilion.
...ather and son elevate
...he noh play.
...is built.
...ccomplishments in
...ink brush painting.
...rality of the daimyo
...ularity as a culture
...presented
...held by
...nd
...ed.

...nswer the following questions from ① to ⑥.

(1): Which hieroglyphics were used in ancient Egypt? Choose from A to D.

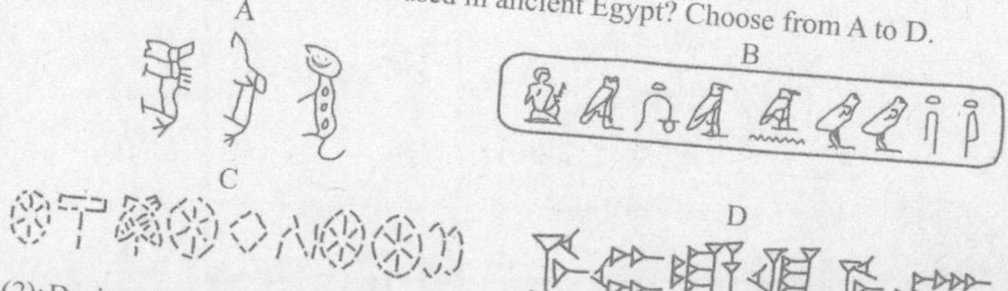

A
B
C
D

(2): During this time period, what is the name of t...
houses of the nobili...

CLASS 170 TIME FOR THE NEXT GENERATION

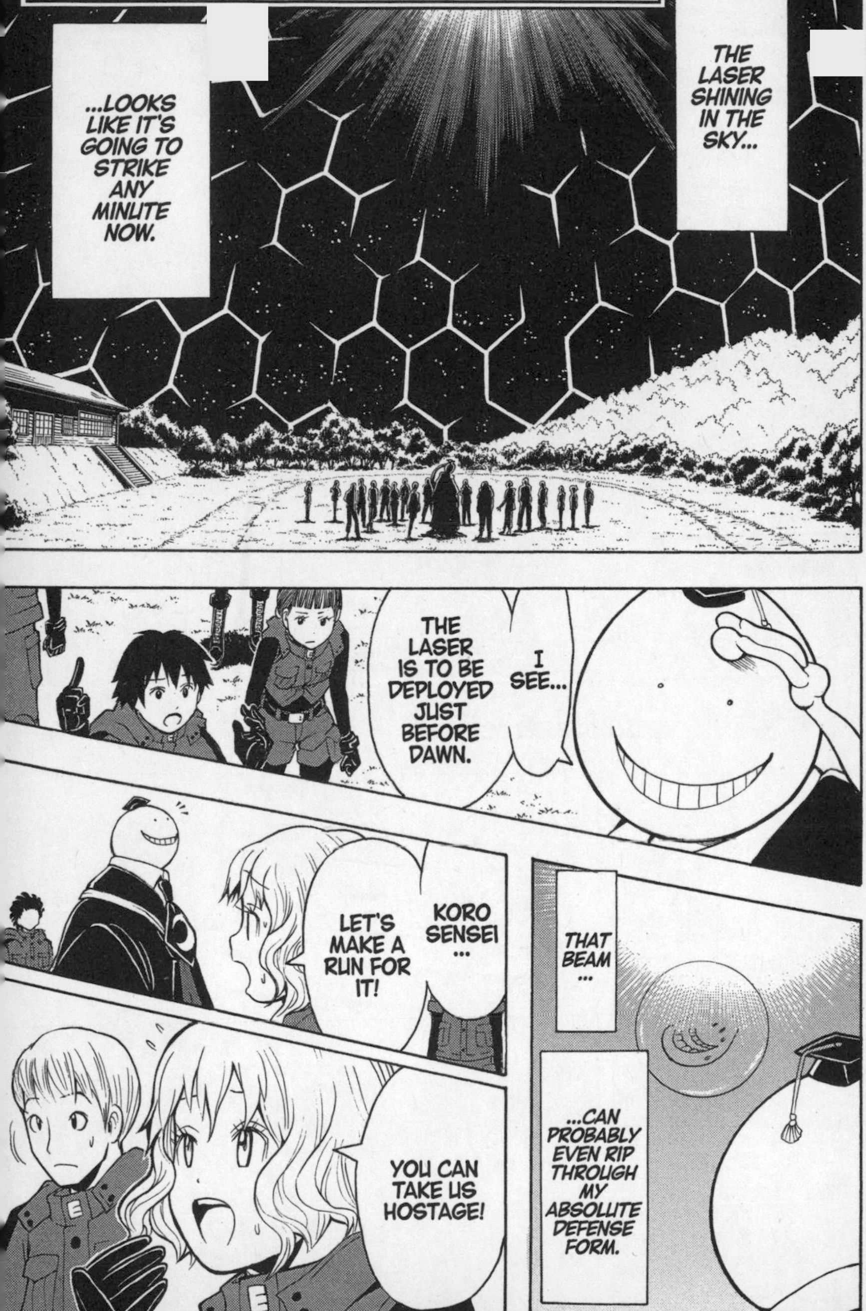
THE LASER SHINING IN THE SKY...
...LOOKS LIKE IT'S GOING TO STRIKE ANY MINUTE NOW.
I SEE...
THE LASER IS TO BE DEPLOYED JUST BEFORE DAWN.
THAT BEAM...
...CAN PROBABLY EVEN RIP THROUGH MY ABSOLUTE DEFENSE FORM.
KORO SENSEI...
LET'S MAKE A RUN FOR IT!
YOU CAN TAKE US HOSTAGE!

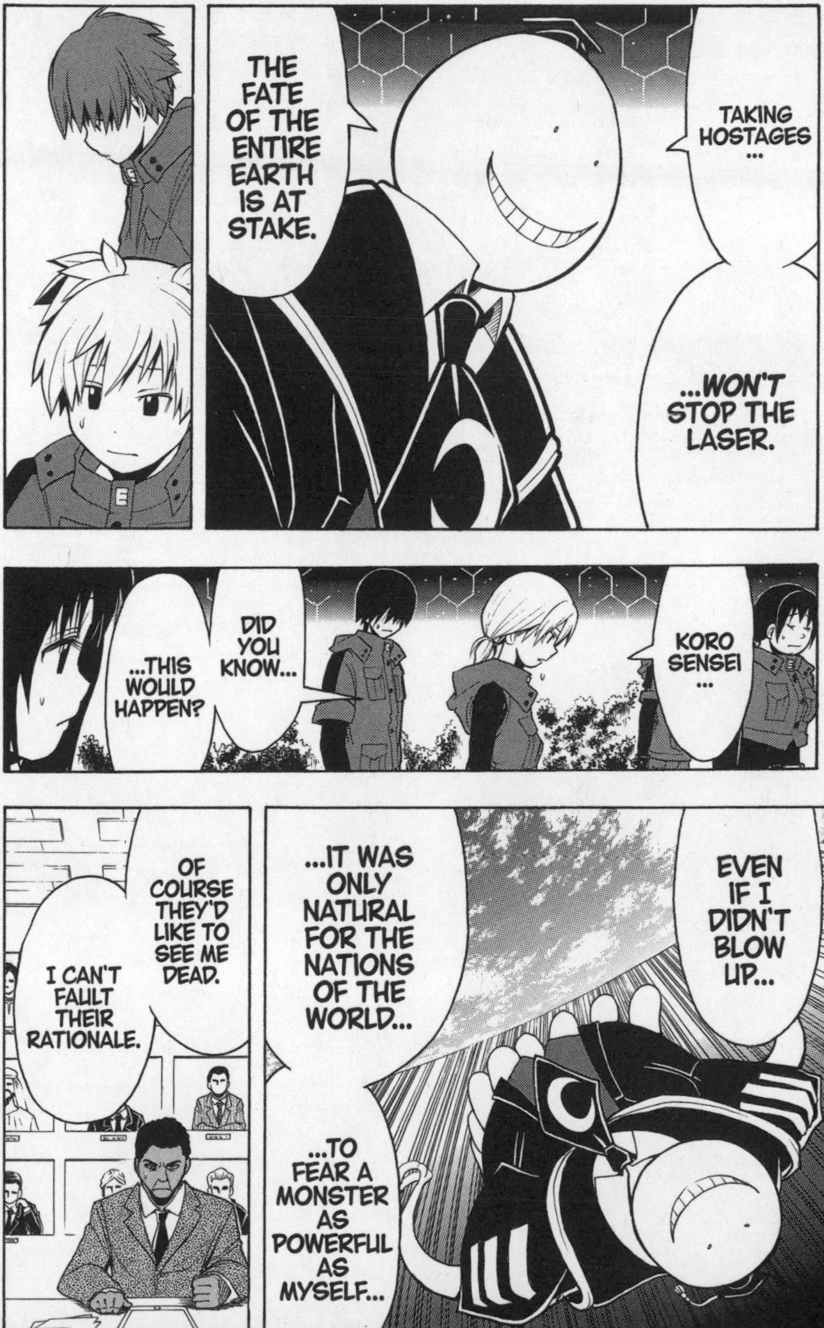
TAKING HOSTAGES ...
...WON'T STOP THE LASER.
THE FATE OF THE ENTIRE EARTH IS AT STAKE.
KORO SENSEI ...
DID YOU KNOW...
...THIS WOULD HAPPEN?
EVEN IF I DIDN'T BLOW UP...
...IT WAS ONLY NATURAL FOR THE NATIONS OF THE WORLD...
...TO FEAR A MONSTER AS POWERFUL AS MYSELF...
OF COURSE THEY'D LIKE TO SEE ME DEAD.
I CAN'T FAULT THEIR RATIONALE.

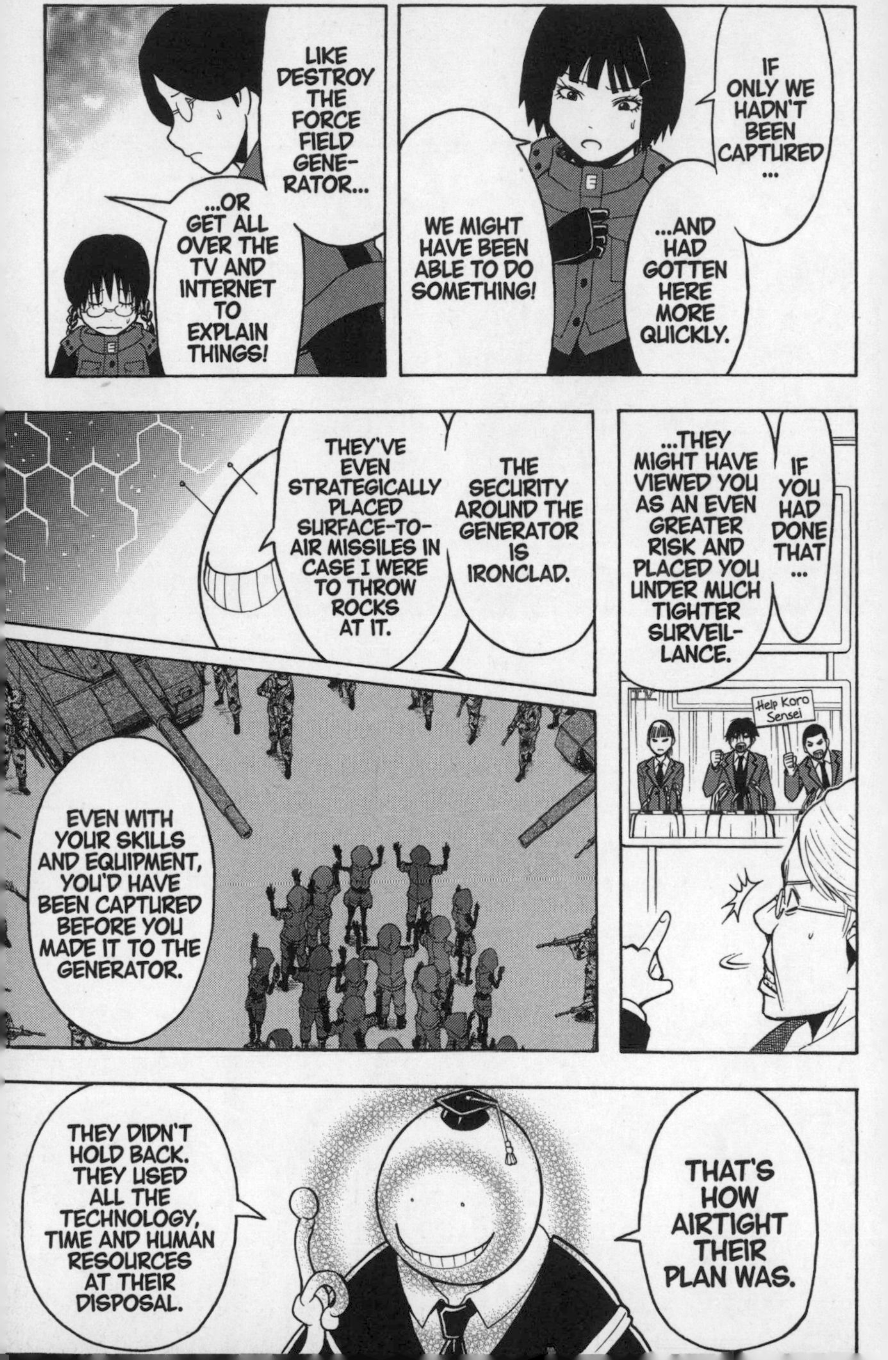
IF ONLY WE HADN'T BEEN CAPTURED...
...AND HAD GOTTEN HERE MORE QUICKLY.
WE MIGHT HAVE BEEN ABLE TO DO SOMETHING!
LIKE DESTROY THE FORCE FIELD GENERATOR...
...OR GET ALL OVER THE TV AND INTERNET TO EXPLAIN THINGS!
IF YOU HAD DONE THAT...
...THEY MIGHT HAVE VIEWED YOU AS AN EVEN GREATER RISK AND PLACED YOU UNDER MUCH TIGHTER SURVEIL-LANCE.
TV
Help Koro Sensei
THE SECURITY AROUND THE GENERATOR IS IRONCLAD.
THEY'VE EVEN STRATEGICALLY PLACED SURFACE-TO-AIR MISSILES IN CASE I WERE TO THROW ROCKS AT IT.
EVEN WITH YOUR SKILLS AND EQUIPMENT, YOU'D HAVE BEEN CAPTURED BEFORE YOU MADE IT TO THE GENERATOR.
THAT'S HOW AIRTIGHT THEIR PLAN WAS.
THEY DIDN'T HOLD BACK. THEY USED ALL THE TECHNOLOGY, TIME AND HUMAN RESOURCES AT THEIR DISPOSAL.

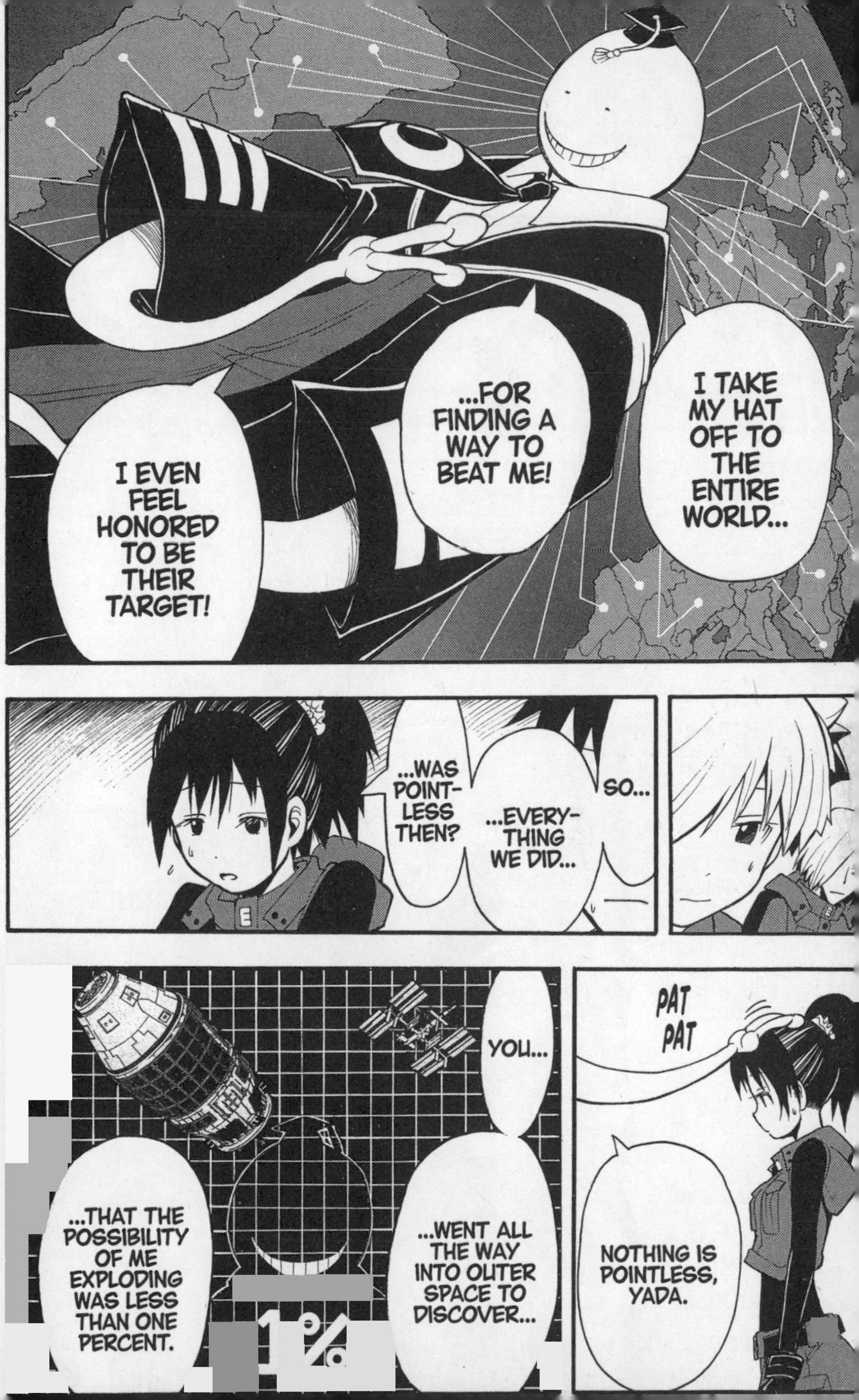
I TAKE MY HAT OFF TO THE ENTIRE WORLD...
...FOR FINDING A WAY TO BEAT ME!
I EVEN FEEL HONORED TO BE THEIR TARGET!
SO...
...EVERYTHING WE DID...
...WAS POINTLESS THEN?
PAT PAT
NOTHING IS POINTLESS, YADA.
YOU...
...WENT ALL THE WAY INTO OUTER SPACE TO DISCOVER...
...THAT THE POSSIBILITY OF ME EXPLODING WAS LESS THAN ONE PERCENT.
1%

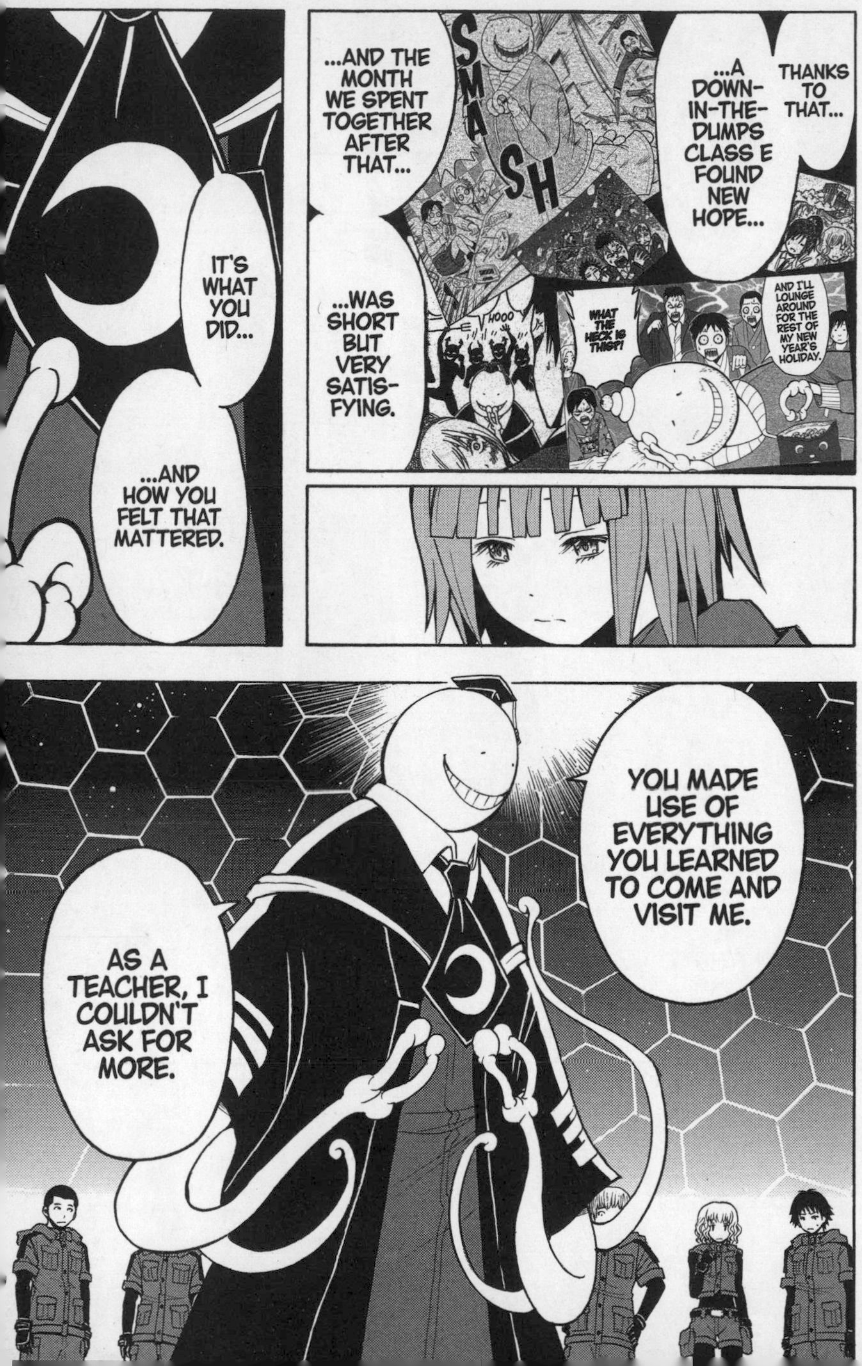
THANKS TO THAT...
...A DOWN-IN-THE-DUMPS CLASS E FOUND NEW HOPE...
...AND THE MONTH WE SPENT TOGETHER AFTER THAT...
SMASH
AND I'LL LOUNGE AROUND FOR THE REST OF MY NEW YEAR'S HOLIDAY.
WHAT THE HECK IS THIS?!
HOOO
...WAS SHORT BUT VERY SATISFYING.
IT'S WHAT YOU DID...
...AND HOW YOU FELT THAT MATTERED.
YOU MADE USE OF EVERYTHING YOU LEARNED TO COME AND VISIT ME.
AS A TEACHER, I COULDN'T ASK FOR MORE.

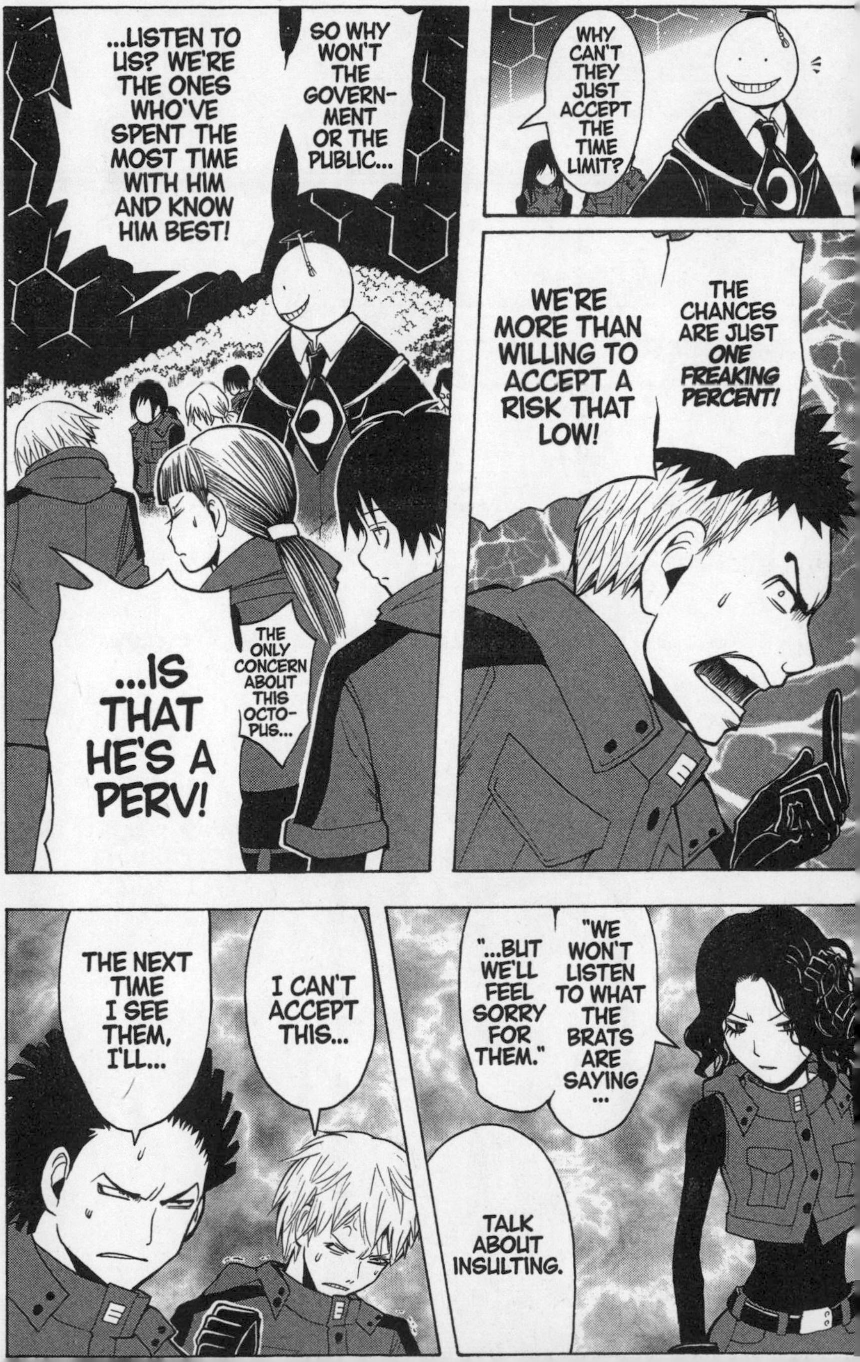
WHY CAN'T THEY JUST ACCEPT THE TIME LIMIT?
THE CHANCES ARE JUST ONE FREAKING PERCENT!
WE'RE MORE THAN WILLING TO ACCEPT A RISK THAT LOW!
SO WHY WON'T THE GOVERNMENT OR THE PUBLIC...
...LISTEN TO US? WE'RE THE ONES WHO'VE SPENT THE MOST TIME WITH HIM AND KNOW HIM BEST!
THE ONLY CONCERN ABOUT THIS OCTOPUS...
...IS THAT HE'S A PERV!
"WE WON'T LISTEN TO WHAT THE BRATS ARE SAYING...
"...BUT WE'LL FEEL SORRY FOR THEM."
TALK ABOUT INSULTING.
I CAN'T ACCEPT THIS...
THE NEXT TIME I SEE THEM, I'LL...

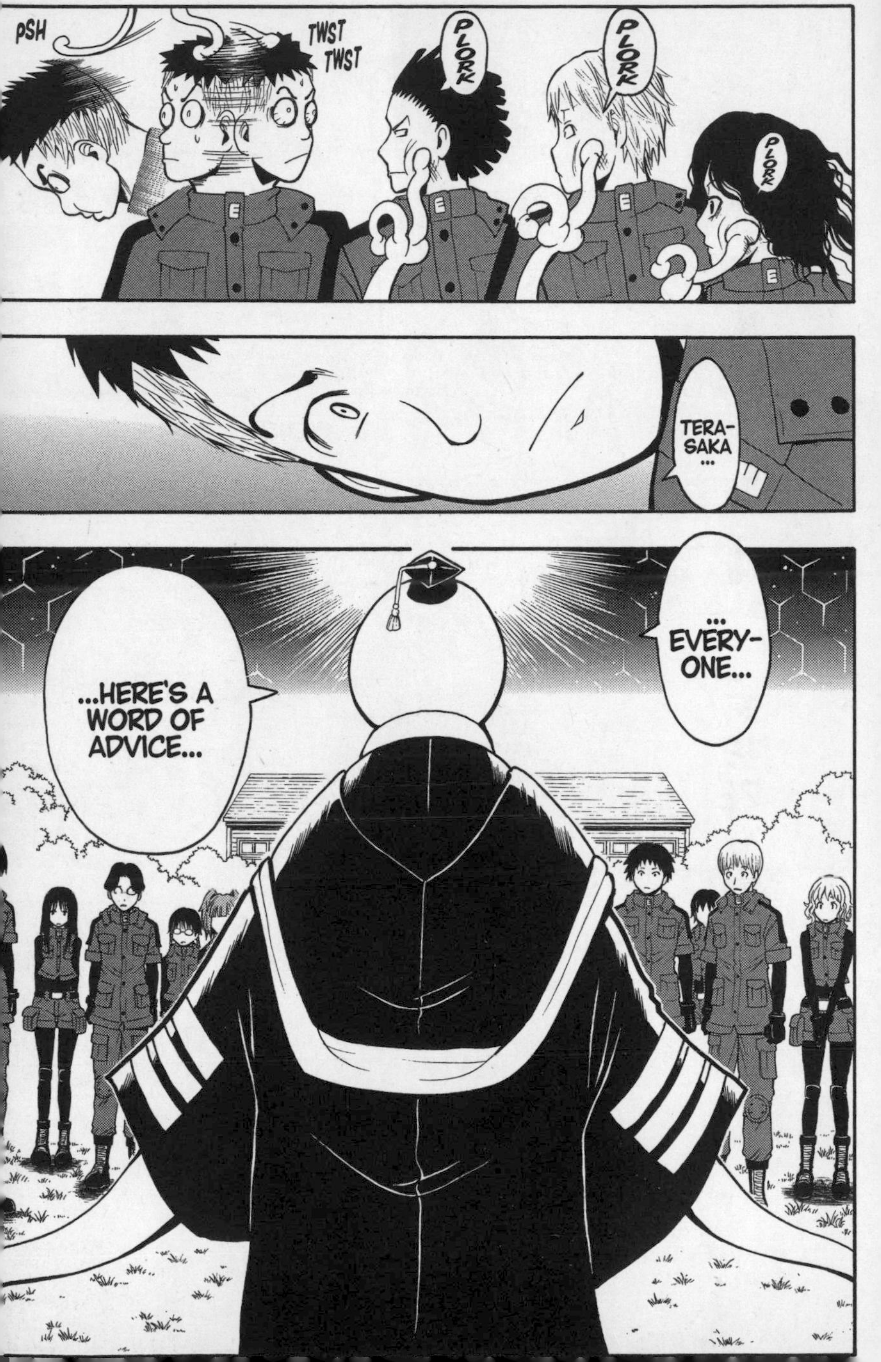
PLORK
PLORK
PLORK
TWST TWST
PSH
TERA-SAKA...
...EVERY-ONE...
...HERE'S A WORD OF ADVICE...

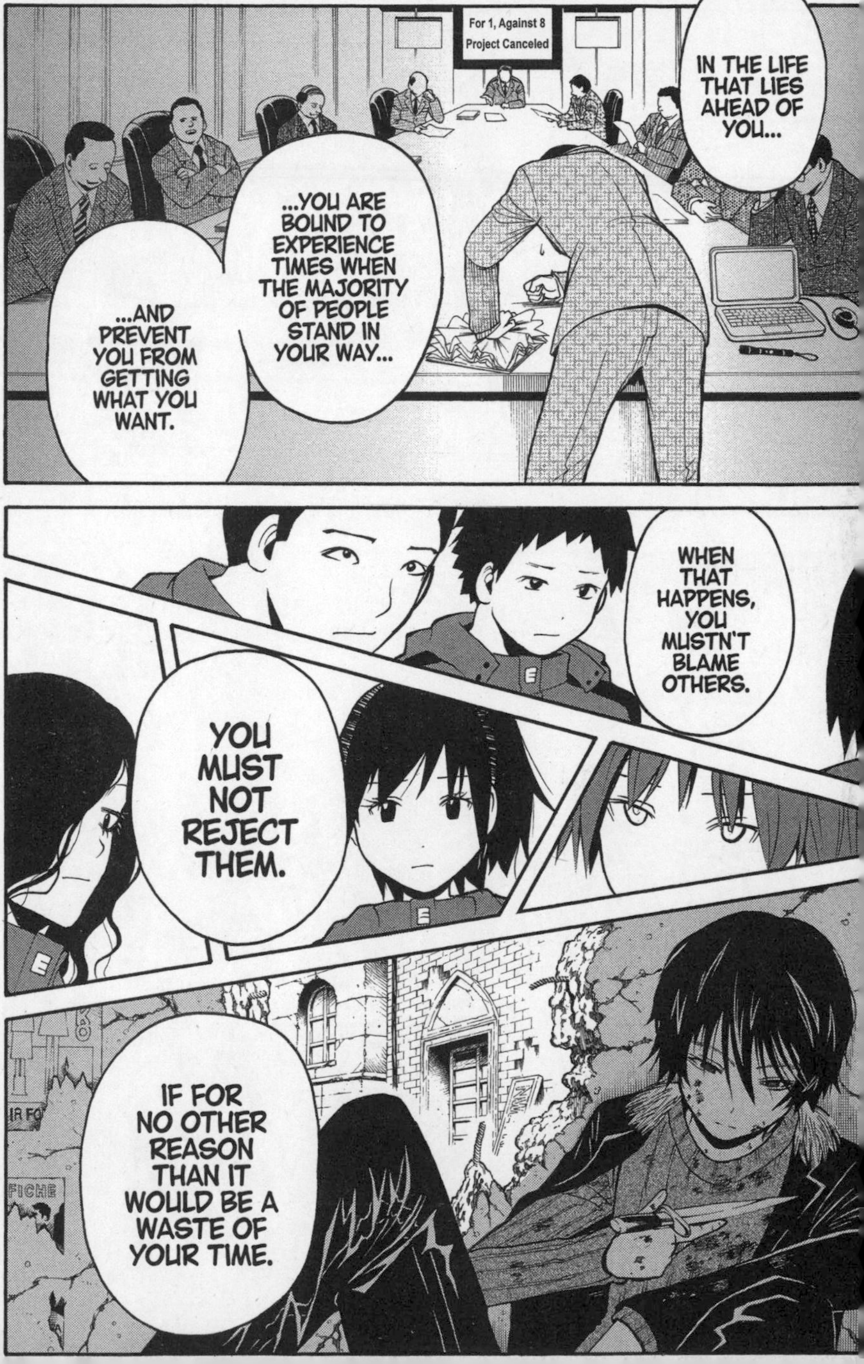
IN THE LIFE THAT LIES AHEAD OF YOU...
For 1, Against 8
Project Canceled
...YOU ARE BOUND TO EXPERIENCE TIMES WHEN THE MAJORITY OF PEOPLE STAND IN YOUR WAY...
...AND PREVENT YOU FROM GETTING WHAT YOU WANT.
WHEN THAT HAPPENS, YOU MUSTN'T BLAME OTHERS.
YOU MUST NOT REJECT THEM.
IF FOR NO OTHER REASON THAN IT WOULD BE A WASTE OF YOUR TIME.

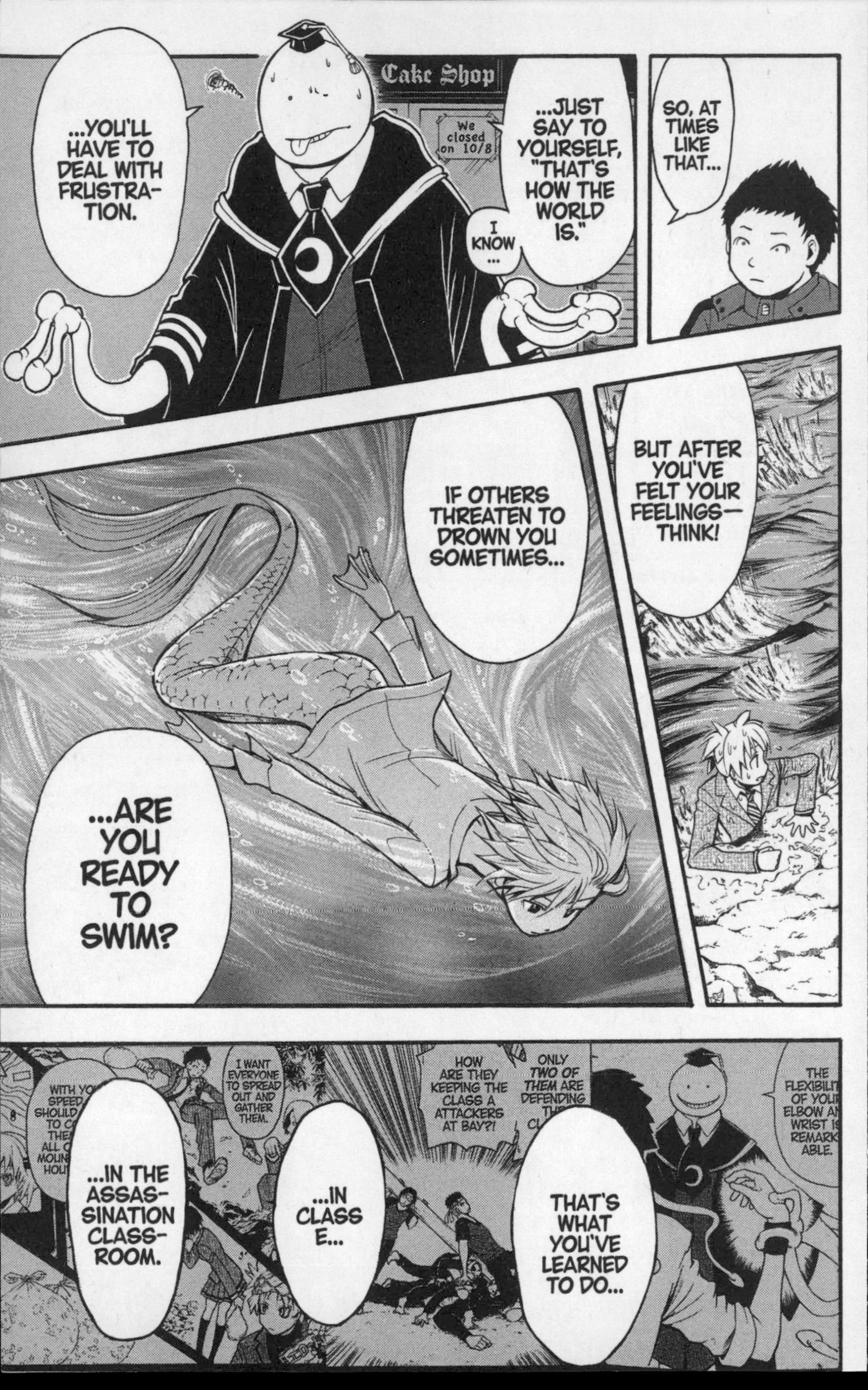
SO, AT TIMES LIKE THAT...
Cake Shop
We closed on 10/8
...JUST SAY TO YOURSELF, "THAT'S HOW THE WORLD IS."
I KNOW ...
...YOU'LL HAVE TO DEAL WITH FRUSTRATION.
BUT AFTER YOU'VE FELT YOUR FEELINGS— THINK!
IF OTHERS THREATEN TO DROWN YOU SOMETIMES...
...ARE YOU READY TO SWIM?
THE FLEXIBILIT OF YOUR ELBOW AN WRIST I REMARK ABLE.
THAT'S WHAT YOU'VE LEARNED TO DO...
ONLY TWO OF THEM ARE DEFENDING TH CL
HOW ARE THEY KEEPING THE CLASS A ATTACKERS AT BAY?!
...IN CLASS E...
I WANT EVERYONE TO SPREAD OUT AND GATHER THEM.
WITH YO SPEED SHOULD TO C THEM ALL C MOUN HOL
...IN THE ASSASSINATION CLASSROOM.

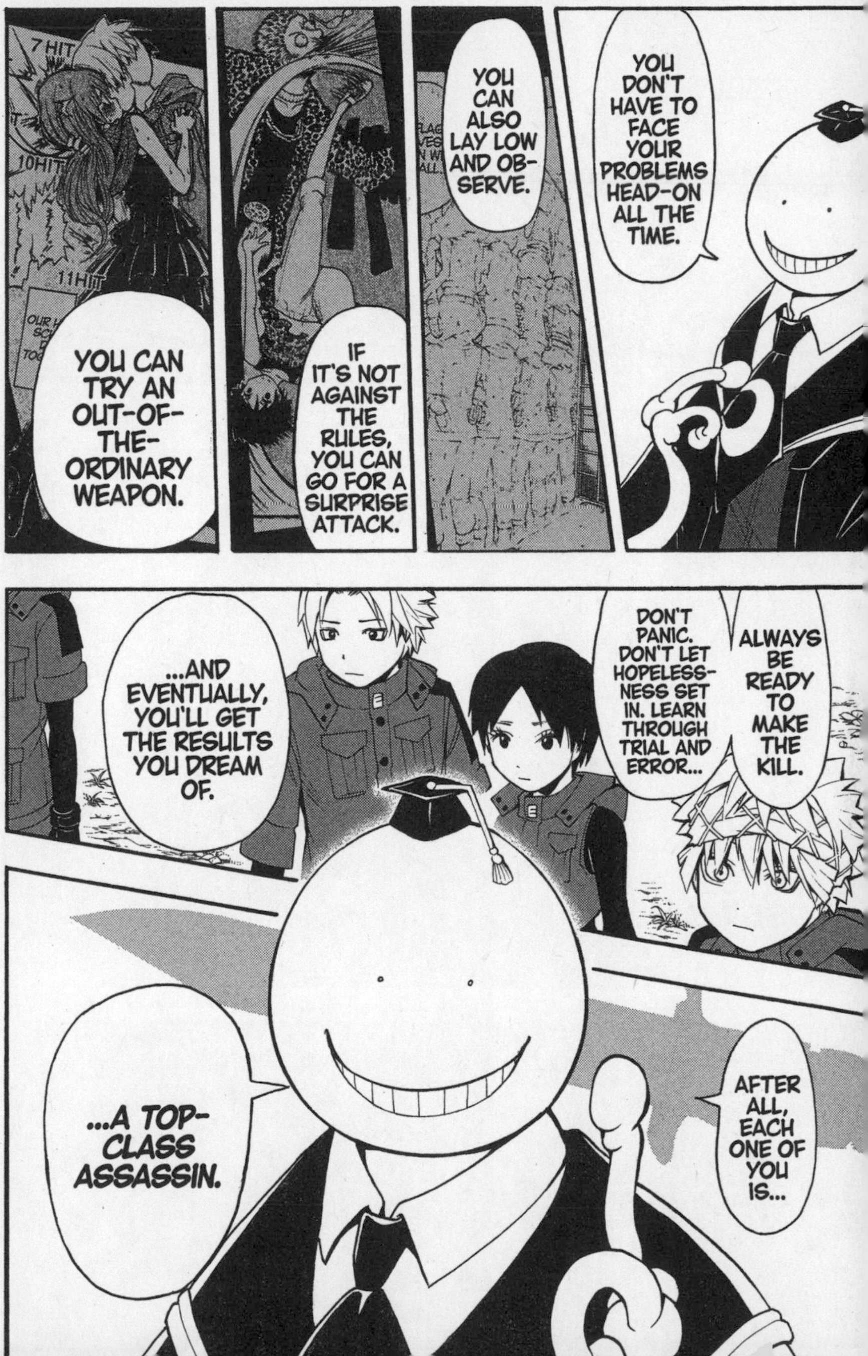
YOU DON'T HAVE TO FACE YOUR PROBLEMS HEAD-ON ALL THE TIME.
YOU CAN ALSO LAY LOW AND OB-SERVE.
IF IT'S NOT AGAINST THE RULES, YOU CAN GO FOR A SURPRISE ATTACK.
7 HIT
10HIT
11HIT
YOU CAN TRY AN OUT-OF-THE-ORDINARY WEAPON.
ALWAYS BE READY TO MAKE THE KILL.
DON'T PANIC. DON'T LET HOPELESS-NESS SET IN. LEARN THROUGH TRIAL AND ERROR...
...AND EVENTUALLY, YOU'LL GET THE RESULTS YOU DREAM OF.
AFTER ALL, EACH ONE OF YOU IS...
...A TOP-CLASS ASSASSIN.

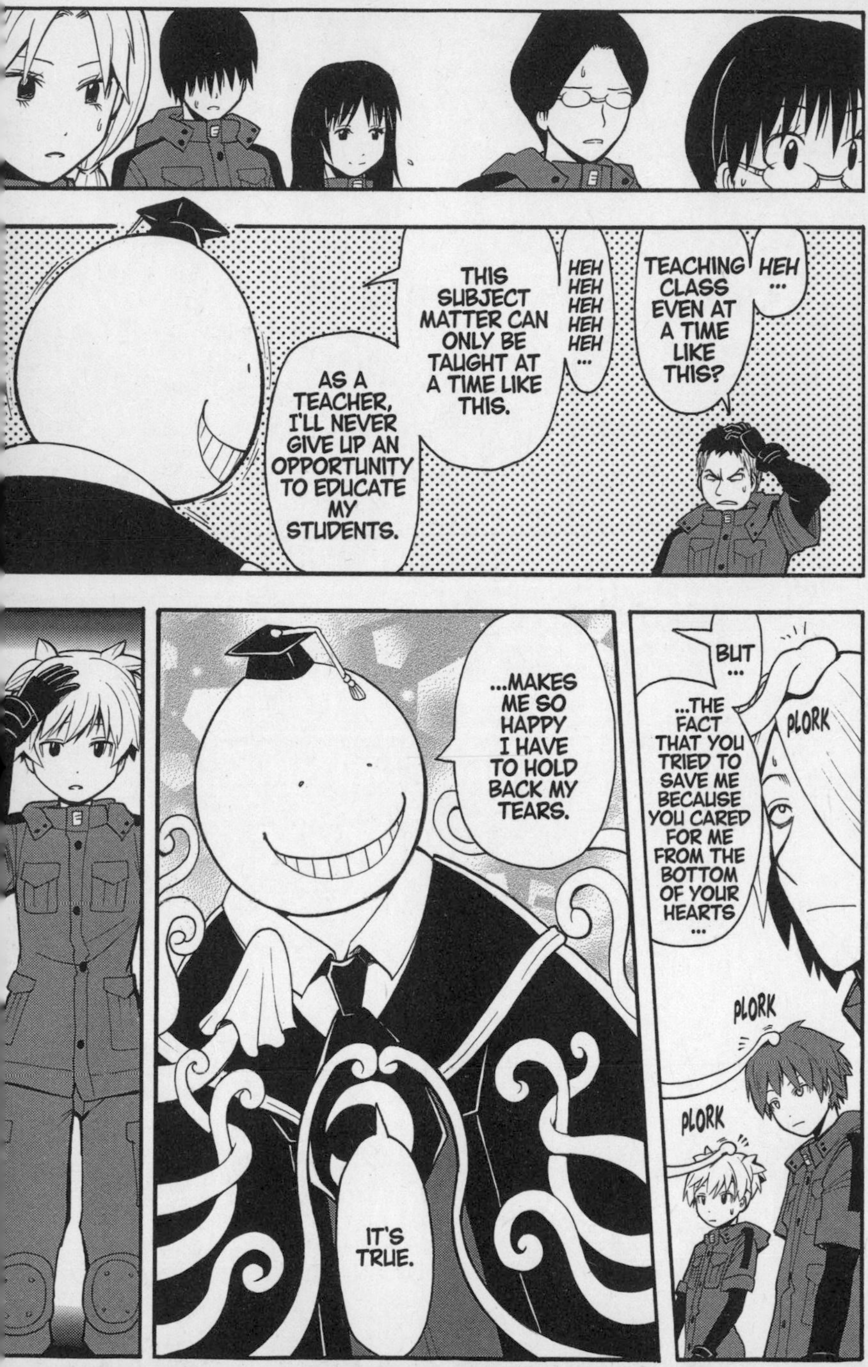
HEH ...
TEACHING CLASS EVEN AT A TIME LIKE THIS?
HEH HEH HEH HEH HEH ...
THIS SUBJECT MATTER CAN ONLY BE TAUGHT AT A TIME LIKE THIS.
AS A TEACHER, I'LL NEVER GIVE UP AN OPPORTUNITY TO EDUCATE MY STUDENTS.
BUT ...
...THE FACT THAT YOU TRIED TO SAVE ME BECAUSE YOU CARED FOR ME FROM THE BOTTOM OF YOUR HEARTS ...
PLORK
PLORK
PLORK
...MAKES ME SO HAPPY I HAVE TO HOLD BACK MY TEARS.
IT'S TRUE.

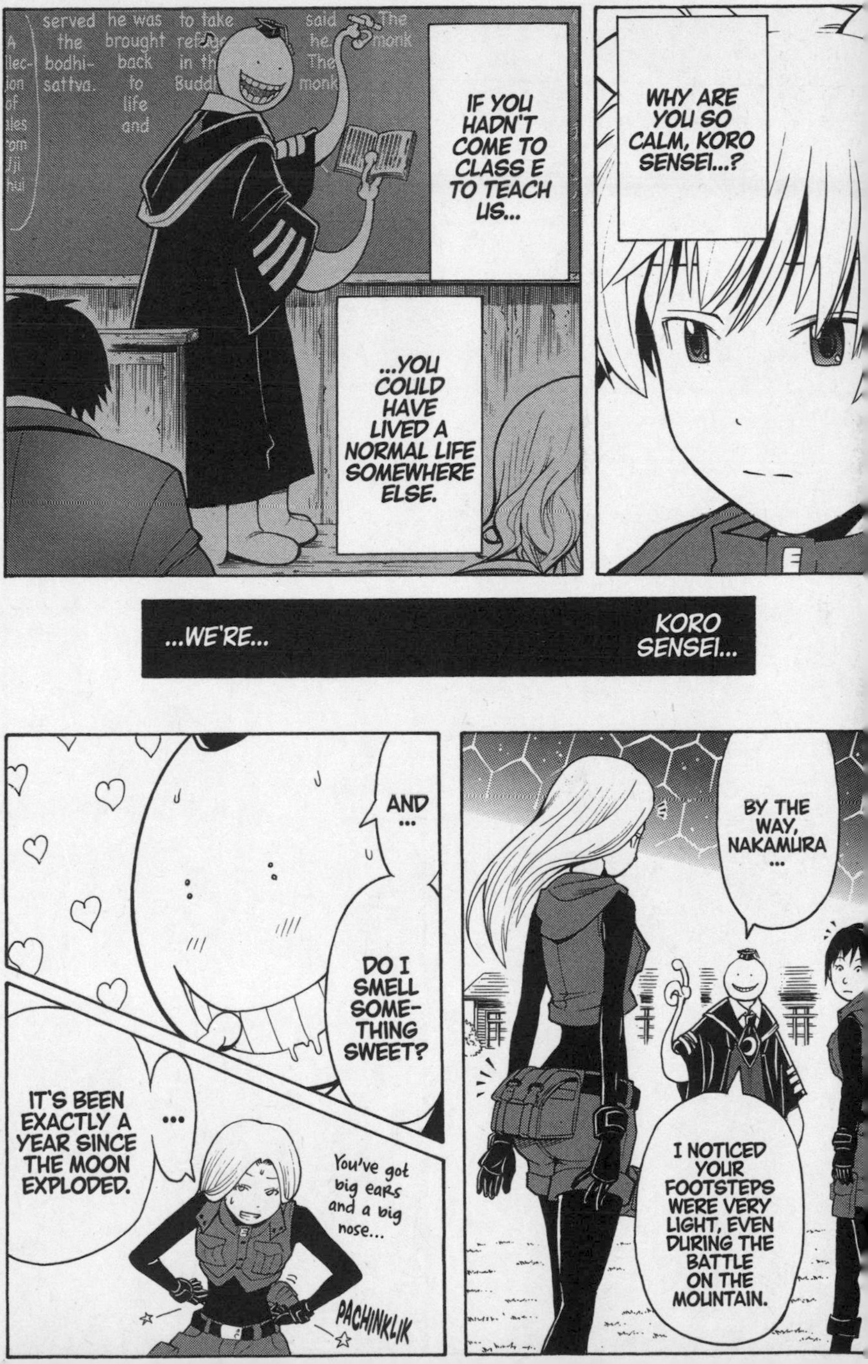
WHY ARE YOU SO CALM, KORO SENSEI...?
IF YOU HADN'T COME TO CLASS E TO TEACH US...
...YOU COULD HAVE LIVED A NORMAL LIFE SOMEWHERE ELSE.
KORO SENSEI...
...WE'RE...
BY THE WAY, NAKAMURA...
I NOTICED YOUR FOOTSTEPS WERE VERY LIGHT, EVEN DURING THE BATTLE ON THE MOUNTAIN.
AND...
DO I SMELL SOMETHING SWEET?
...
IT'S BEEN EXACTLY A YEAR SINCE THE MOON EXPLODED.
You've got big ears and a big nose...
PACHINKLIK

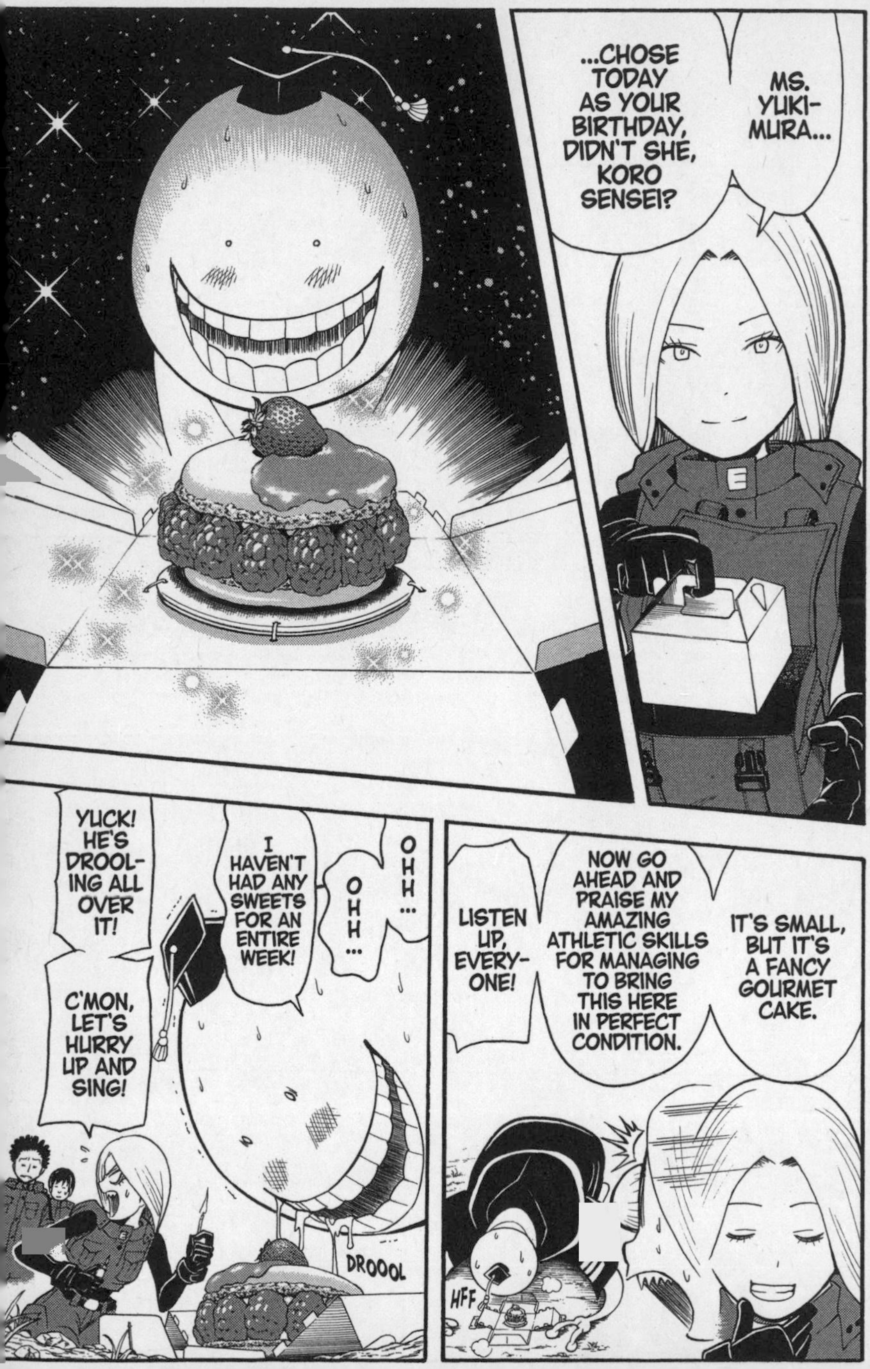
MS. YUKI-MURA...
...CHOSE TODAY AS YOUR BIRTHDAY, DIDN'T SHE, KORO SENSEI?
IT'S SMALL, BUT IT'S A FANCY GOURMET CAKE.
NOW GO AHEAD AND PRAISE MY AMAZING ATHLETIC SKILLS FOR MANAGING TO BRING THIS HERE IN PERFECT CONDITION.
LISTEN UP, EVERY-ONE!
HFF
OHH...
OHH...
I HAVEN'T HAD ANY SWEETS FOR AN ENTIRE WEEK!
YUCK! HE'S DROOL-ING ALL OVER IT!
C'MON, LET'S HURRY UP AND SING!
DROOOL

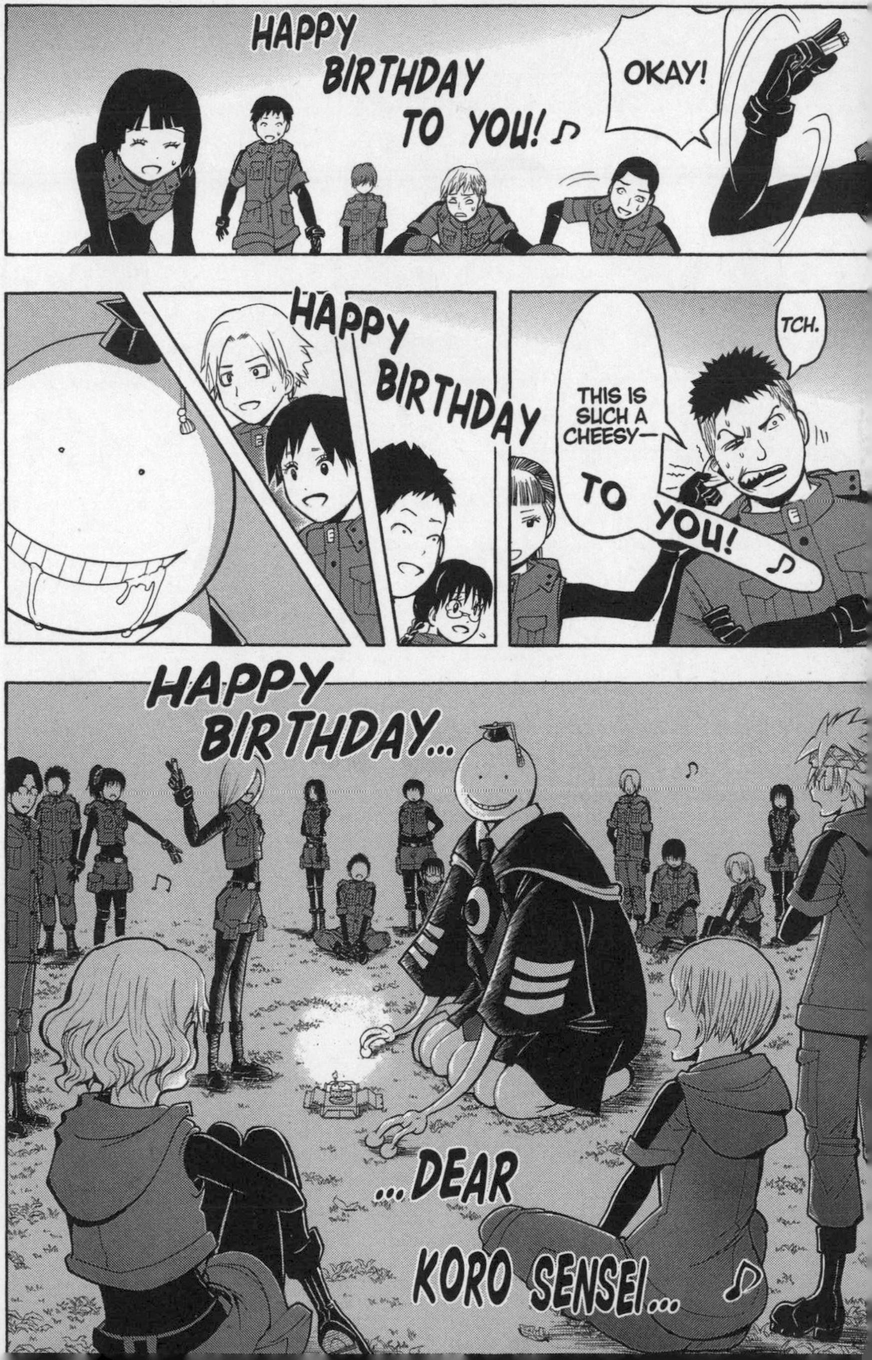

OKAY!
HAPPY BIRTHDAY TO YOU! ♪
TCH.
THIS IS SUCH A CHEESY—
HAPPY BIRTHDAY
TO YOU! ♪
HAPPY BIRTHDAY...
...DEAR
KORO SENSEI... ♪

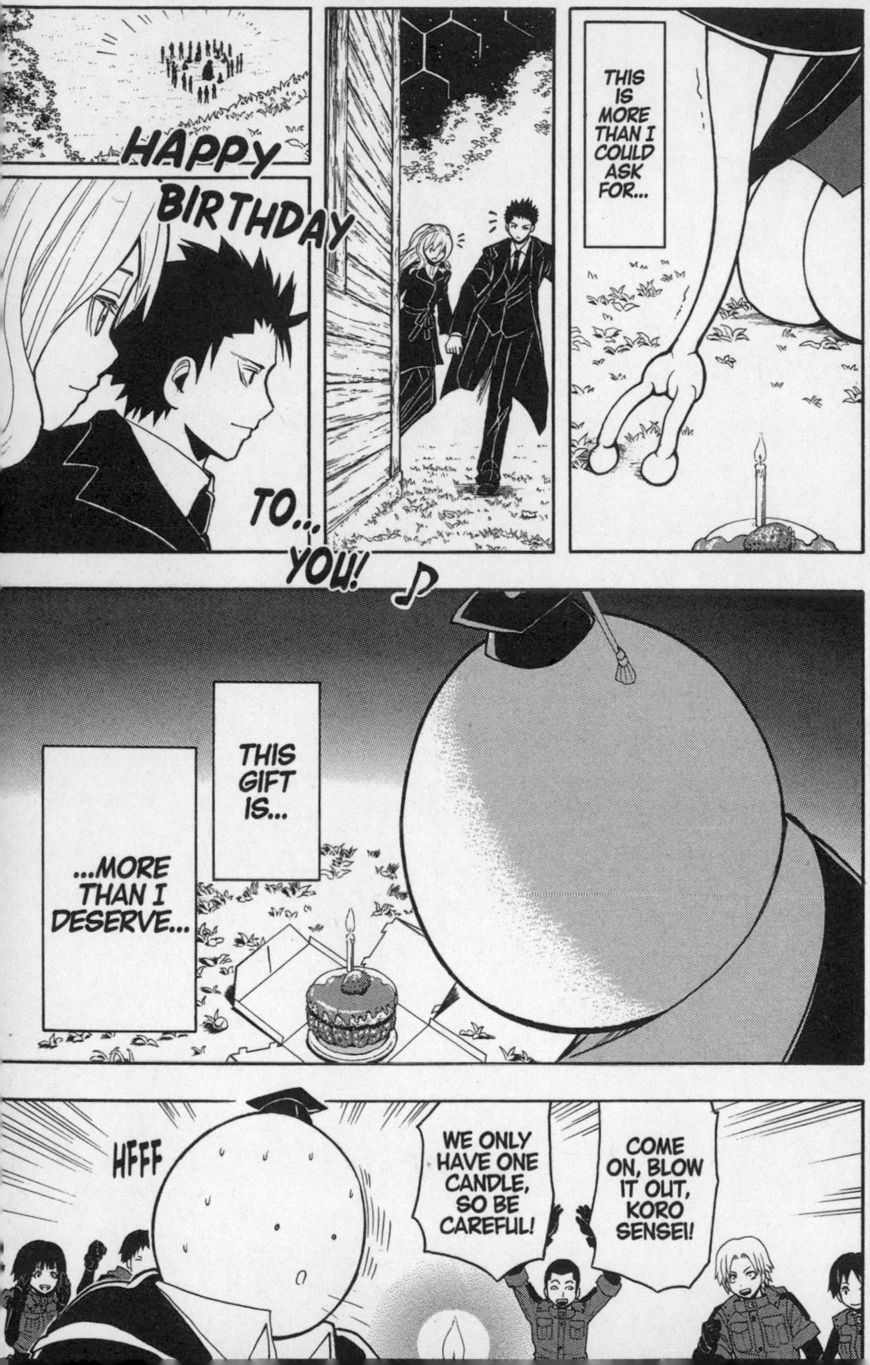
THIS IS MORE THAN I COULD ASK FOR...
HAPPY BIRTHDAY
TO...
YOU!
THIS GIFT IS...
...MORE THAN I DESERVE...
COME ON, BLOW IT OUT, KORO SENSEI!
WE ONLY HAVE ONE CANDLE, SO BE CAREFUL!
HFFF

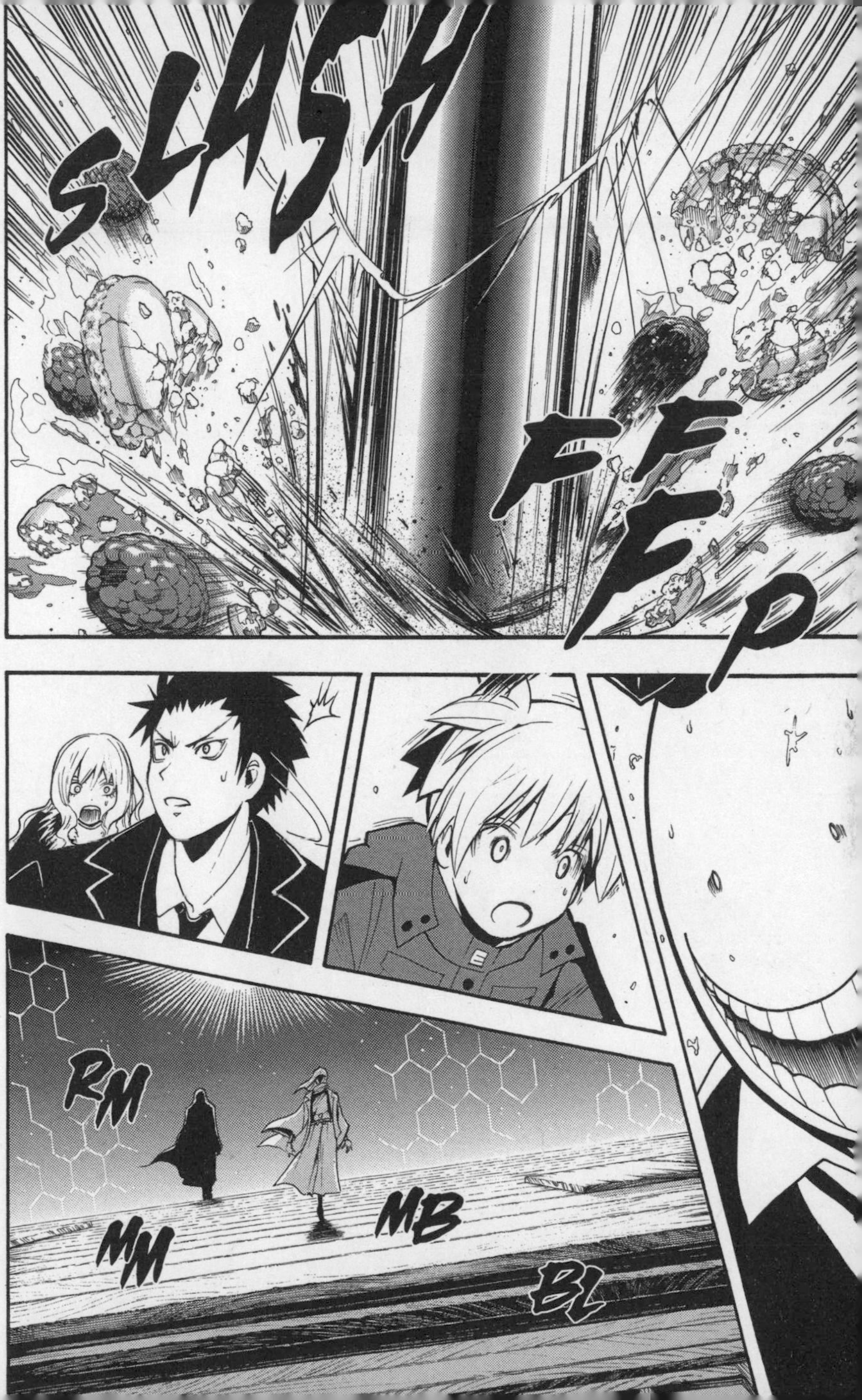
SLASH
FFFP
RM
MM
MB
BL

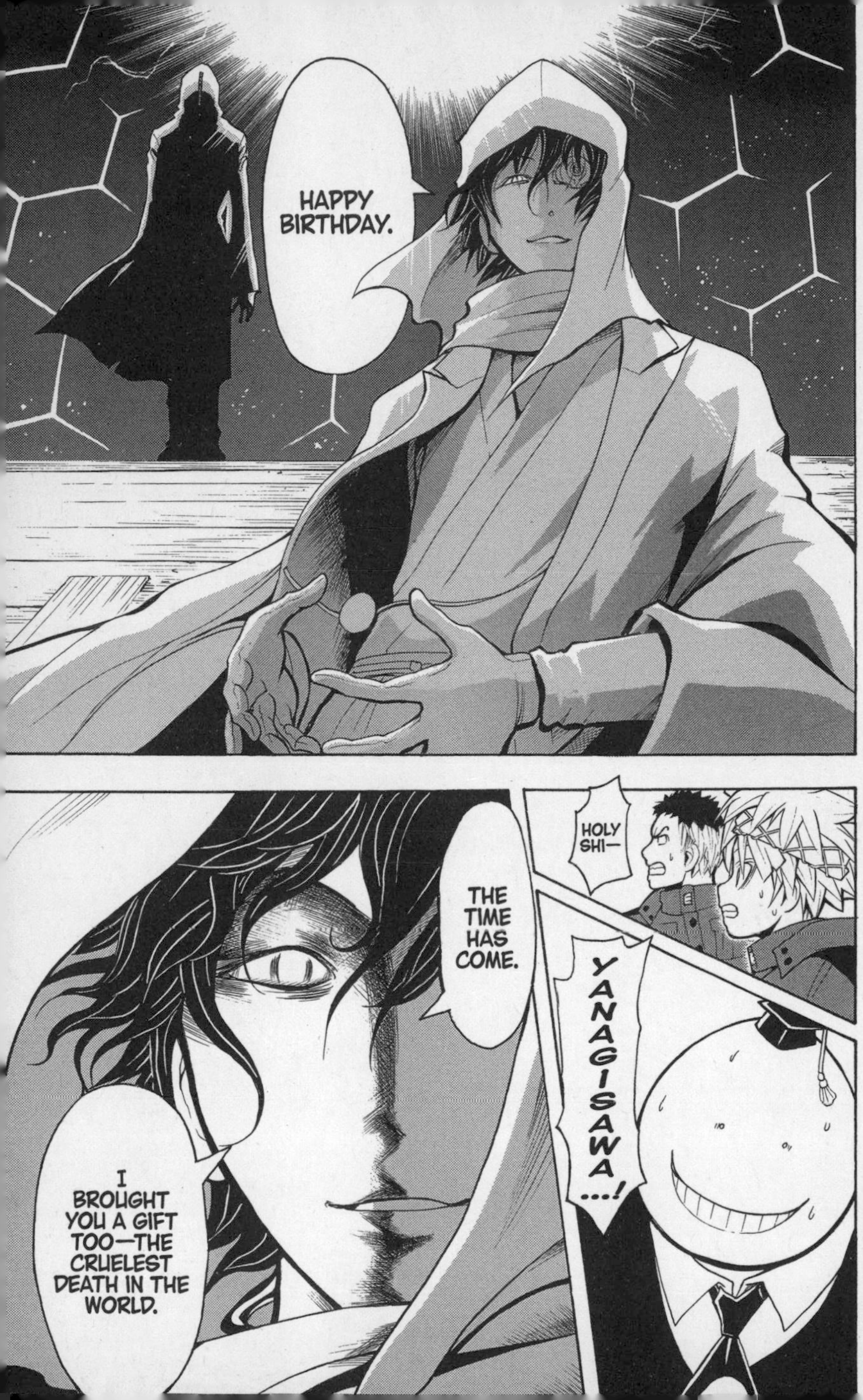
HAPPY BIRTHDAY.
HOLY SHI—
YANAGISAWA...!
THE TIME HAS COME.
I BROUGHT YOU A GIFT TOO—THE CRUELEST DEATH IN THE WORLD.

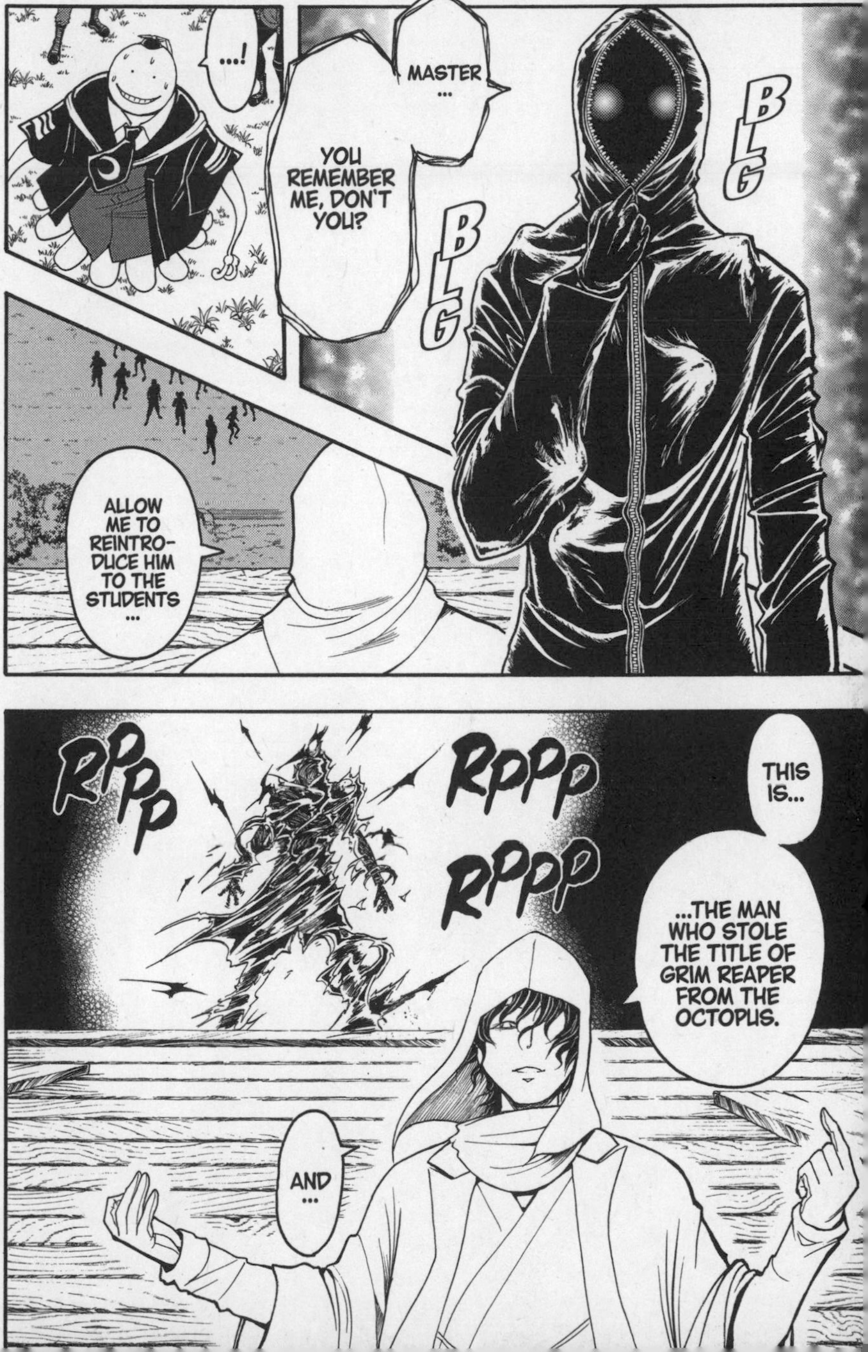
MASTER...
YOU REMEMBER ME, DON'T YOU?
BLG
BLG
...!
ALLOW ME TO REINTRODUCE HIM TO THE STUDENTS...
THIS IS...
RPPP
RPPP
RPPP
...THE MAN WHO STOLE THE TITLE OF GRIM REAPER FROM THE OCTOPUS.
AND...

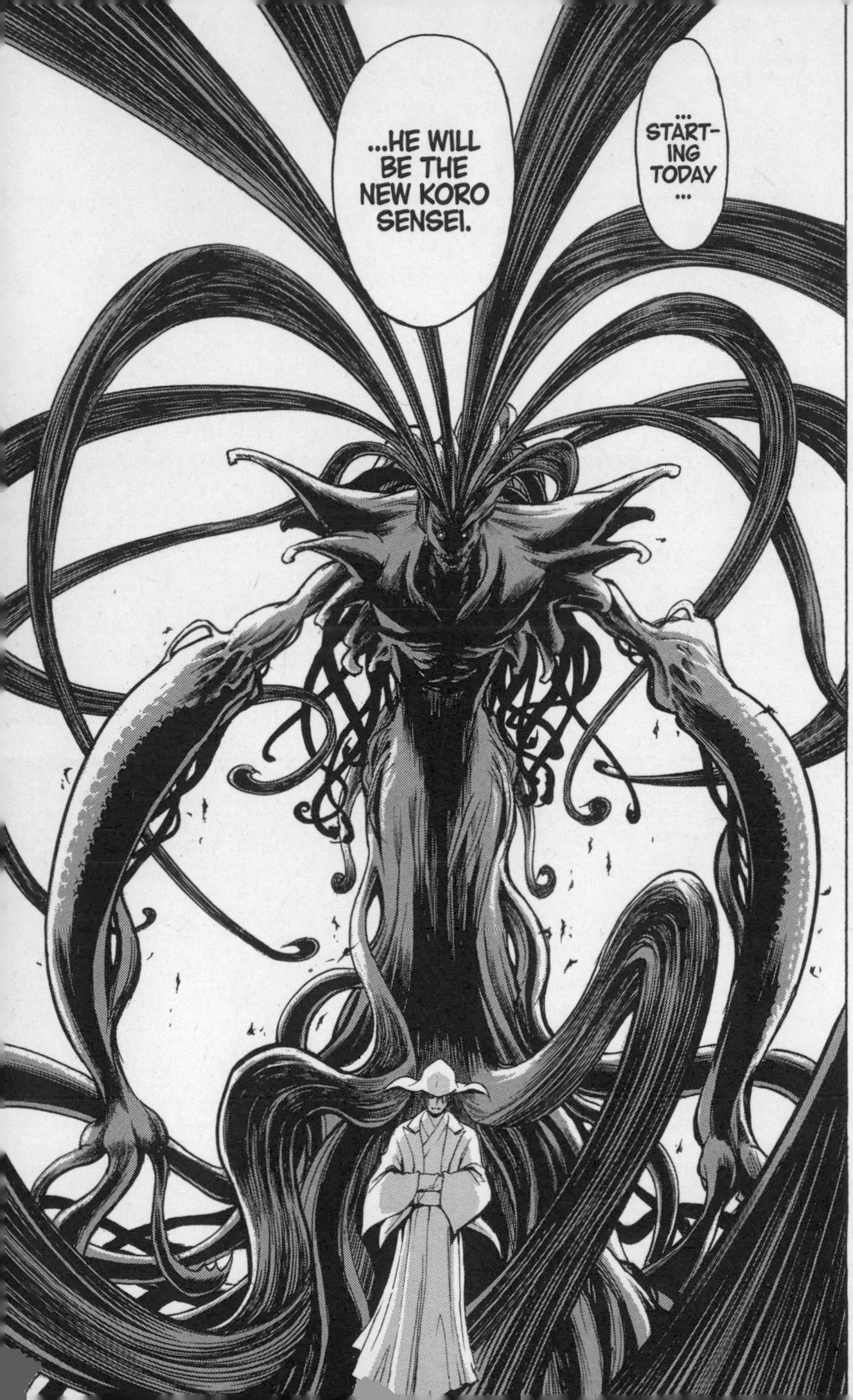
...STARTING TODAY...
...HE WILL BE THE NEW KORO SENSEI.

Next Issue

I decided to change Koro Sensei's look from this volume on. What do you think? The designer of the front cover complained, "The new design is such a pain to work on..." And we're left with a huge surplus stock of the previous version. But have no fear, the now jobless predecessor will go around handing them out for free!

Yusei Matsui

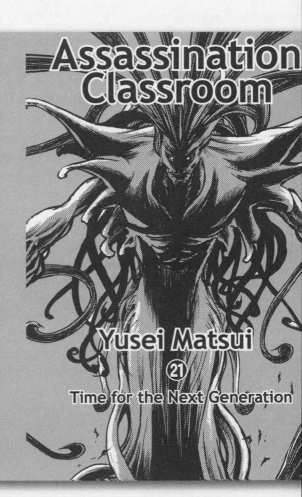

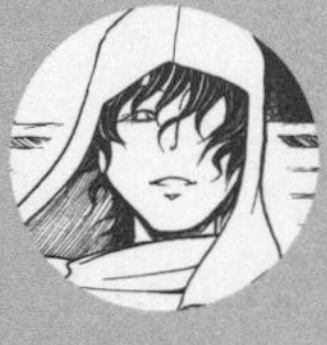

Assassination Classroom
Yusei Matsui
21
Time for the Next Generation

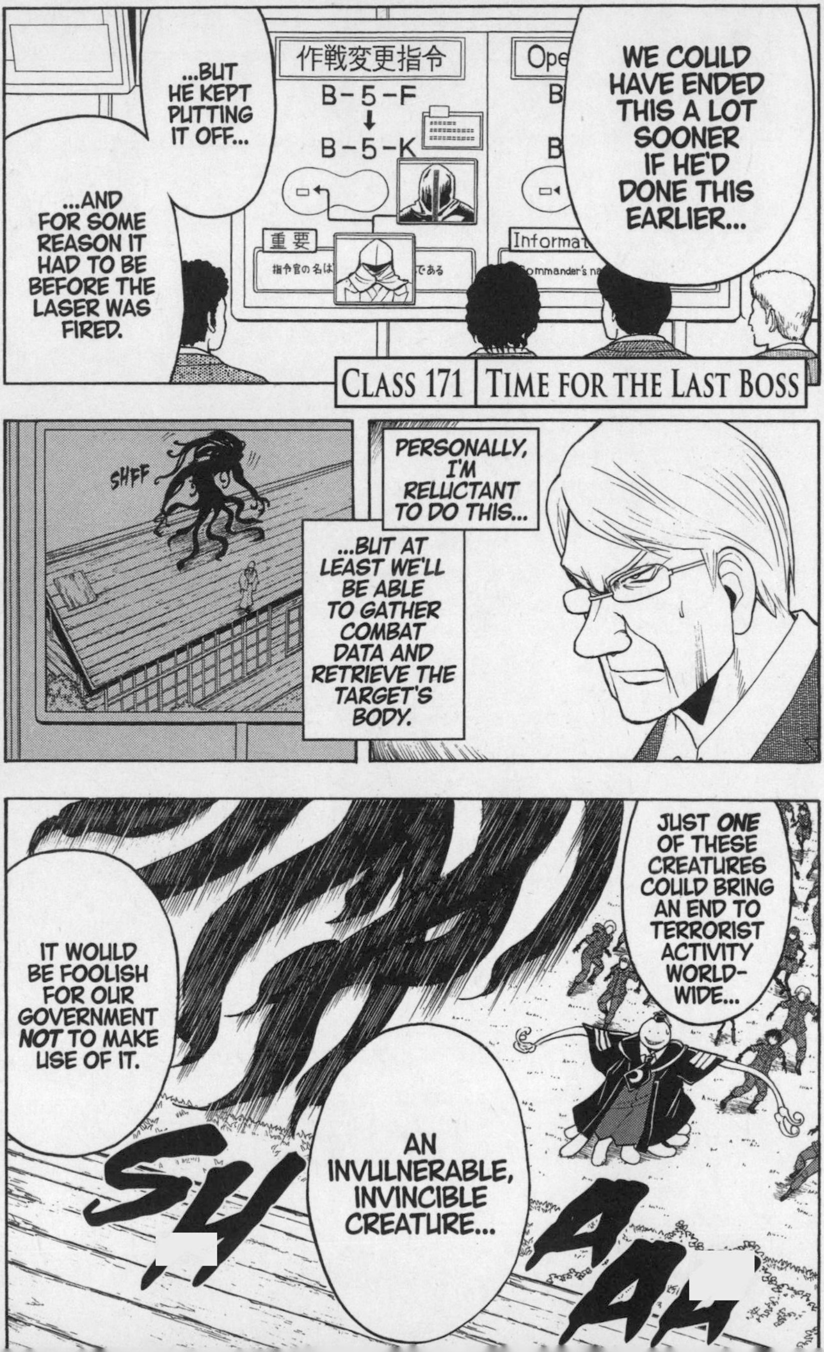
WE COULD HAVE ENDED THIS A LOT SOONER IF HE'D DONE THIS EARLIER...
作戦変更指令
B-5-F
B-5-K
重要
指令官の名は
である
Ope
Informat
Commander's na
...BUT HE KEPT PUTTING IT OFF...
...AND FOR SOME REASON IT HAD TO BE BEFORE THE LASER WAS FIRED.
CLASS 171 TIME FOR THE LAST BOSS
PERSONALLY, I'M RELUCTANT TO DO THIS...
...BUT AT LEAST WE'LL BE ABLE TO GATHER COMBAT DATA AND RETRIEVE THE TARGET'S BODY.
SHFF
JUST ONE OF THESE CREATURES COULD BRING AN END TO TERRORIST ACTIVITY WORLD-WIDE...
AN INVULNERABLE, INVINCIBLE CREATURE...
IT WOULD BE FOOLISH FOR OUR GOVERNMENT NOT TO MAKE USE OF IT.
SH
AA

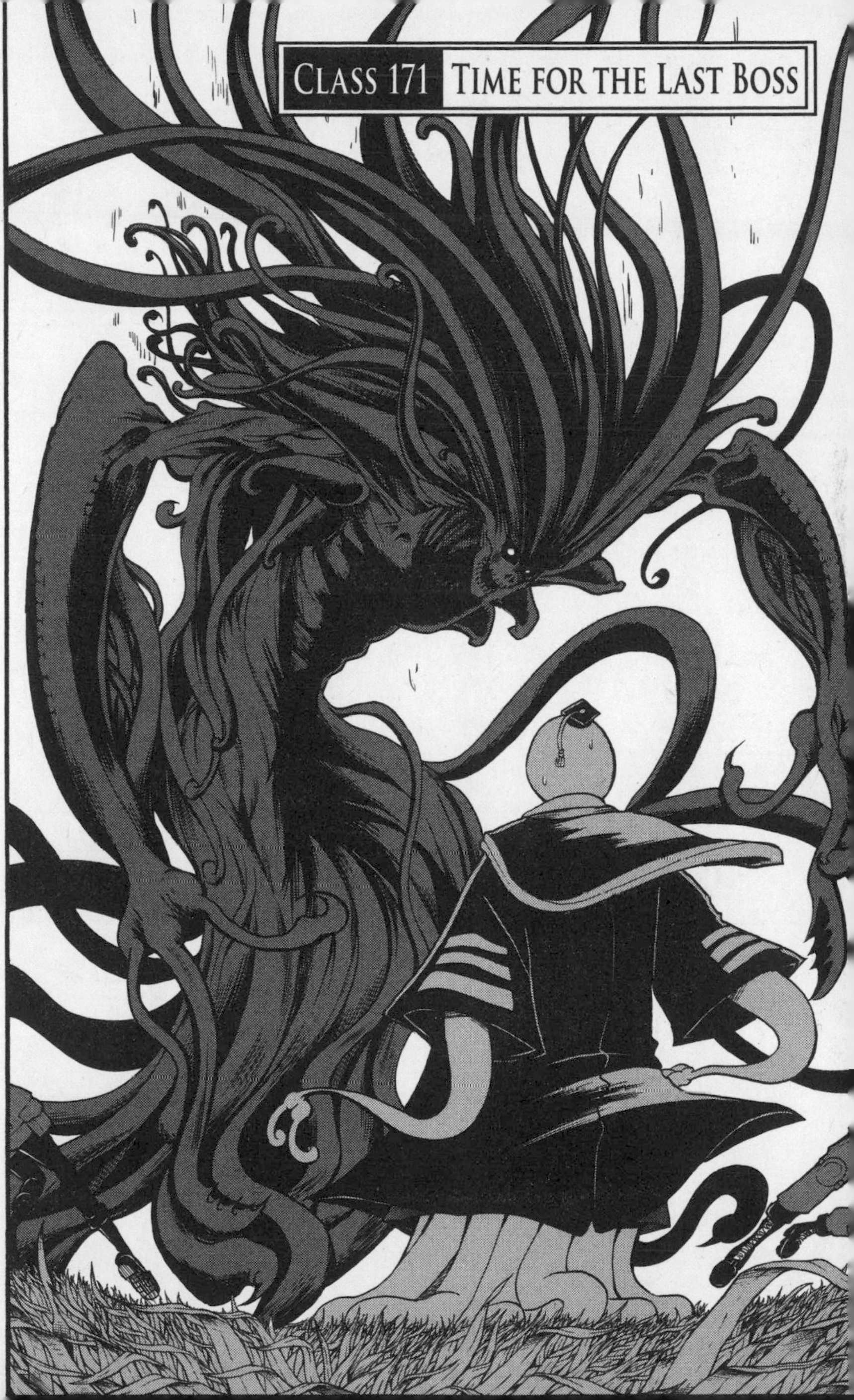

Class 171
Time for the Last Boss

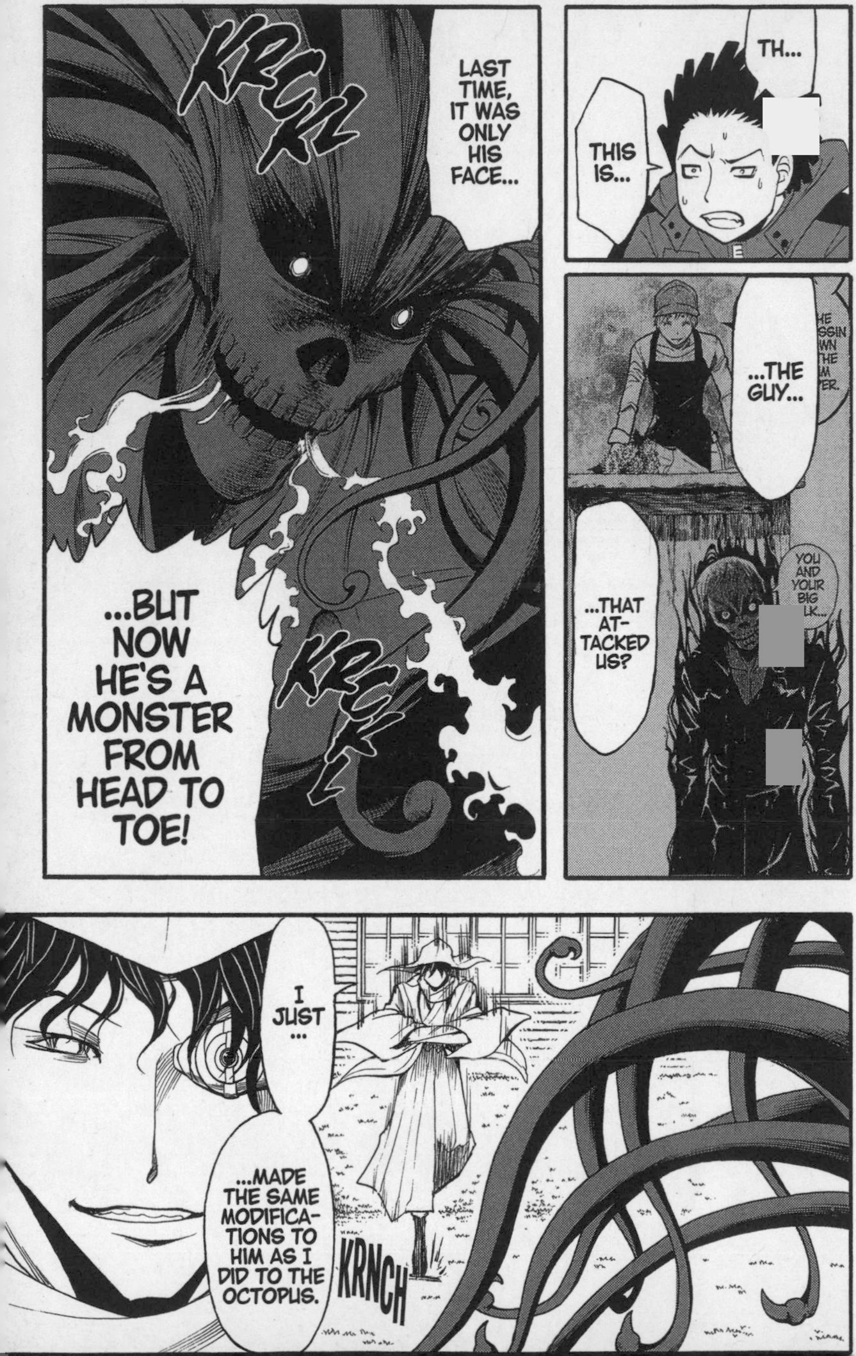
TH...
THIS IS...
...THE GUY...
YOU AND YOUR BIG
...THAT AT-TACKED US?
KRCKL
LAST TIME, IT WAS ONLY HIS FACE...
...BUT NOW HE'S A MONSTER FROM HEAD TO TOE!
KRCKL
I JUST...
...MADE THE SAME MODIFICA-TIONS TO HIM AS I DID TO THE OCTOPUS.
KRNCH

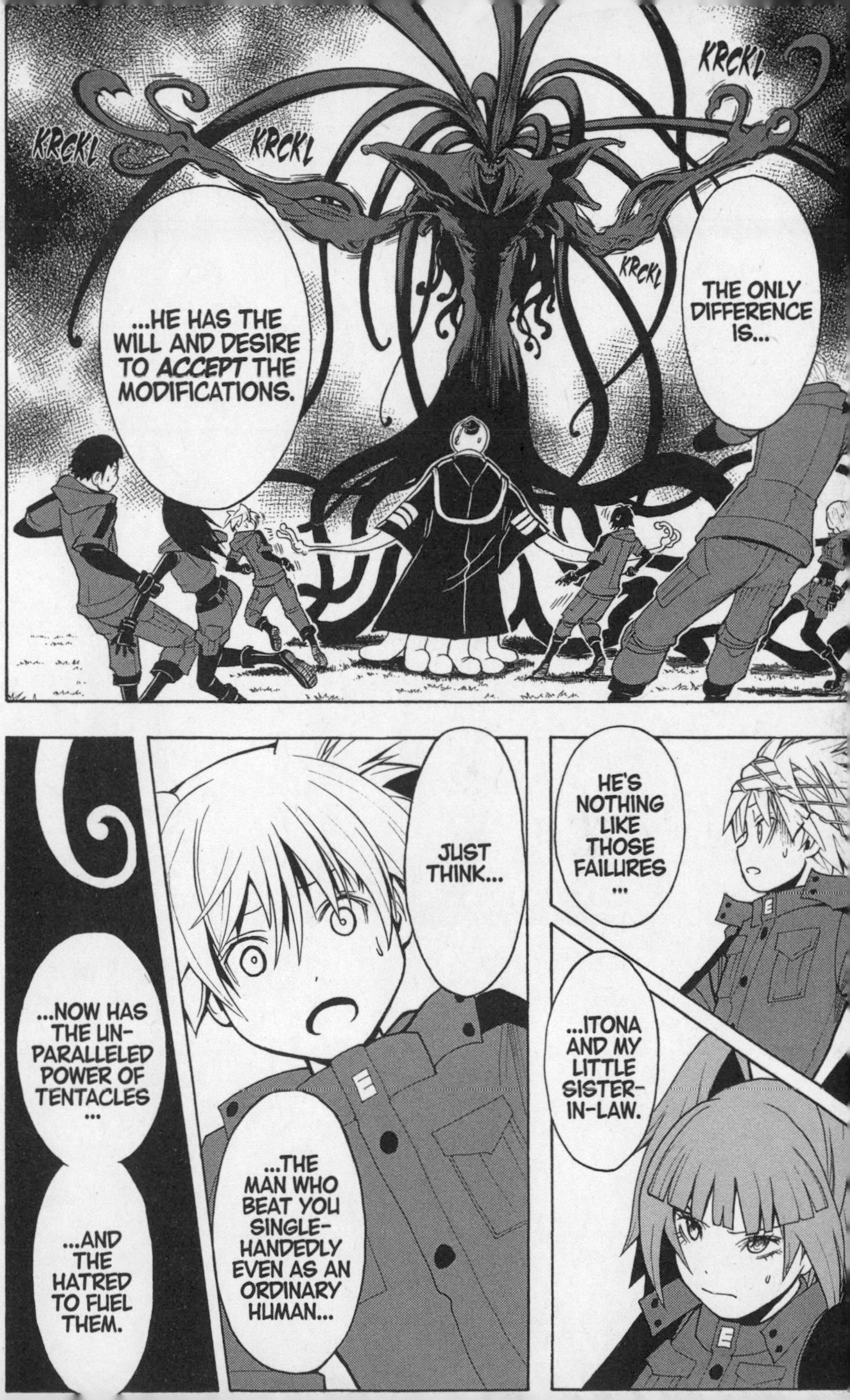
KRCKL
KRCKL
THE ONLY DIFFERENCE IS...
KRCKL
KRCKL
...HE HAS THE WILL AND DESIRE TO *ACCEPT* THE MODIFICATIONS.
HE'S NOTHING LIKE THOSE FAILURES ...
...ITONA AND MY LITTLE SISTER-IN-LAW.
JUST THINK...
...THE MAN WHO BEAT YOU SINGLE-HANDEDLY EVEN AS AN ORDINARY HUMAN...
...NOW HAS THE UN-PARALLELED POWER OF TENTACLES ...
...AND THE HATRED TO FUEL THEM.

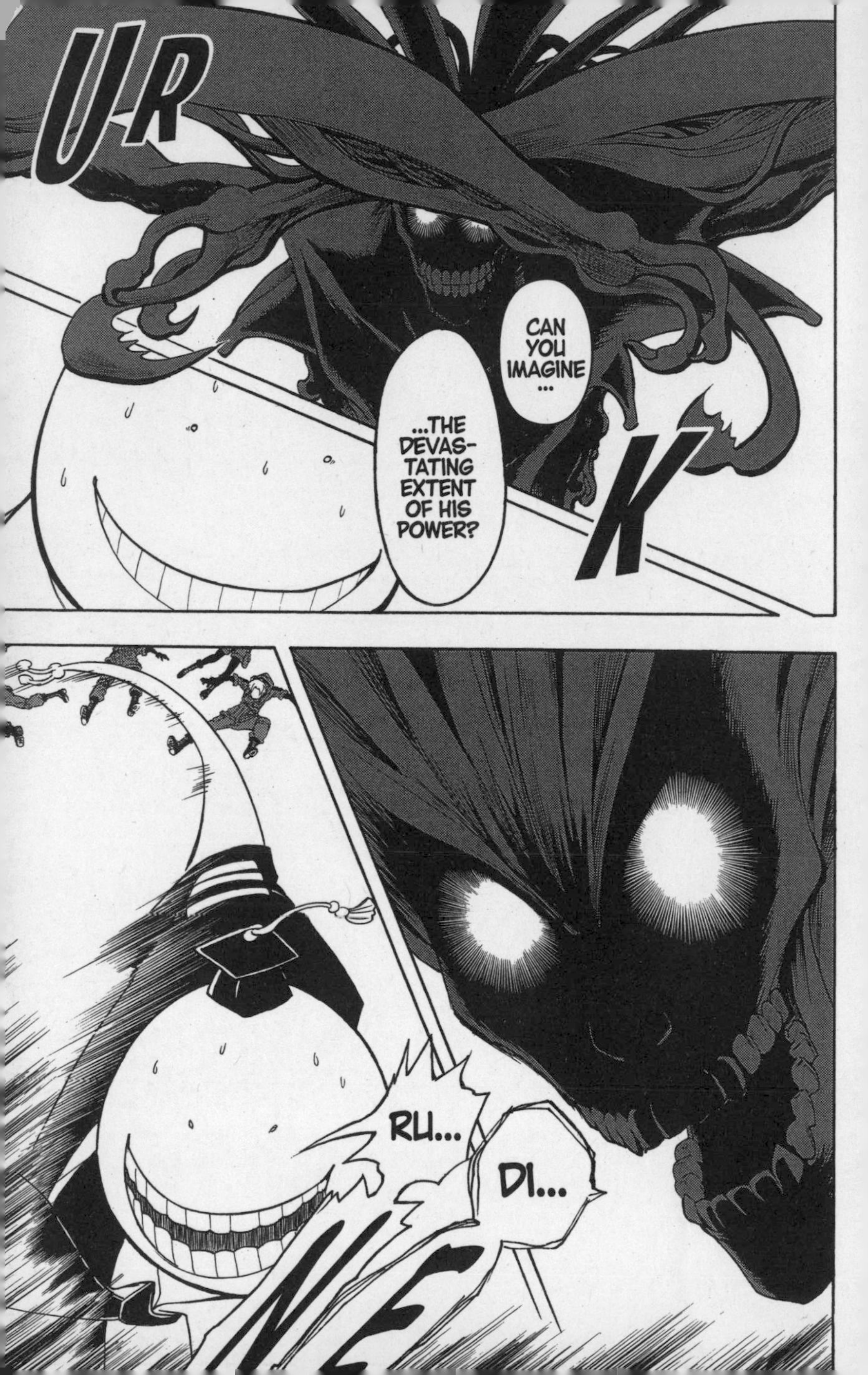
UR
CAN YOU IMAGINE...
...THE DEVAS-TATING EXTENT OF HIS POWER?
K
RU...
DI...

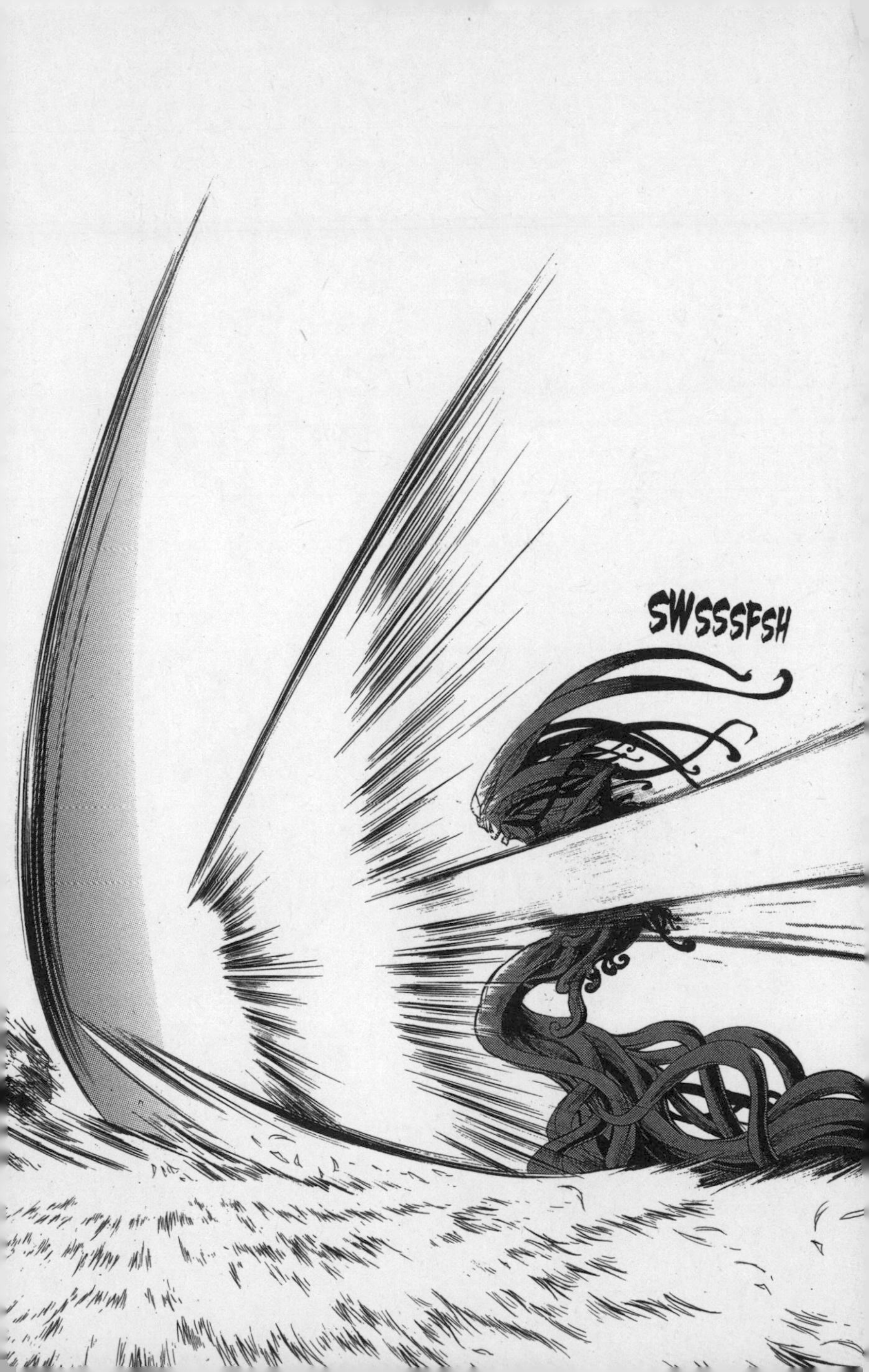
SWSSSFSH

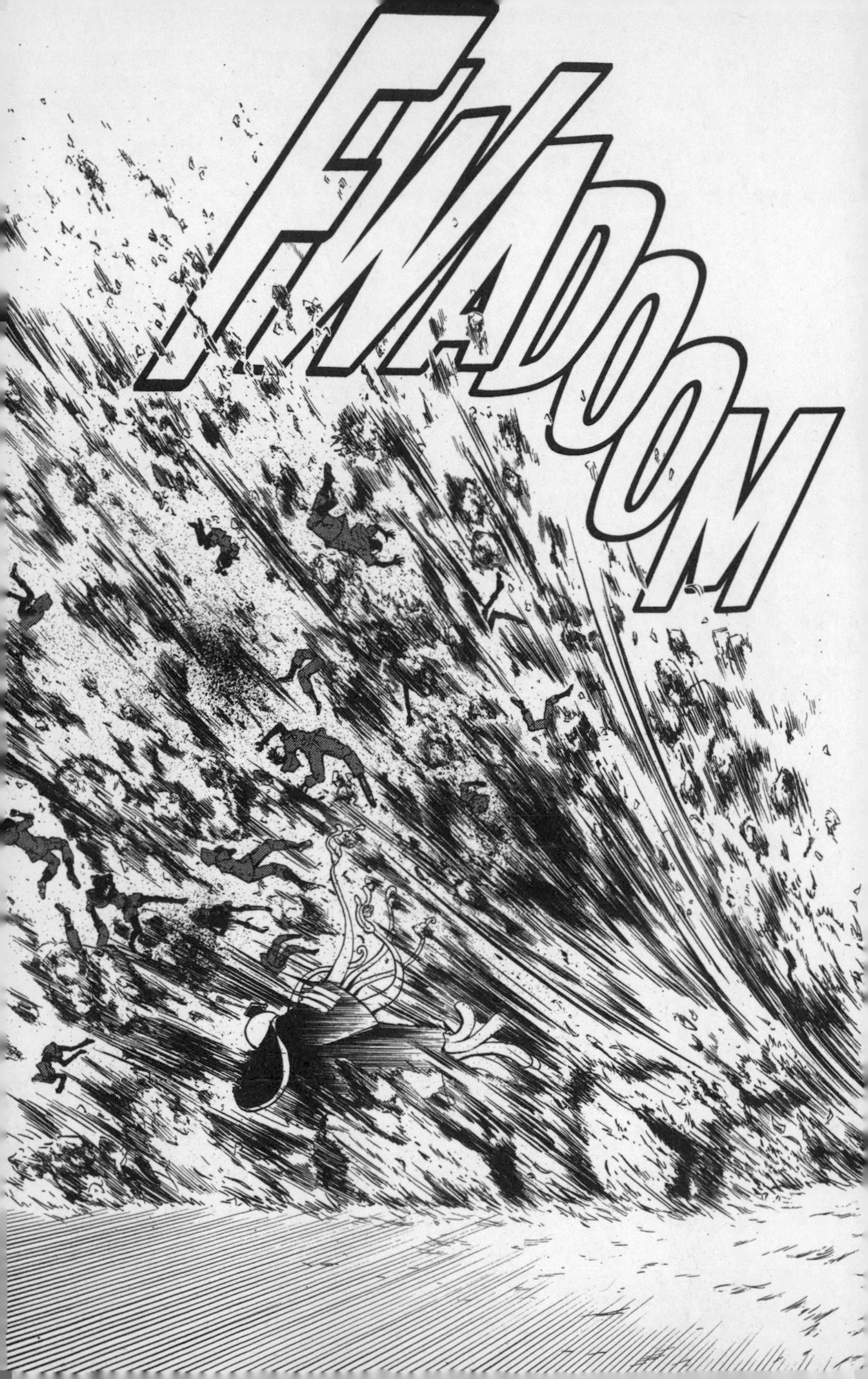
FWADOOM

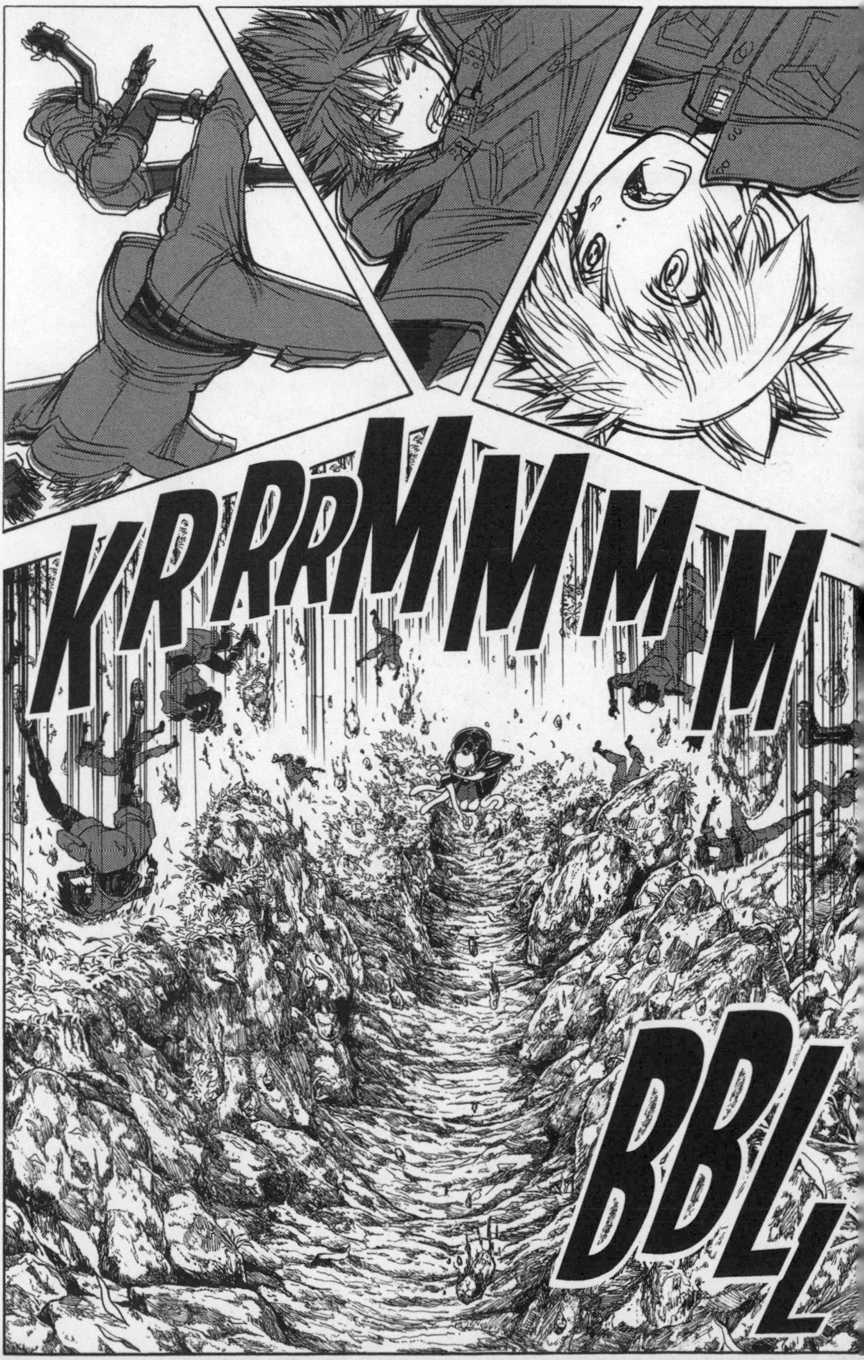
KRRRMMMMM
BBLL

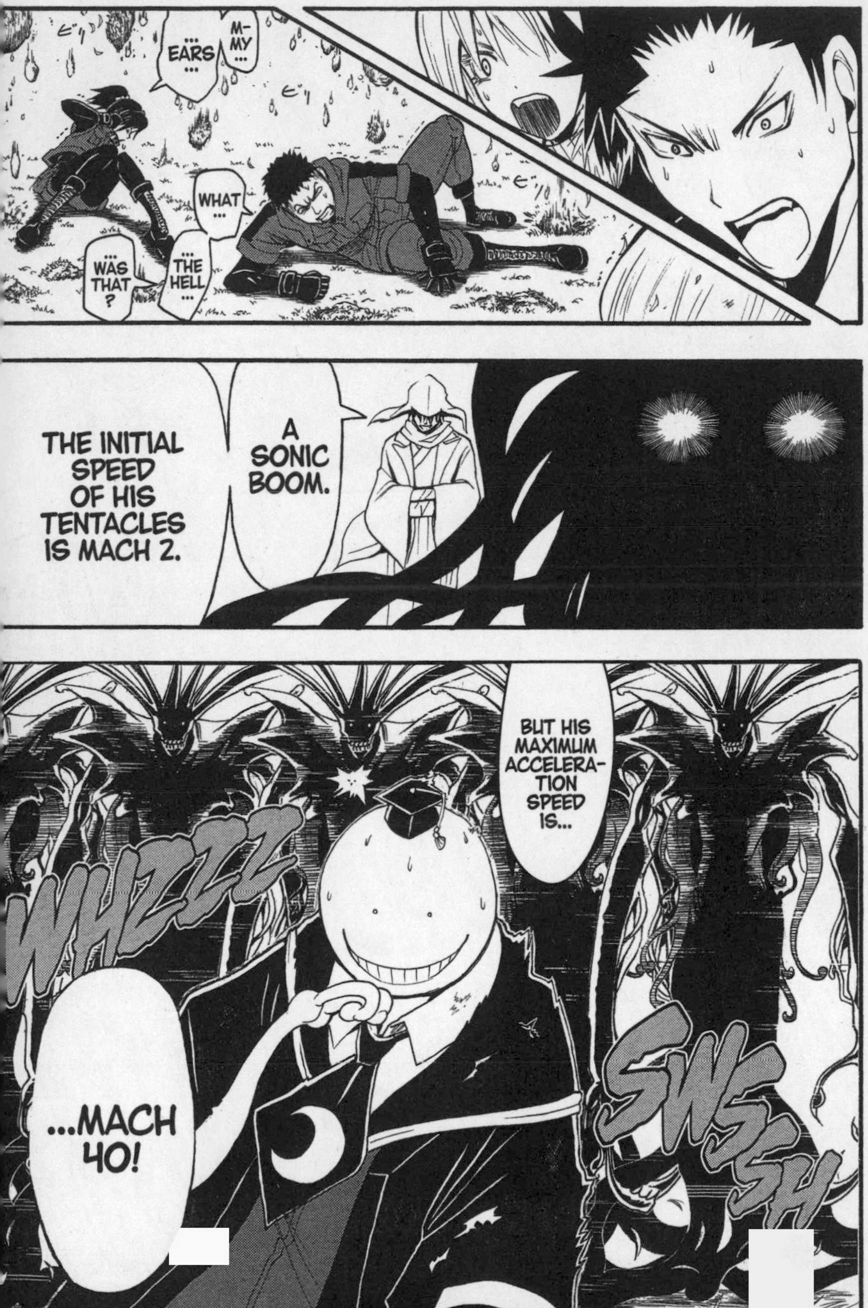
M-MY ...
... EARS ...
WHAT ...
... THE HELL ...
... WAS THAT ?
A SONIC BOOM.
THE INITIAL SPEED OF HIS TENTACLES IS MACH 2.
BUT HIS MAXIMUM ACCELERA-TION SPEED IS...
SWSSH
WHZZZ
...MACH 40!

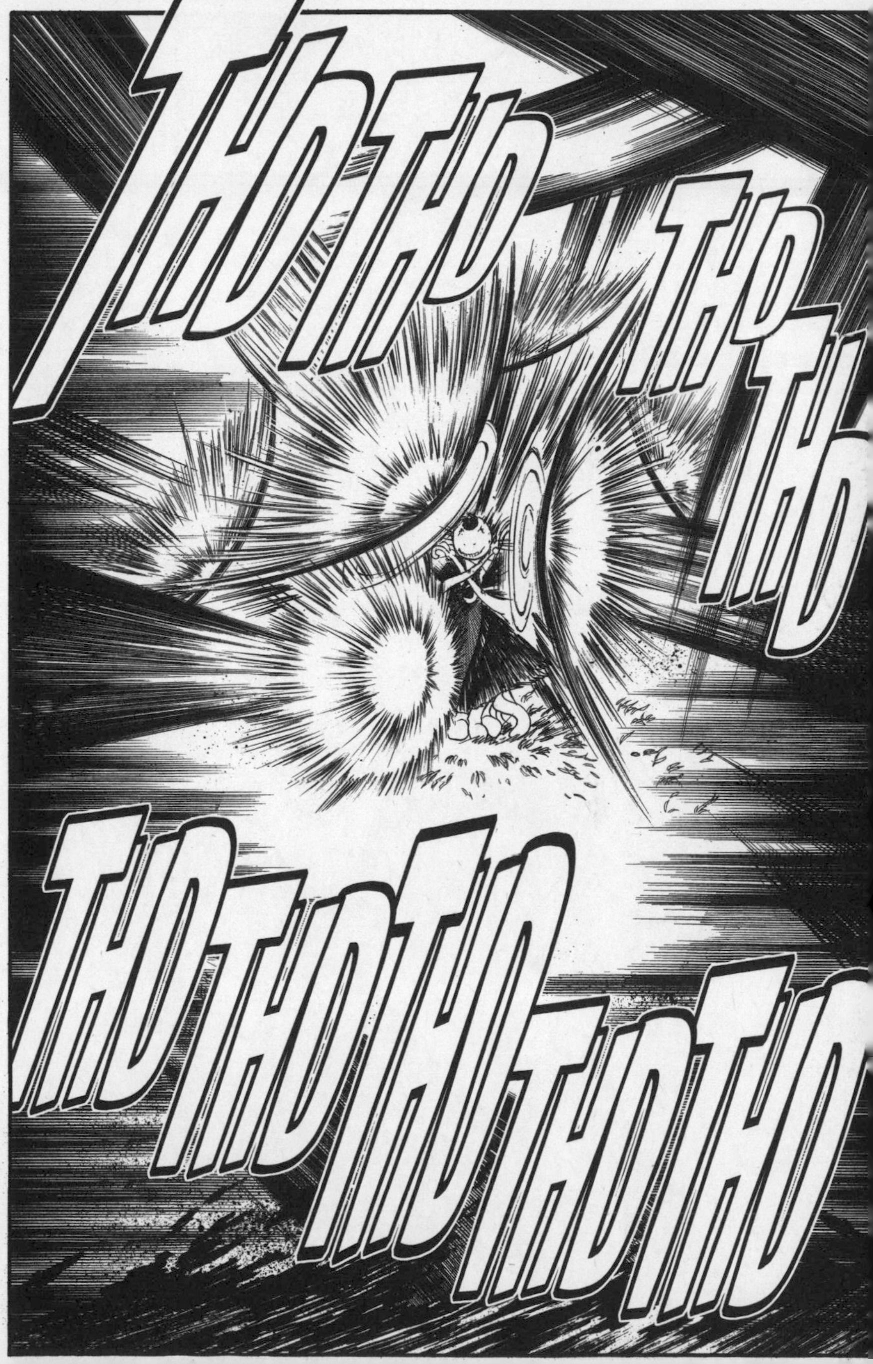
THD THD THD
THD THD THD
THD THD THD THD THD THD THD

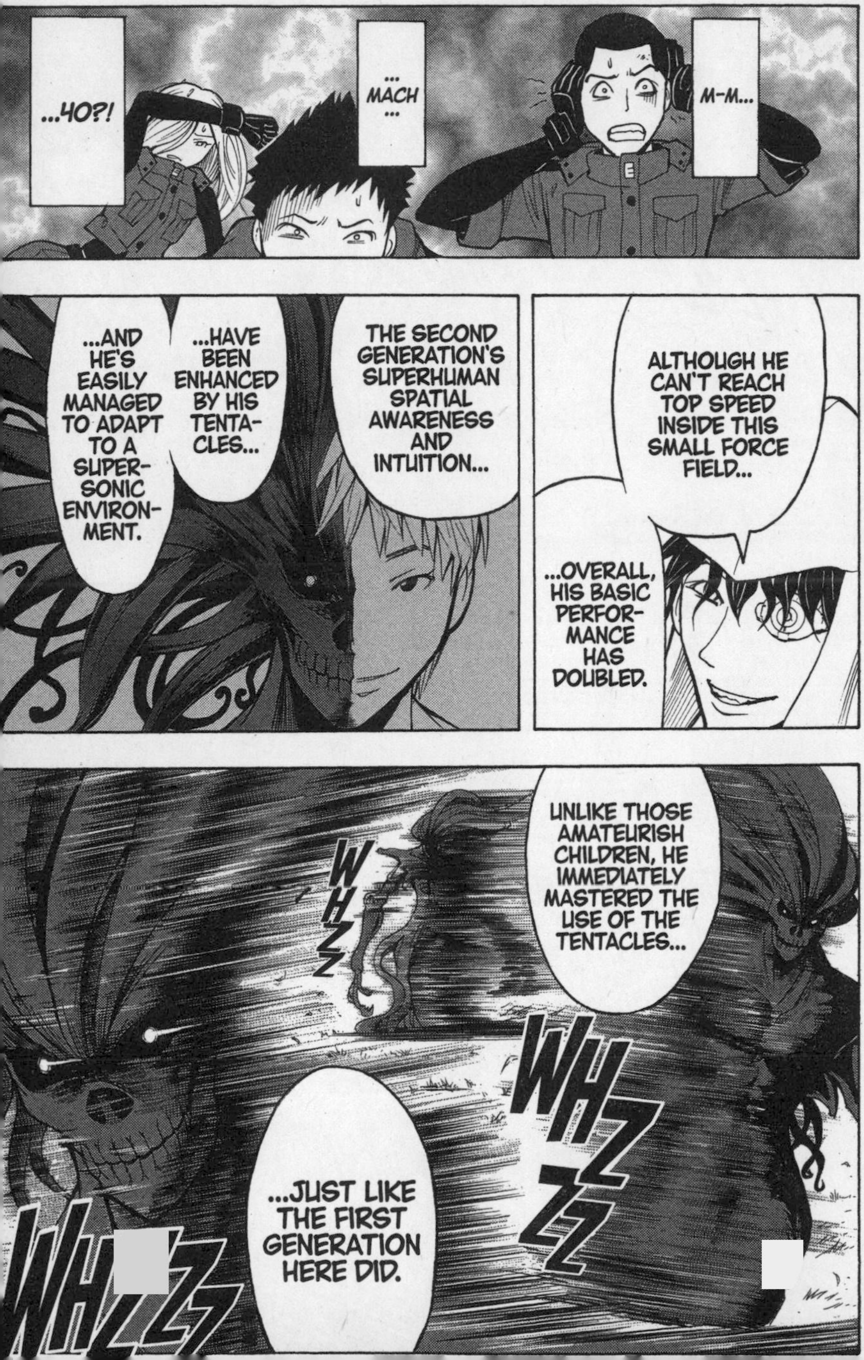
M-M...
...MACH...
...40?!
ALTHOUGH HE CAN'T REACH TOP SPEED INSIDE THIS SMALL FORCE FIELD...
...OVERALL, HIS BASIC PERFORMANCE HAS DOUBLED.
THE SECOND GENERATION'S SUPERHUMAN SPATIAL AWARENESS AND INTUITION...
...HAVE BEEN ENHANCED BY HIS TENTACLES...
...AND HE'S EASILY MANAGED TO ADAPT TO A SUPERSONIC ENVIRONMENT.
UNLIKE THOSE AMATEURISH CHILDREN, HE IMMEDIATELY MASTERED THE USE OF THE TENTACLES...
WHZZ
WHZZZ
...JUST LIKE THE FIRST GENERATION HERE DID.
WHZZS

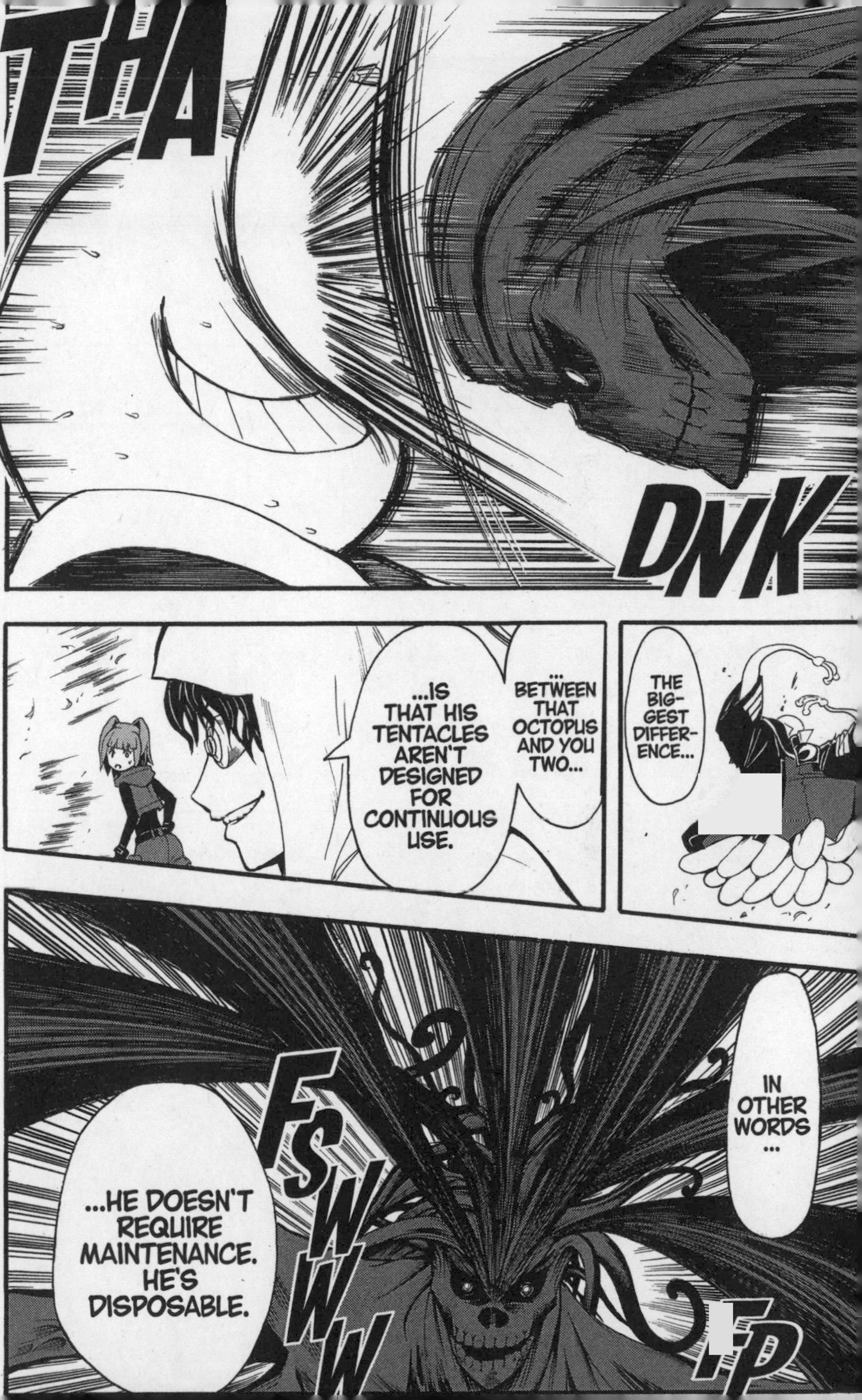
THA
DNK
THE BIGGEST DIFFERENCE...
...BETWEEN THAT OCTOPUS AND YOU TWO...
...IS THAT HIS TENTACLES AREN'T DESIGNED FOR CONTINUOUS USE.
IN OTHER WORDS...
...HE DOESN'T REQUIRE MAINTENANCE. HE'S DISPOSABLE.
FSWWW
FP

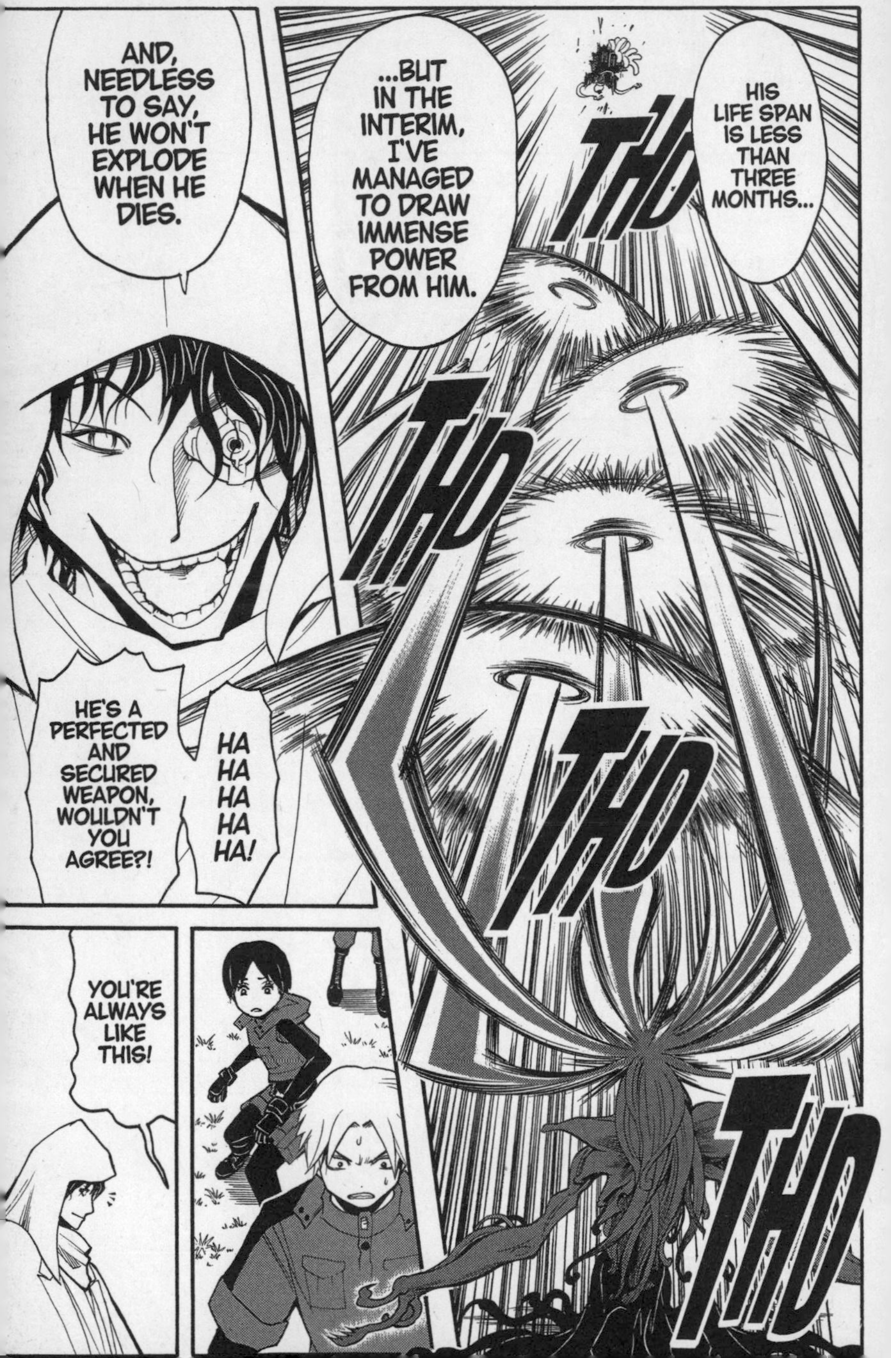
HIS LIFE SPAN IS LESS THAN THREE MONTHS...
...BUT IN THE INTERIM, I'VE MANAGED TO DRAW IMMENSE POWER FROM HIM.
THD
THD
THD
THD
AND, NEEDLESS TO SAY, HE WON'T EXPLODE WHEN HE DIES.
HE'S A PERFECTED AND SECURED WEAPON, WOULDN'T YOU AGREE?!
HA HA HA HA HA!
YOU'RE ALWAYS LIKE THIS!

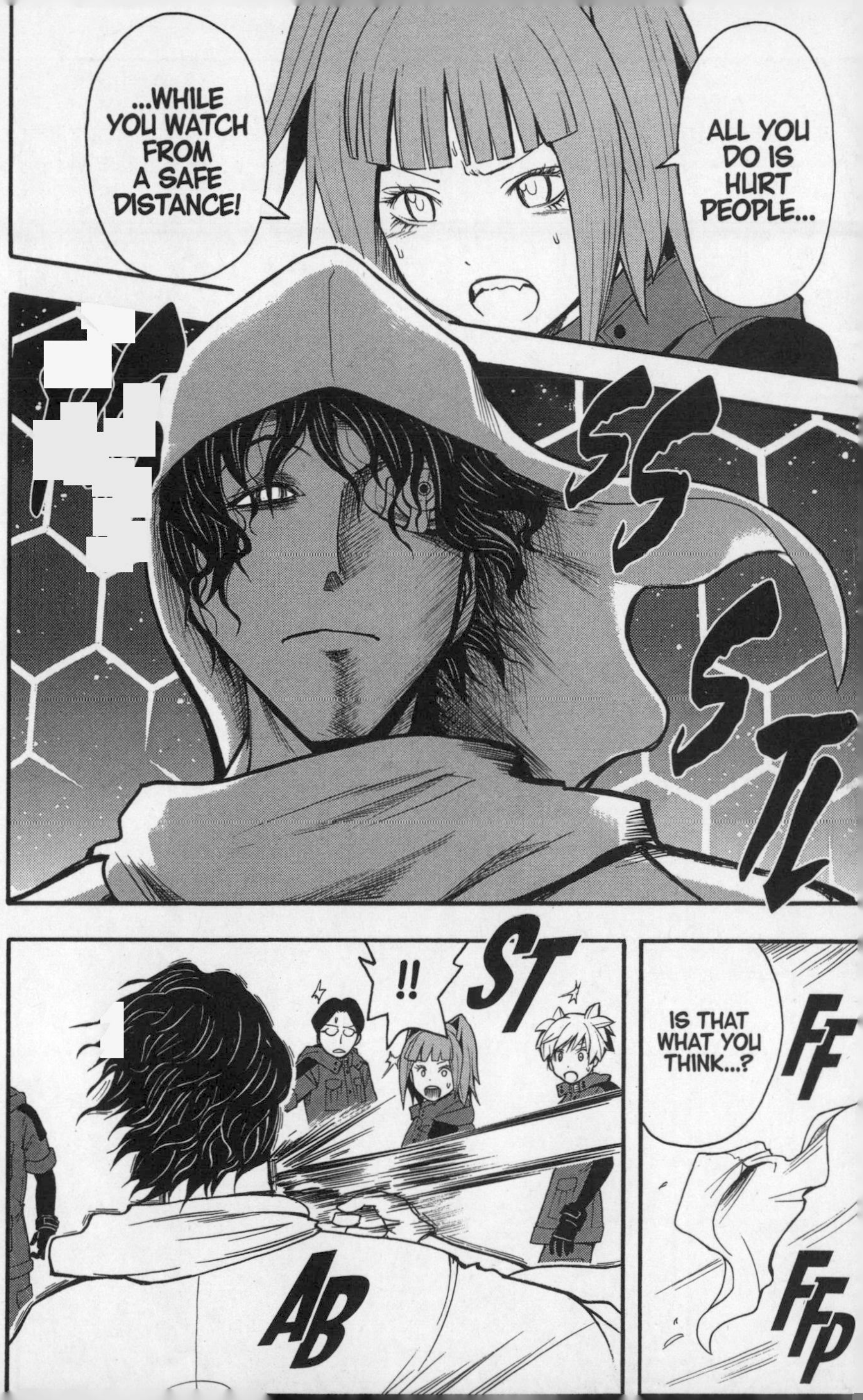
ALL YOU DO IS HURT PEOPLE...
...WHILE YOU WATCH FROM A SAFE DISTANCE!
SS
STL
IS THAT WHAT YOU THINK...?
FF
FFP
!!
ST
AB

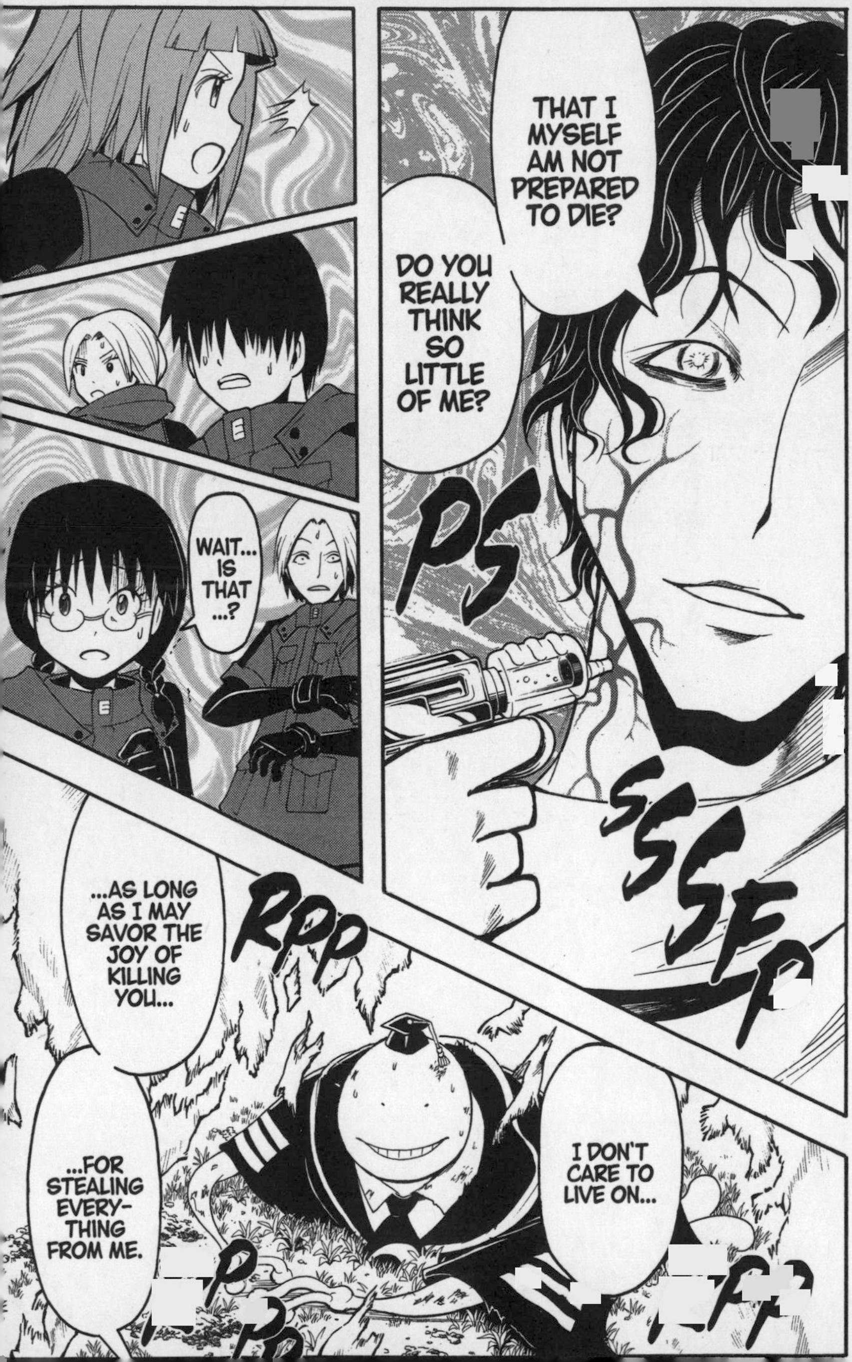
THAT I MYSELF AM NOT PREPARED TO DIE?
DO YOU REALLY THINK SO LITTLE OF ME?
PS
SSSFP
WAIT... IS THAT ...?
RPP
I DON'T CARE TO LIVE ON...
...AS LONG AS I MAY SAVOR THE JOY OF KILLING YOU...
...FOR STEALING EVERY-THING FROM ME.

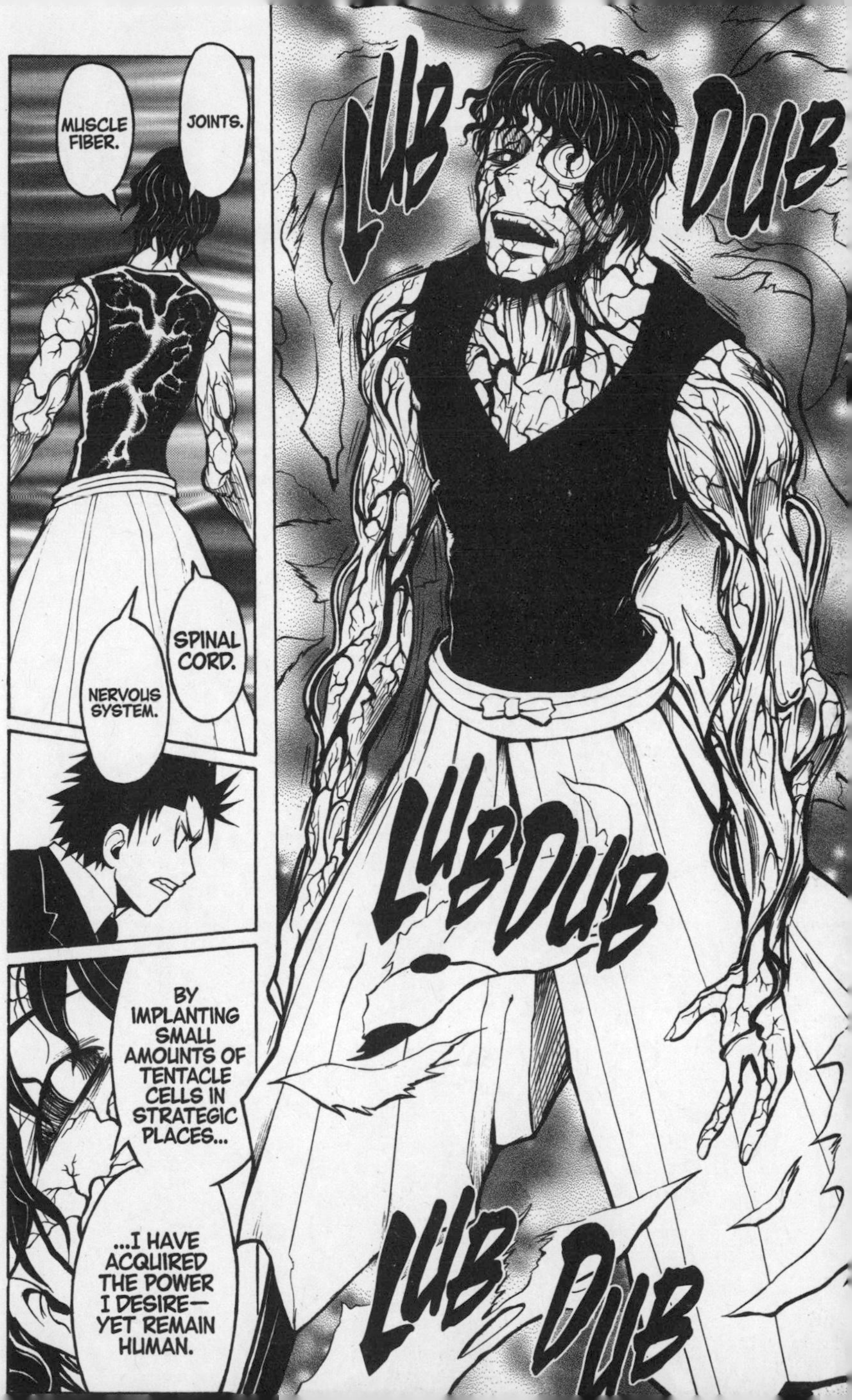
LUB DUB
LUB DUB
LUB DUB
JOINTS.
MUSCLE FIBER.
SPINAL CORD.
NERVOUS SYSTEM.
BY IMPLANTING SMALL AMOUNTS OF TENTACLE CELLS IN STRATEGIC PLACES...
...I HAVE ACQUIRED THE POWER I DESIRE—YET REMAIN HUMAN.

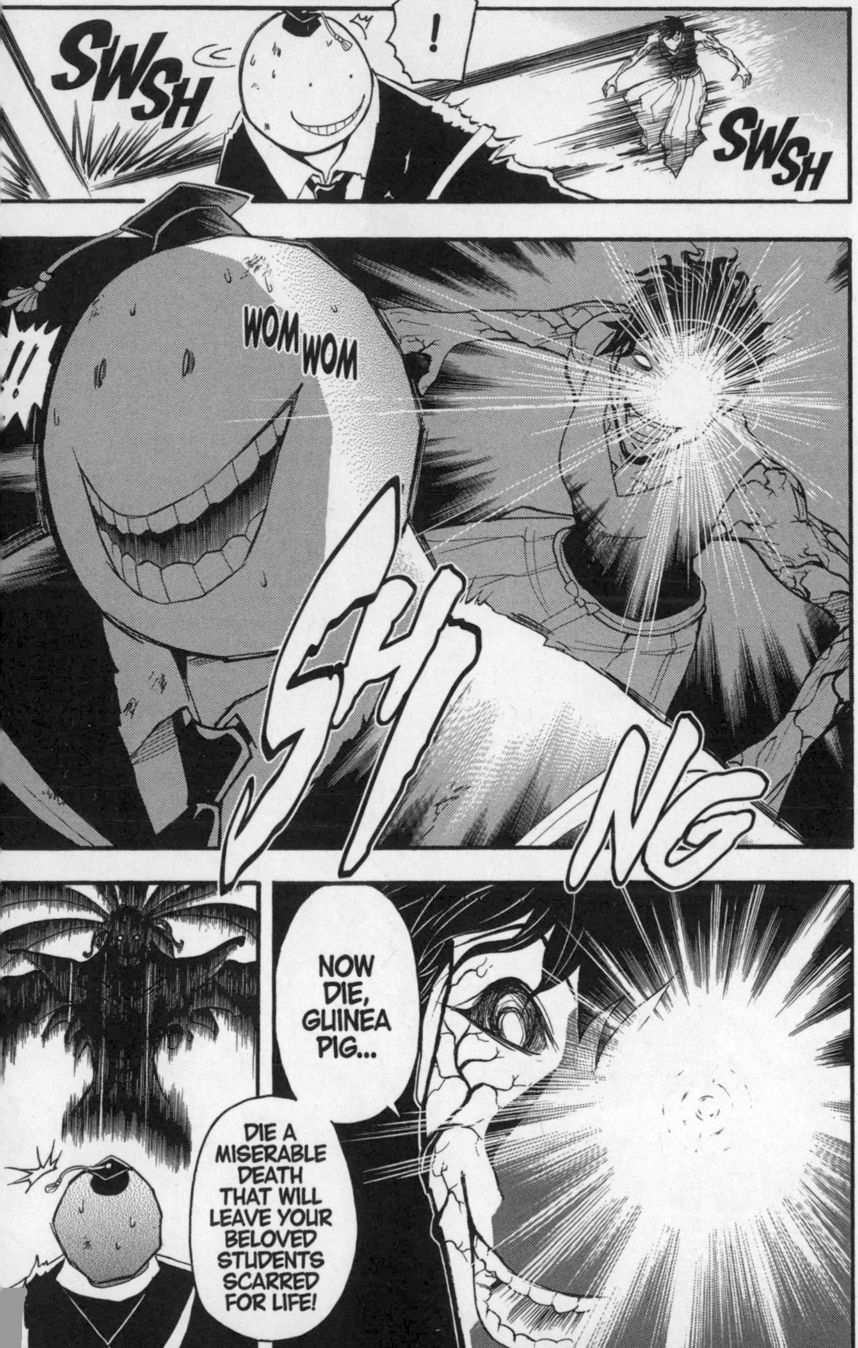
!
SWSH
SWSH
!!
WOM WOM
SHING
NOW DIE, GUINEA PIG...
DIE A MISERABLE DEATH THAT WILL LEAVE YOUR BELOVED STUDENTS SCARRED FOR LIFE!

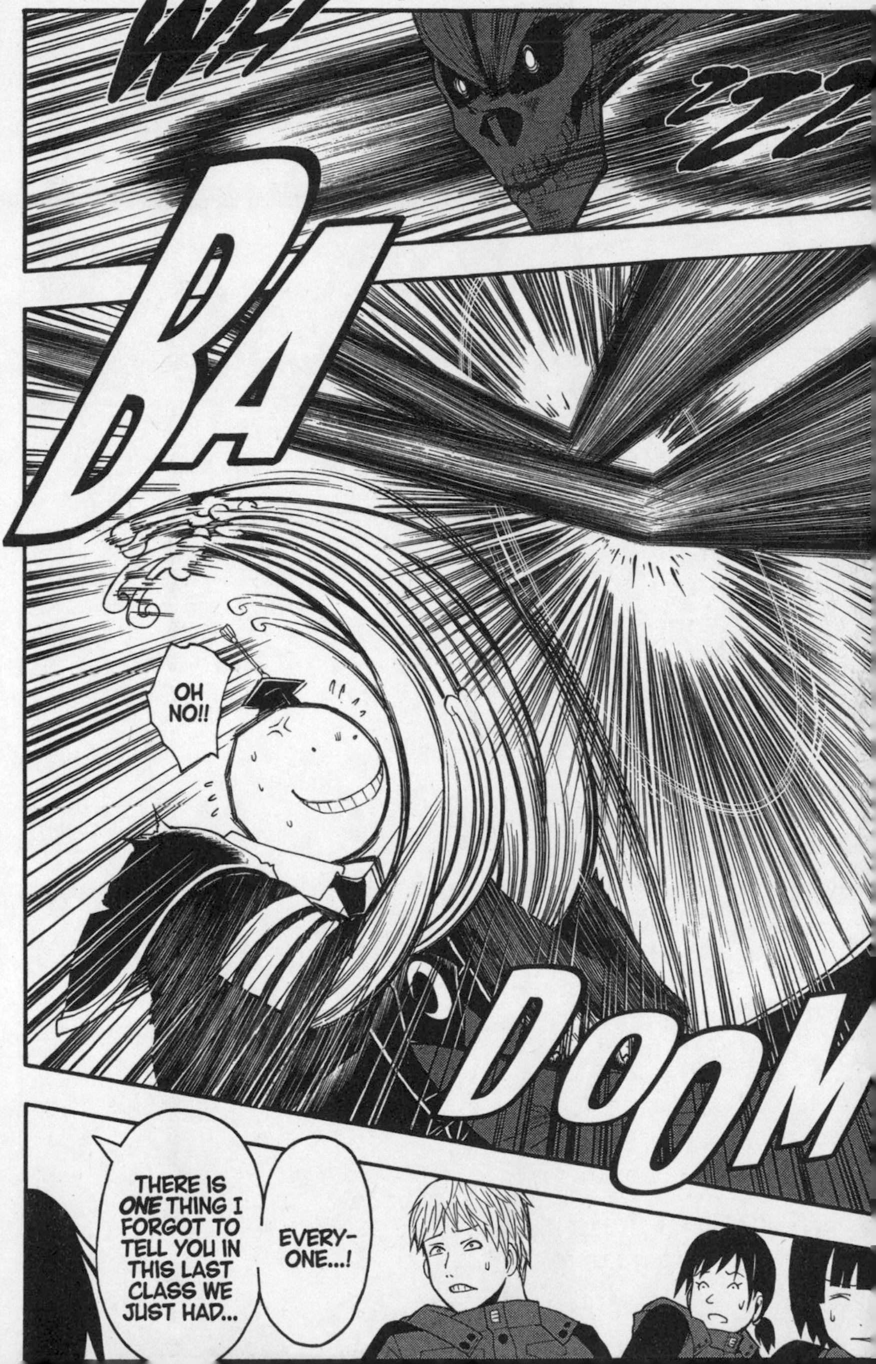
WHIZZZ
BA
OH NO!!
DOOM
EVERY-ONE...!
THERE IS ONE THING I FORGOT TO TELL YOU IN THIS LAST CLASS WE JUST HAD...

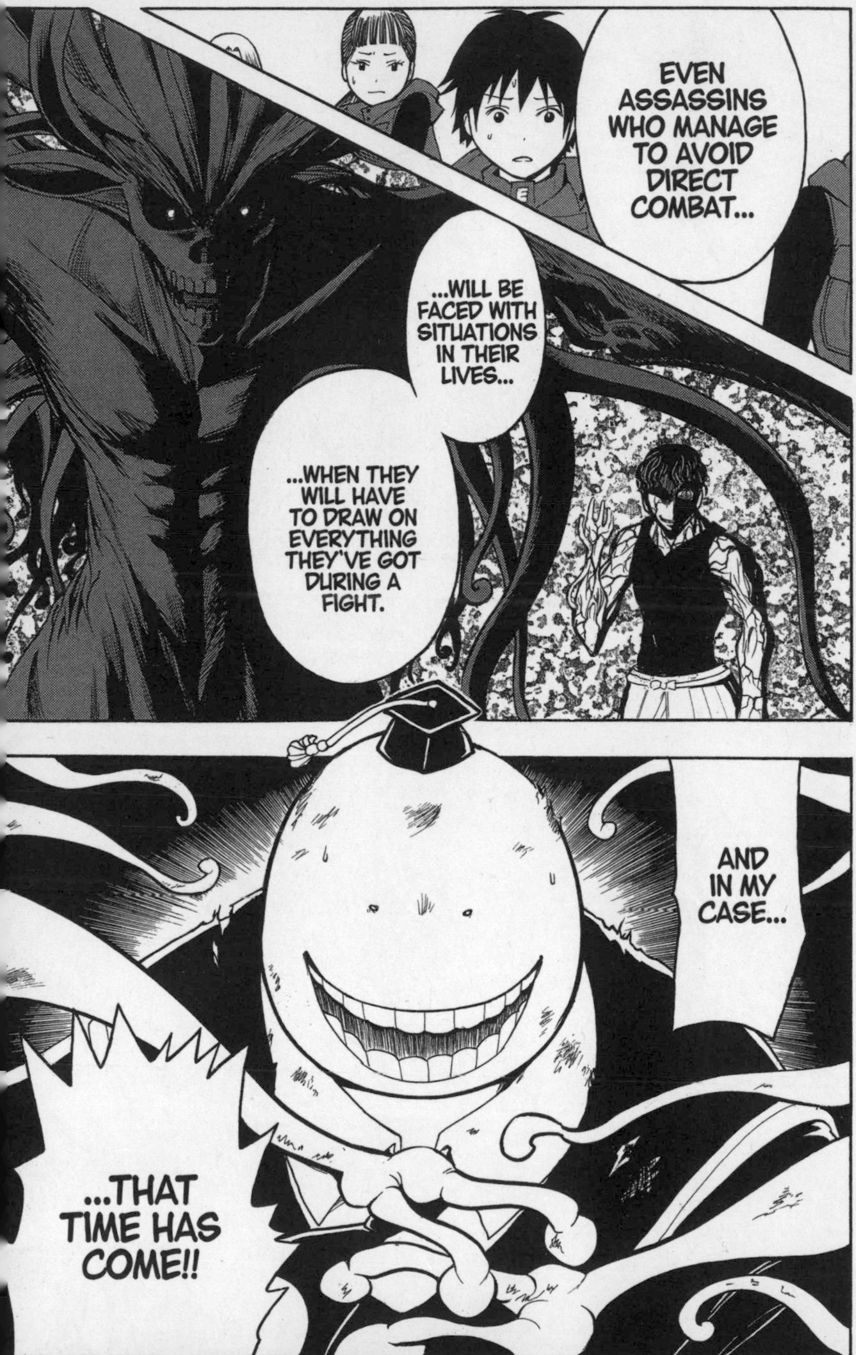
EVEN ASSASSINS WHO MANAGE TO AVOID DIRECT COMBAT...
...WILL BE FACED WITH SITUATIONS IN THEIR LIVES...
...WHEN THEY WILL HAVE TO DRAW ON EVERYTHING THEY'VE GOT DURING A FIGHT.
AND IN MY CASE...
...THAT TIME HAS COME!!

Breakdown of Reasons Why He Has to Fight

As Revenge for my cake!
To settle the score!
To protect the school!
To protect my students!

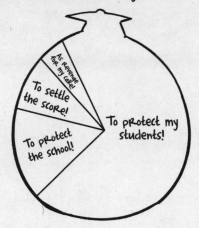

Class 172 Time for the Students

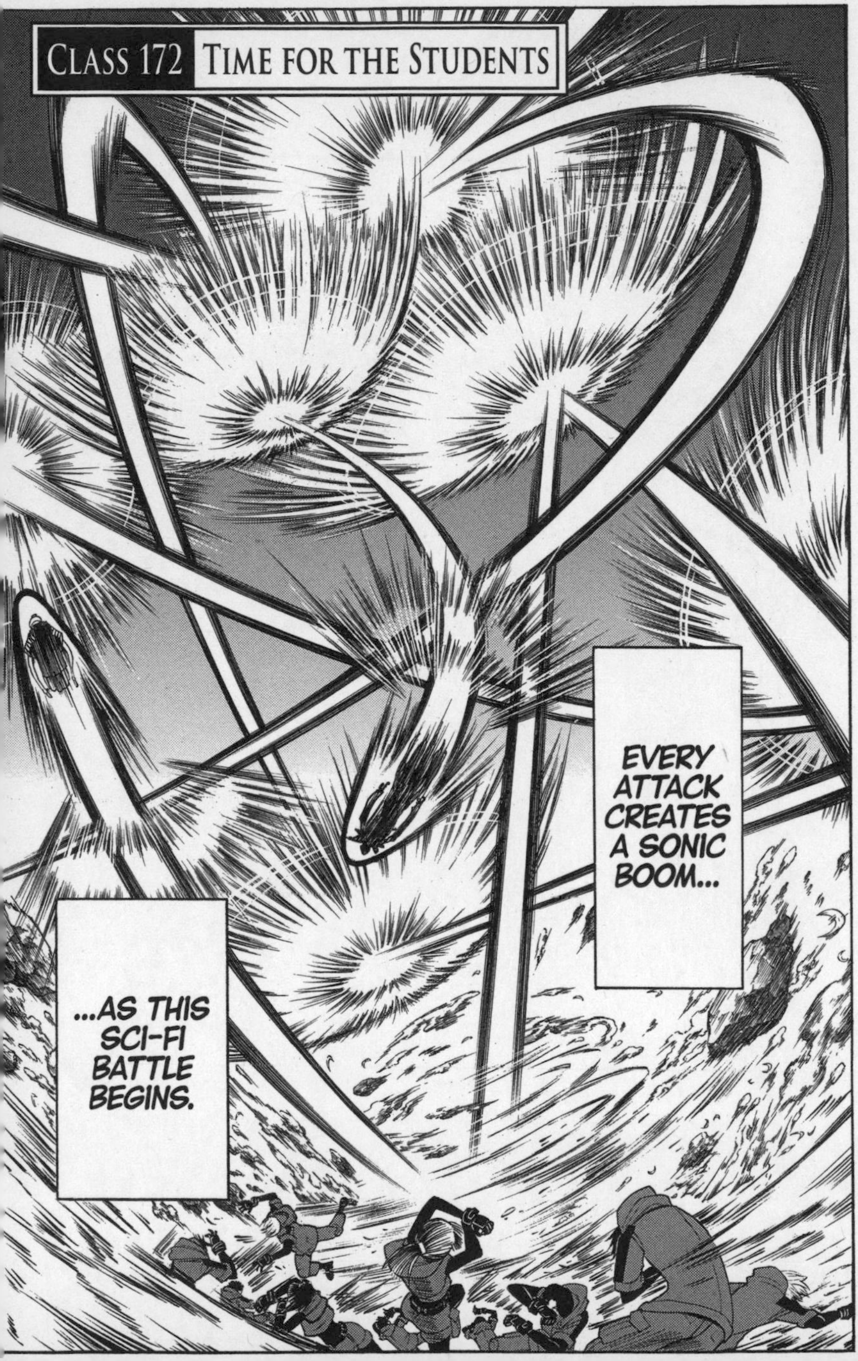
EVERY ATTACK CREATES A SONIC BOOM...
...AS THIS SCI-FI BATTLE BEGINS.

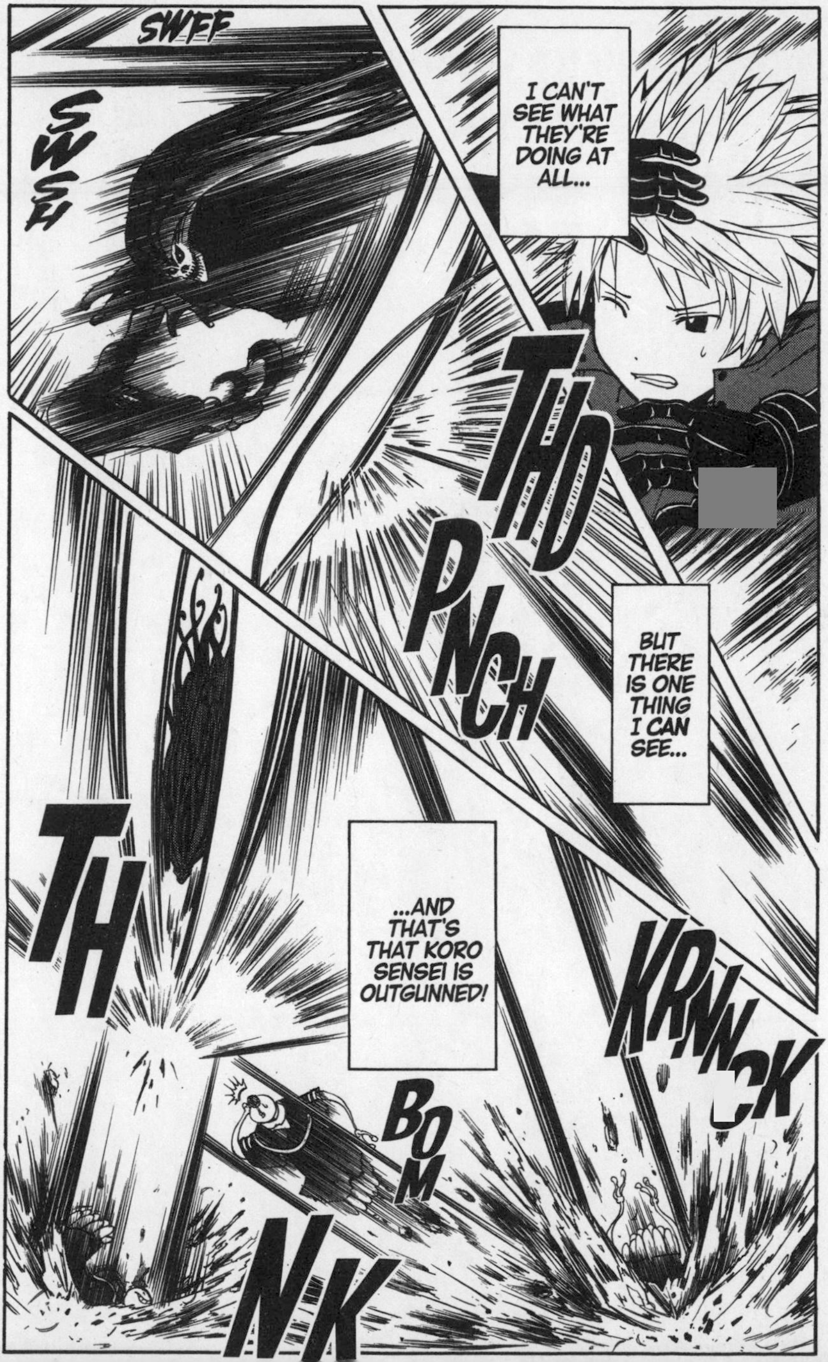
I CAN'T SEE WHAT THEY'RE DOING AT ALL...
SWFF
SWSH
THD
PNCH
BUT THERE IS ONE THING I CAN SEE...
KRNNCK
...AND THAT'S THAT KORO SENSEI IS OUTGUNNED!
BOM
TH
NK

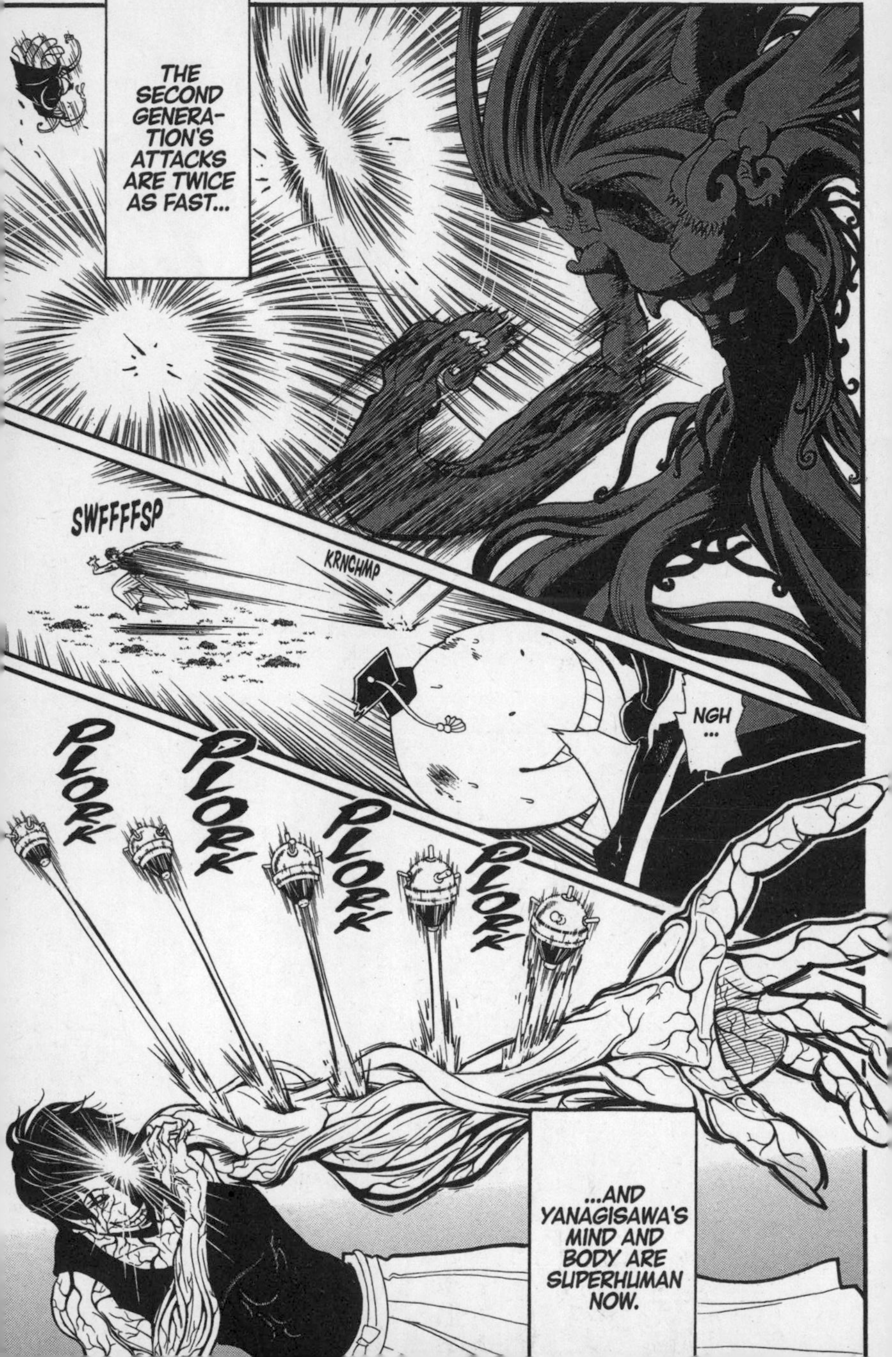
THE SECOND GENERATION'S ATTACKS ARE TWICE AS FAST...
KRNCHMP
SWFFFFSP
NGH...
PLORK
PLORK
PLORK
PLORK
PLORK
...AND YANAGISAWA'S MIND AND BODY ARE SUPERHUMAN NOW.

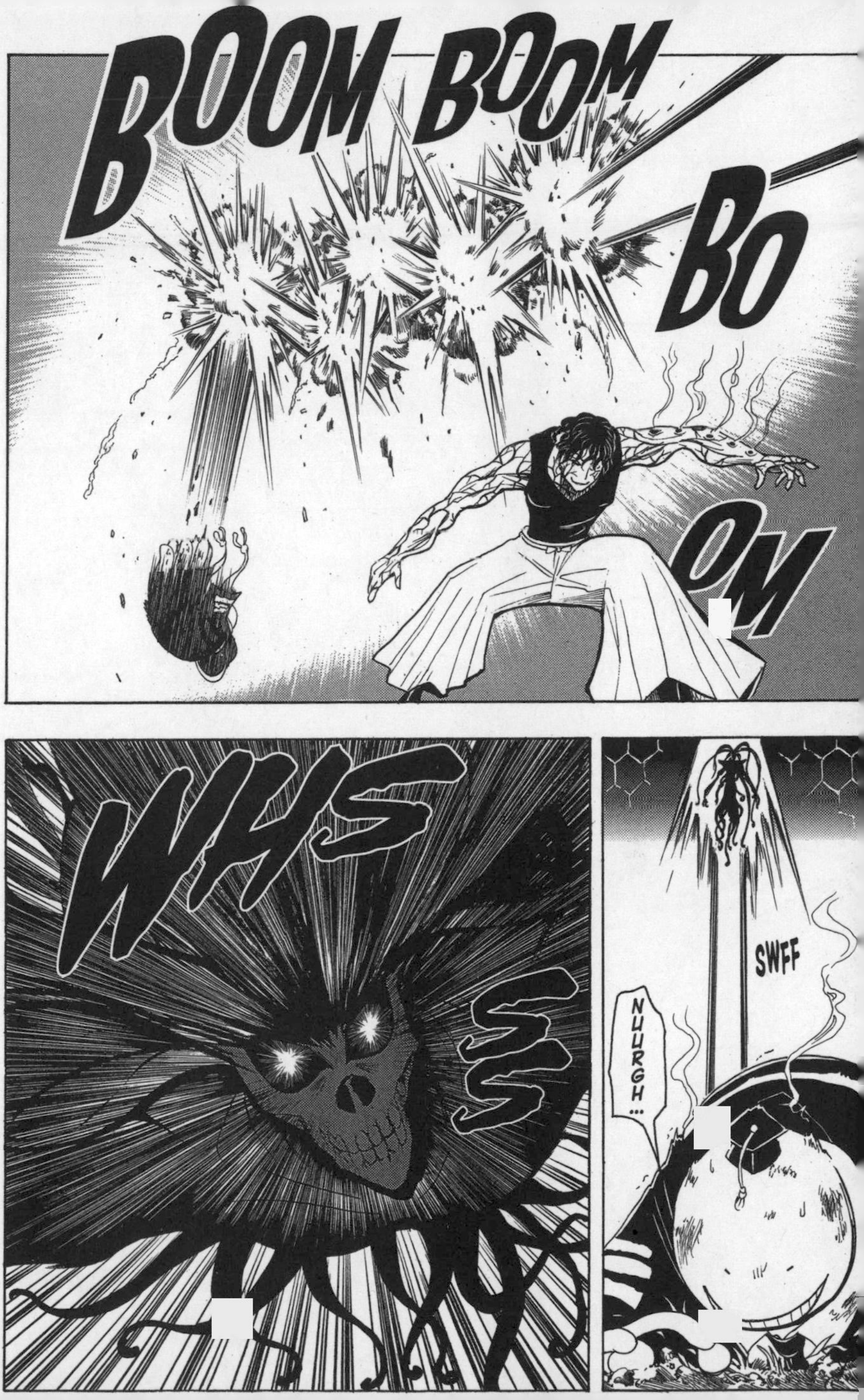
BOOM BOOM
BO
OM
SWFF
NUURGH...
WHS
SS

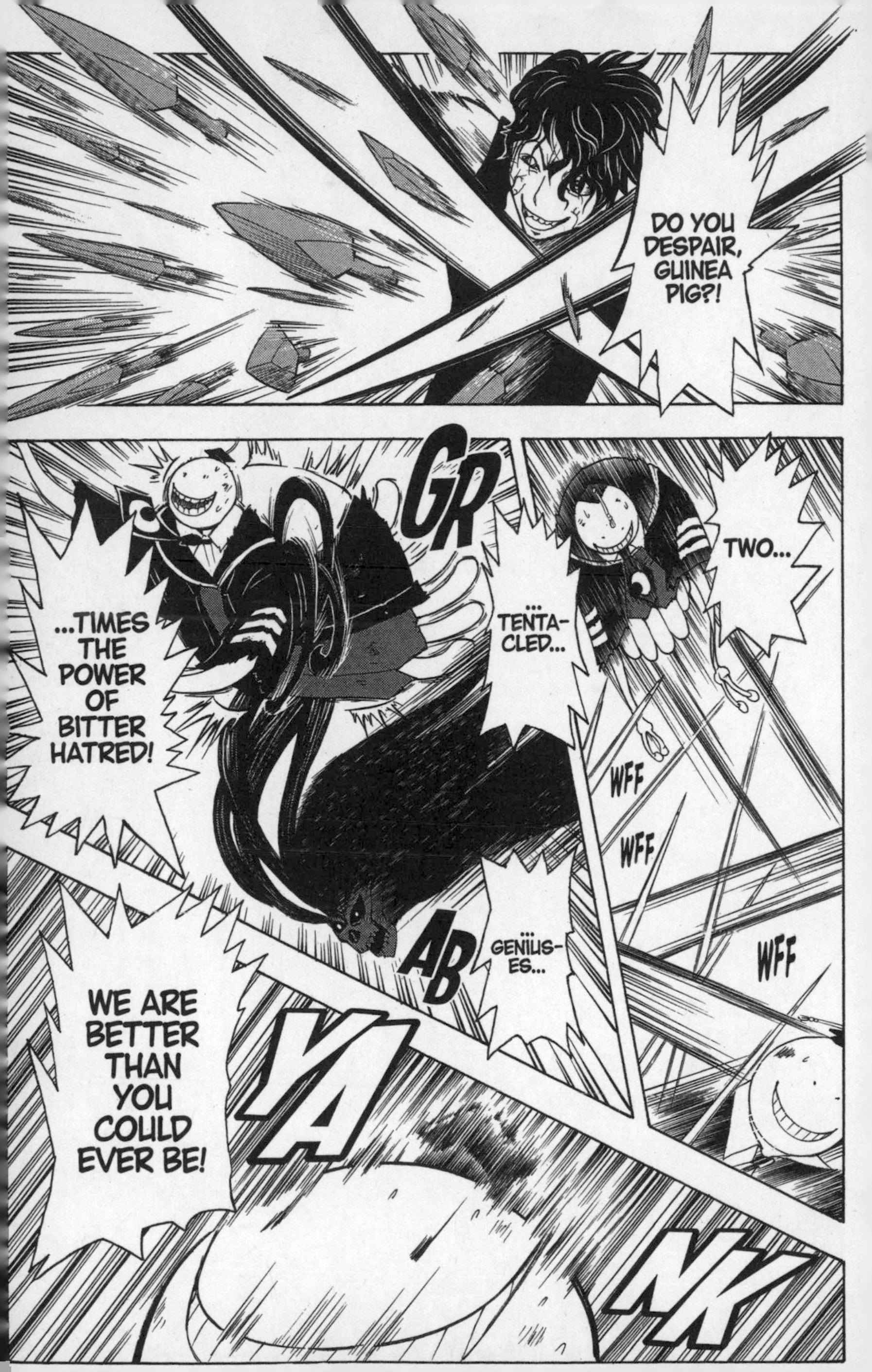
DO YOU DESPAIR, GUINEA PIG?!
TWO...
WFF
WFF
WFF
...TENTACLED...
GR
AB
GENIUSES...
...TIMES THE POWER OF BITTER HATRED!
WE ARE BETTER THAN YOU COULD EVER BE!
YA
NK

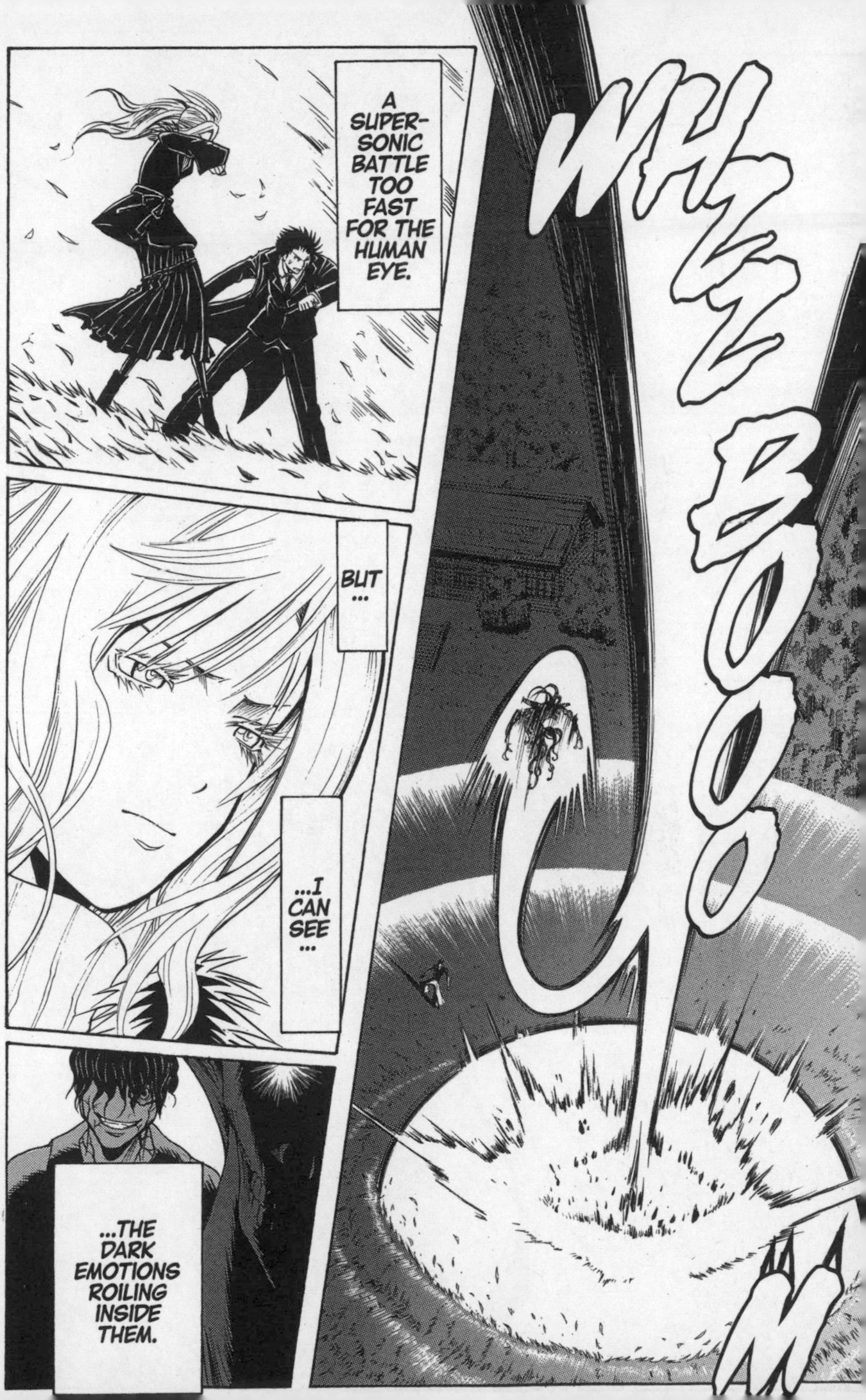
WHUBOOOOM
A SUPER-SONIC BATTLE TOO FAST FOR THE HUMAN EYE.
BUT...
...I CAN SEE...
...THE DARK EMOTIONS ROILING INSIDE THEM.

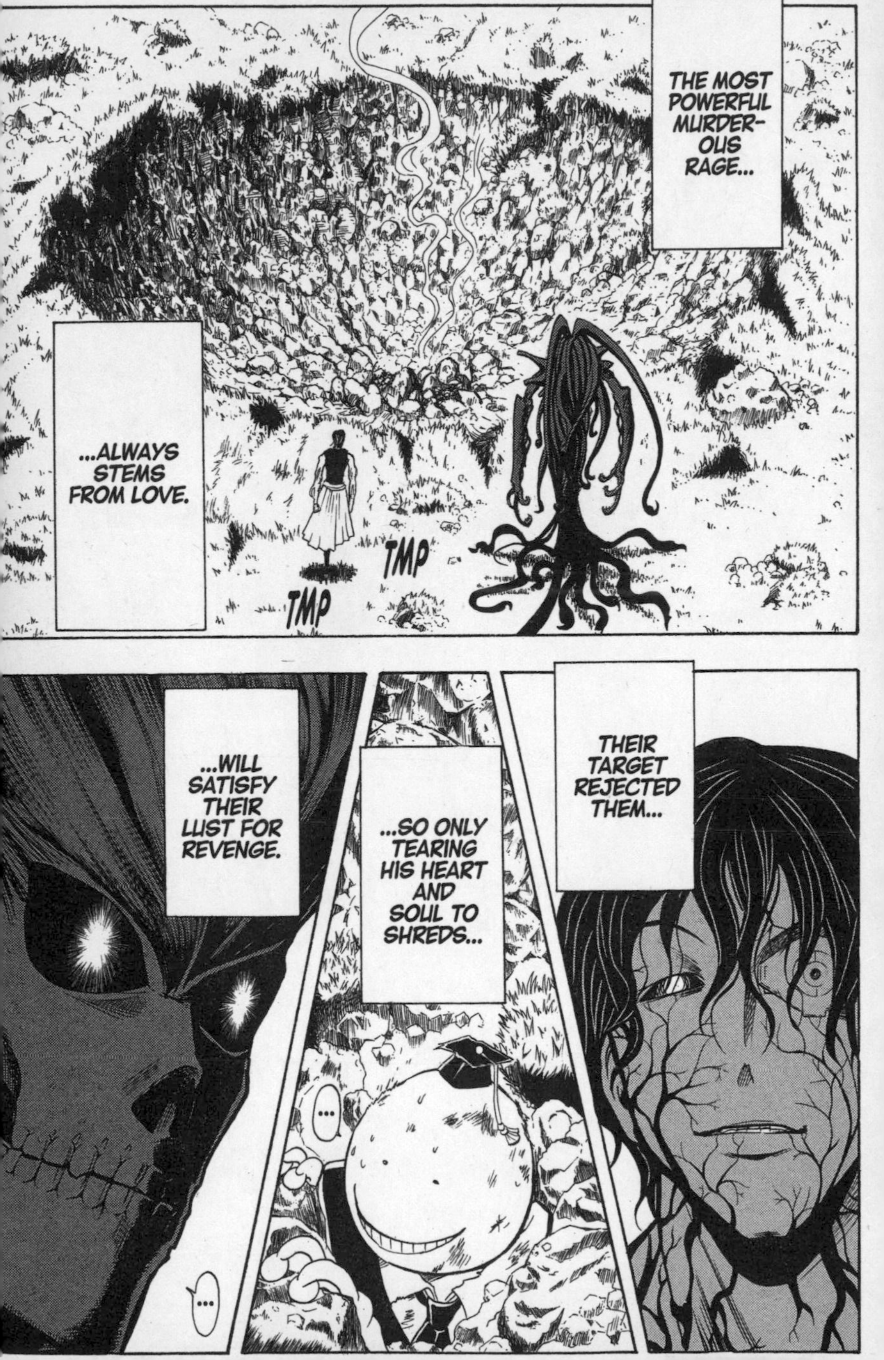
THE MOST POWERFUL MURDER-OUS RAGE...
TMP
TMP
...ALWAYS STEMS FROM LOVE.
THEIR TARGET REJECTED THEM...
...SO ONLY TEARING HIS HEART AND SOUL TO SHREDS...
...
...WILL SATISFY THEIR LUST FOR REVENGE.
...

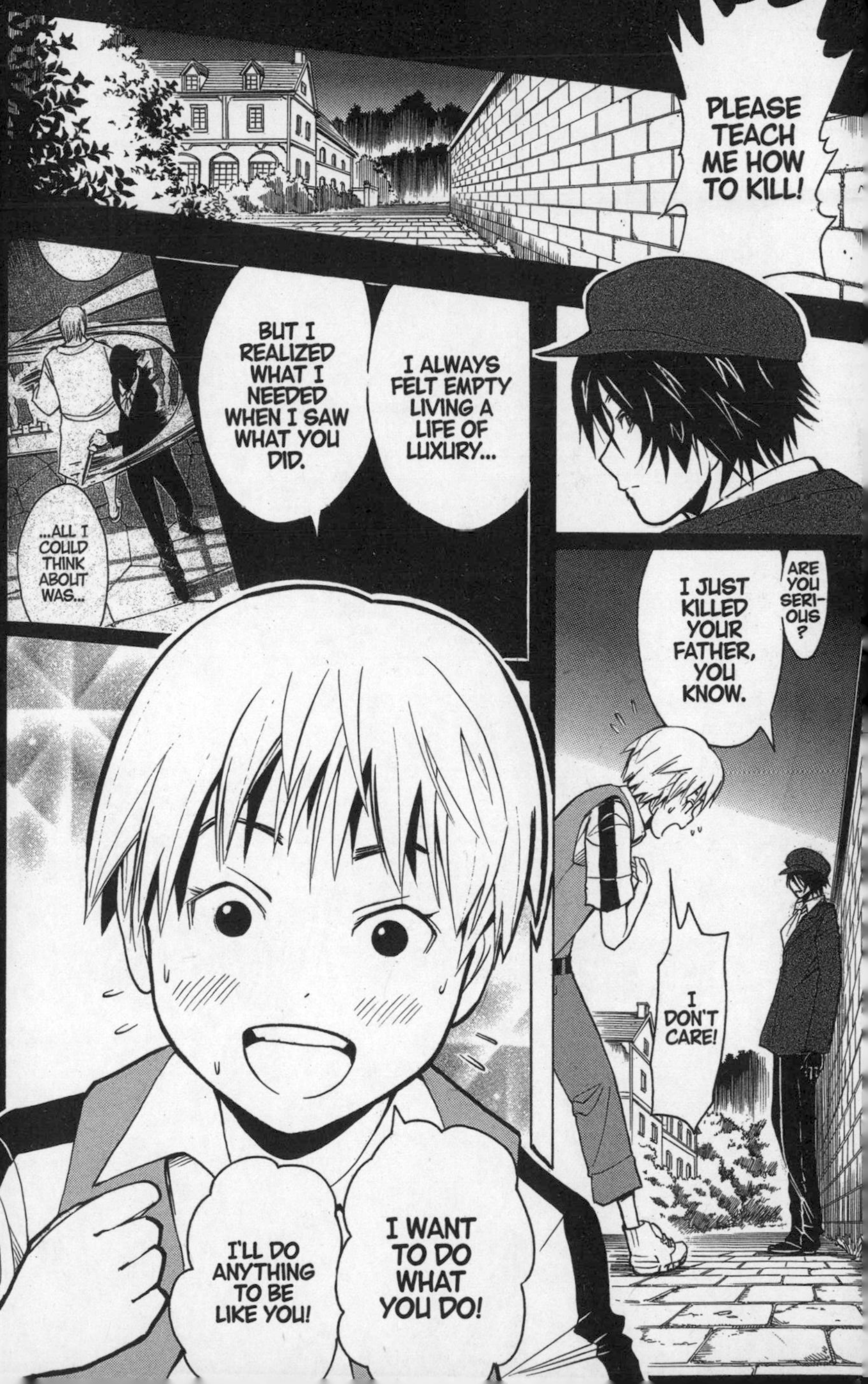
PLEASE TEACH ME HOW TO KILL!
I ALWAYS FELT EMPTY LIVING A LIFE OF LUXURY...
BUT I REALIZED WHAT I NEEDED WHEN I SAW WHAT YOU DID.
...ALL I COULD THINK ABOUT WAS...
ARE YOU SERIOUS?
I JUST KILLED YOUR FATHER, YOU KNOW.
I DON'T CARE!
I WANT TO DO WHAT YOU DO!
I'LL DO ANYTHING TO BE LIKE YOU!

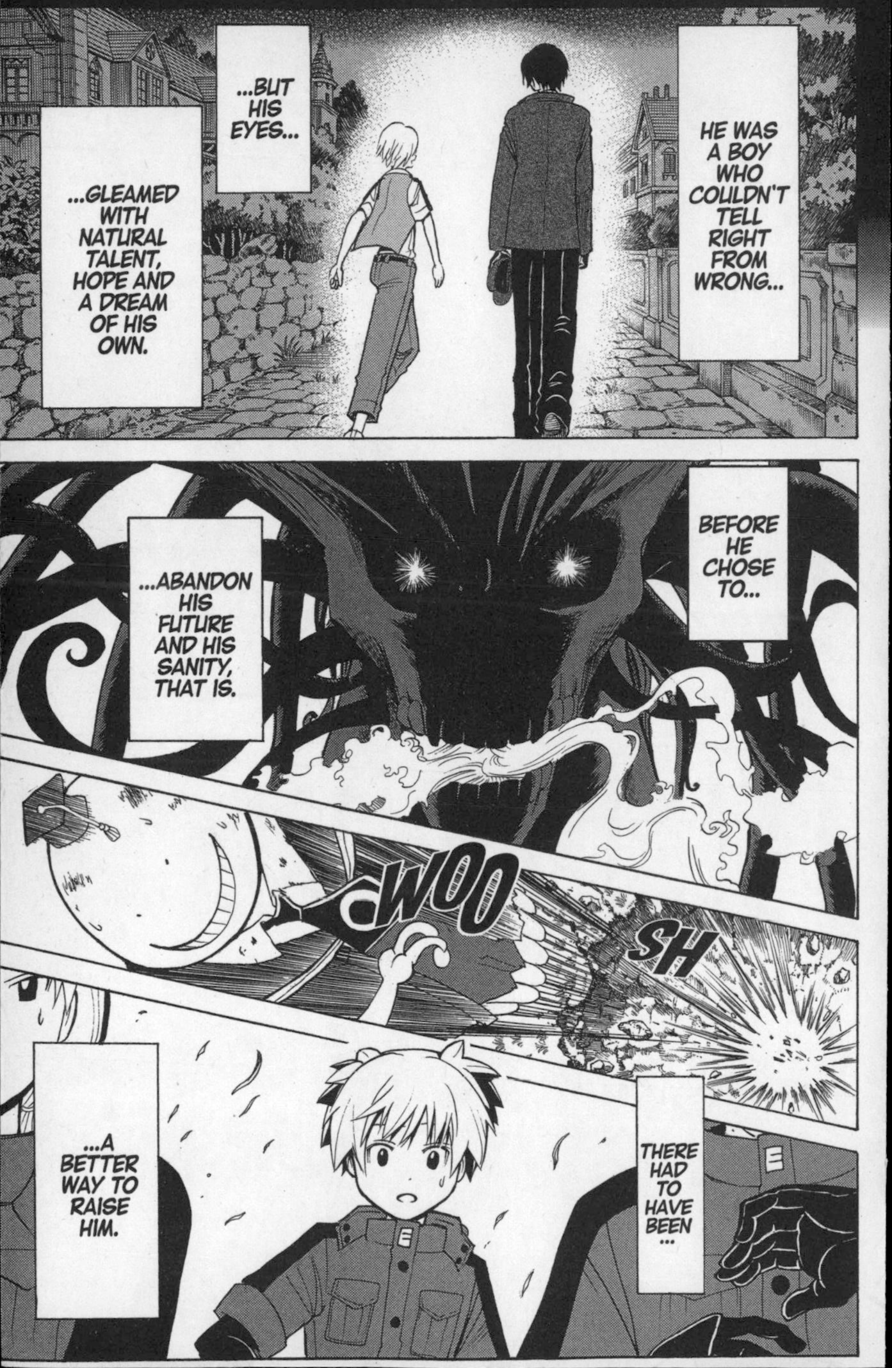
HE WAS A BOY WHO COULDN'T TELL RIGHT FROM WRONG...
...BUT HIS EYES...
...GLEAMED WITH NATURAL TALENT, HOPE AND A DREAM OF HIS OWN.
BEFORE HE CHOSE TO...
...ABANDON HIS FUTURE AND HIS SANITY, THAT IS.
WOO
SH
THERE HAD TO HAVE BEEN...
...A BETTER WAY TO RAISE HIM.

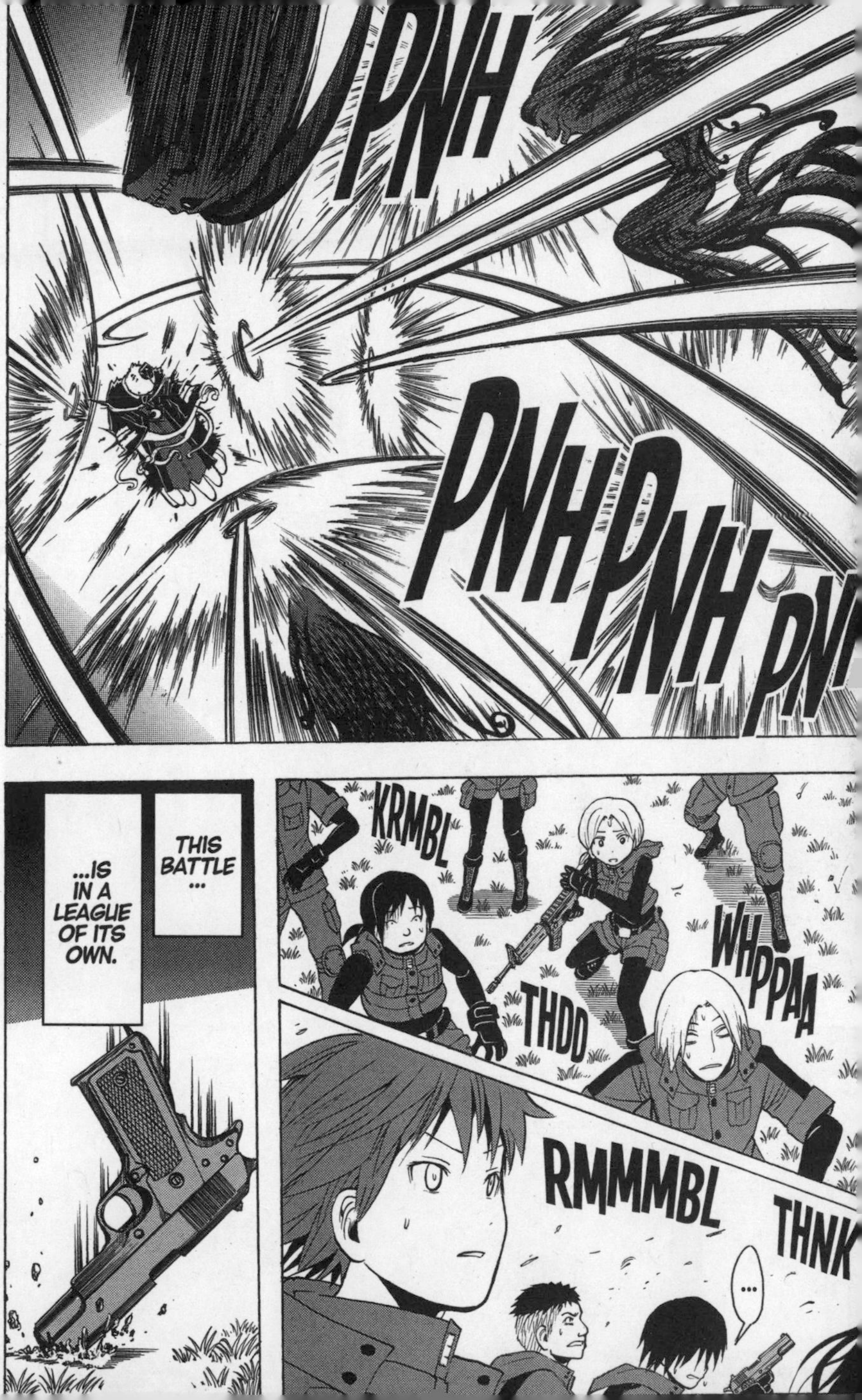
PNH
PNHPNH PN
KRMBL
WHPPAA
THDD
RMMMBL
THNK
...
THIS BATTLE ...
...IS IN A LEAGUE OF ITS OWN.

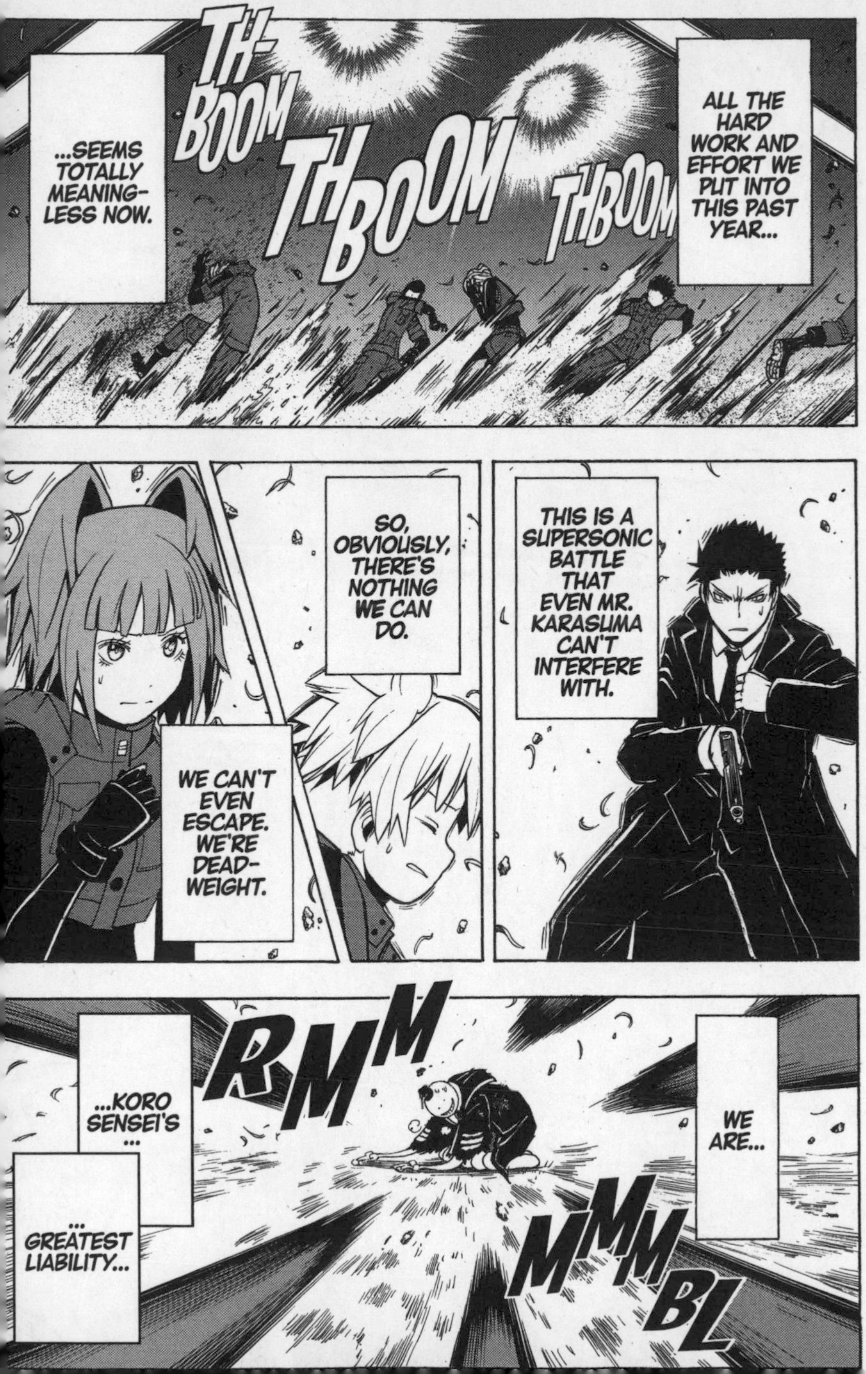
ALL THE HARD WORK AND EFFORT WE PUT INTO THIS PAST YEAR...
THBOOM
THBOOM
TH-BOOM
...SEEMS TOTALLY MEANING-LESS NOW.
THIS IS A SUPERSONIC BATTLE THAT EVEN MR. KARASUMA CAN'T INTERFERE WITH.
SO, OBVIOUSLY, THERE'S NOTHING WE CAN DO.
WE CAN'T EVEN ESCAPE. WE'RE DEAD-WEIGHT.
WE ARE...
RMMM
...KORO SENSEI'S...
...GREATEST LIABILITY...
MMMMBL

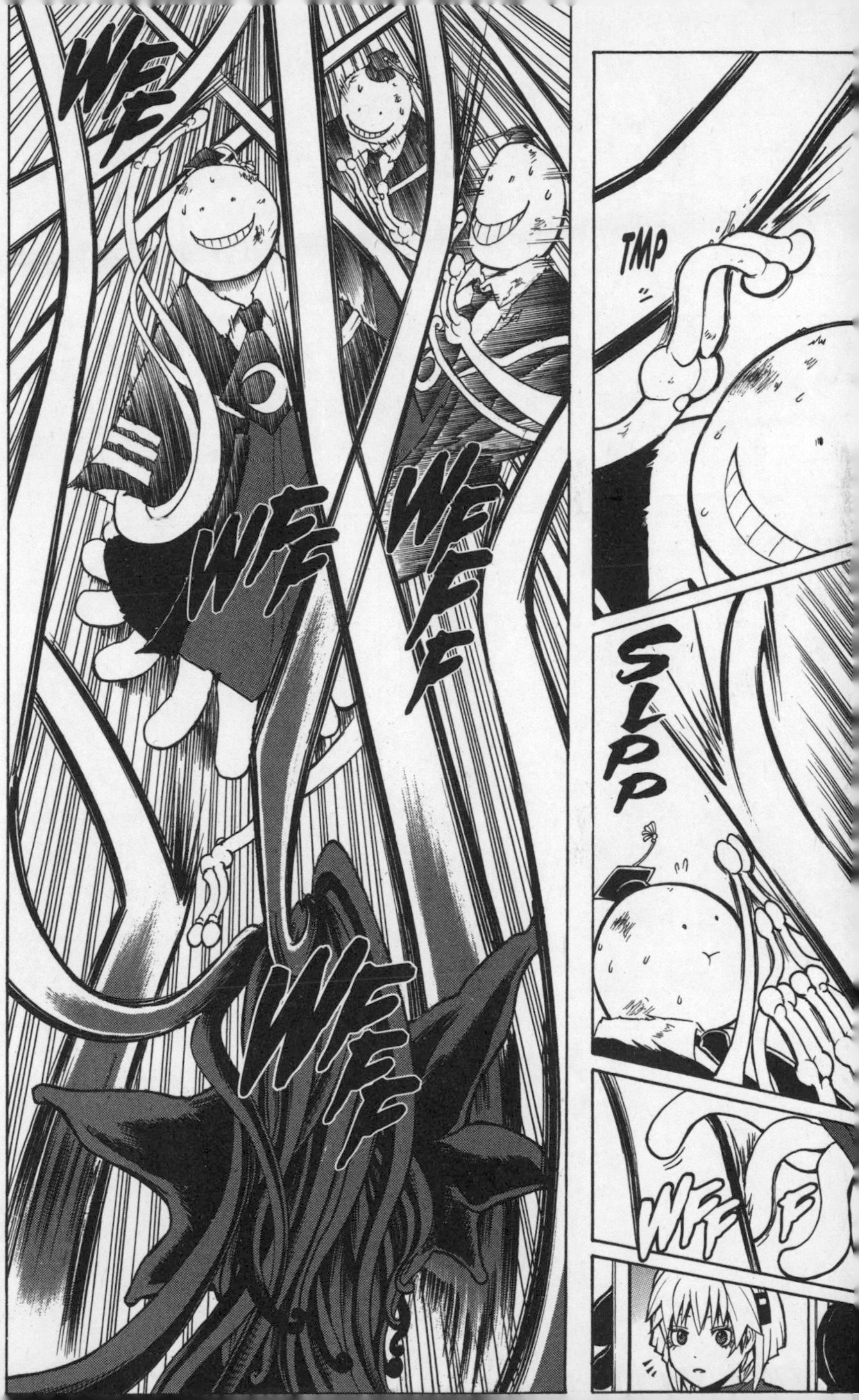
TMP
SLIPP
WFF F
WFF
WFF
WFF
WFF

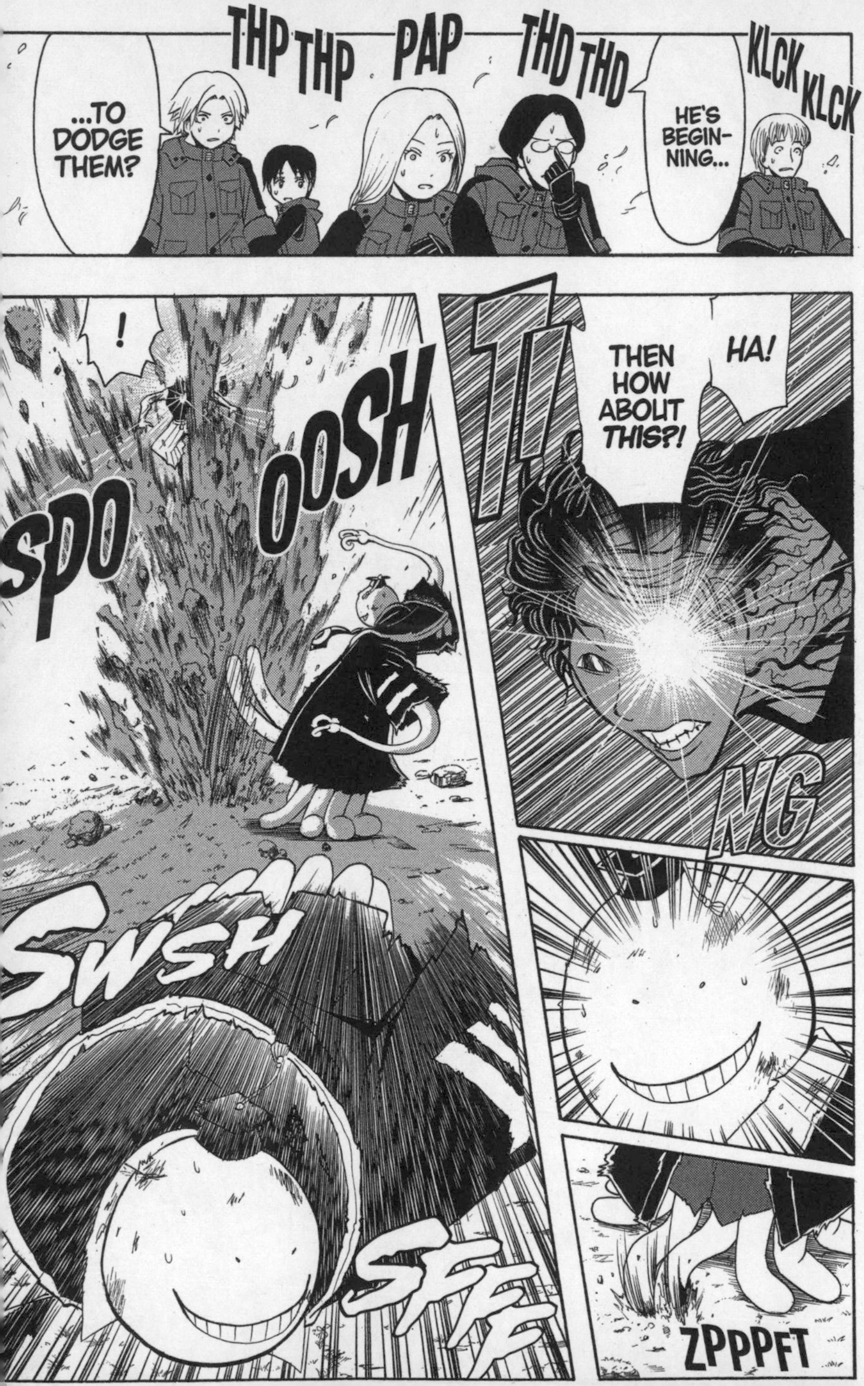
KLCK KLCK
HE'S BEGIN-NING...
THD THD
PAP
THP THP
...TO DODGE THEM?
HA!
THEN HOW ABOUT THIS?!
TI
NG
ZPPPFT
!
SPO
OOSH
SWSH
SFF

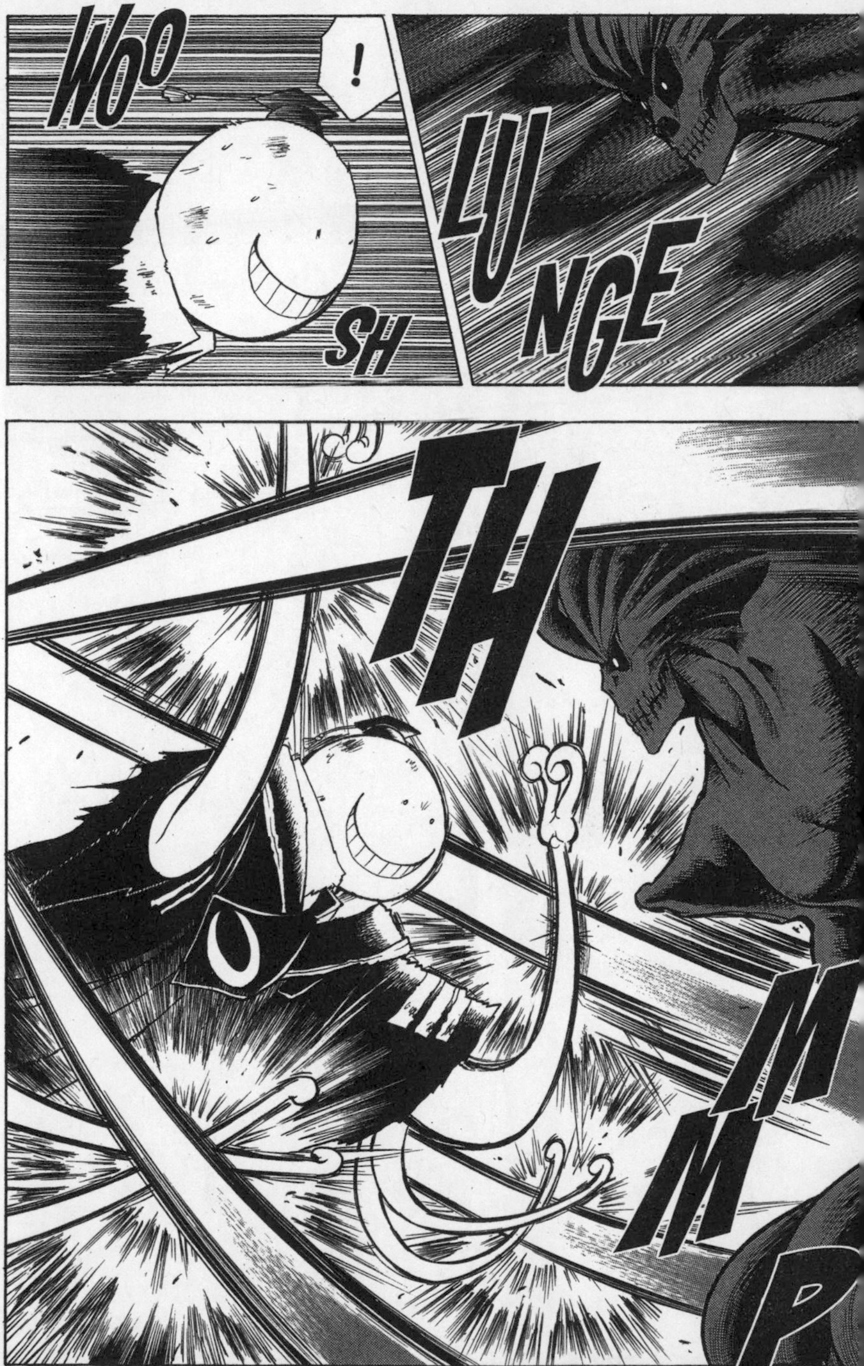
LUNGE
!
WOO
SH
TH
MMP

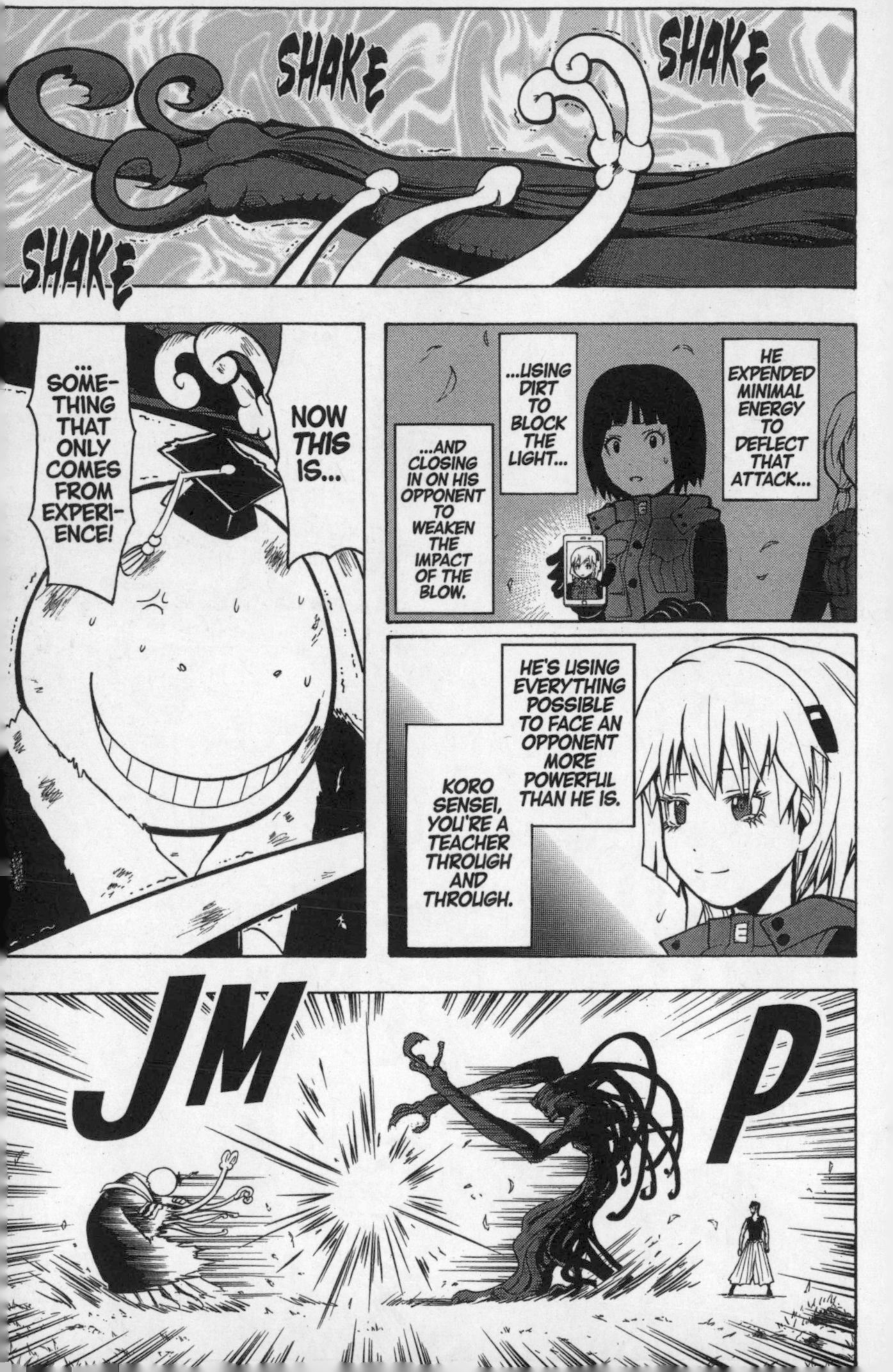
SHAKE
SHAKE
SHAKE
HE EXPENDED MINIMAL ENERGY TO DEFLECT THAT ATTACK...
...USING DIRT TO BLOCK THE LIGHT...
...AND CLOSING IN ON HIS OPPONENT TO WEAKEN THE IMPACT OF THE BLOW.
HE'S USING EVERYTHING POSSIBLE TO FACE AN OPPONENT MORE POWERFUL THAN HE IS.
KORO SENSEI, YOU'RE A TEACHER THROUGH AND THROUGH.
NOW THIS IS...
...SOME-THING THAT ONLY COMES FROM EXPERI-ENCE!
JM
P

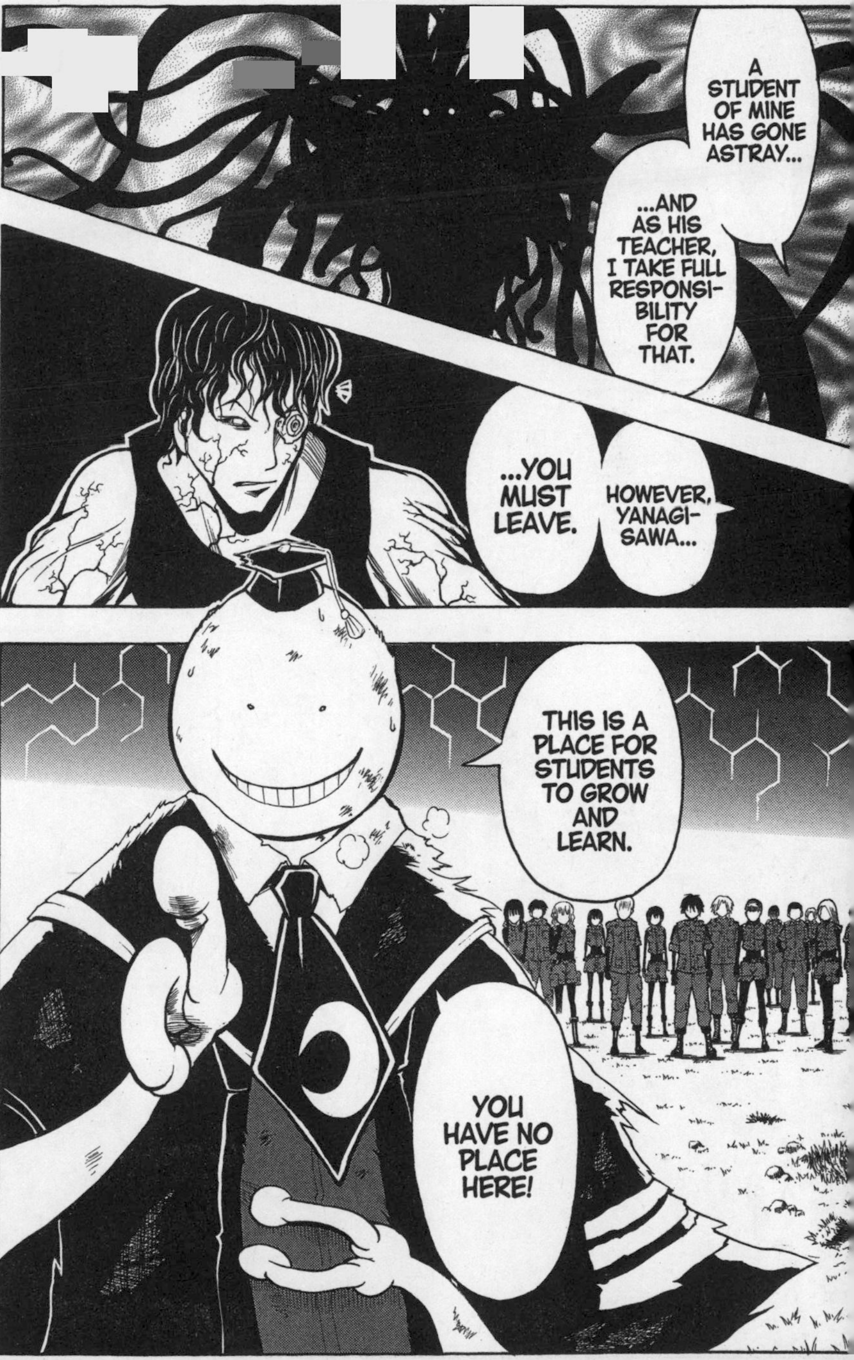
A STUDENT OF MINE HAS GONE ASTRAY...
...AND AS HIS TEACHER, I TAKE FULL RESPONSIBILITY FOR THAT.
HOWEVER, YANAGISAWA...
...YOU MUST LEAVE.
THIS IS A PLACE FOR STUDENTS TO GROW AND LEARN.
YOU HAVE NO PLACE HERE!

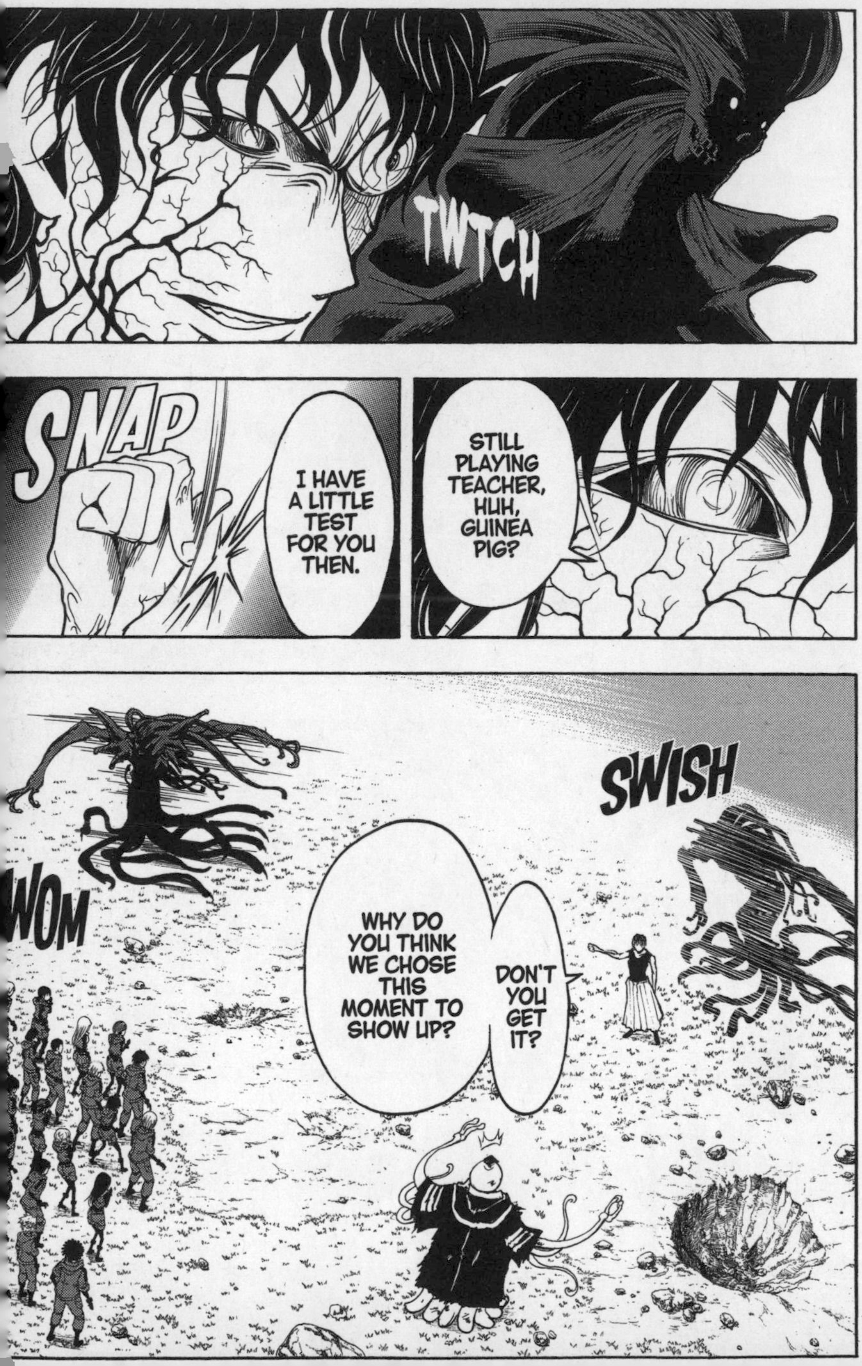
TWTCH
STILL PLAYING TEACHER, HUH, GUINEA PIG?
SNAP
I HAVE A LITTLE TEST FOR YOU THEN.
SWISH
DON'T YOU GET IT?
WHY DO YOU THINK WE CHOSE THIS MOMENT TO SHOW UP?
WOM

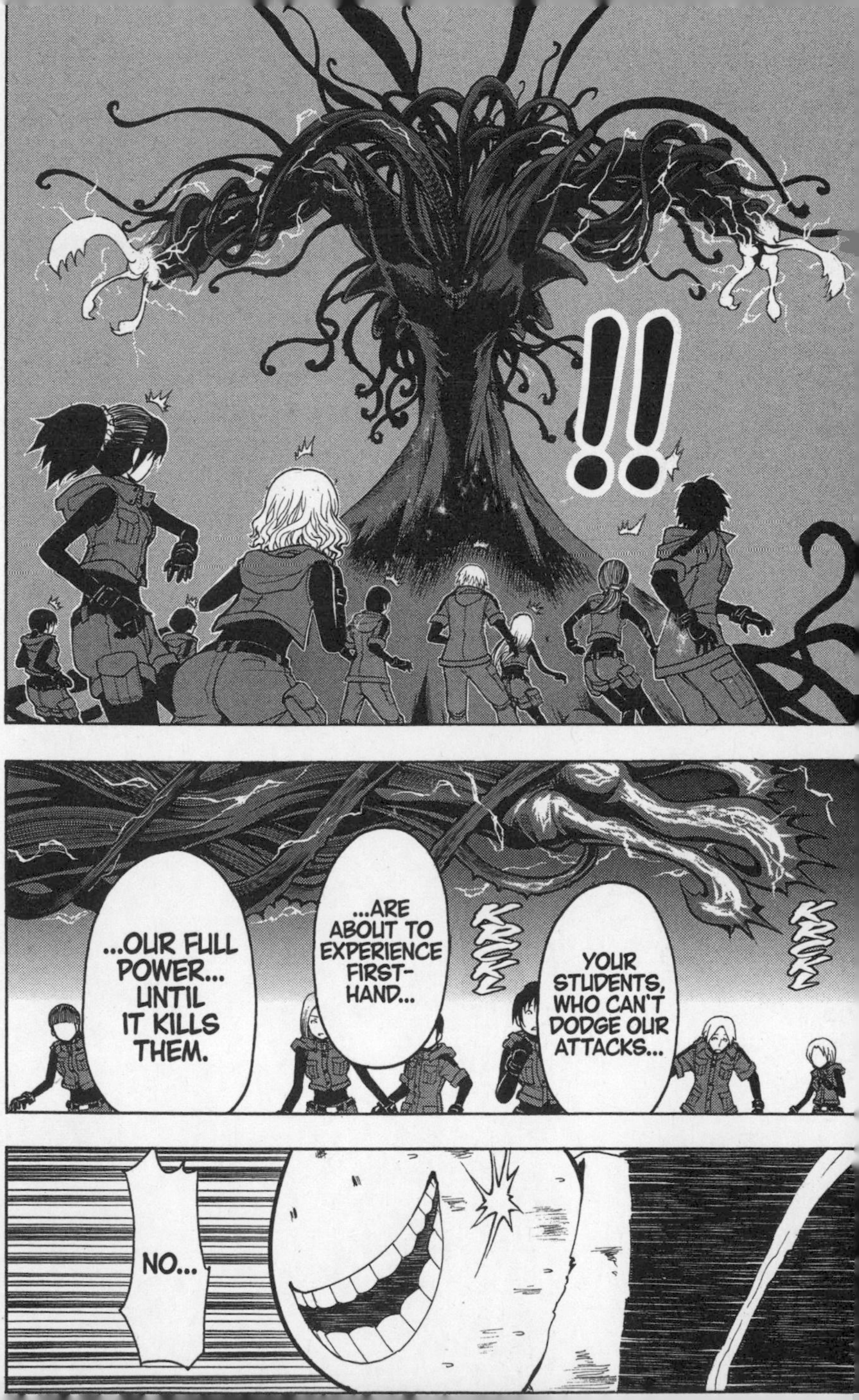
!!
YOUR STUDENTS, WHO CAN'T DODGE OUR ATTACKS...
...ARE ABOUT TO EXPERIENCE FIRST-HAND...
...OUR FULL POWER... UNTIL IT KILLS THEM.
NO...

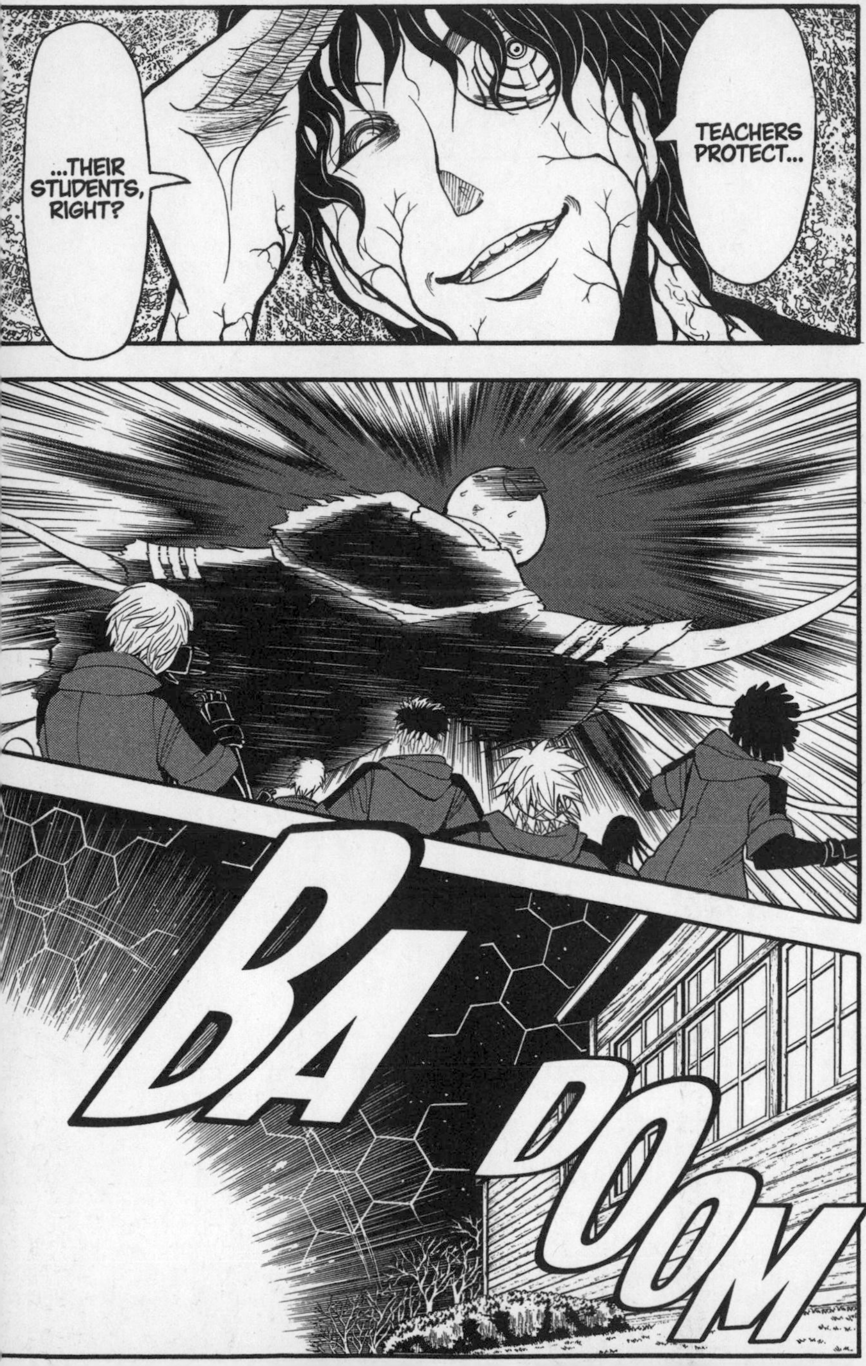
TEACHERS PROTECT...
...THEIR STUDENTS, RIGHT?
BA DOOM

YANAGISAWA

◕ APPEARANCE: HEIGHT AND WEIGHT: SLIGHTLY SHORTER
      THAN AVERAGE. TO SOME, HE SEEMS LIKE
      A YOUNG BOY.

◕ ABILITY: A VERSATILE GENIUS WHO SURPASSES HUMANS.
      SOME PEOPLE THOUGHT THEY SAW HIM FLY
      THROUGH THE SKY WITH WINGS.

◕ PERSONALITY: EXTREMELY RUTHLESS, COLDHEARTED AND
      LOGICAL TO AN INHUMAN EXTENT. BUT ONE
      WOMAN IMAGINED HE WAS A KIND YET
      SOCIALLY INEPT, TRUSTWORTHY MAN.

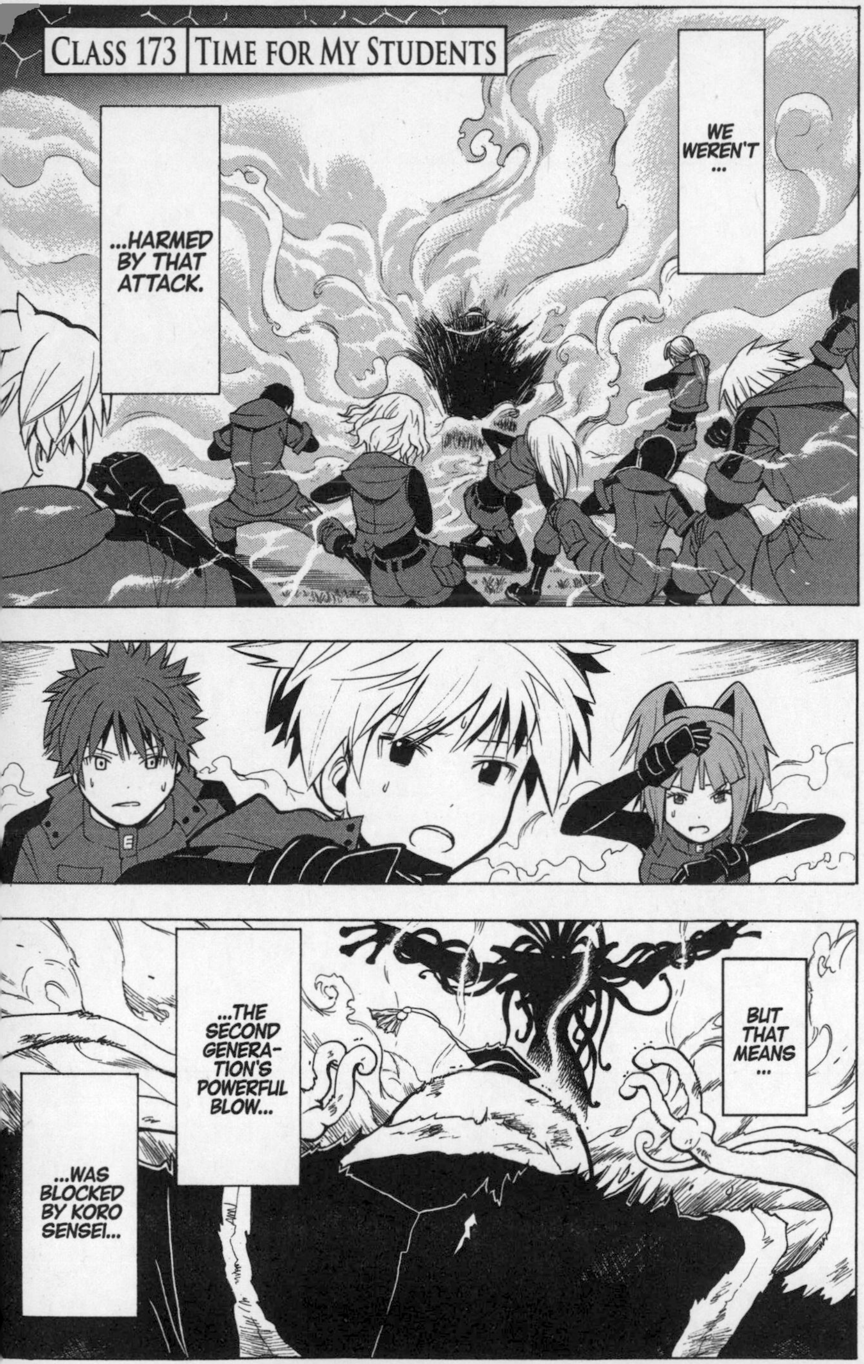
CLASS 173 TIME FOR MY STUDENTS
WE WEREN'T ...
...HARMED BY THAT ATTACK.
BUT THAT MEANS ...
...THE SECOND GENERATION'S POWERFUL BLOW...
...WAS BLOCKED BY KORO SENSEI...

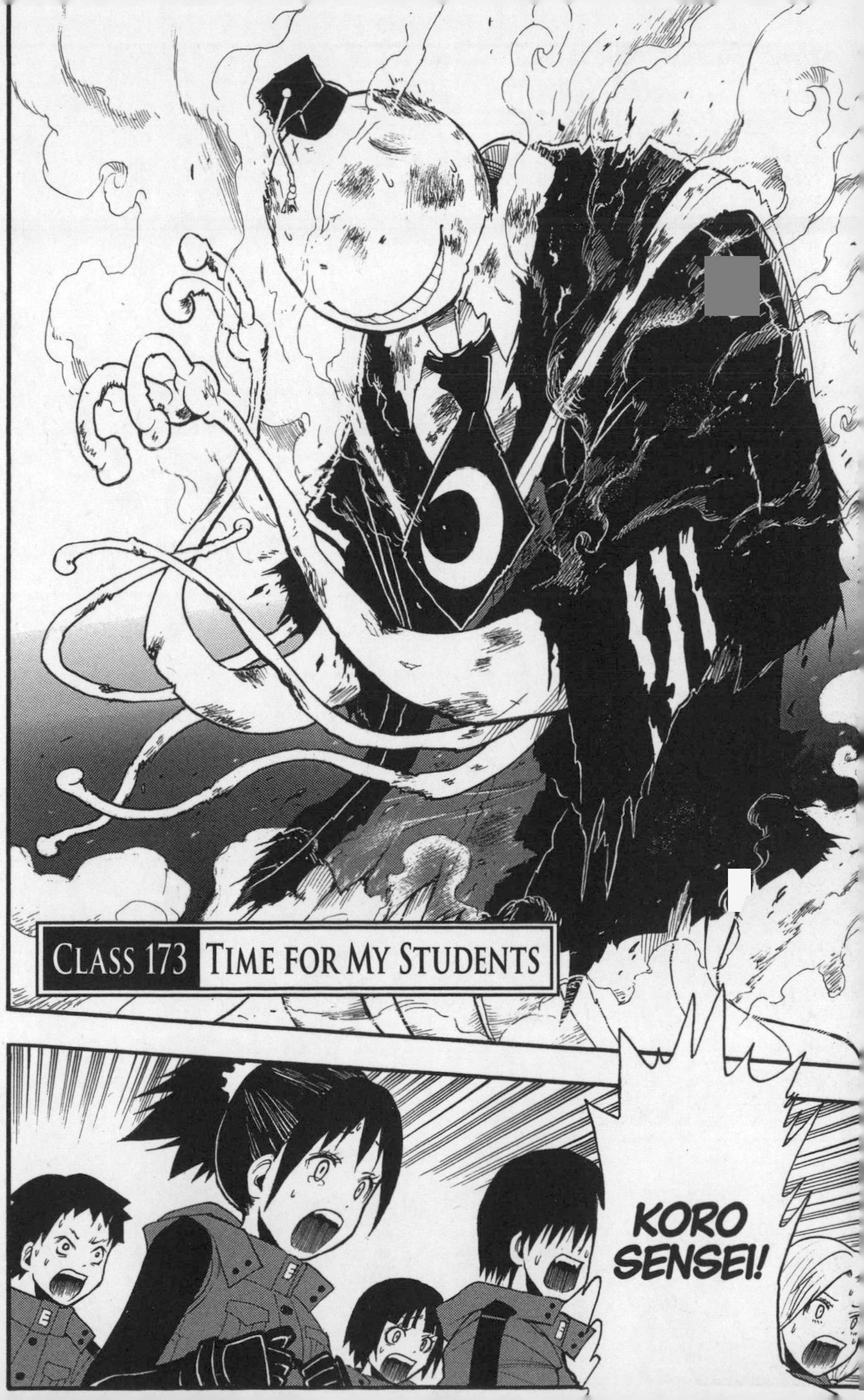
CLASS 173 TIME FOR MY STUDENTS
KORO SENSEI!

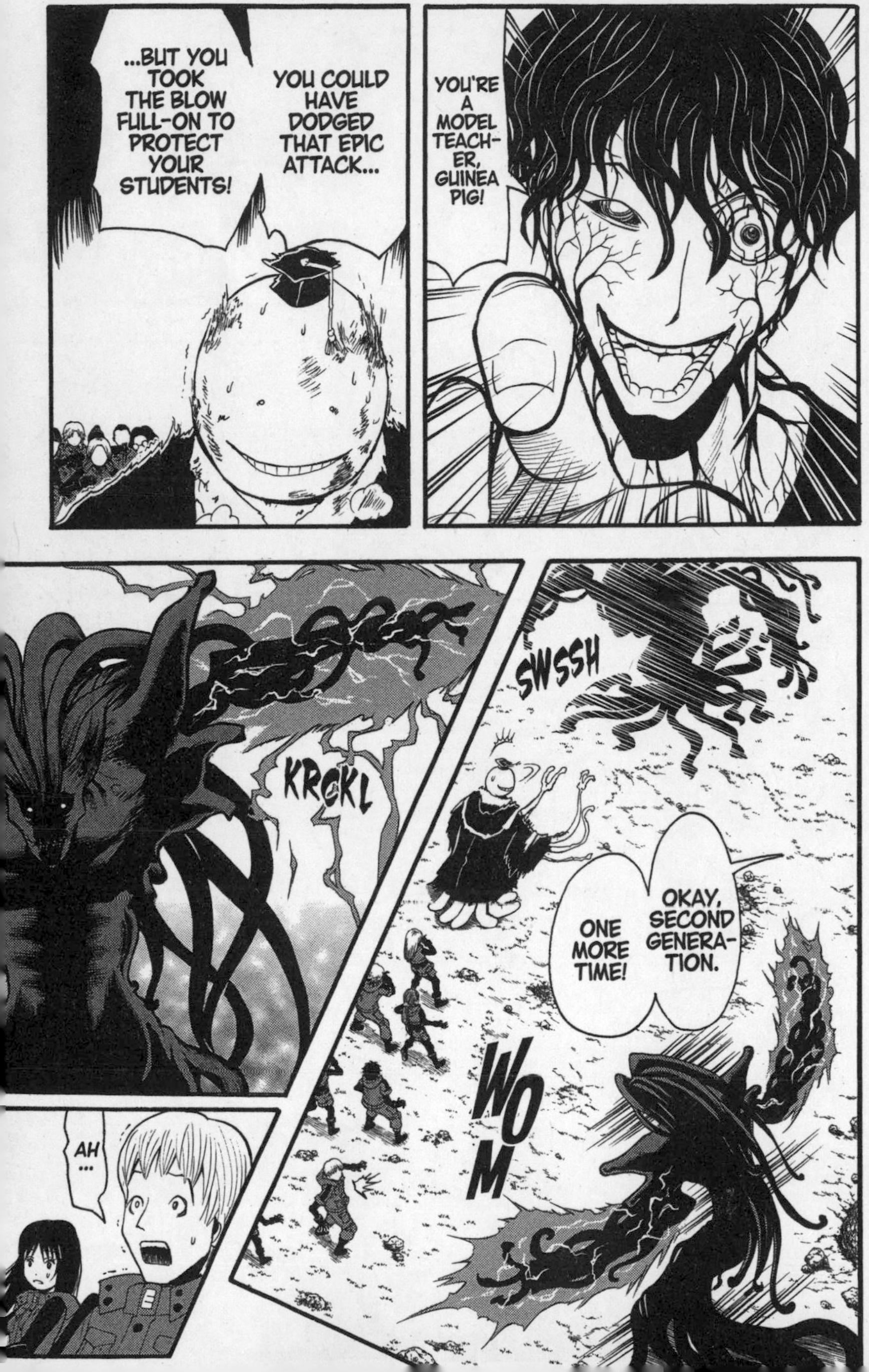
YOU'RE A MODEL TEACHER, GUINEA PIG!
YOU COULD HAVE DODGED THAT EPIC ATTACK...
...BUT YOU TOOK THE BLOW FULL-ON TO PROTECT YOUR STUDENTS!
SWSSH
OKAY, SECOND GENERATION.
ONE MORE TIME!
WOM
KRCKL
AH...

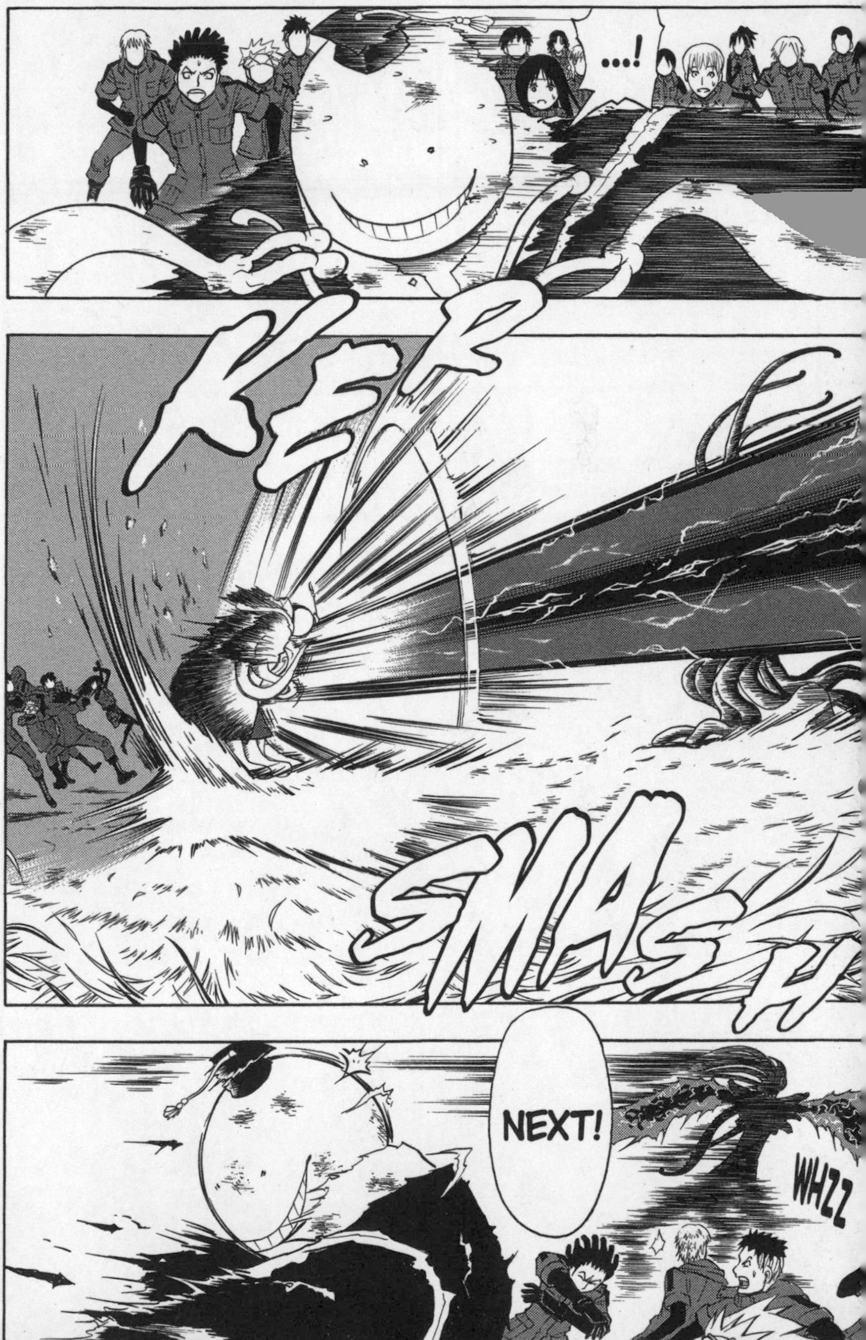
...!
KER
SMASH
NEXT!
WHZZ

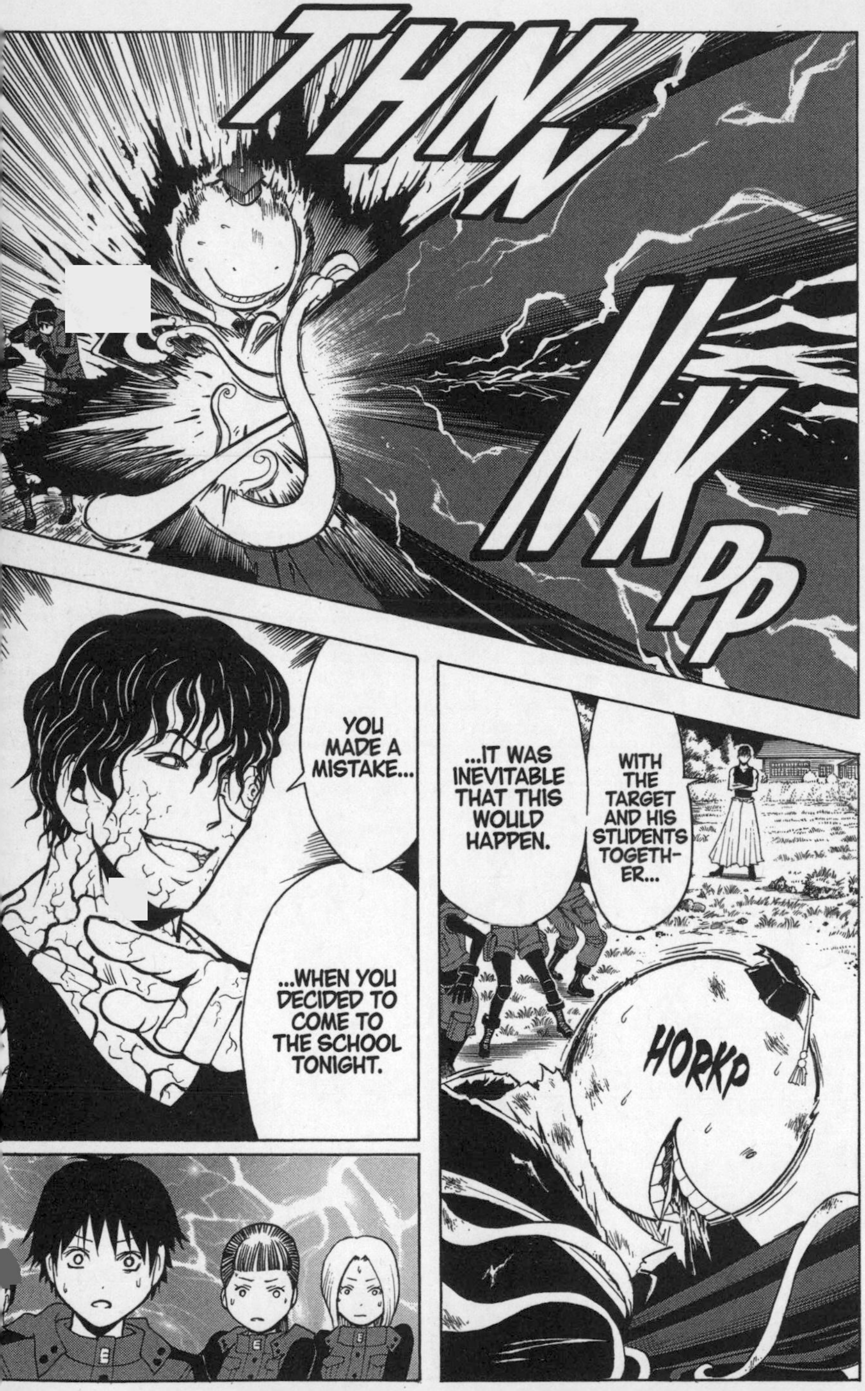
THINNKPP
WITH THE TARGET AND HIS STUDENTS TOGETHER...
...IT WAS INEVITABLE THAT THIS WOULD HAPPEN.
HORKP
YOU MADE A MISTAKE...
...WHEN YOU DECIDED TO COME TO THE SCHOOL TONIGHT.

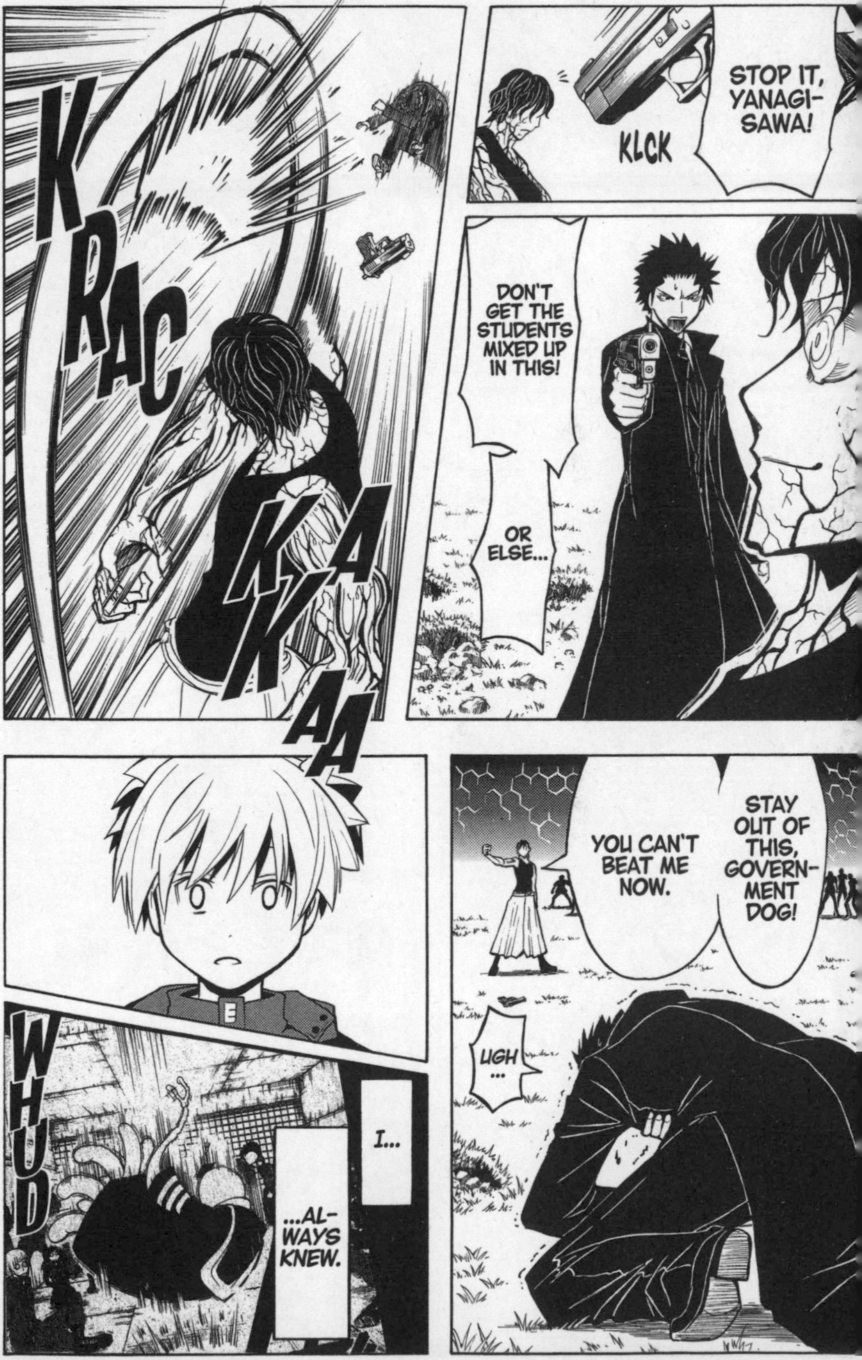
STOP IT, YANAGI-SAWA!
KLCK
DON'T GET THE STUDENTS MIXED UP IN THIS!
OR ELSE...
KRAC
KAKAAA
STAY OUT OF THIS, GOVERNMENT DOG!
YOU CAN'T BEAT ME NOW.
UGH...
E
WHUD
I...
...AL-WAYS KNEW.

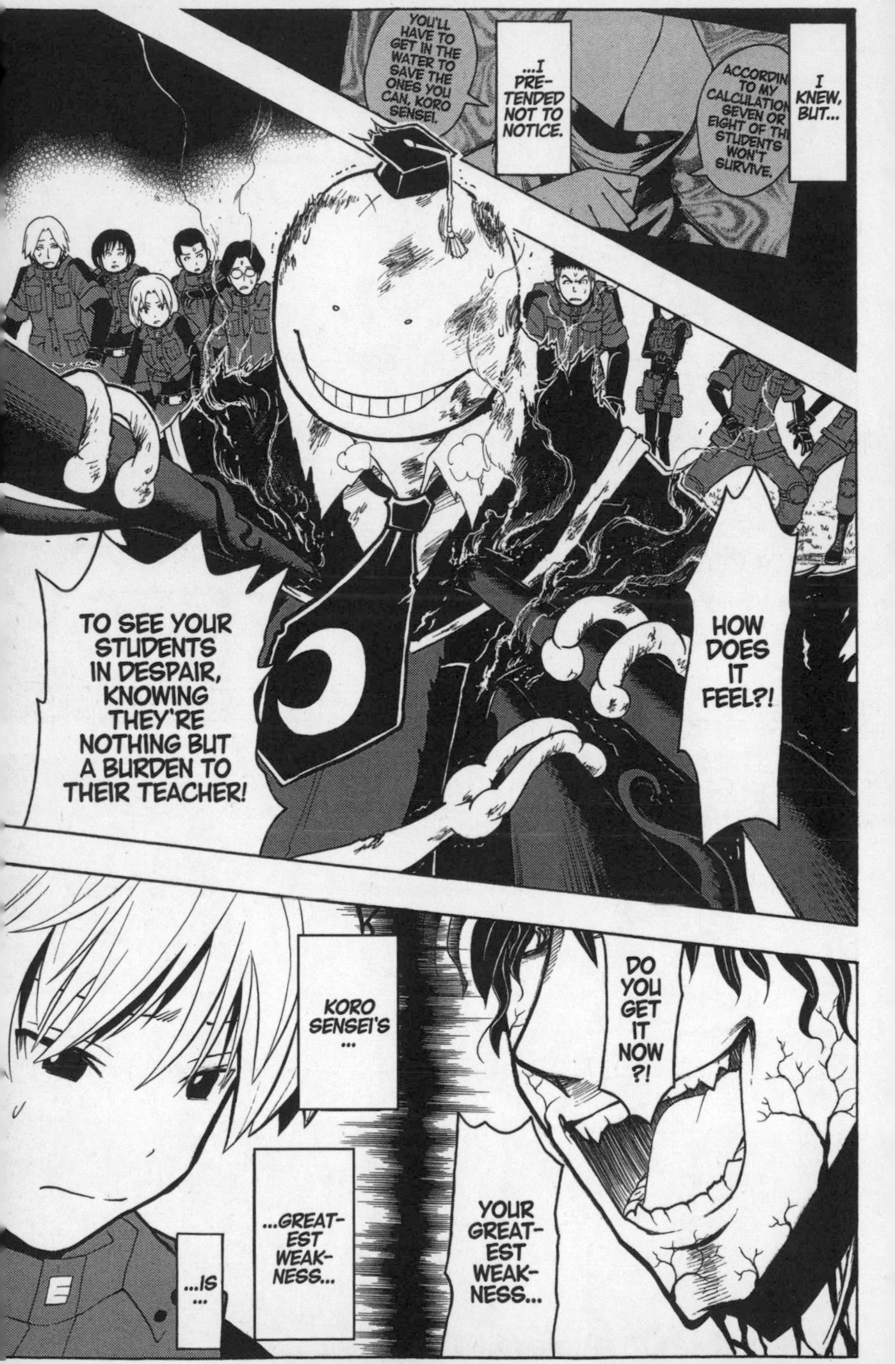
I KNEW, BUT...
ACCORDIN TO MY CALCULATION SEVEN OR EIGHT OF TH STUDENTS WON'T SURVIVE.
...I PRE-TENDED NOT TO NOTICE.
YOU'LL HAVE TO GET IN THE WATER TO SAVE THE ONES YOU CAN, KORO SENSEI.
HOW DOES IT FEEL?!
TO SEE YOUR STUDENTS IN DESPAIR, KNOWING THEY'RE NOTHING BUT A BURDEN TO THEIR TEACHER!
DO YOU GET IT NOW?!
YOUR GREAT-EST WEAK-NESS...
KORO SENSEI'S...
...GREAT-EST WEAK-NESS...
...IS...

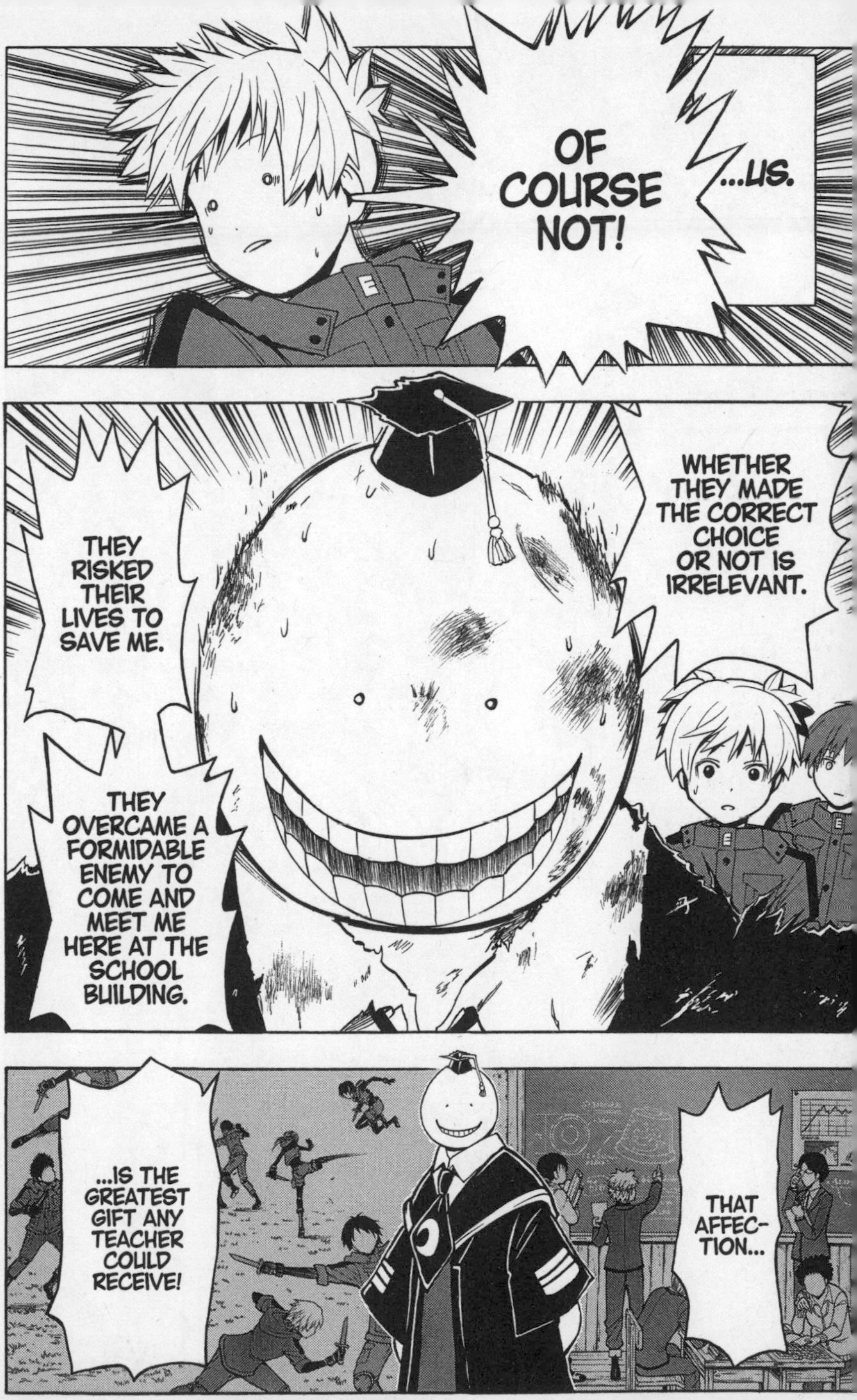
...US.
OF COURSE NOT!
WHETHER THEY MADE THE CORRECT CHOICE OR NOT IS IRRELEVANT.
THEY RISKED THEIR LIVES TO SAVE ME.
THEY OVERCAME A FORMIDABLE ENEMY TO COME AND MEET ME HERE AT THE SCHOOL BUILDING.
THAT AFFEC-TION...
...IS THE GREATEST GIFT ANY TEACHER COULD RECEIVE!

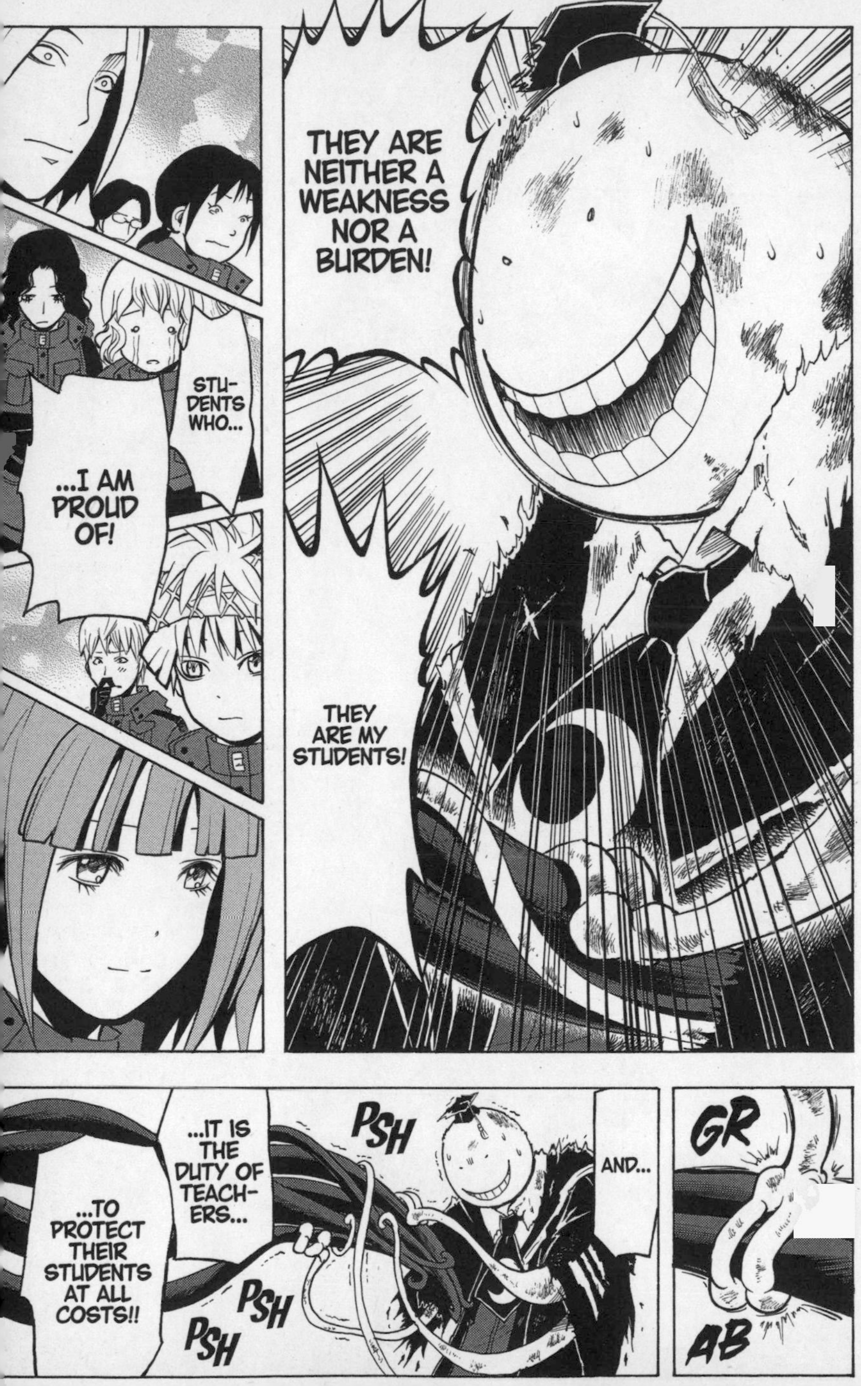
THEY ARE NEITHER A WEAKNESS NOR A BURDEN!
THEY ARE MY STUDENTS!
STU-DENTS WHO...
...I AM PROUD OF!
GR
AB
AND...
PSH
...IT IS THE DUTY OF TEACH-ERS...
PSH
PSH
...TO PROTECT THEIR STUDENTS AT ALL COSTS!!

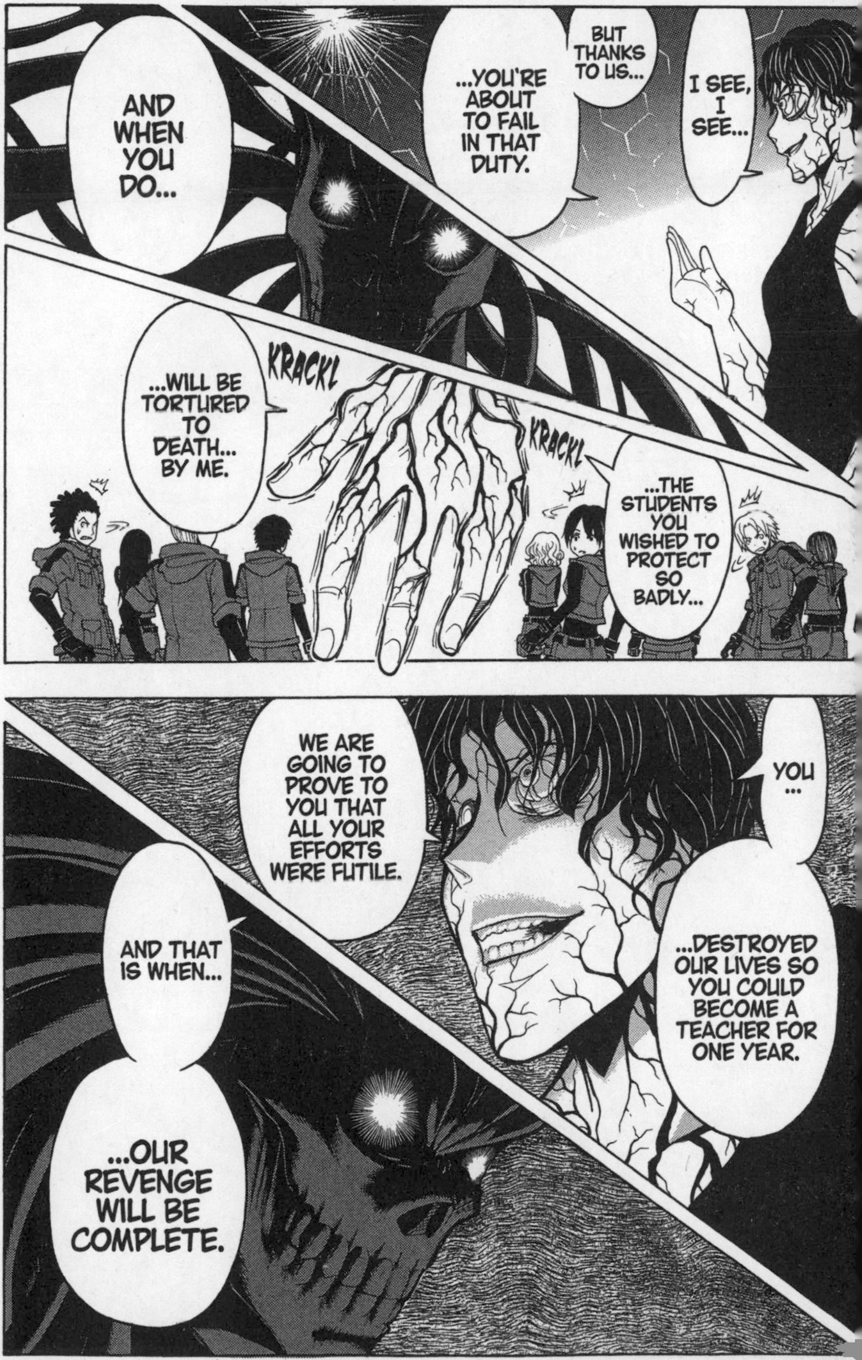
I SEE, I SEE...
BUT THANKS TO US...
...YOU'RE ABOUT TO FAIL IN THAT DUTY.
AND WHEN YOU DO...
KRACKL
KRACKL
...THE STUDENTS YOU WISHED TO PROTECT SO BADLY...
...WILL BE TORTURED TO DEATH... BY ME.
YOU...
...DESTROYED OUR LIVES SO YOU COULD BECOME A TEACHER FOR ONE YEAR.
WE ARE GOING TO PROVE TO YOU THAT ALL YOUR EFFORTS WERE FUTILE.
AND THAT IS WHEN...
...OUR REVENGE WILL BE COMPLETE.

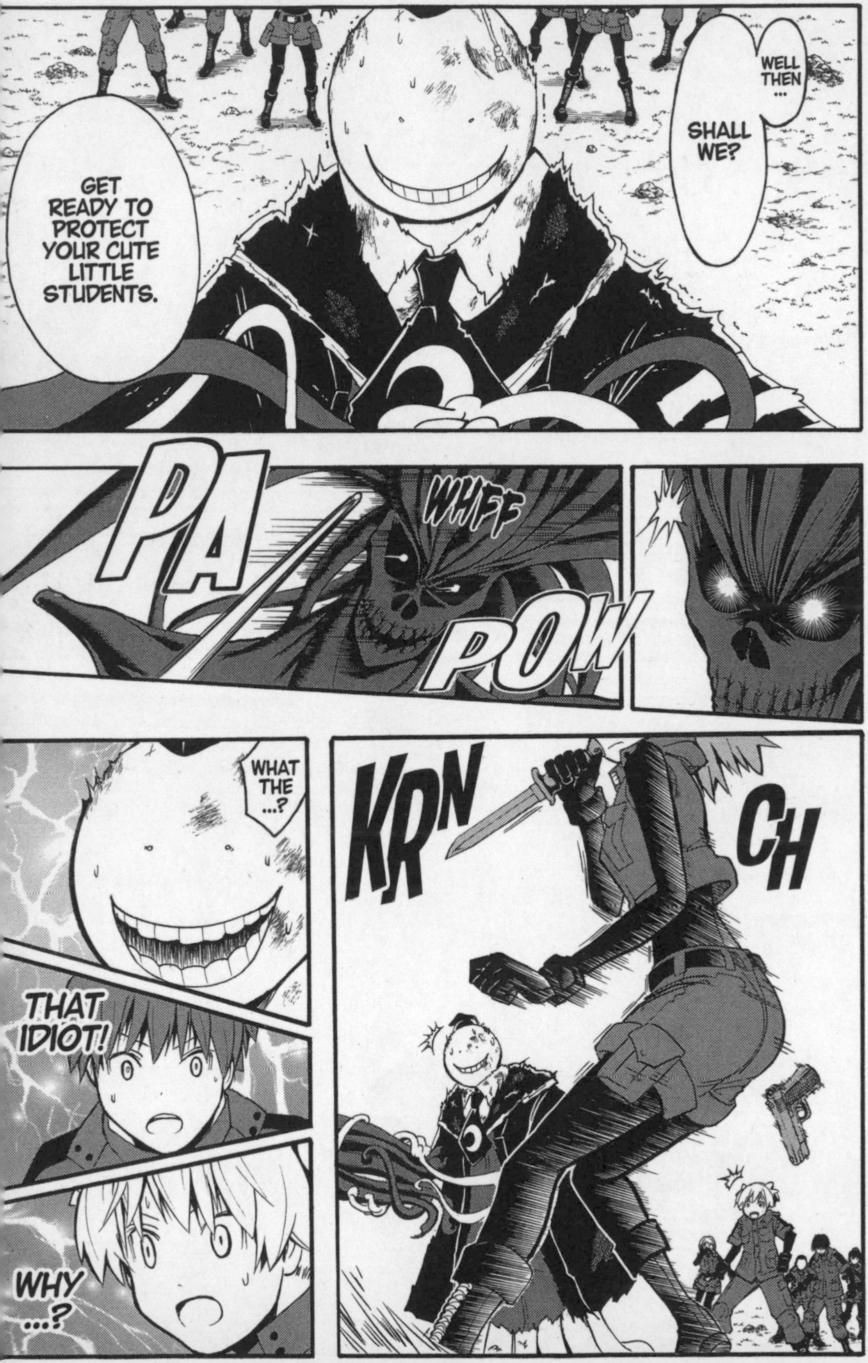
WELL THEN ...
SHALL WE?
GET READY TO PROTECT YOUR CUTE LITTLE STUDENTS.
WHFF
PA
POW
KRN
CH
WHAT THE ...?
THAT IDIOT!
WHY ...?

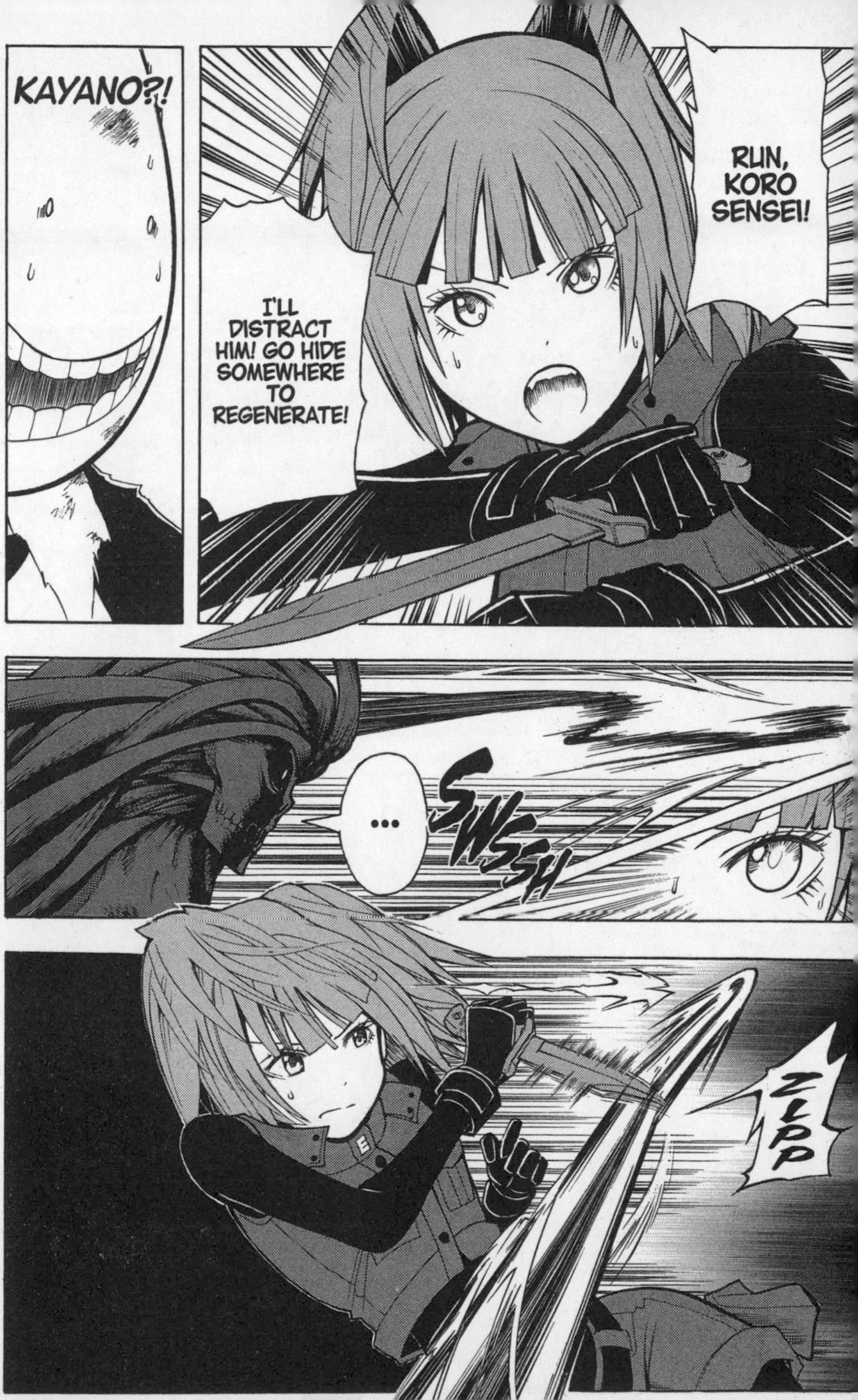
RUN, KORO SENSEI!
I'LL DISTRACT HIM! GO HIDE SOMEWHERE TO REGENERATE!
KAYANO?!
SWSSH
...
ZIPP

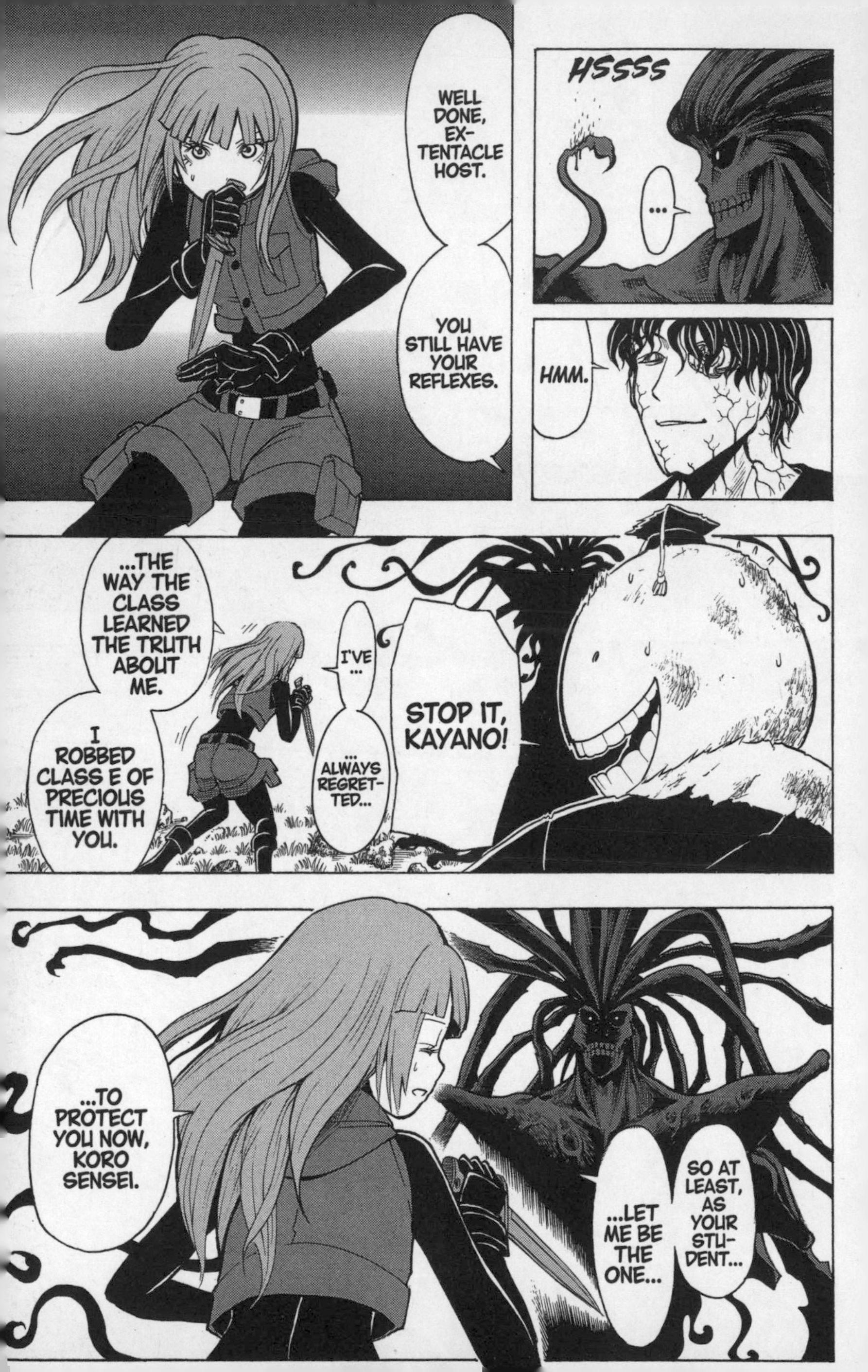
HSSSS
...
HMM.
WELL DONE, EX-TENTACLE HOST.
YOU STILL HAVE YOUR REFLEXES.
STOP IT, KAYANO!
I'VE ...
... ALWAYS REGRET-TED...
...THE WAY THE CLASS LEARNED THE TRUTH ABOUT ME.
I ROBBED CLASS E OF PRECIOUS TIME WITH YOU.
SO AT LEAST, AS YOUR STU-DENT...
...LET ME BE THE ONE...
...TO PROTECT YOU NOW, KORO SENSEI.

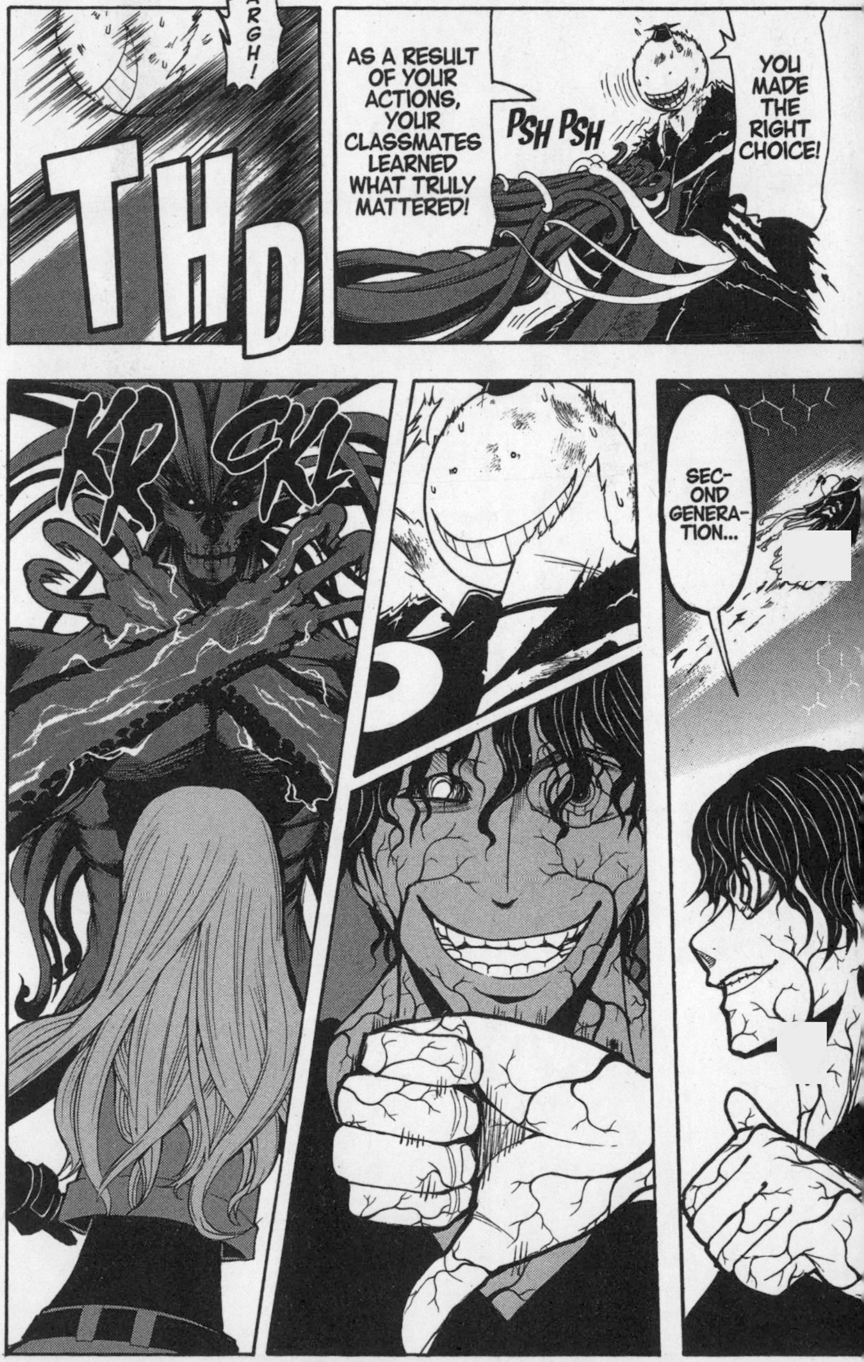
YOU MADE THE RIGHT CHOICE!
PSH PSH
AS A RESULT OF YOUR ACTIONS, YOUR CLASSMATES LEARNED WHAT TRULY MATTERED!
ARGH!
THD
SEC-OND GENERA-TION...
KR CKL

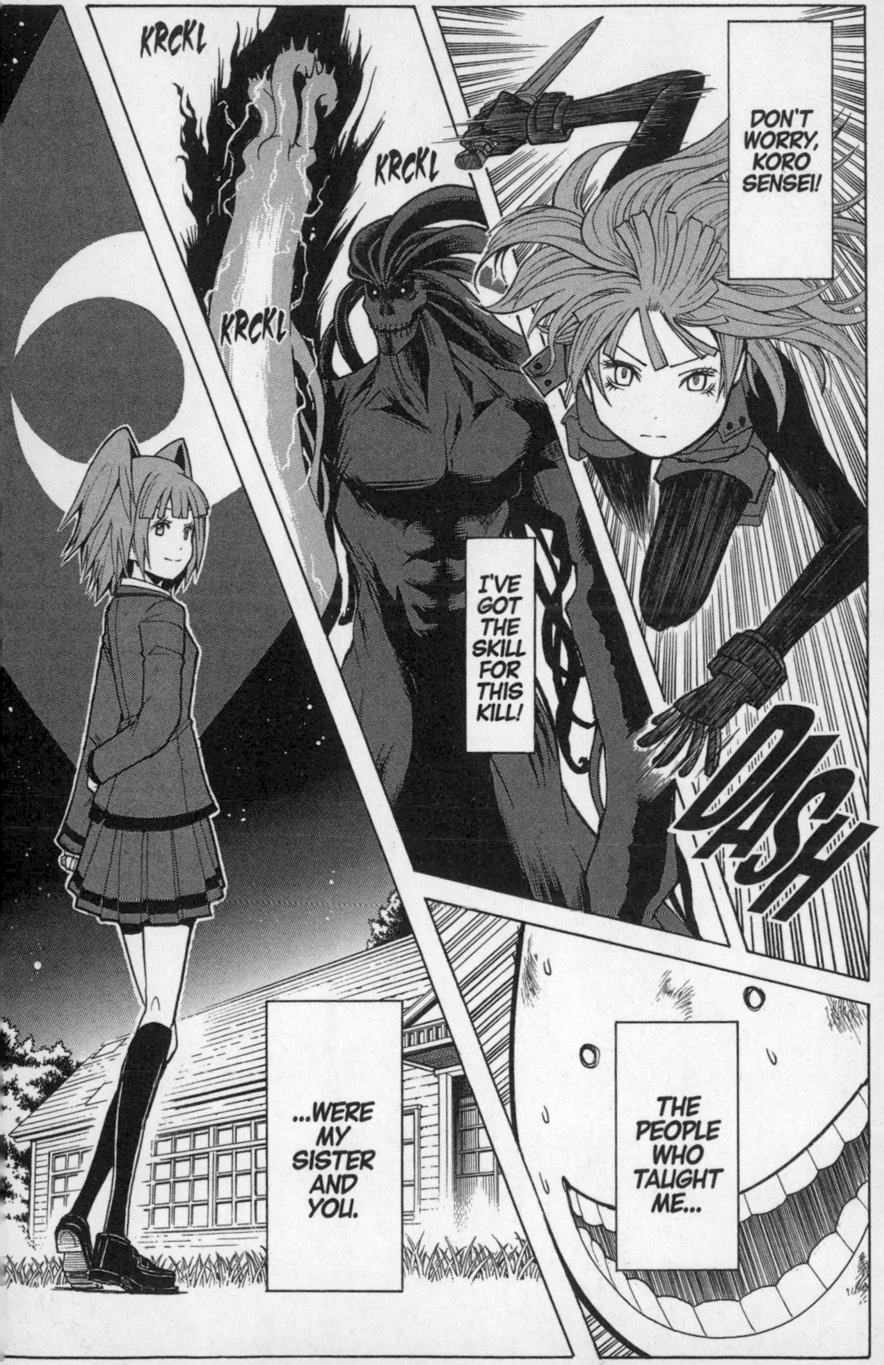
DON'T WORRY, KORO SENSEI!
DASH
KRCKL
KRCKL
KRCKL
I'VE GOT THE SKILL FOR THIS KILL!
THE PEOPLE WHO TAUGHT ME...
...WERE MY SISTER AND YOU.

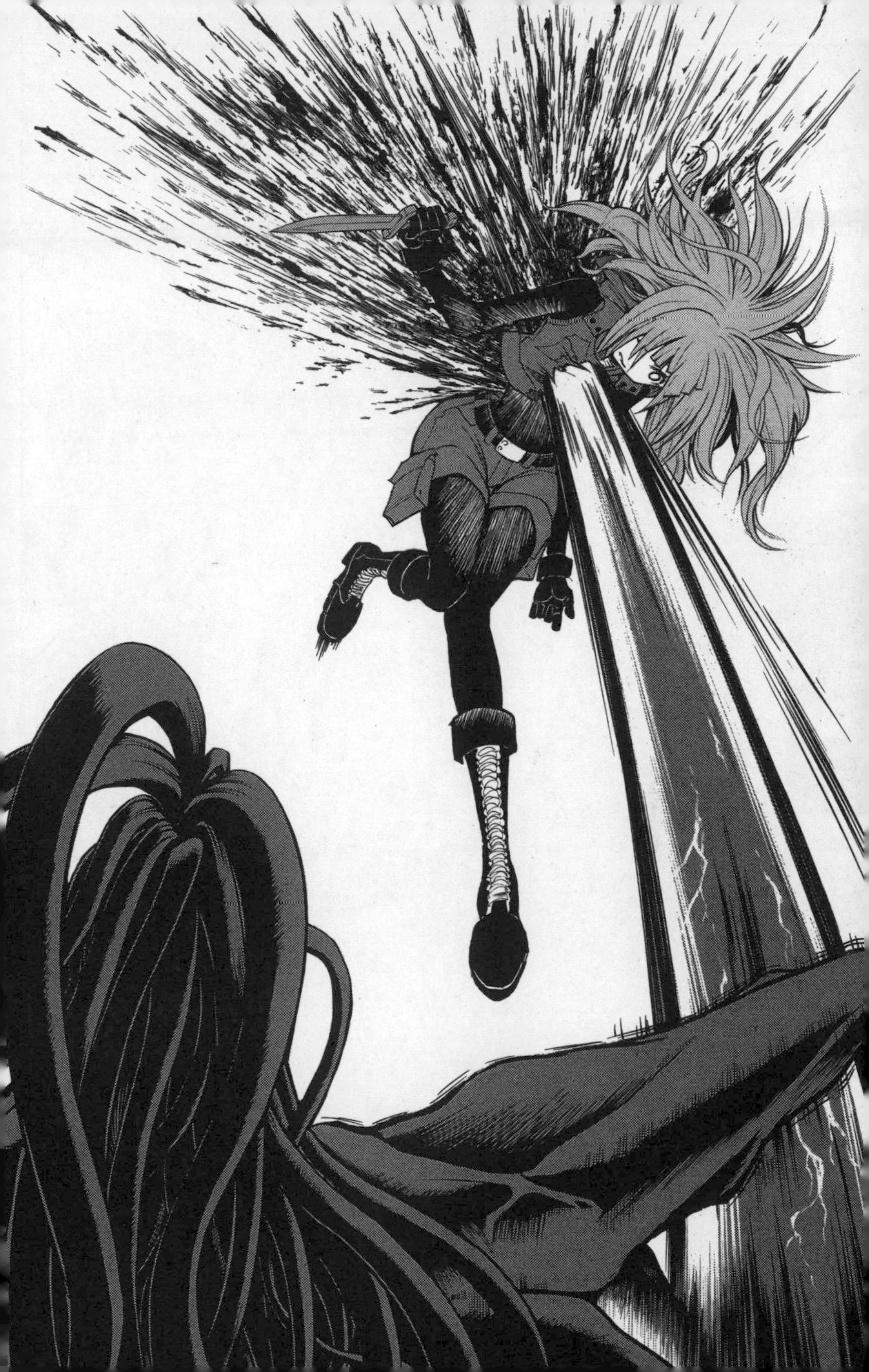

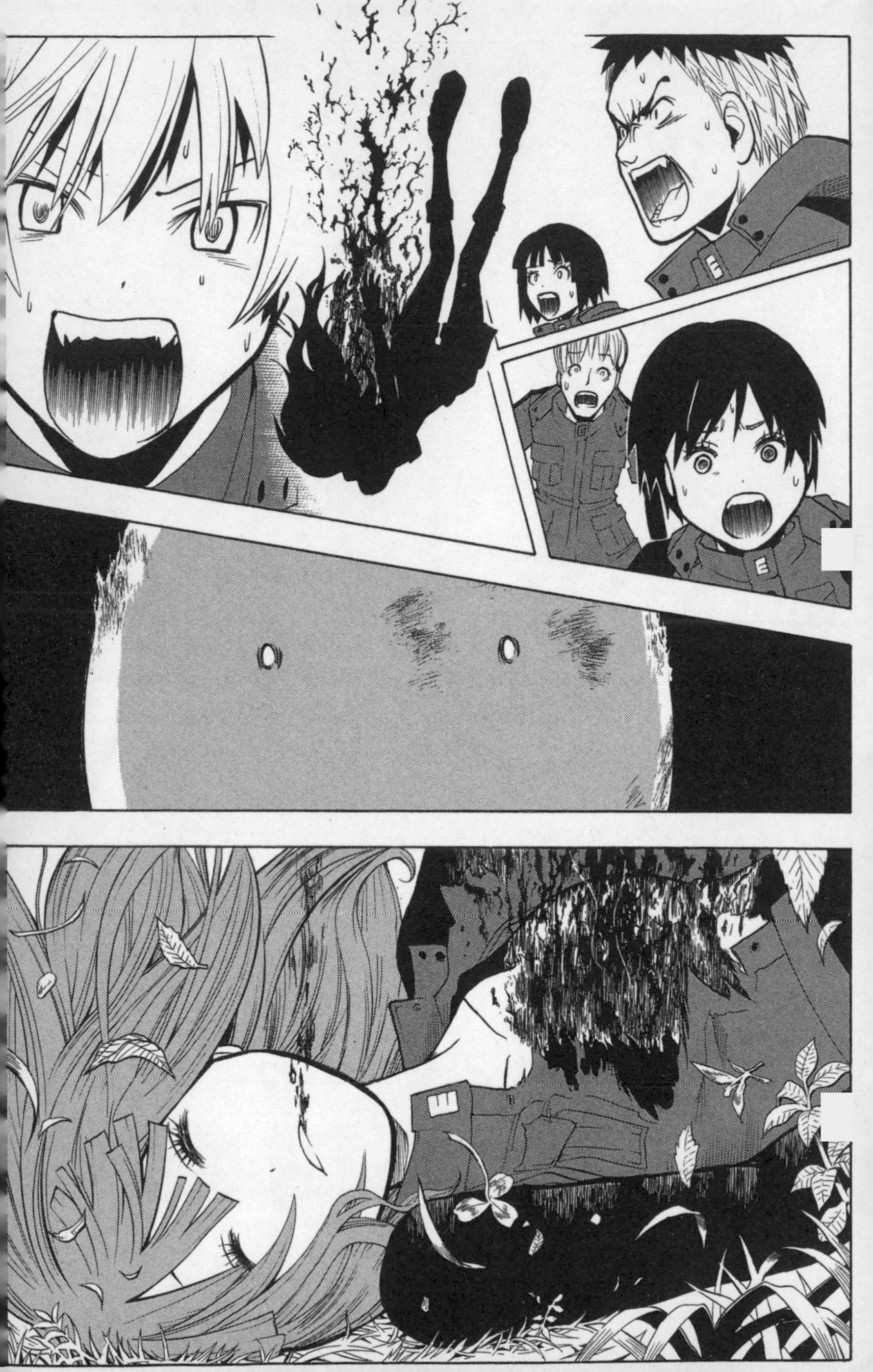

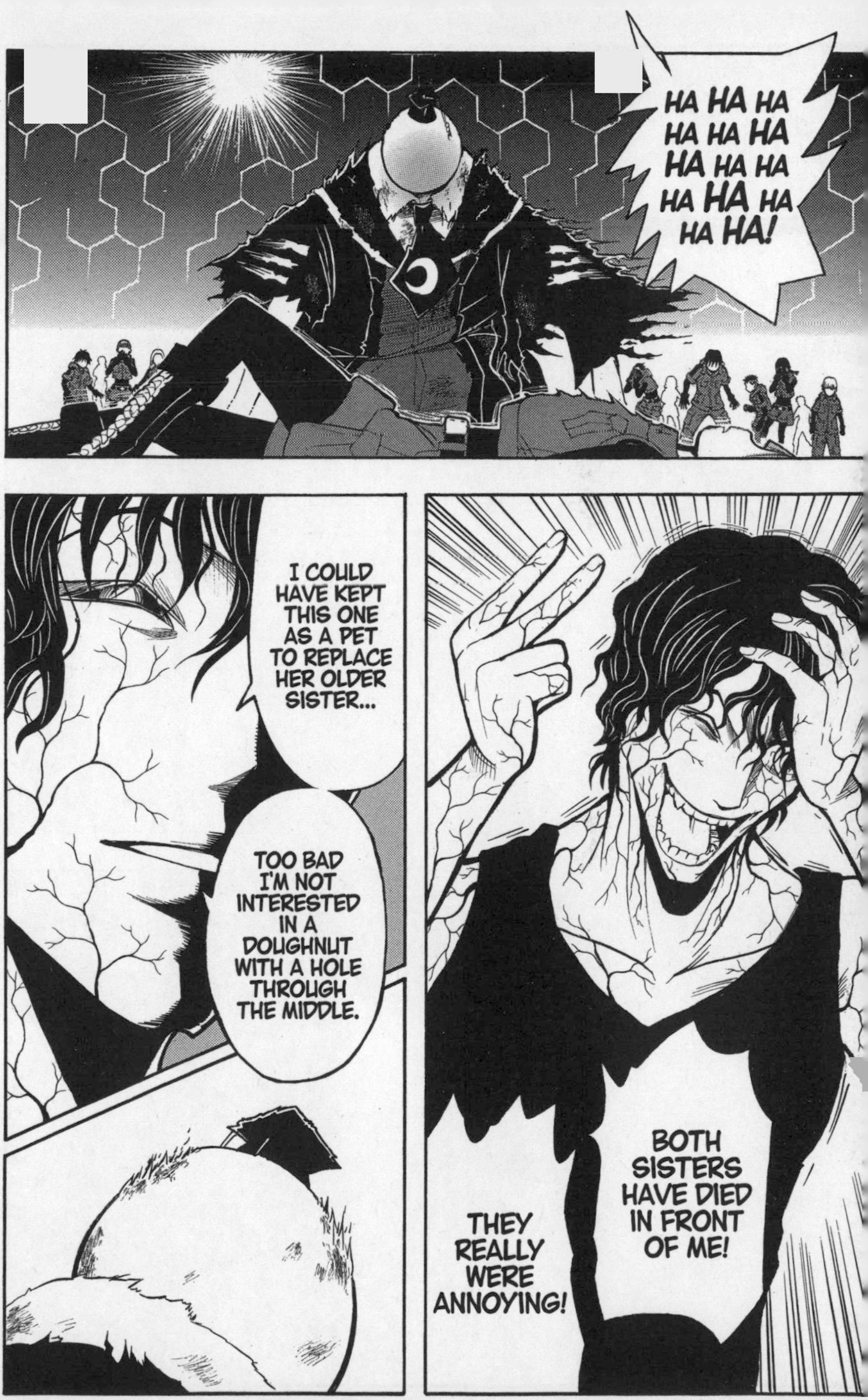
HA HA HA HA HA HA HA HA HA HA HA HA HA HA HA HA HA!
BOTH SISTERS HAVE DIED IN FRONT OF ME!
THEY REALLY WERE ANNOYING!
I COULD HAVE KEPT THIS ONE AS A PET TO REPLACE HER OLDER SISTER...
TOO BAD I'M NOT INTERESTED IN A DOUGHNUT WITH A HOLE THROUGH THE MIDDLE.

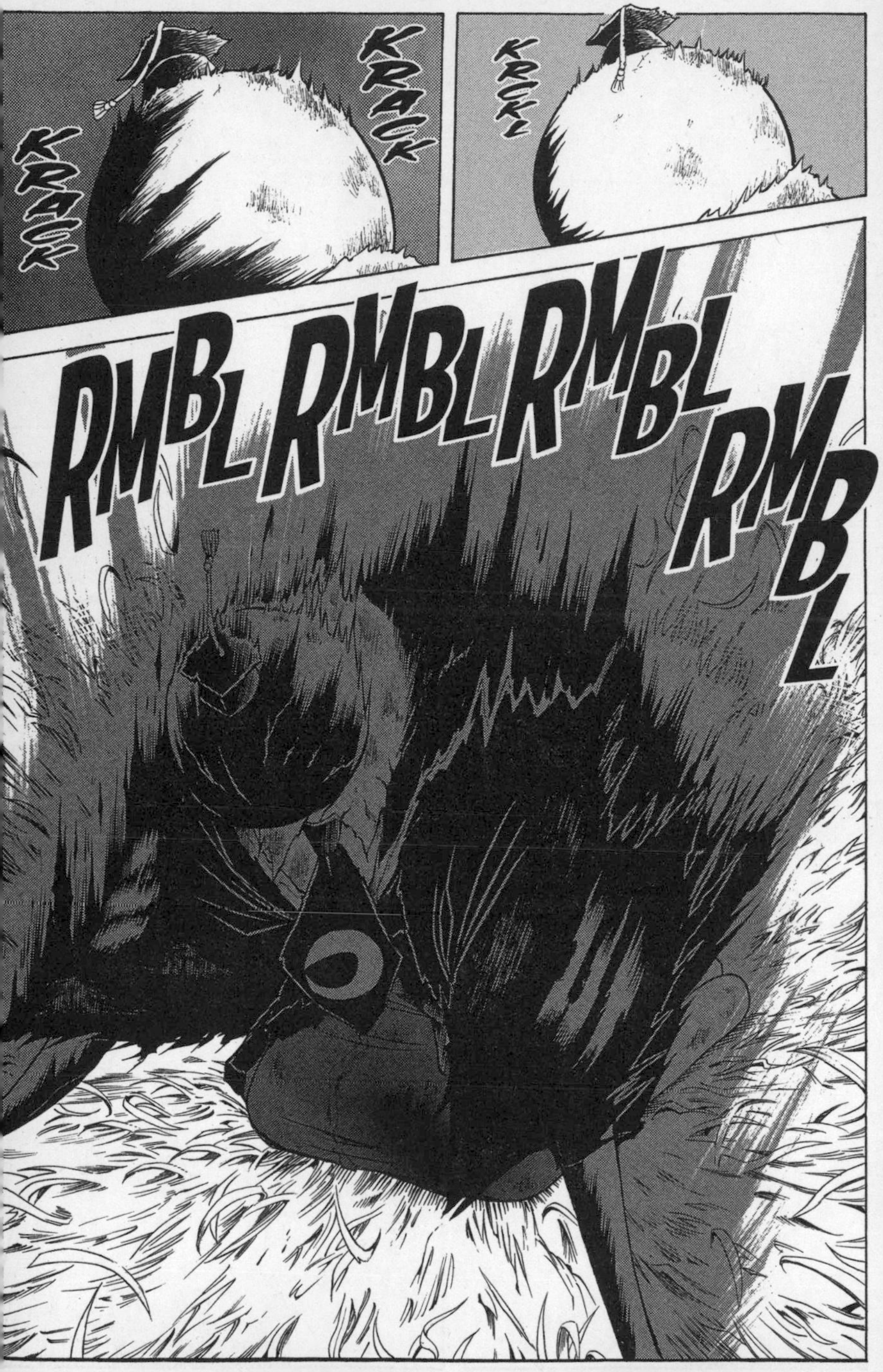
KRACKL
KRACK
KRACK
RMBL RMBL RMBL RMBL

Class 174 Time for Facial Colors

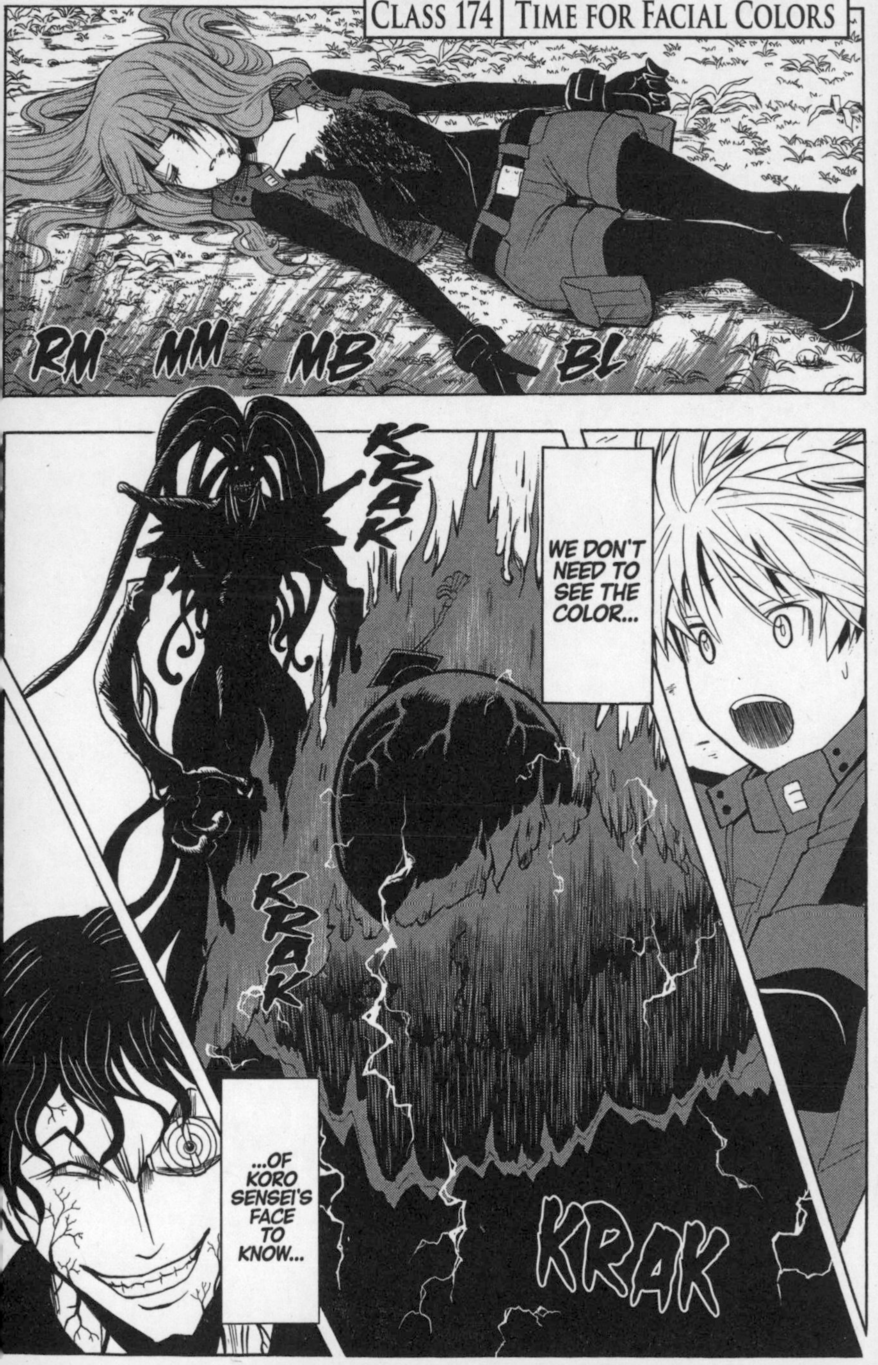
RM MM MB BL
WE DON'T NEED TO SEE THE COLOR...
KRAK KRAK
KRAK
KRAK KRAK
...OF KORO SENSEI'S FACE TO KNOW...

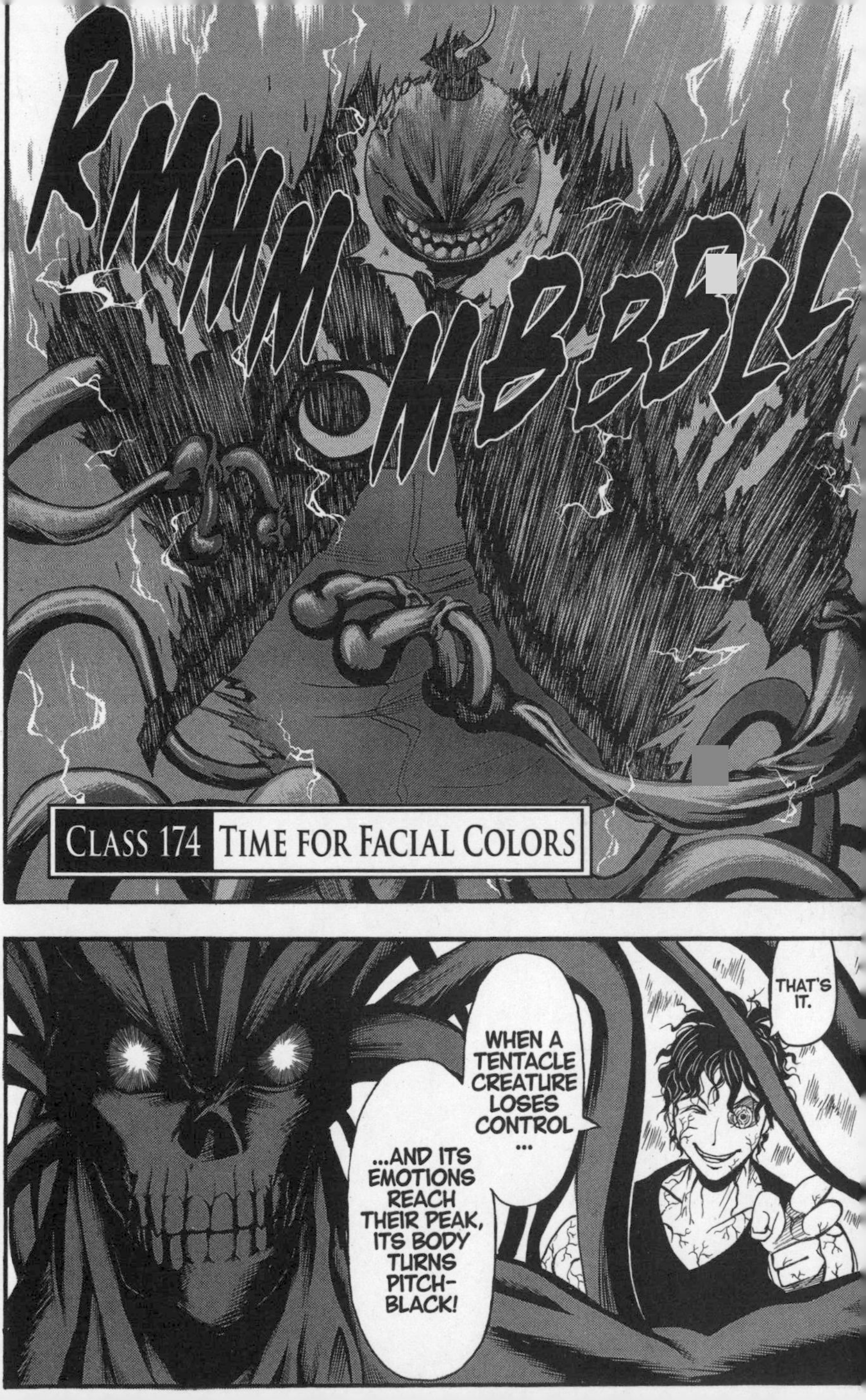
CLASS 174 TIME FOR FACIAL COLORS
THAT'S IT.
WHEN A TENTACLE CREATURE LOSES CONTROL...
...AND ITS EMOTIONS REACH THEIR PEAK, ITS BODY TURNS PITCH-BLACK!

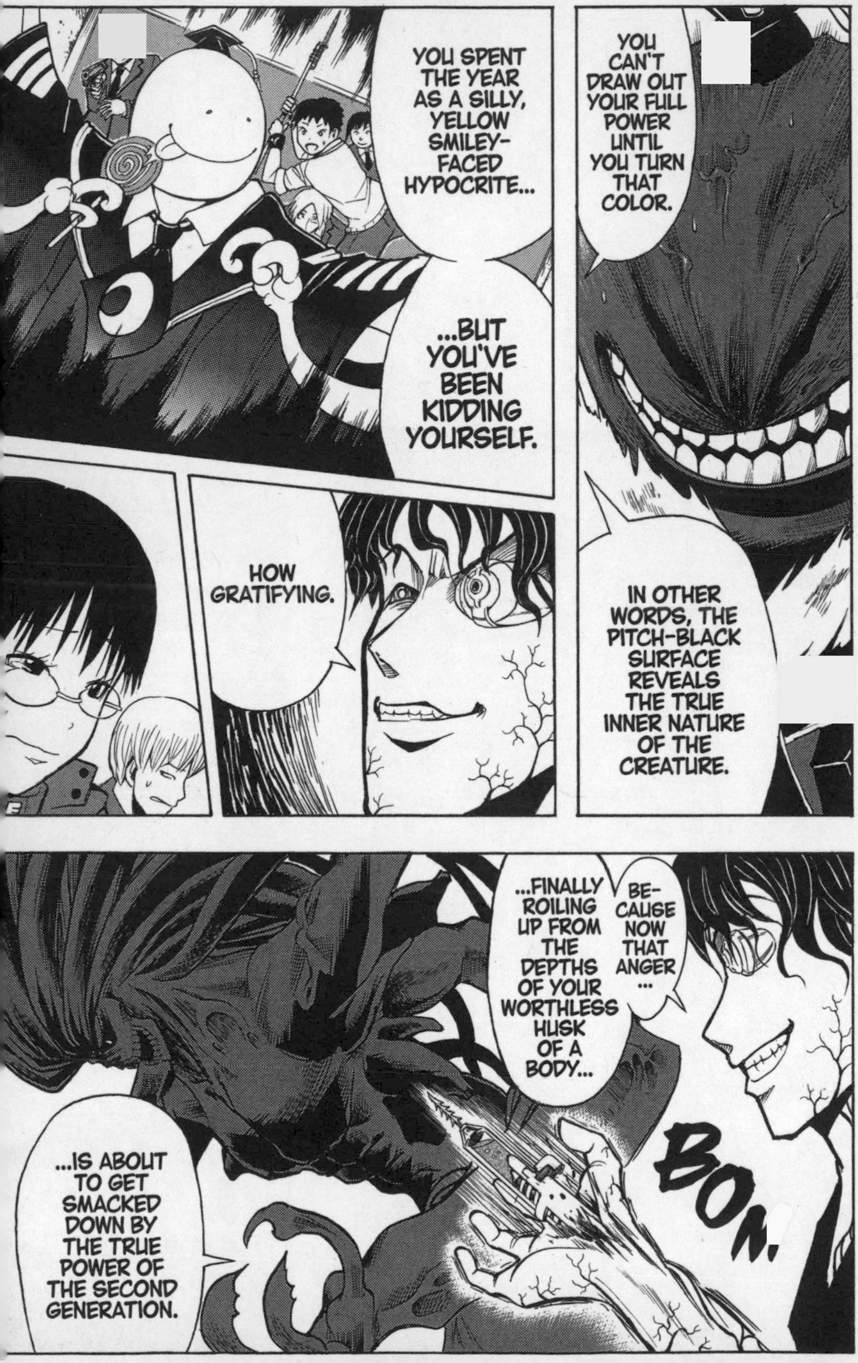
YOU CAN'T DRAW OUT YOUR FULL POWER UNTIL YOU TURN THAT COLOR.
IN OTHER WORDS, THE PITCH-BLACK SURFACE REVEALS THE TRUE INNER NATURE OF THE CREATURE.
YOU SPENT THE YEAR AS A SILLY, YELLOW SMILEY-FACED HYPOCRITE...
...BUT YOU'VE BEEN KIDDING YOURSELF.
HOW GRATIFYING.
BE-CAUSE NOW THAT ANGER...
...FINALLY ROILING UP FROM THE DEPTHS OF YOUR WORTHLESS HUSK OF A BODY...
BOM!
...IS ABOUT TO GET SMACKED DOWN BY THE TRUE POWER OF THE SECOND GENERATION.

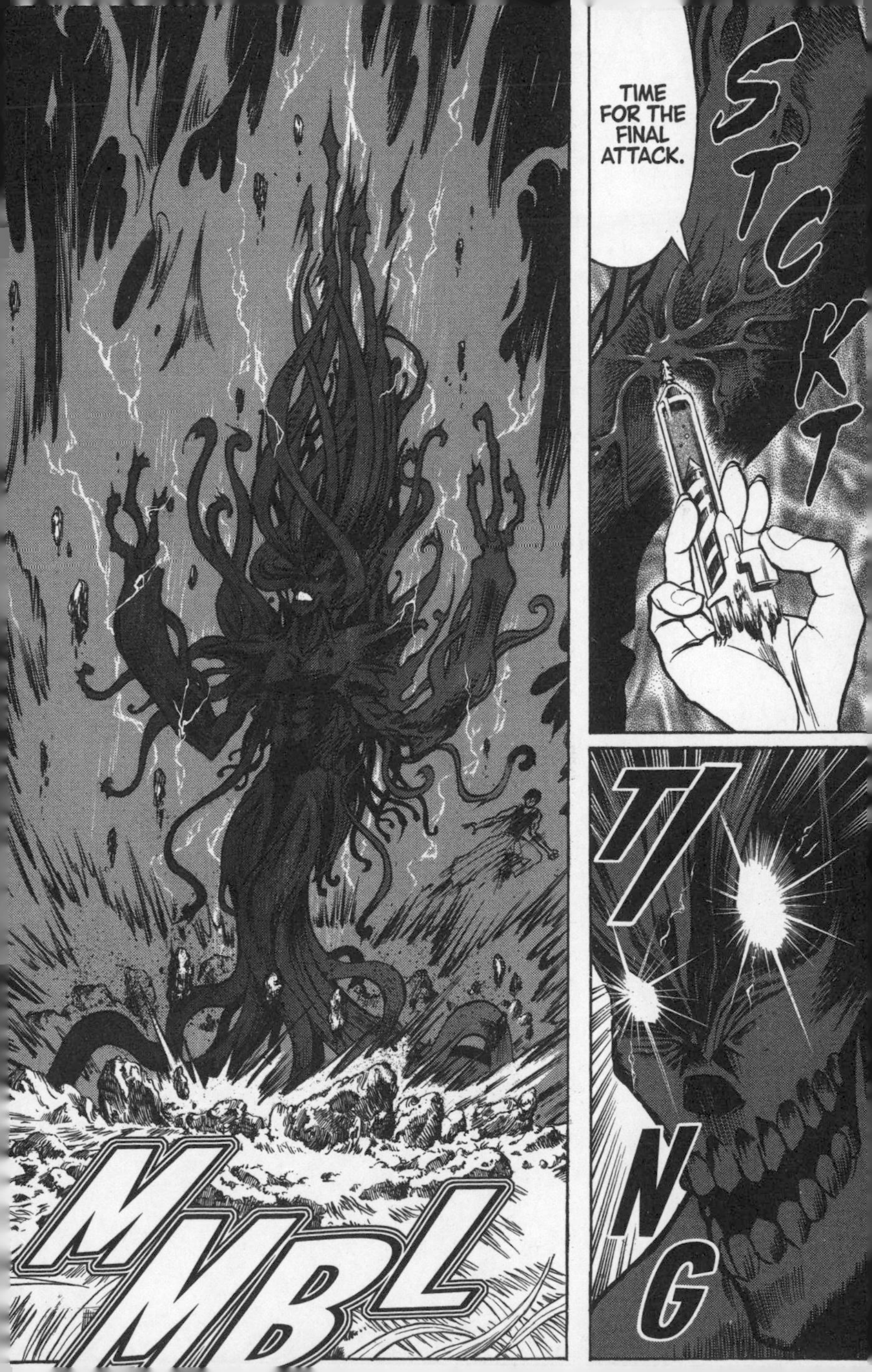
TIME FOR THE FINAL ATTACK.
STCKT
TING
MMBL

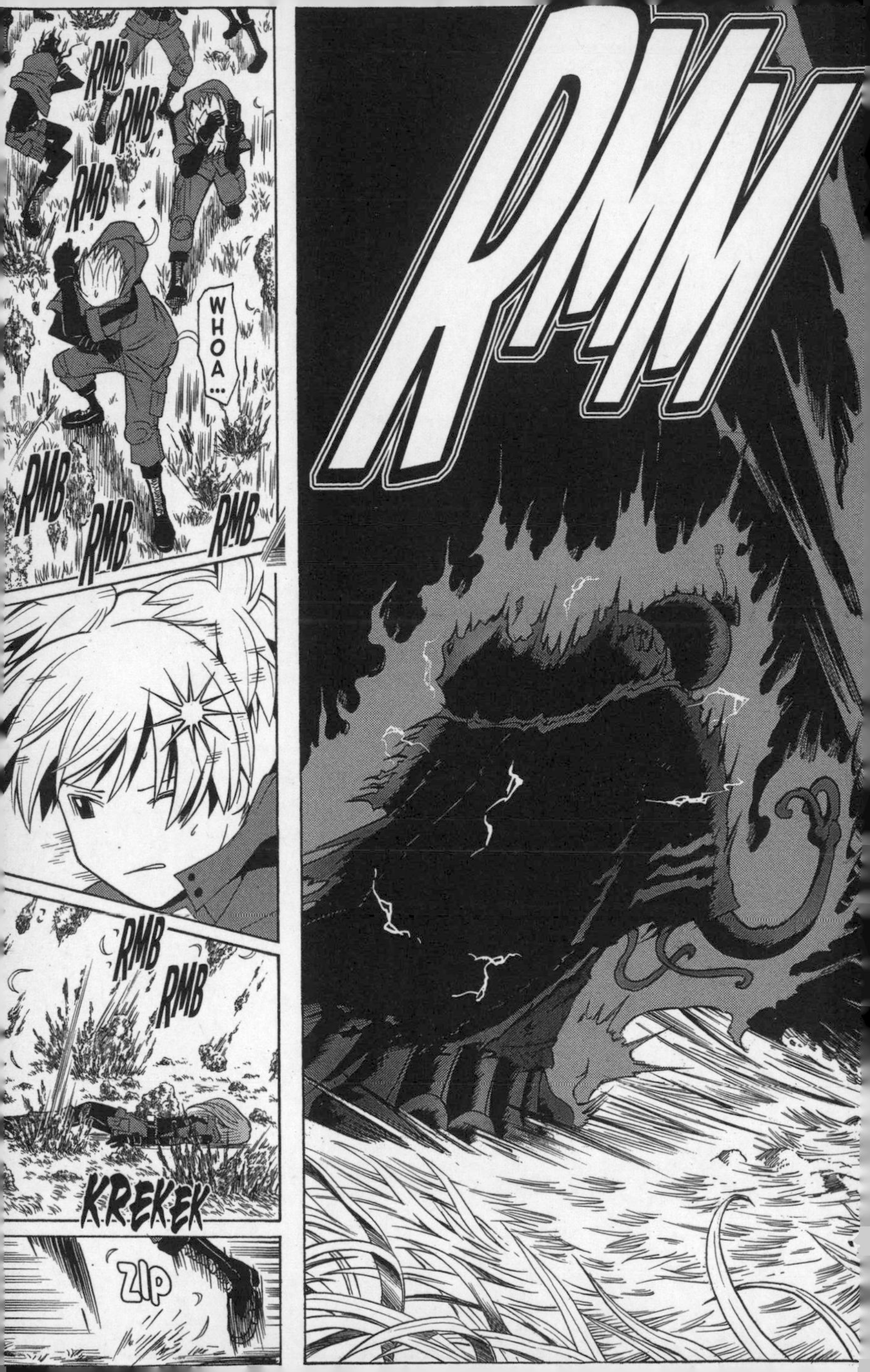
RMM
RMB
RMB
RMB
WHOA...
RMB
RMB
RMB
RMB
RMB
KREKEK
ZIP

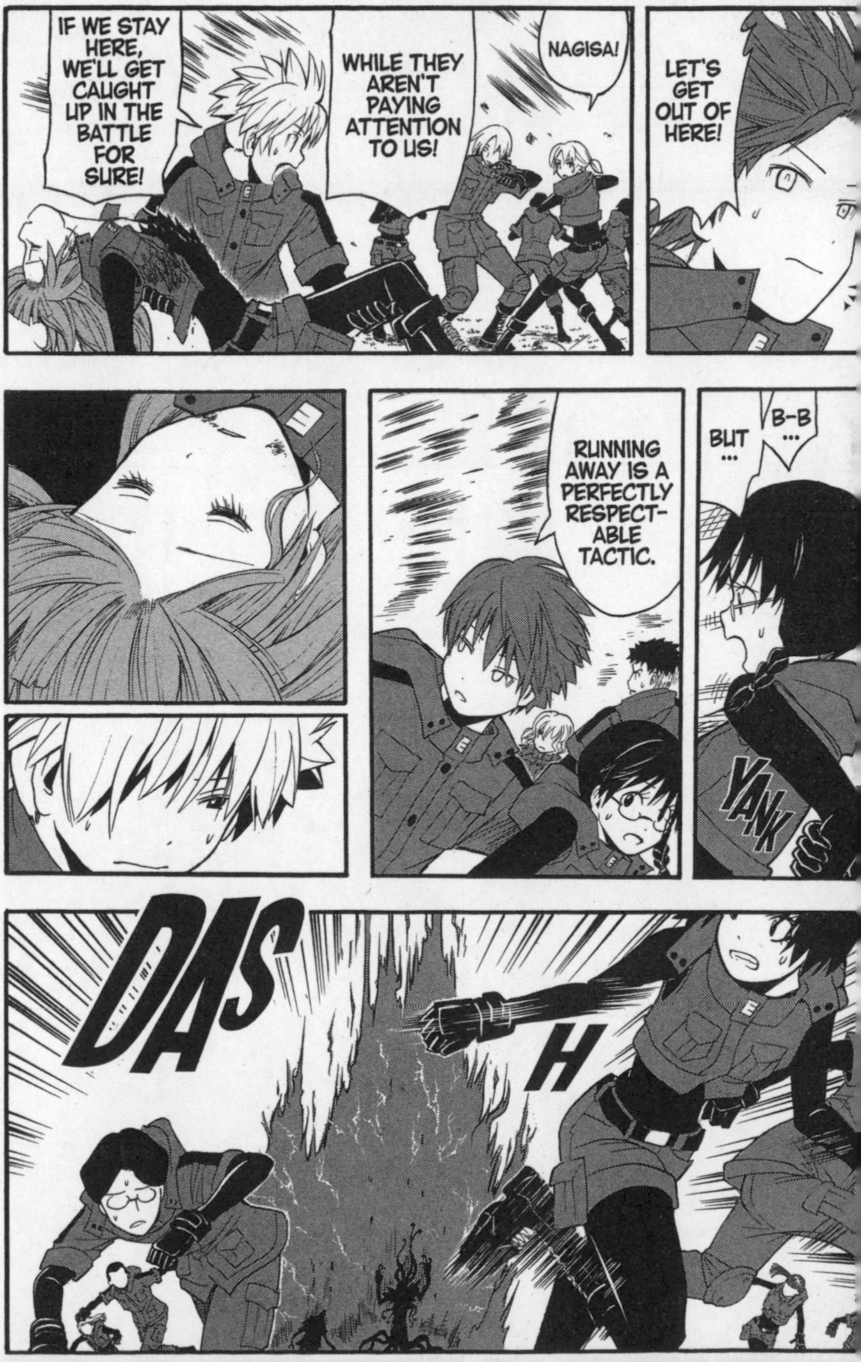
LET'S GET OUT OF HERE!
NAGISA!
WHILE THEY AREN'T PAYING ATTENTION TO US!
IF WE STAY HERE, WE'LL GET CAUGHT UP IN THE BATTLE FOR SURE!
B-B...
BUT...
YANK
RUNNING AWAY IS A PERFECTLY RESPECTABLE TACTIC.
DASH

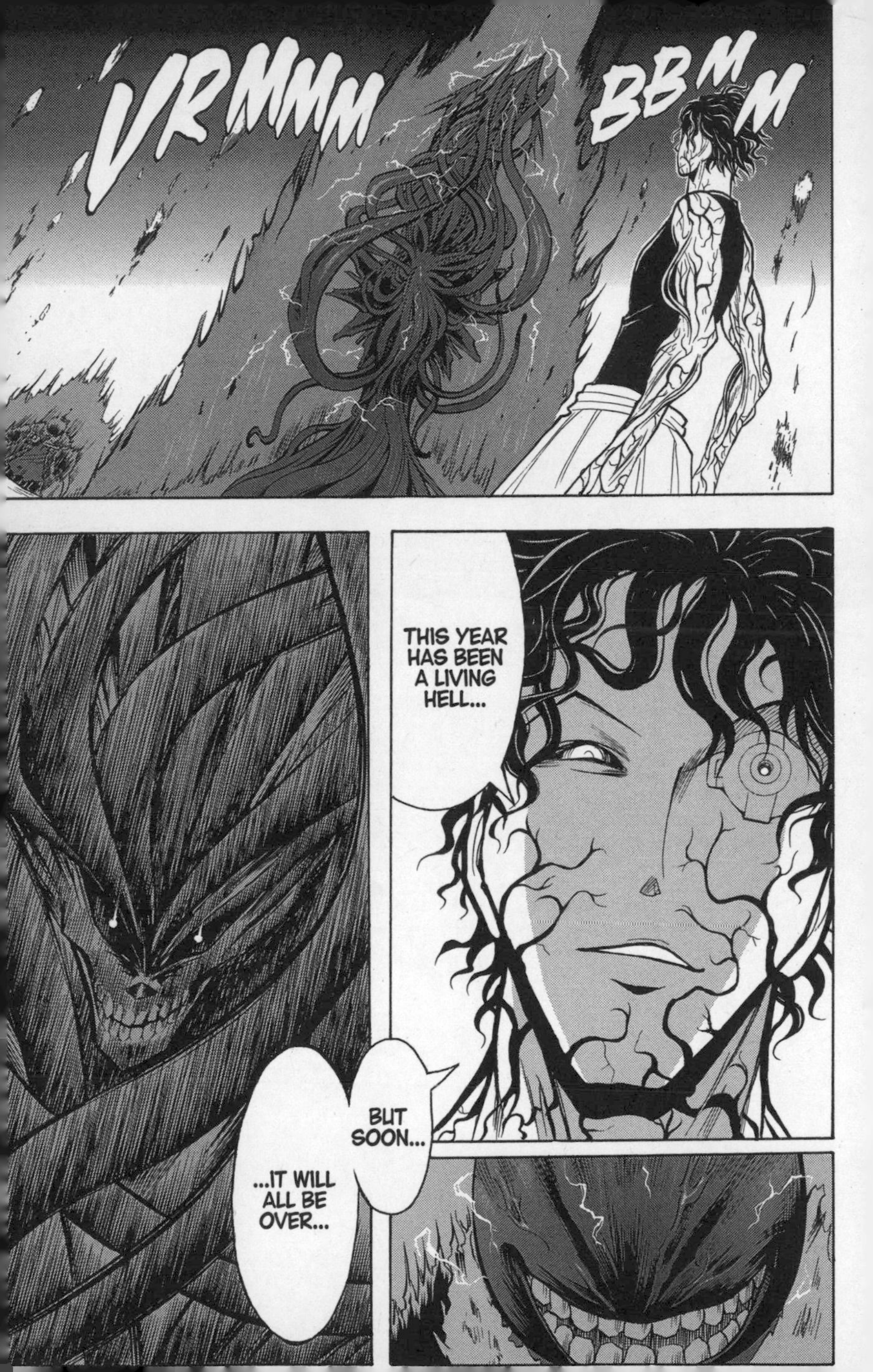
BBMMM
VRMMMM
THIS YEAR HAS BEEN A LIVING HELL...
BUT SOON...
...IT WILL ALL BE OVER...

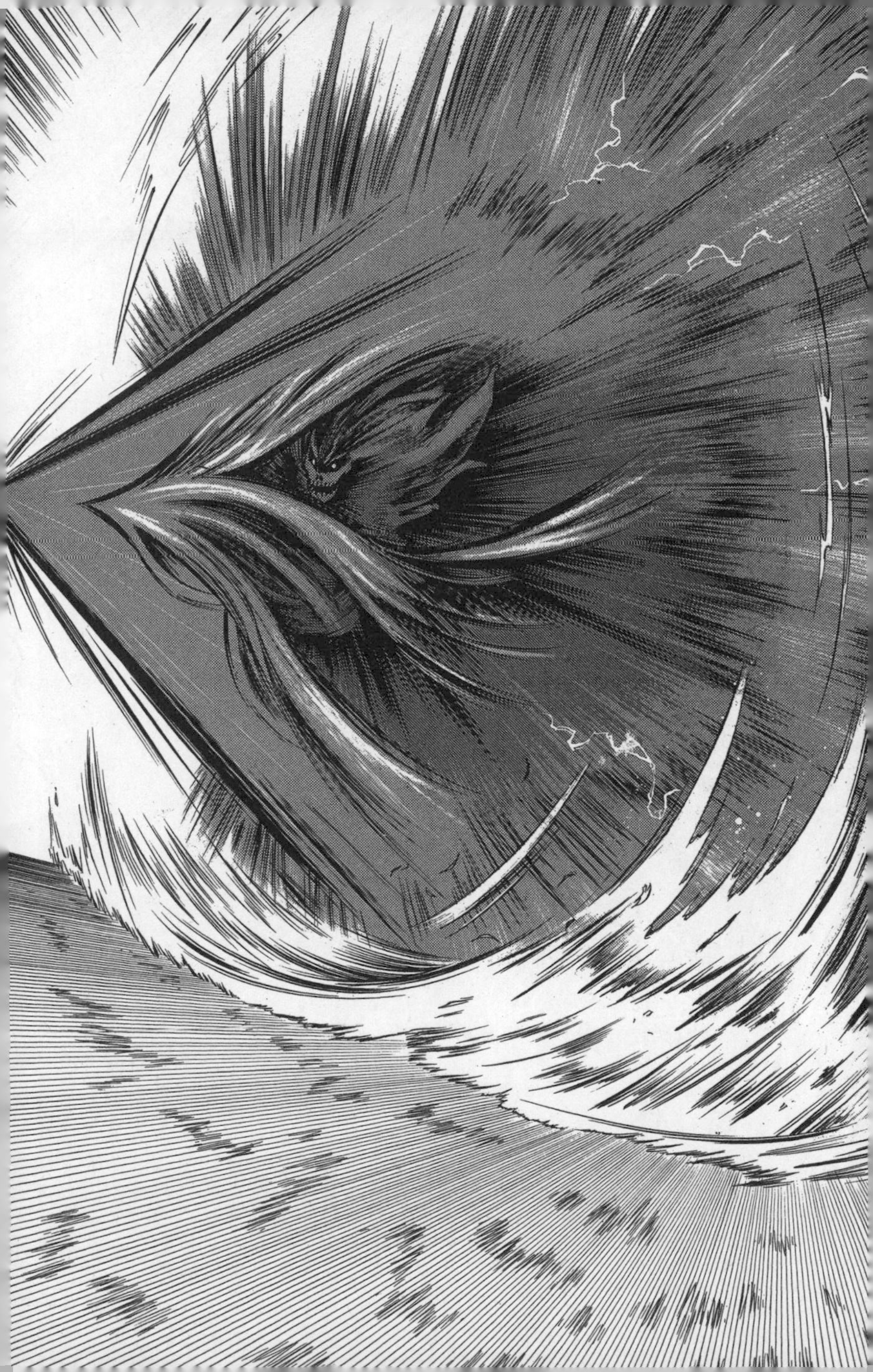

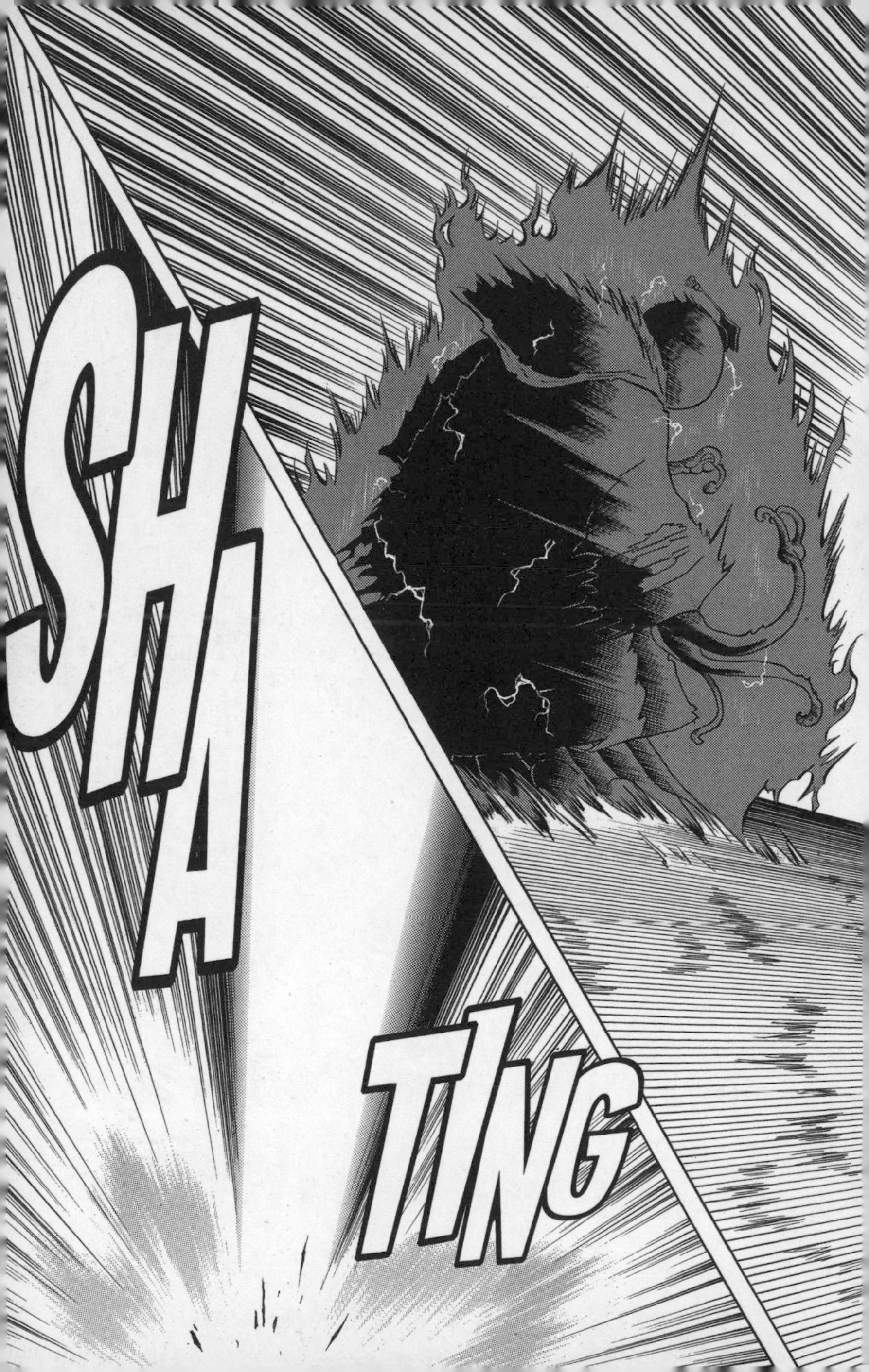
SHA
TING

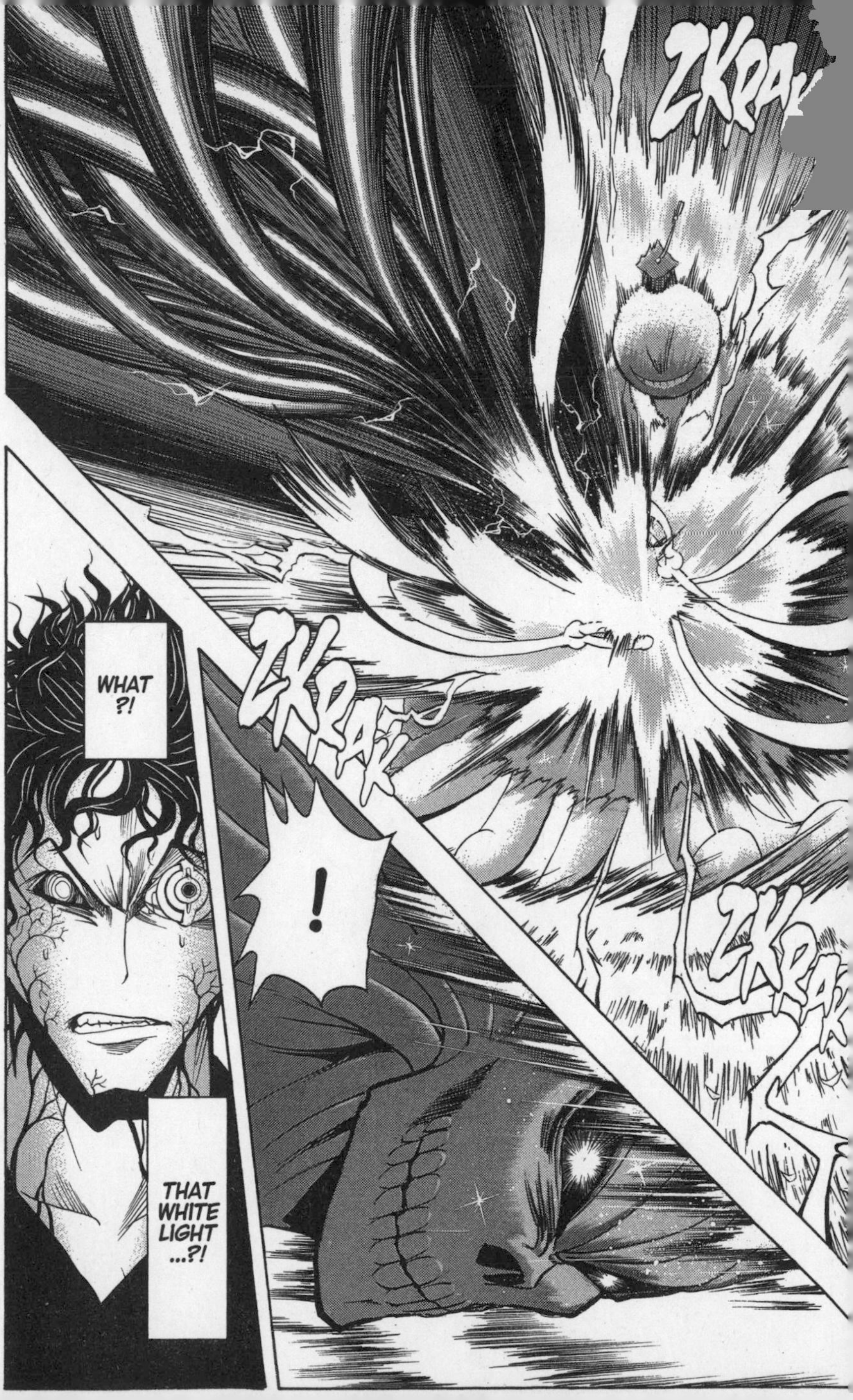
ZKRA
ZKRAK
ZKRAK
!
WHAT ?!
THAT WHITE LIGHT ...?!

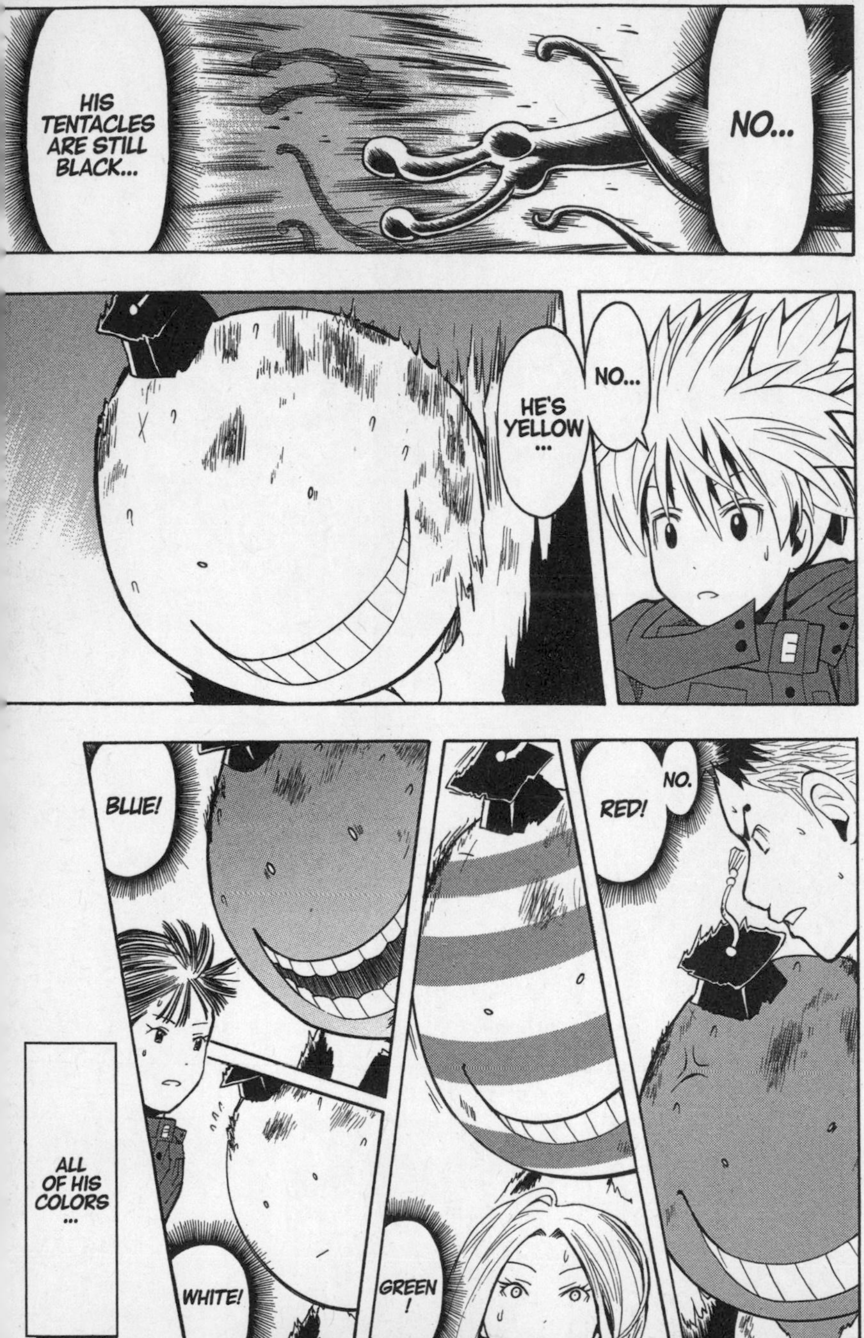
NO...
HIS TENTACLES ARE STILL BLACK...
NO...
HE'S YELLOW ...
NO.
RED!
GREEN !
BLUE!
WHITE!
ALL OF HIS COLORS ...

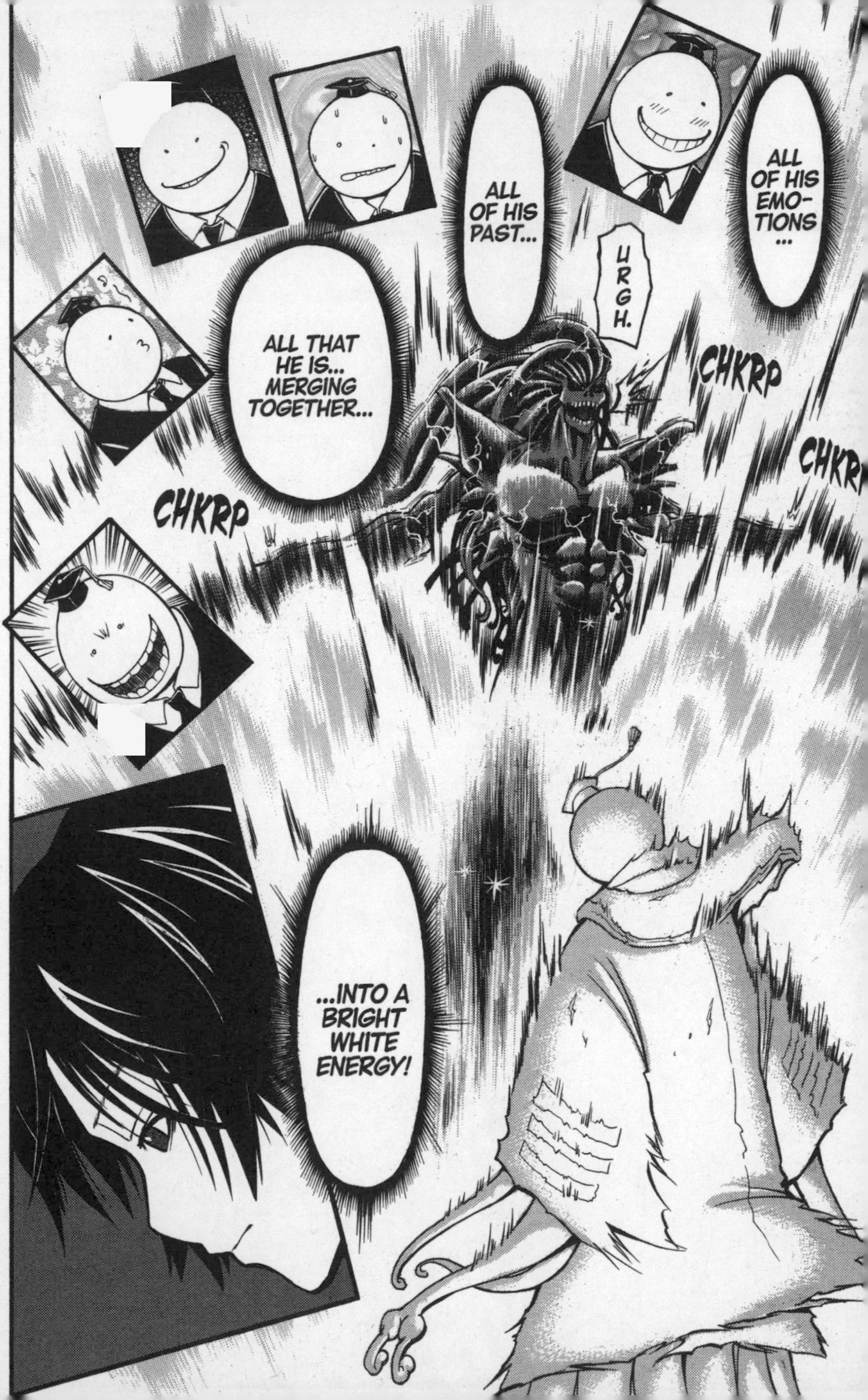
ALL OF HIS EMO-TIONS ...
ALL OF HIS PAST...
URGH.
CHKRP
CHKR
ALL THAT HE IS... MERGING TOGETHER...
CHKRP
...INTO A BRIGHT WHITE ENERGY!

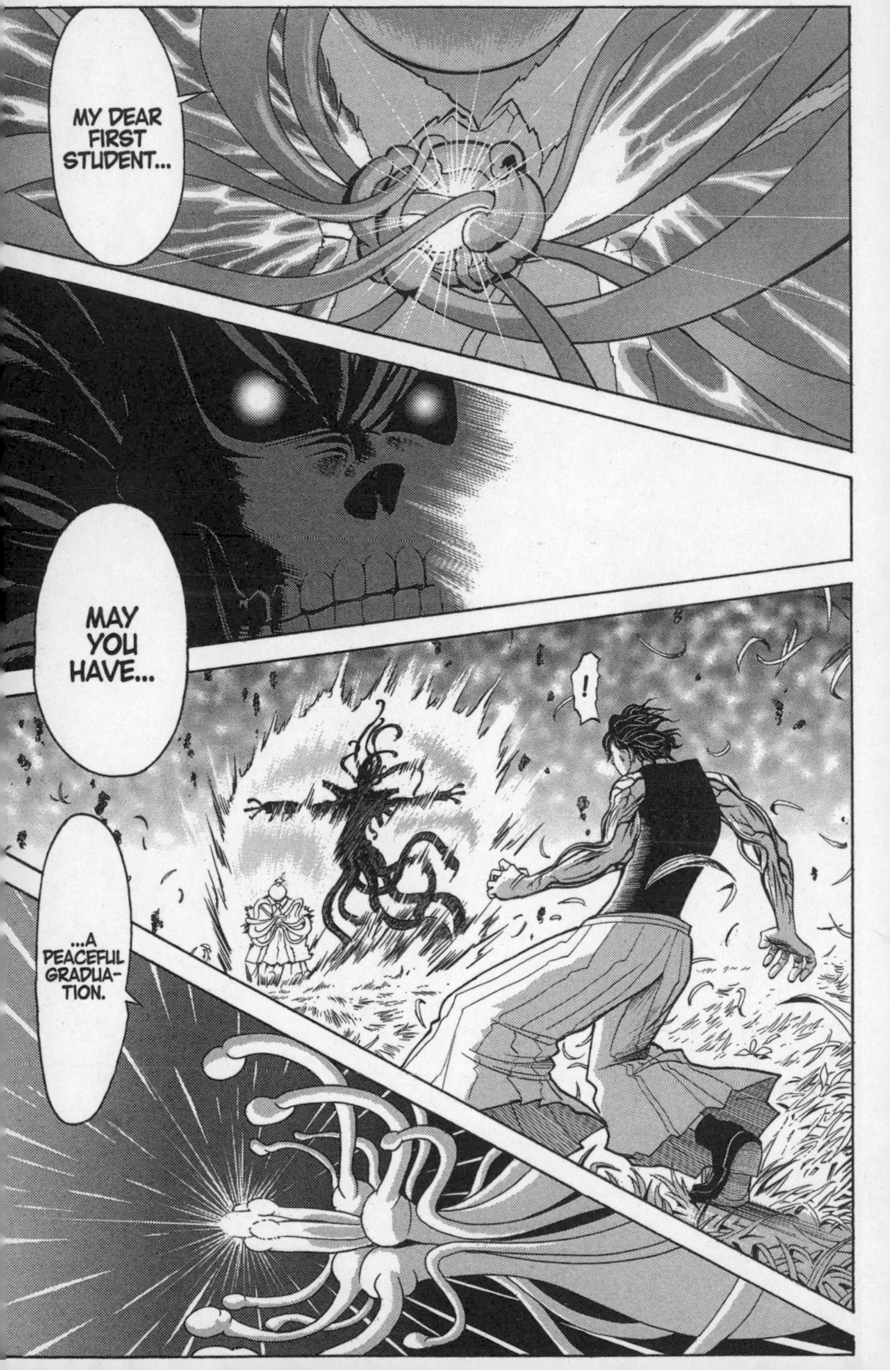
MY DEAR FIRST STUDENT...
MAY YOU HAVE...
!
...A PEACEFUL GRADUATION.

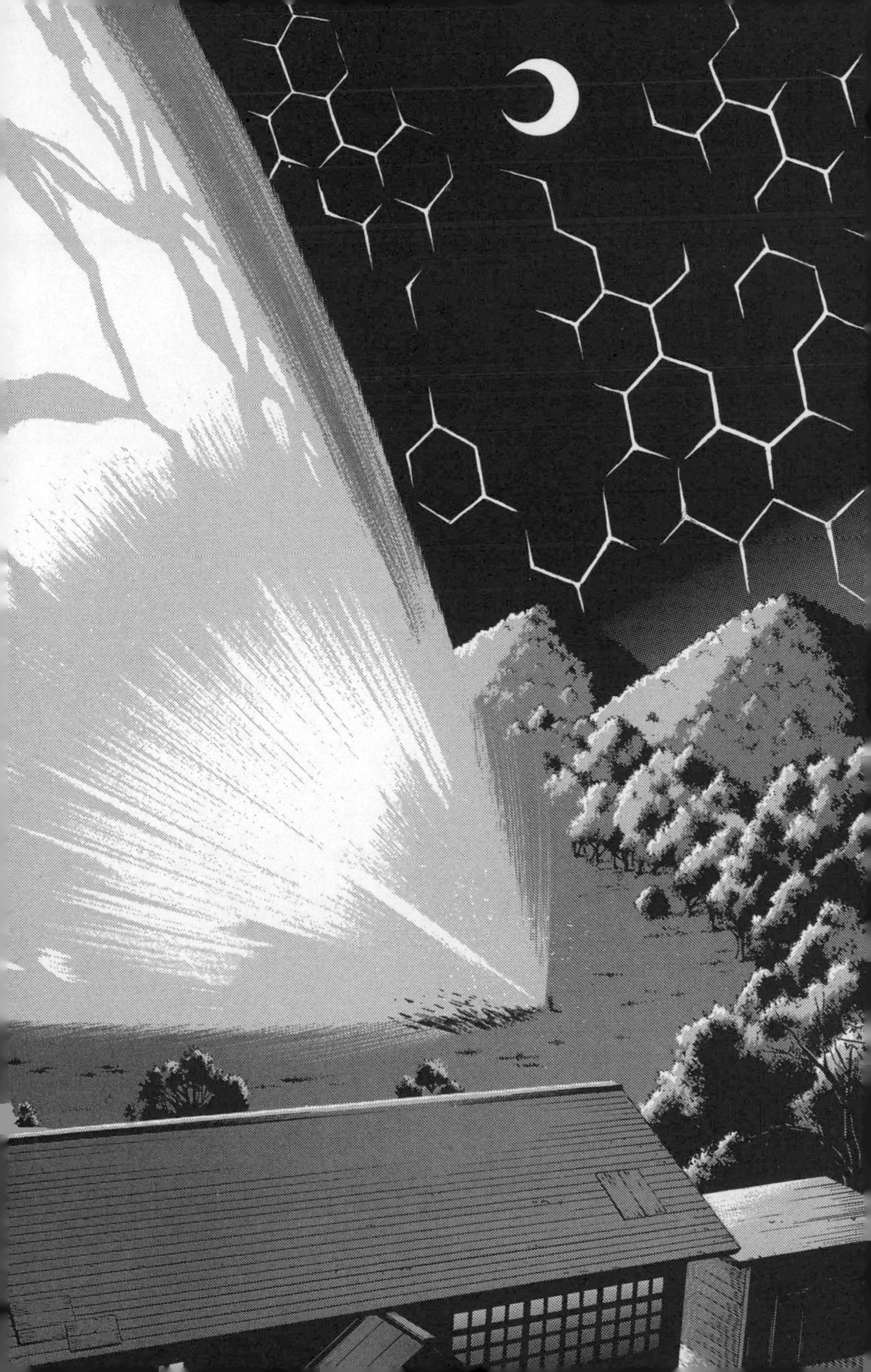

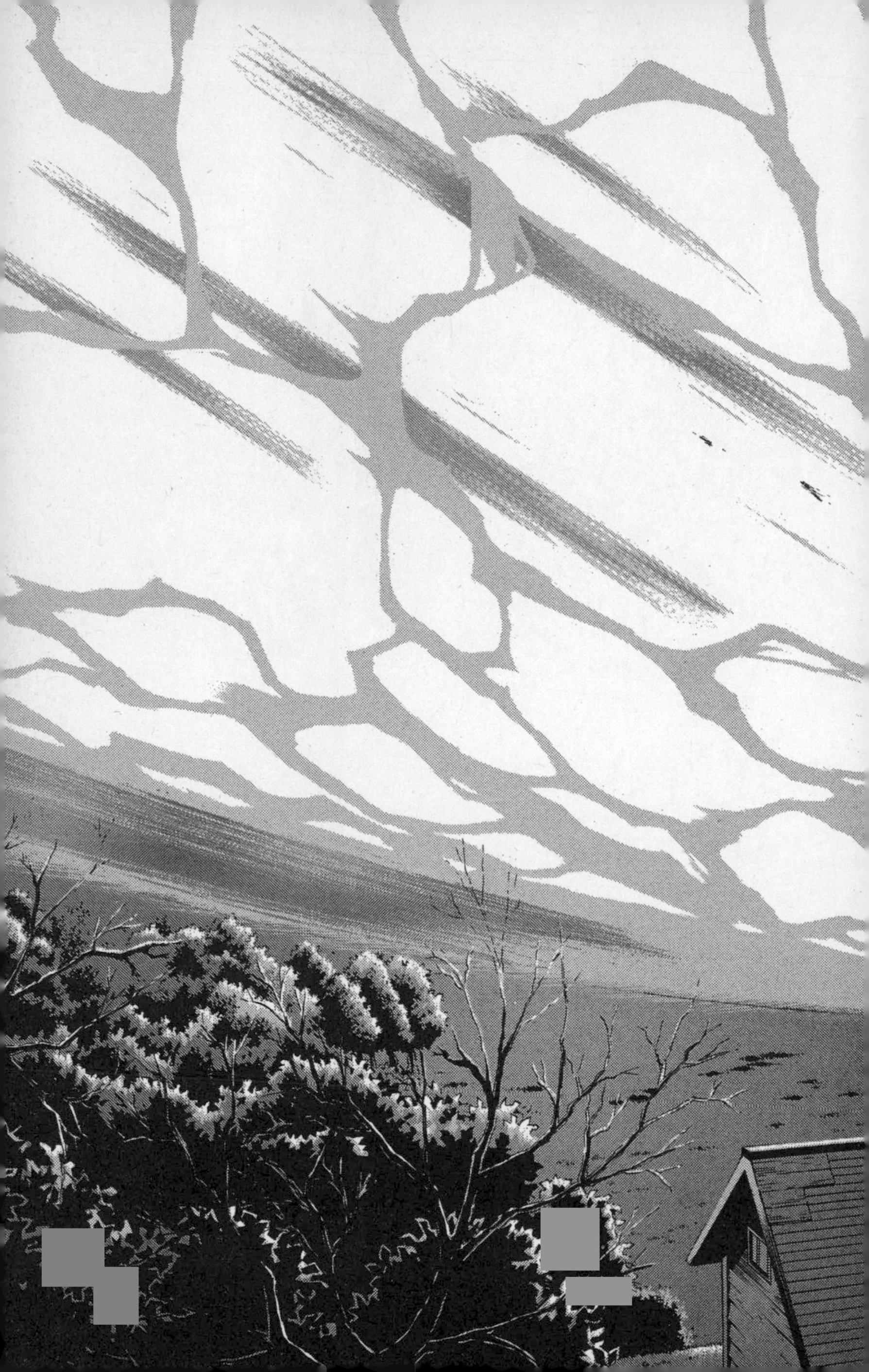

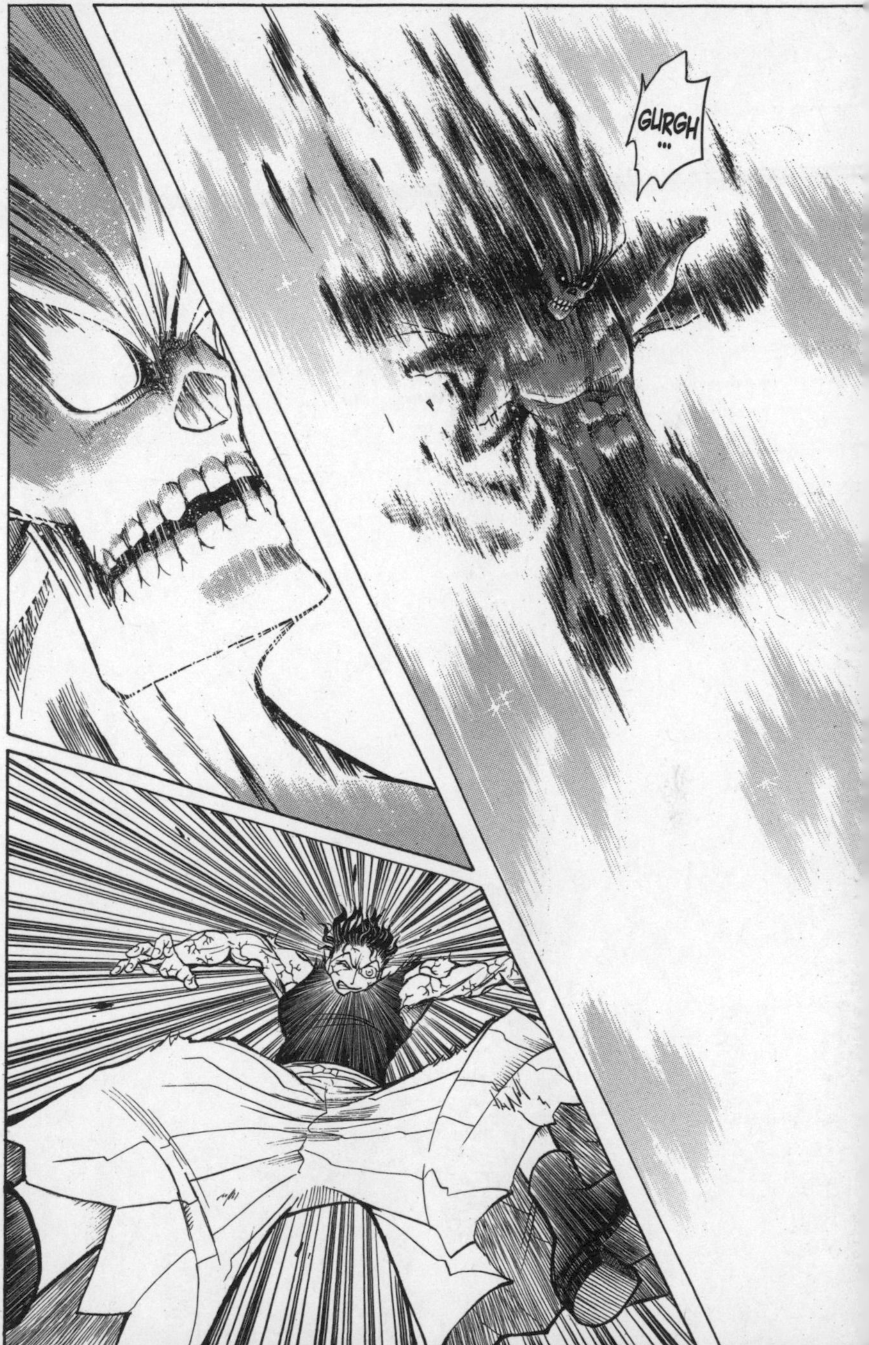
GURGH
...

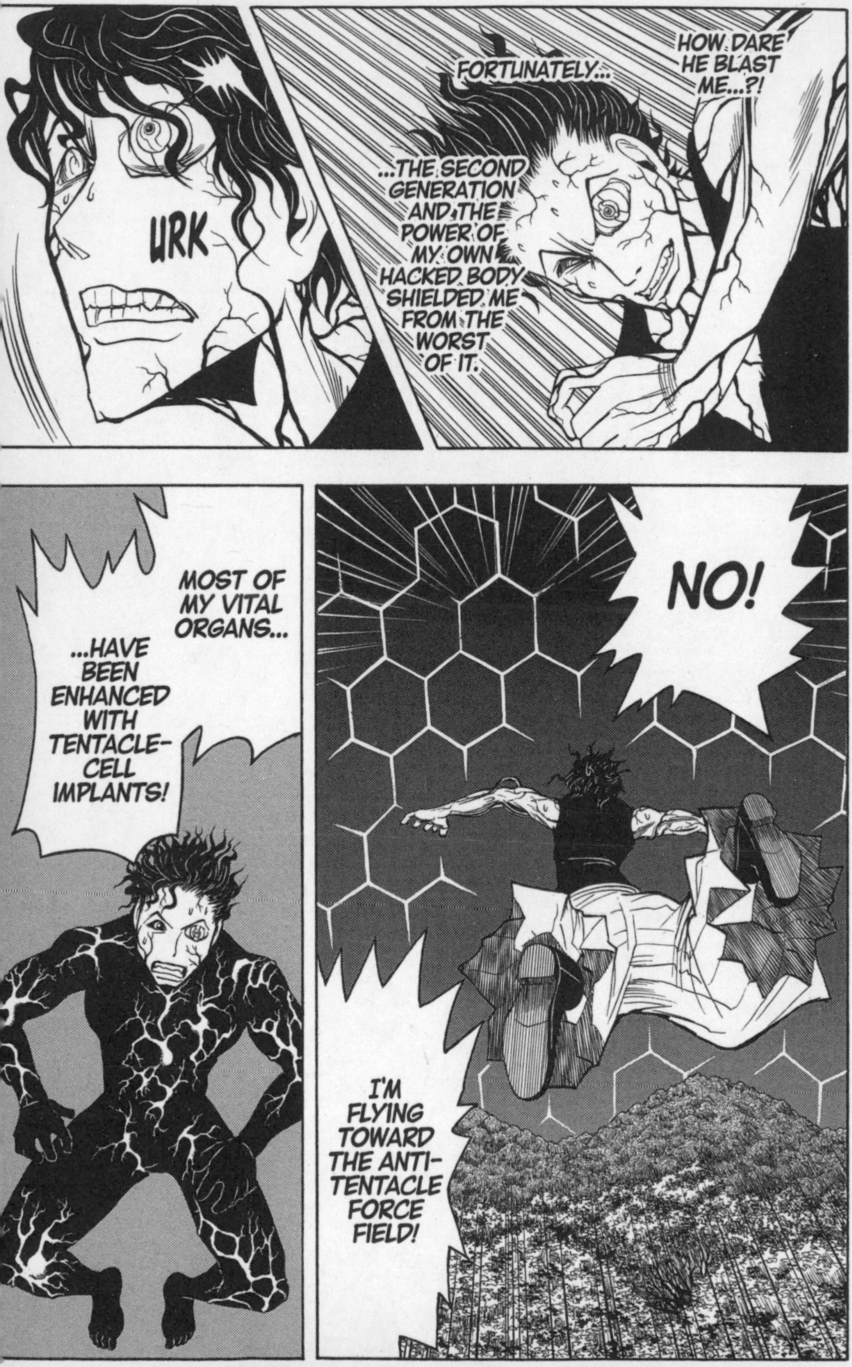
HOW DARE HE BLAST ME...?!
FORTUNATELY...
...THE SECOND GENERATION AND THE POWER OF MY OWN HACKED BODY SHIELDED ME FROM THE WORST OF IT.
URK
NO!
I'M FLYING TOWARD THE ANTI-TENTACLE FORCE FIELD!
MOST OF MY VITAL ORGANS...
...HAVE BEEN ENHANCED WITH TENTACLE-CELL IMPLANTS!

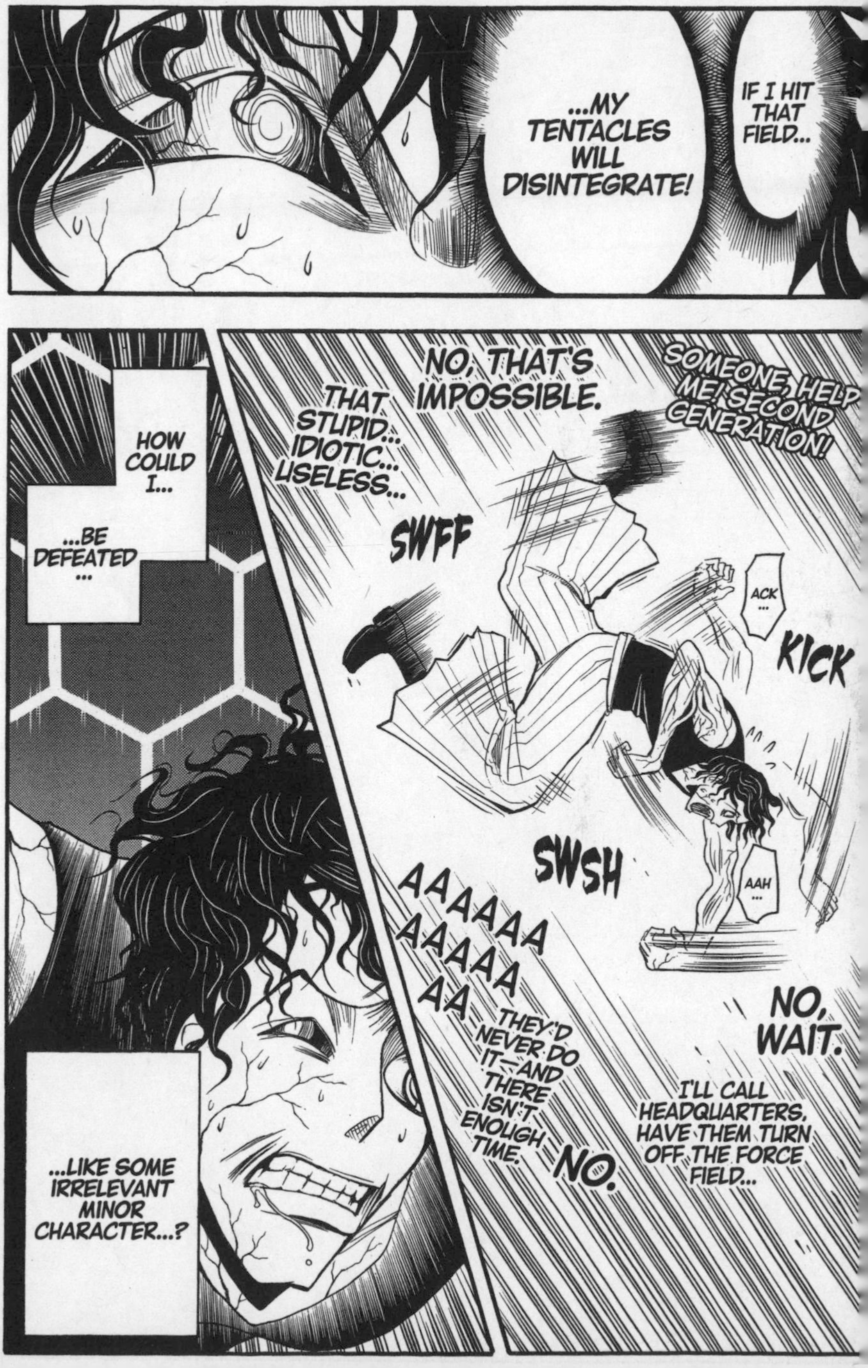
IF I HIT THAT FIELD...
...MY TENTACLES WILL DISINTEGRATE!
SOMEONE, HELP ME! SECOND GENERATION!
NO, THAT'S IMPOSSIBLE.
THAT STUPID... IDIOTIC... USELESS...
SWFF
ACK...
KICK
SWSH
AAH...
NO, WAIT.
AAAAAA AAAAAA AAAAA AA
I'LL CALL HEADQUARTERS, HAVE THEM TURN OFF THE FORCE FIELD...
THEY'D NEVER DO IT—AND THERE ISN'T ENOUGH TIME.
NO.
HOW COULD I...
...BE DEFEATED...
...LIKE SOME IRRELEVANT MINOR CHARACTER...?

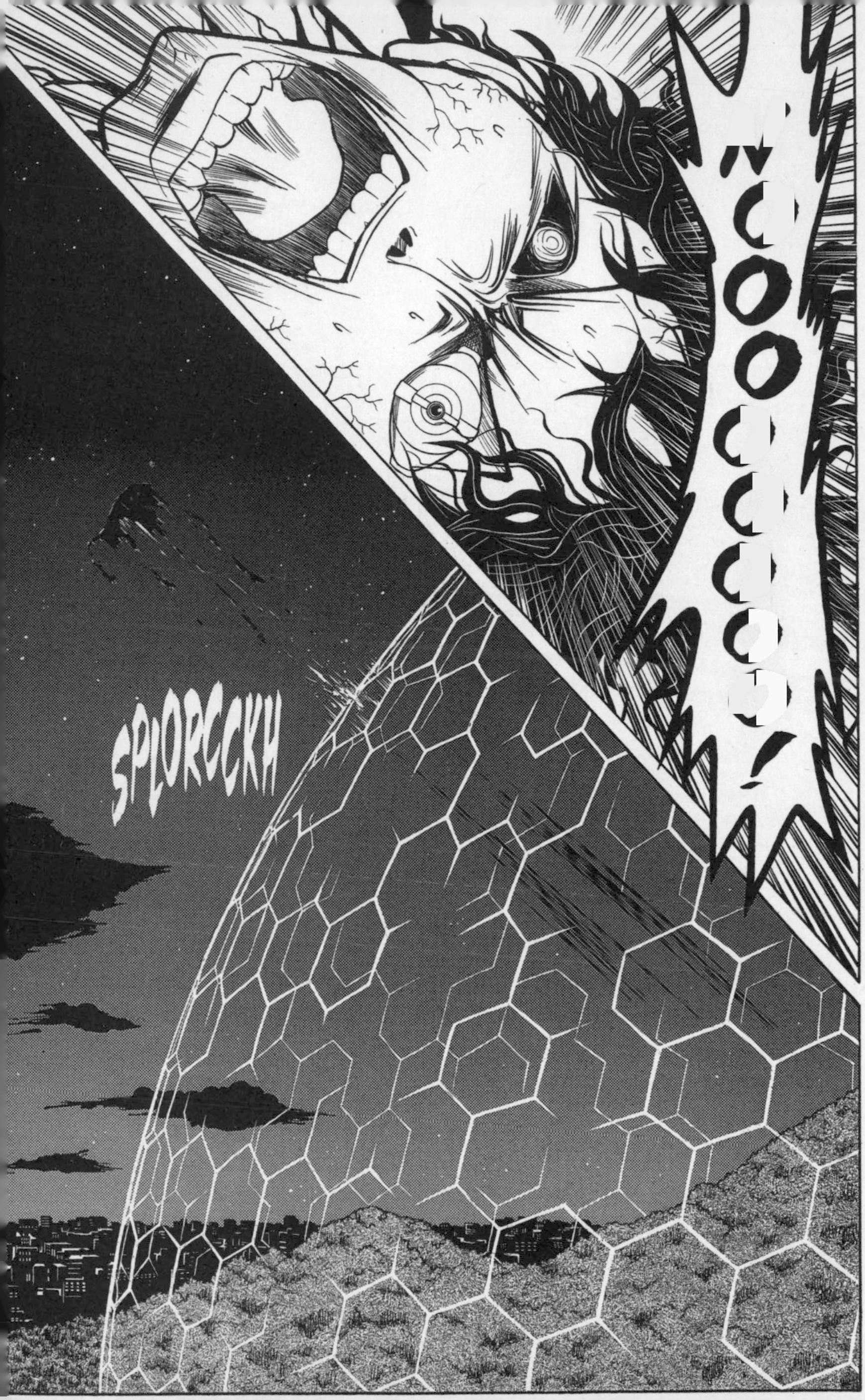
NOOOOOOOO!
SPLORCCKH

Welcome,
Yanagisawa.

LOSER'S
FIELD

Have a seat.

CLASS 175 | TIMELESS

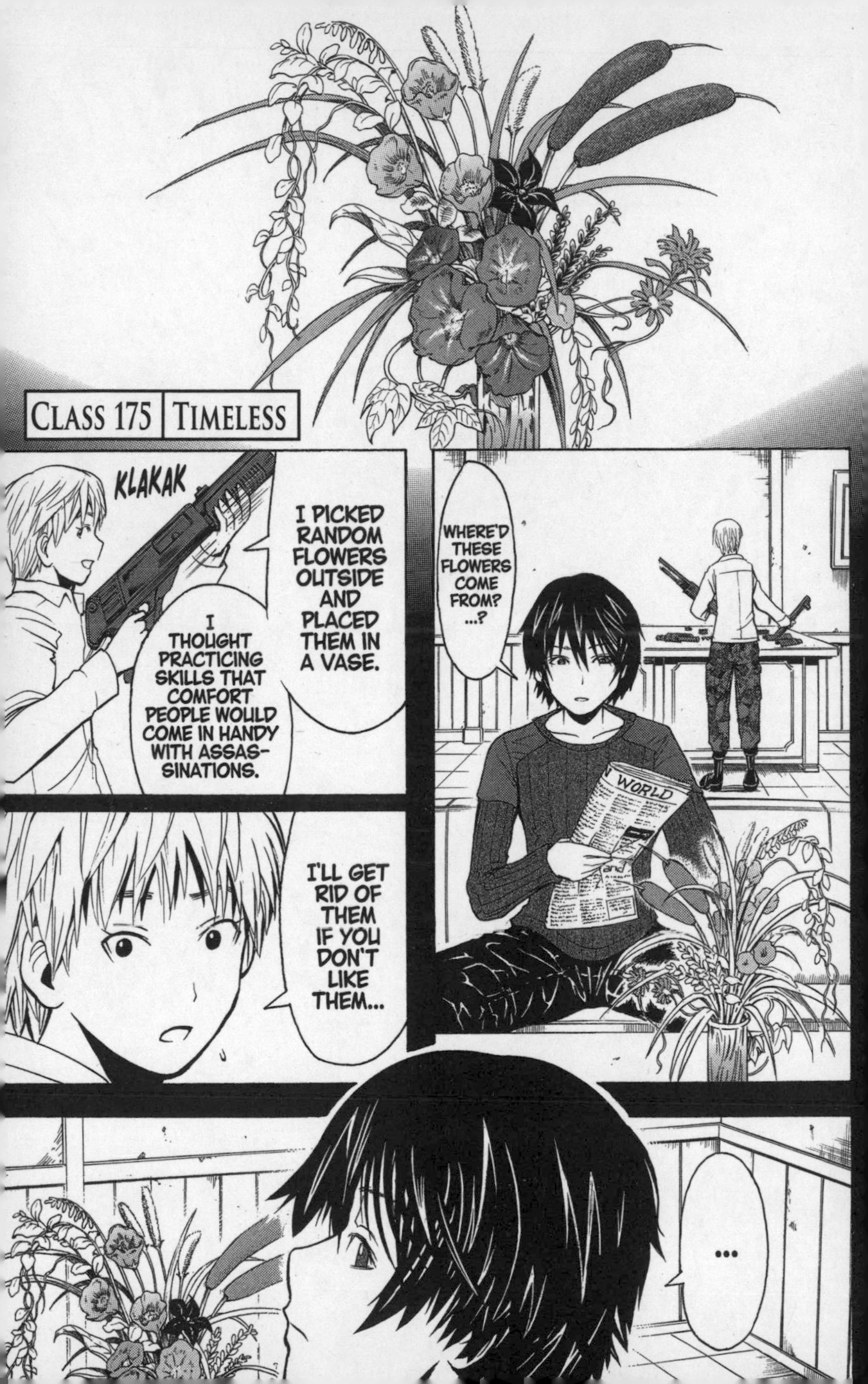

WHERE'D THESE FLOWERS COME FROM? ...?
WORLD
KLAKAK
I PICKED RANDOM FLOWERS OUTSIDE AND PLACED THEM IN A VASE.
I THOUGHT PRACTICING SKILLS THAT COMFORT PEOPLE WOULD COME IN HANDY WITH ASSAS-SINATIONS.
I'LL GET RID OF THEM IF YOU DON'T LIKE THEM...
...

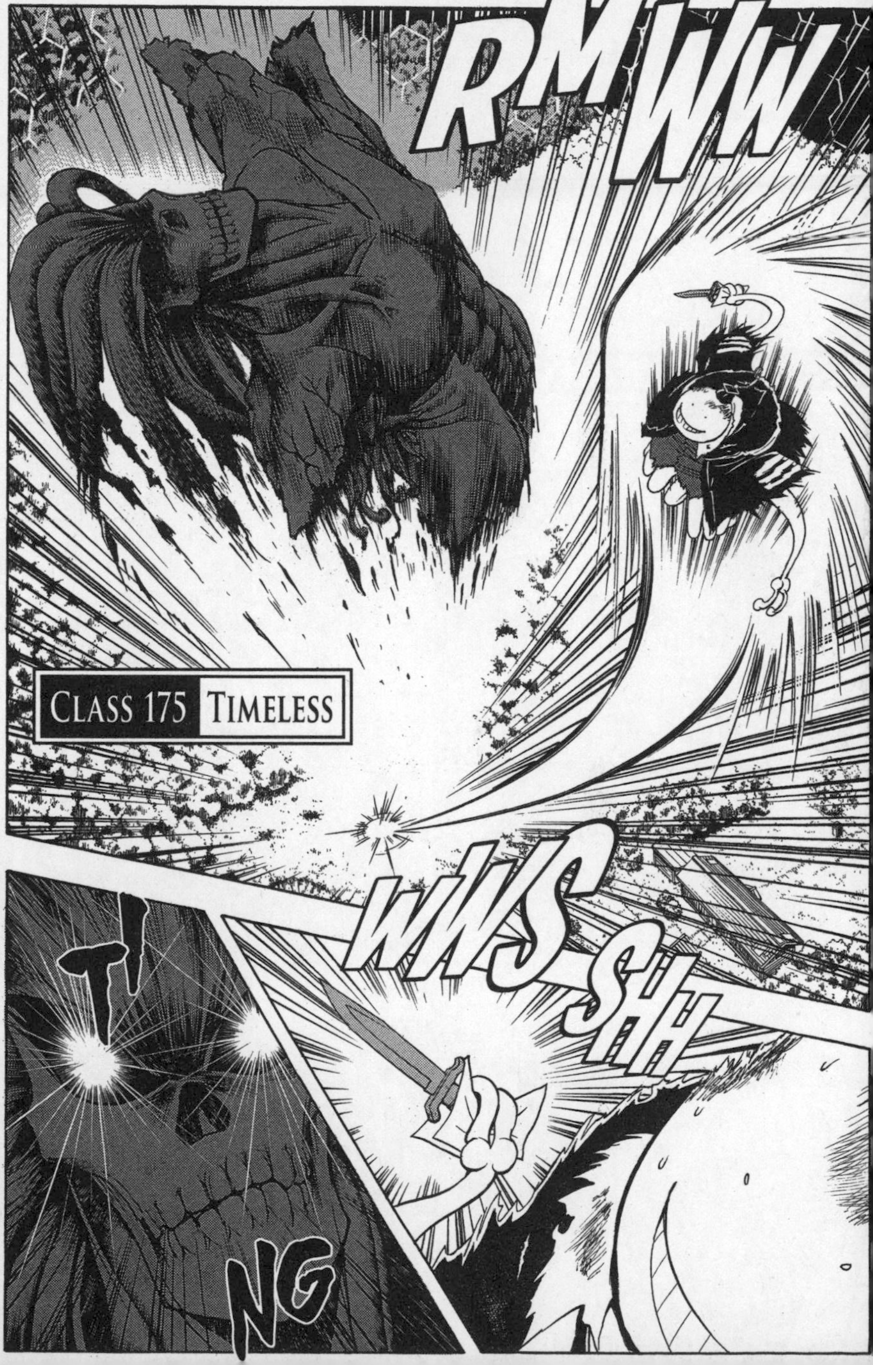
RMWW
CLASS 175 TIMELESS
WHSSH
TH
NG

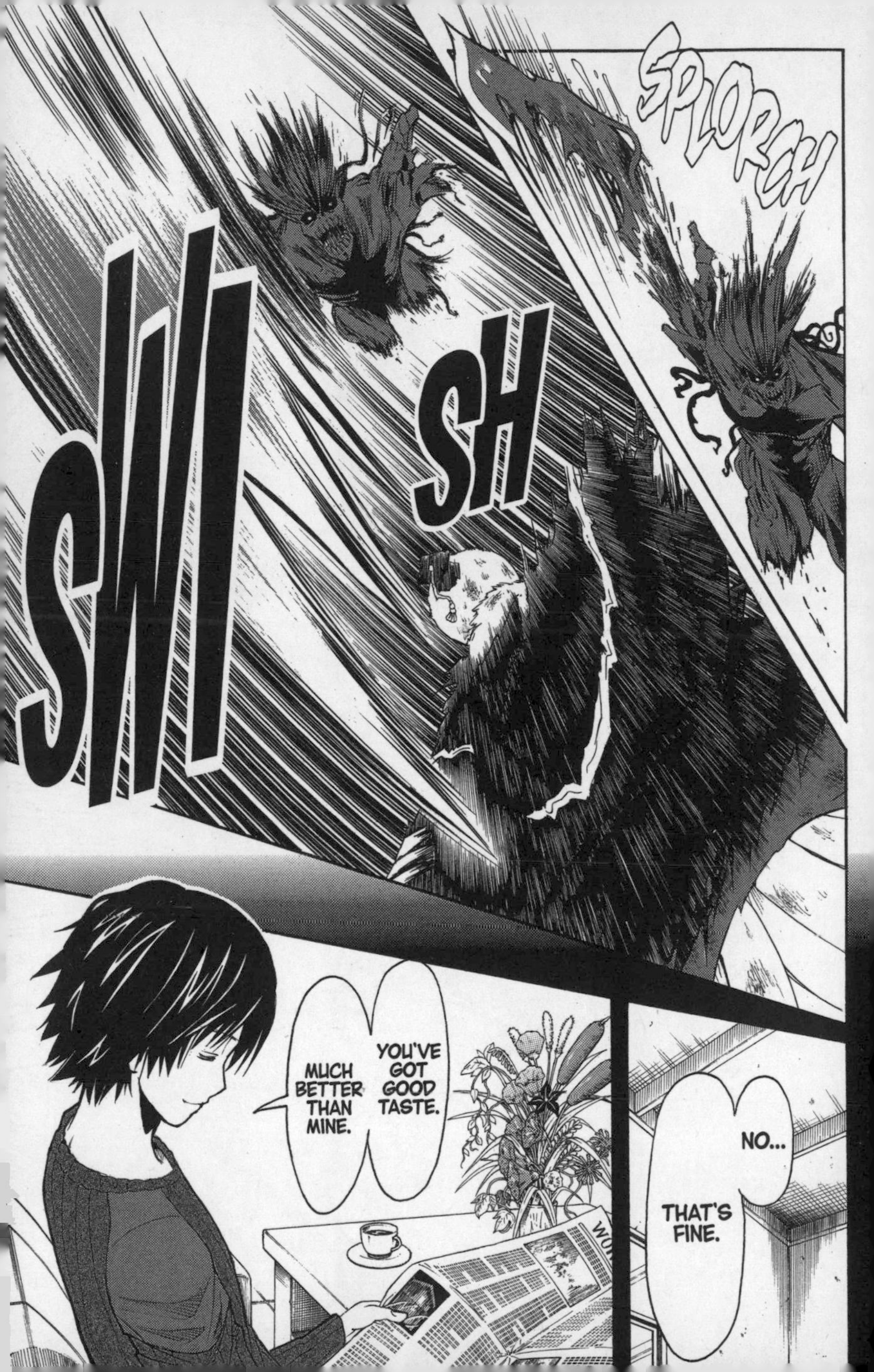
SPLORCH
SWISH
NO...
THAT'S FINE.
YOU'VE GOT GOOD TASTE.
MUCH BETTER THAN MINE.

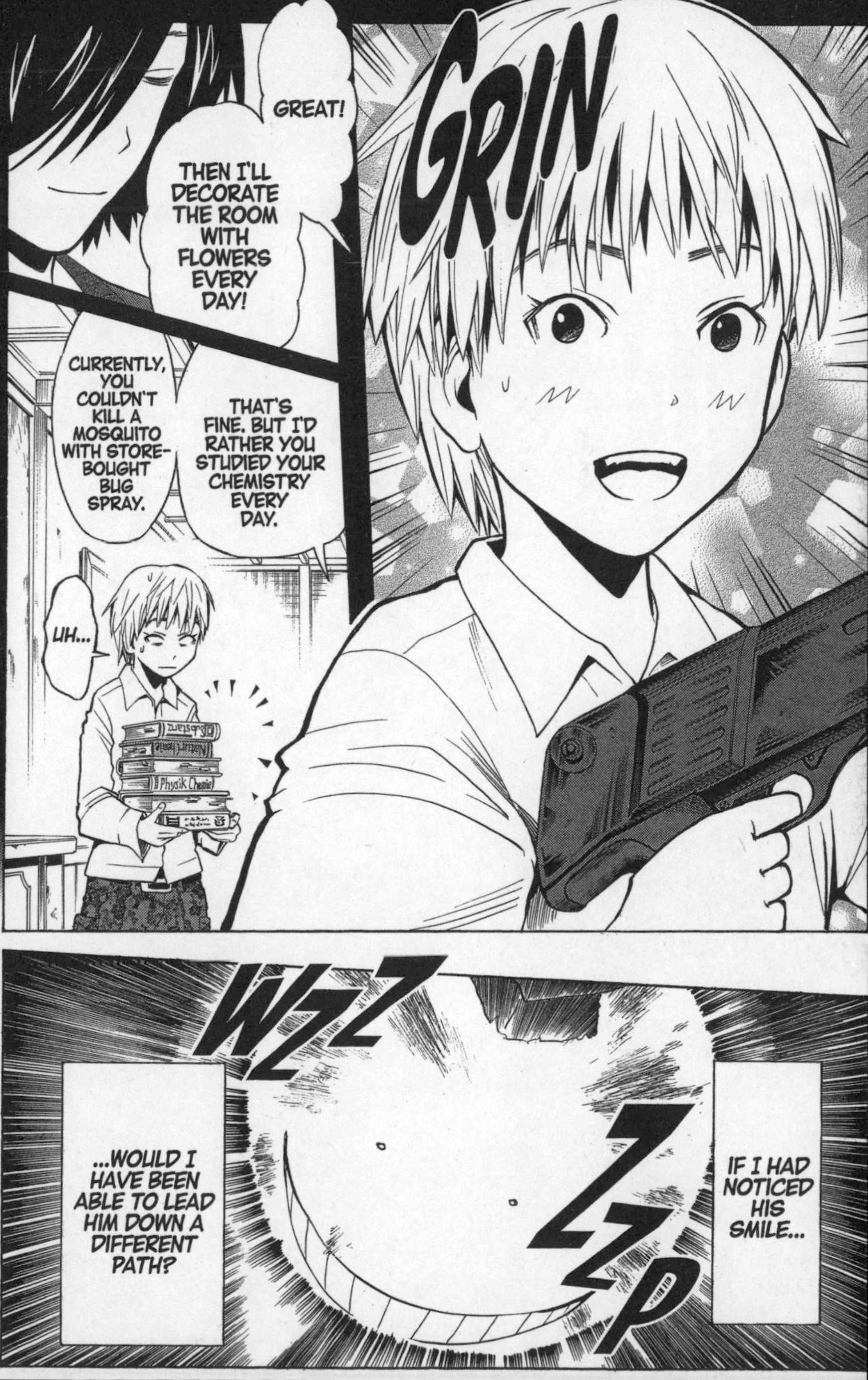
GRIN
GREAT!
THEN I'LL DECORATE THE ROOM WITH FLOWERS EVERY DAY!
THAT'S FINE. BUT I'D RATHER YOU STUDIED YOUR CHEMISTRY EVERY DAY.
CURRENTLY, YOU COULDN'T KILL A MOSQUITO WITH STORE-BOUGHT BUG SPRAY.
UH...
Physik Chemie
WZZ
ZZP
IF I HAD NOTICED HIS SMILE...
...WOULD I HAVE BEEN ABLE TO LEAD HIM DOWN A DIFFERENT PATH?

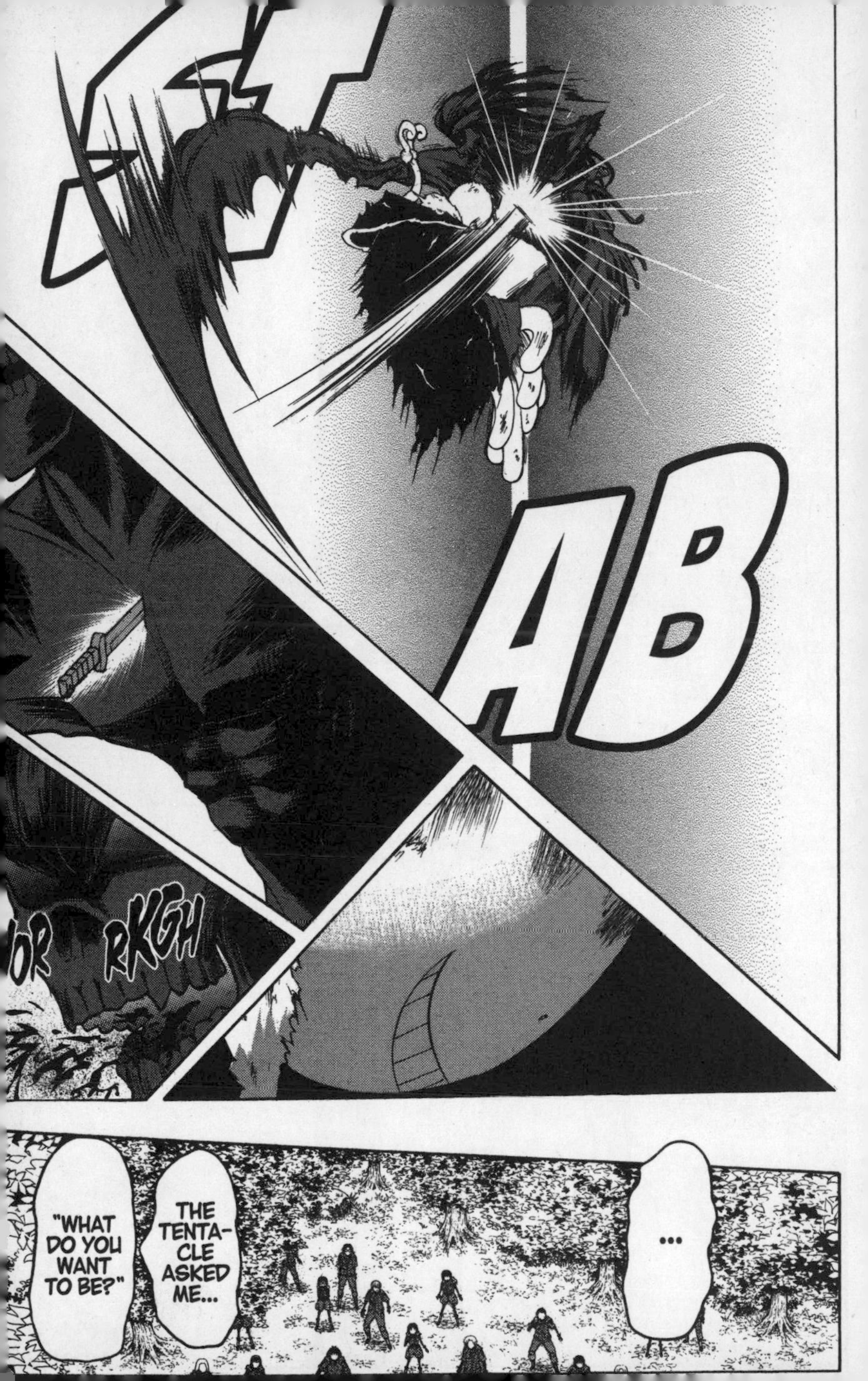
AB
RKGH
...
THE TENTACLE ASKED ME...
"WHAT DO YOU WANT TO BE?"

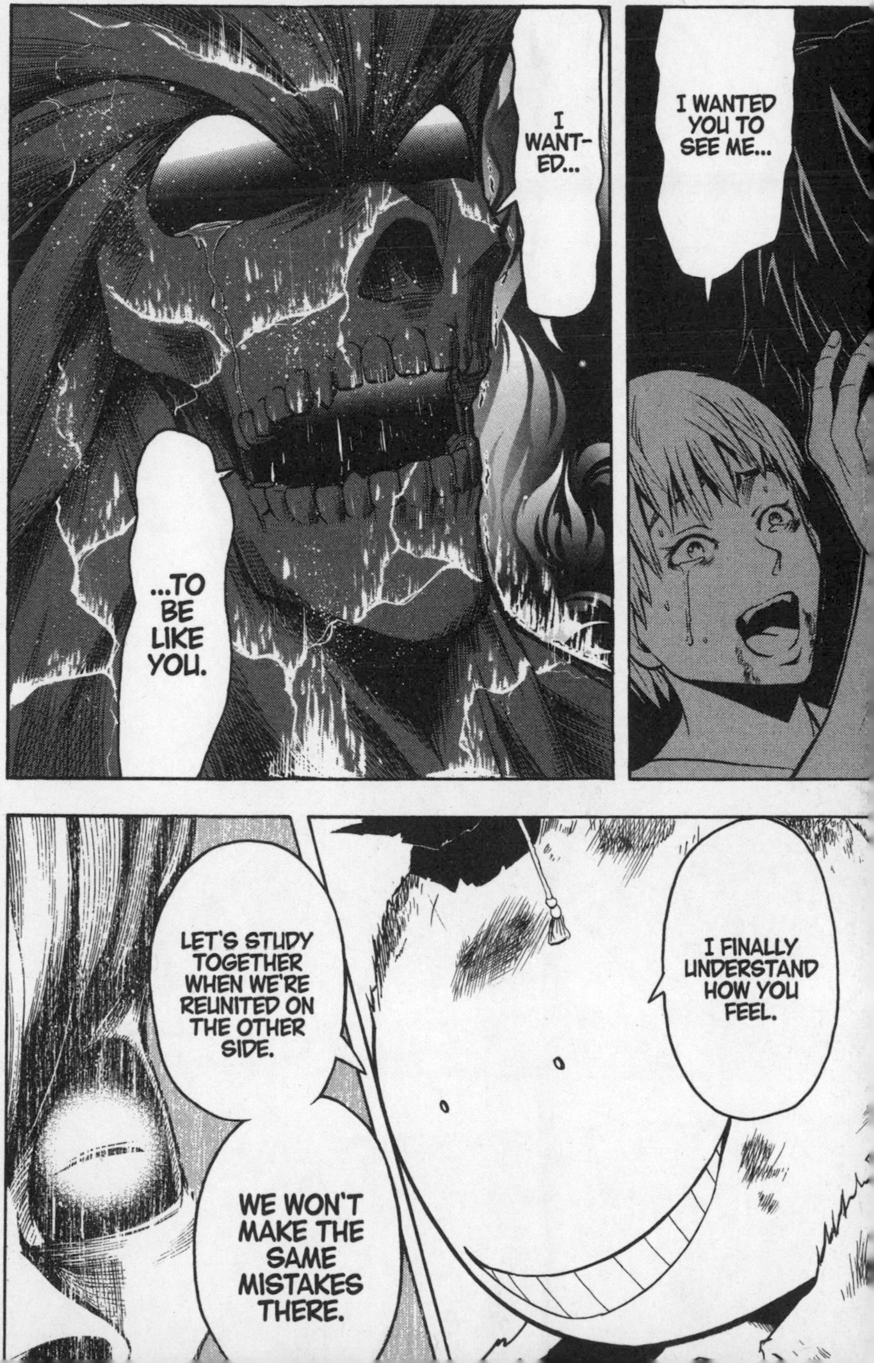
I WANTED YOU TO SEE ME...
I WANTED...
...TO BE LIKE YOU.
I FINALLY UNDERSTAND HOW YOU FEEL.
LET'S STUDY TOGETHER WHEN WE'RE REUNITED ON THE OTHER SIDE.
WE WON'T MAKE THE SAME MISTAKES THERE.

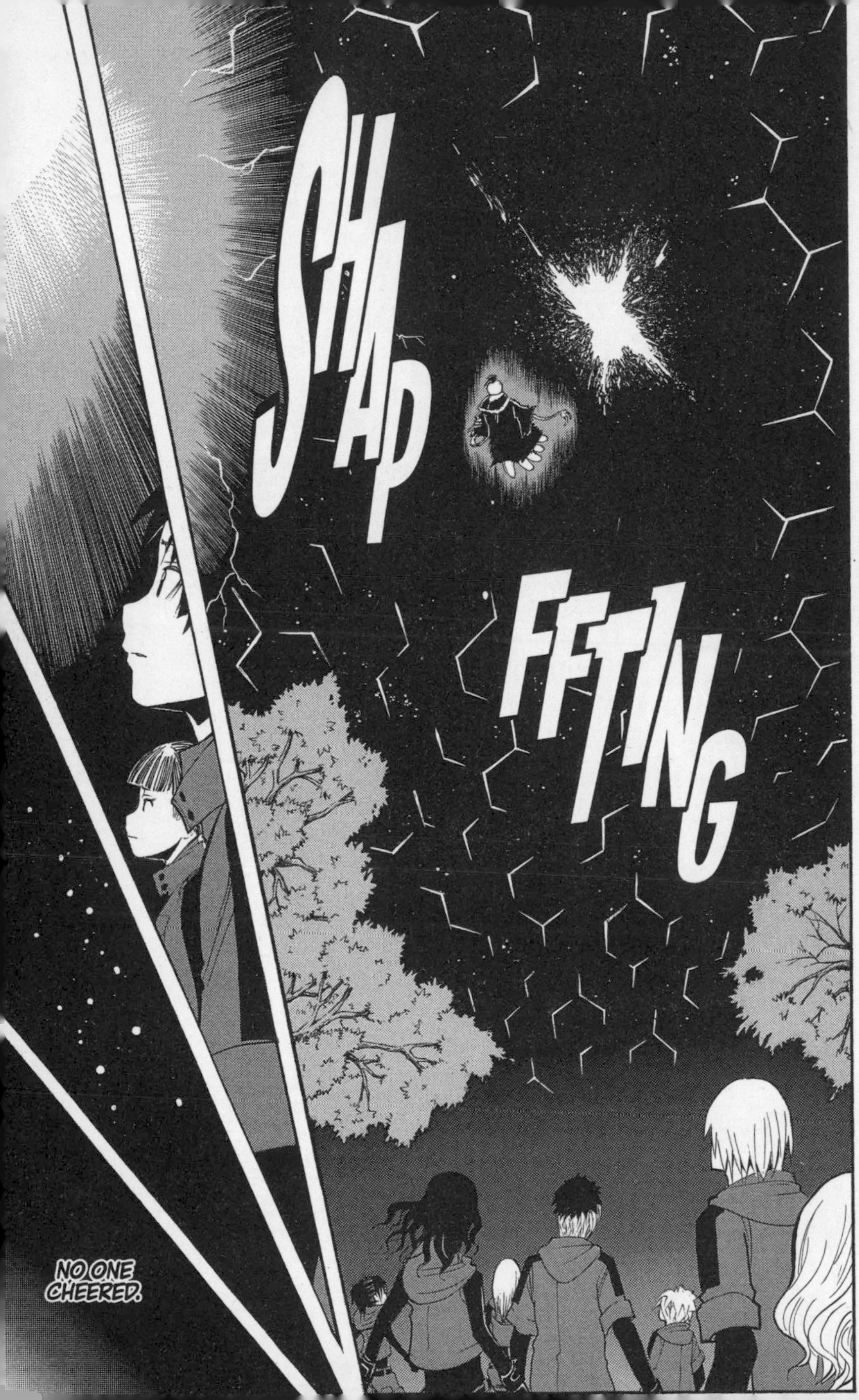
SHAP
FFTING
NO ONE CHEERED.

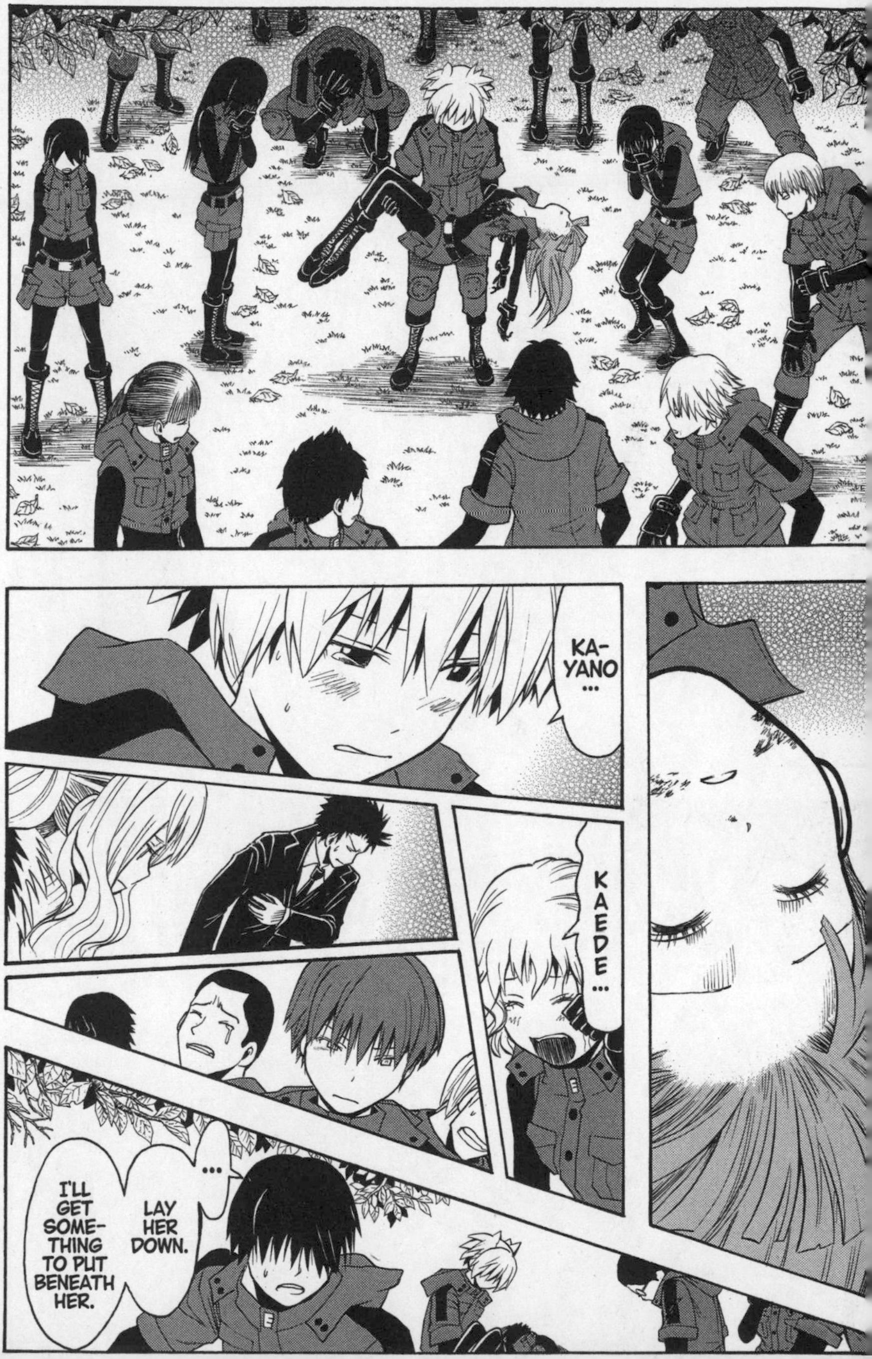
KA-YANO...
KAEDE...
...
LAY HER DOWN.
I'LL GET SOME-THING TO PUT BENEATH HER.

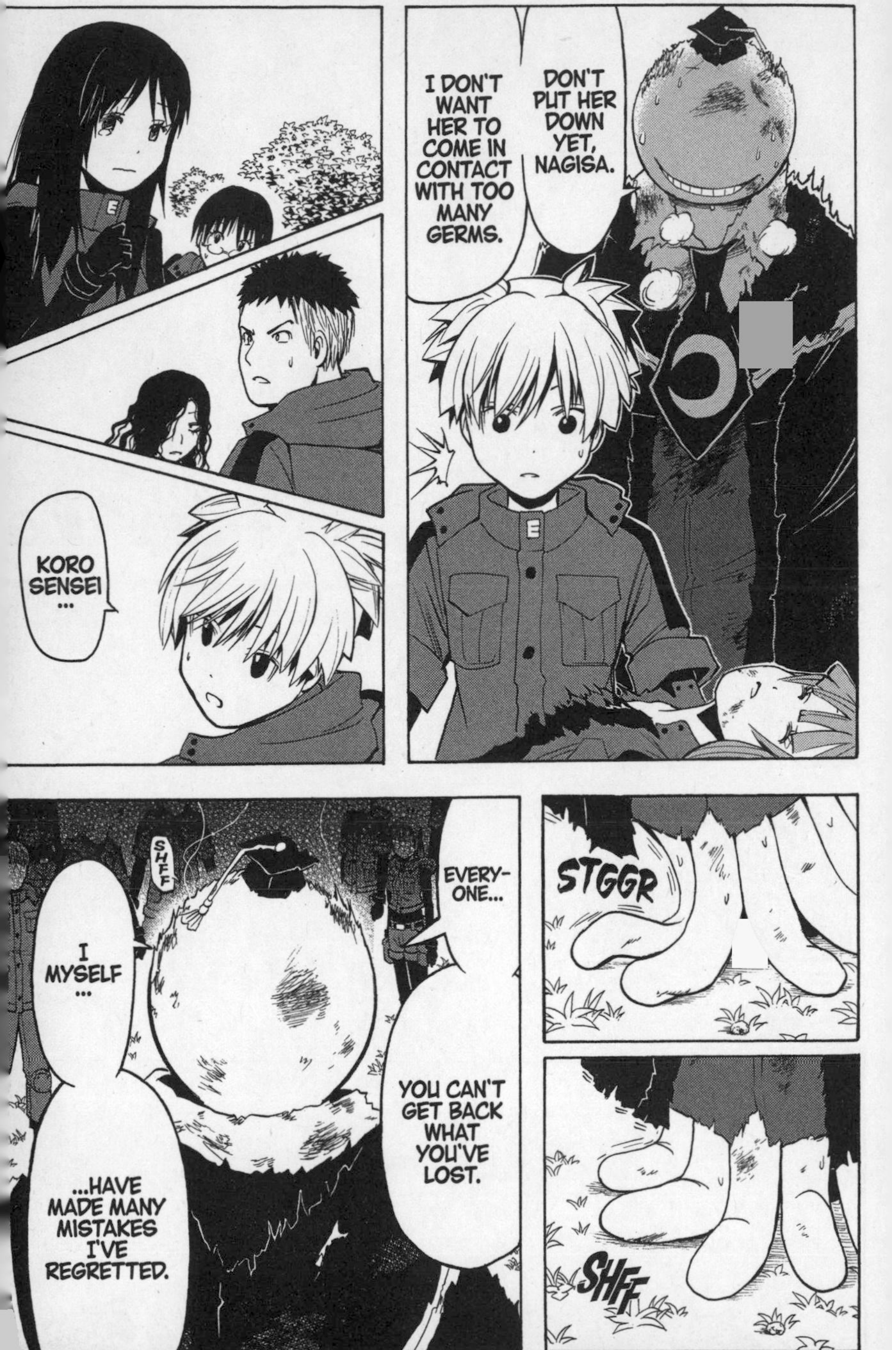
DON'T PUT HER DOWN YET, NAGISA.
I DON'T WANT HER TO COME IN CONTACT WITH TOO MANY GERMS.
KORO SENSEI ...
STGGR
SHFF
EVERY-ONE...
YOU CAN'T GET BACK WHAT YOU'VE LOST.
SHFF
I MYSELF ...
...HAVE MADE MANY MISTAKES I'VE REGRETTED.

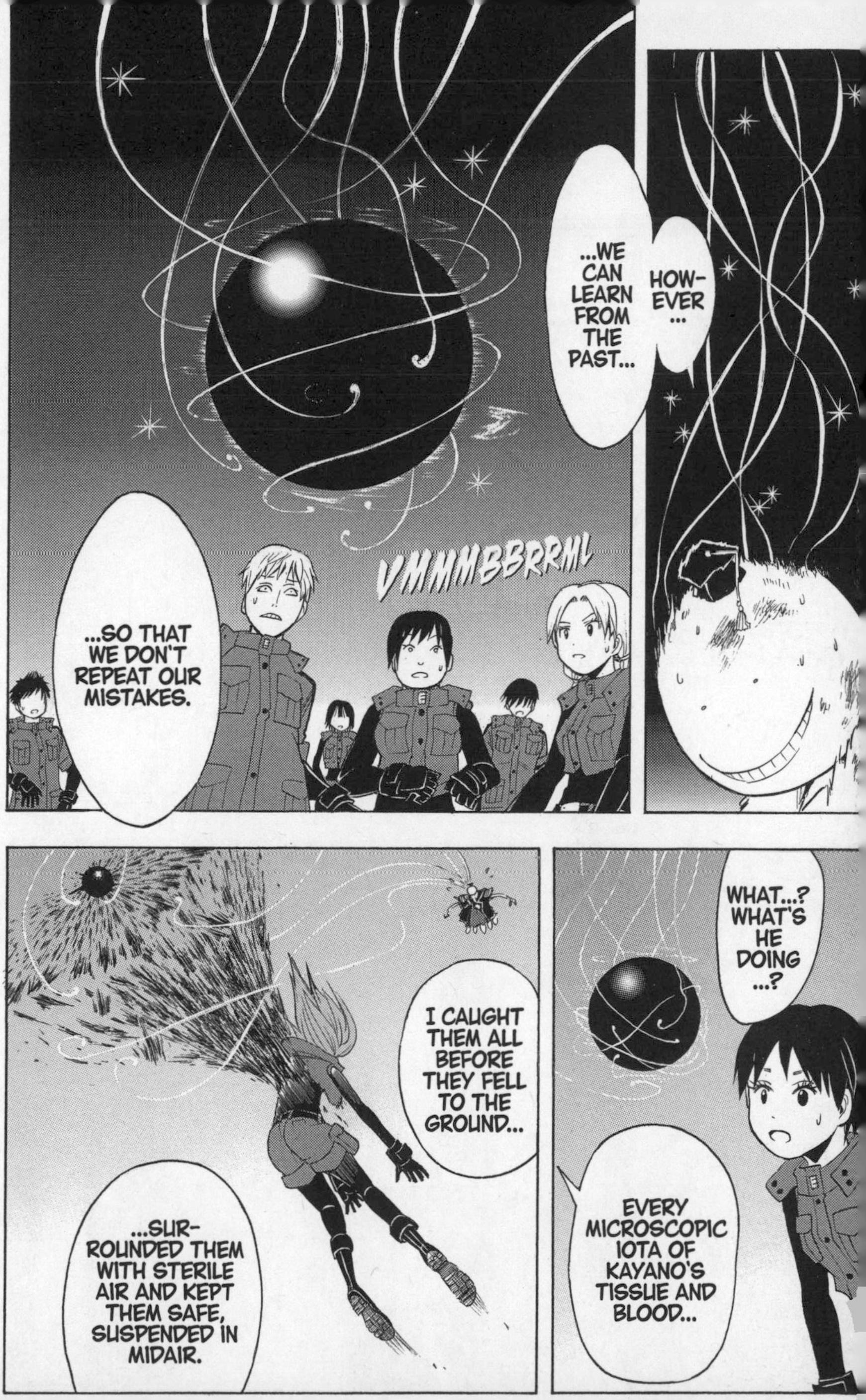
HOW-EVER...
...WE CAN LEARN FROM THE PAST...
VMMMBBRRML
...SO THAT WE DON'T REPEAT OUR MISTAKES.
WHAT...? WHAT'S HE DOING...?
EVERY MICROSCOPIC IOTA OF KAYANO'S TISSUE AND BLOOD...
I CAUGHT THEM ALL BEFORE THEY FELL TO THE GROUND...
...SUR-ROUNDED THEM WITH STERILE AIR AND KEPT THEM SAFE, SUSPENDED IN MIDAIR.

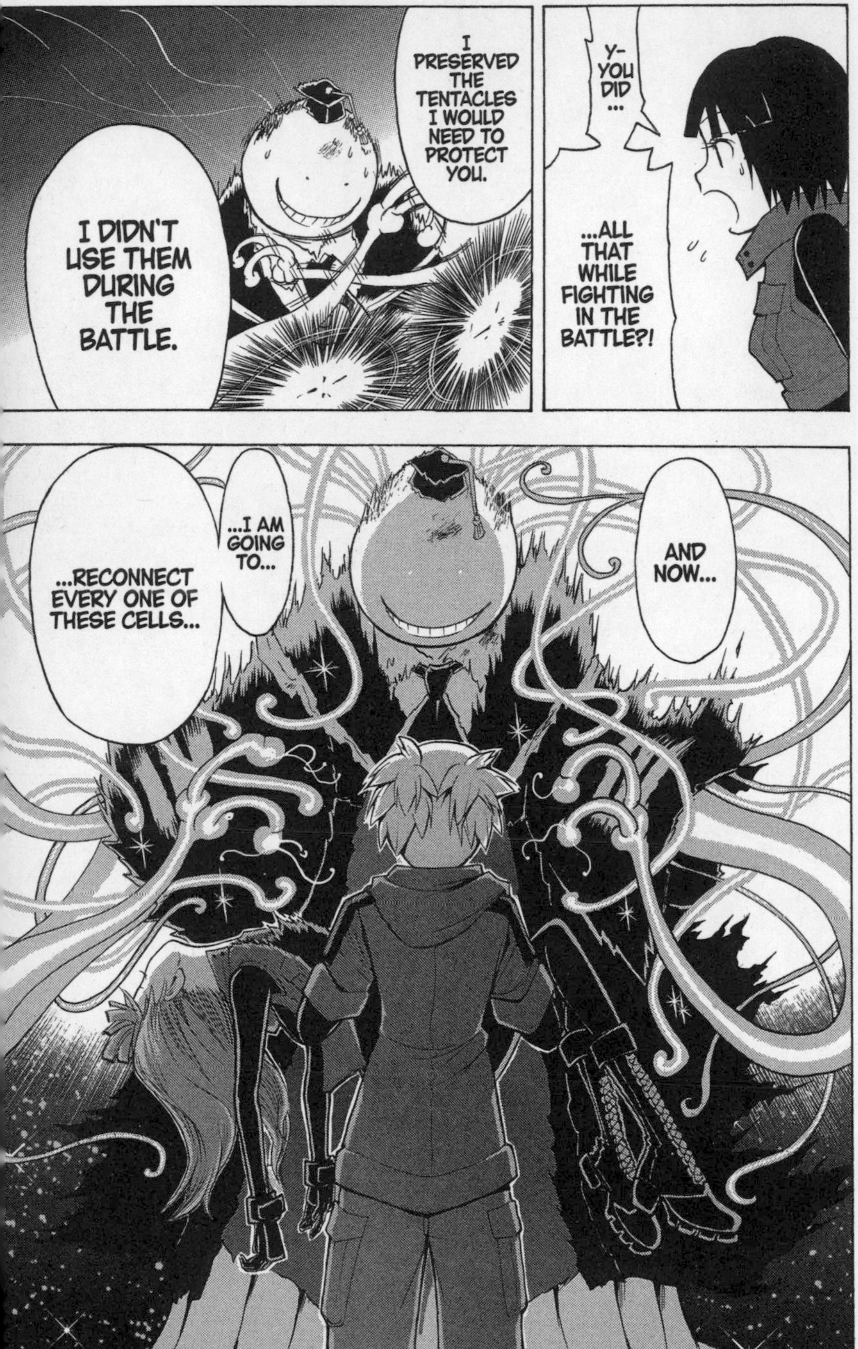
Y-YOU DID...
...ALL THAT WHILE FIGHTING IN THE BATTLE?!
I PRESERVED THE TENTACLES I WOULD NEED TO PROTECT YOU.
I DIDN'T USE THEM DURING THE BATTLE.
AND NOW...
...I AM GOING TO...
...RECONNECT EVERY ONE OF THESE CELLS...

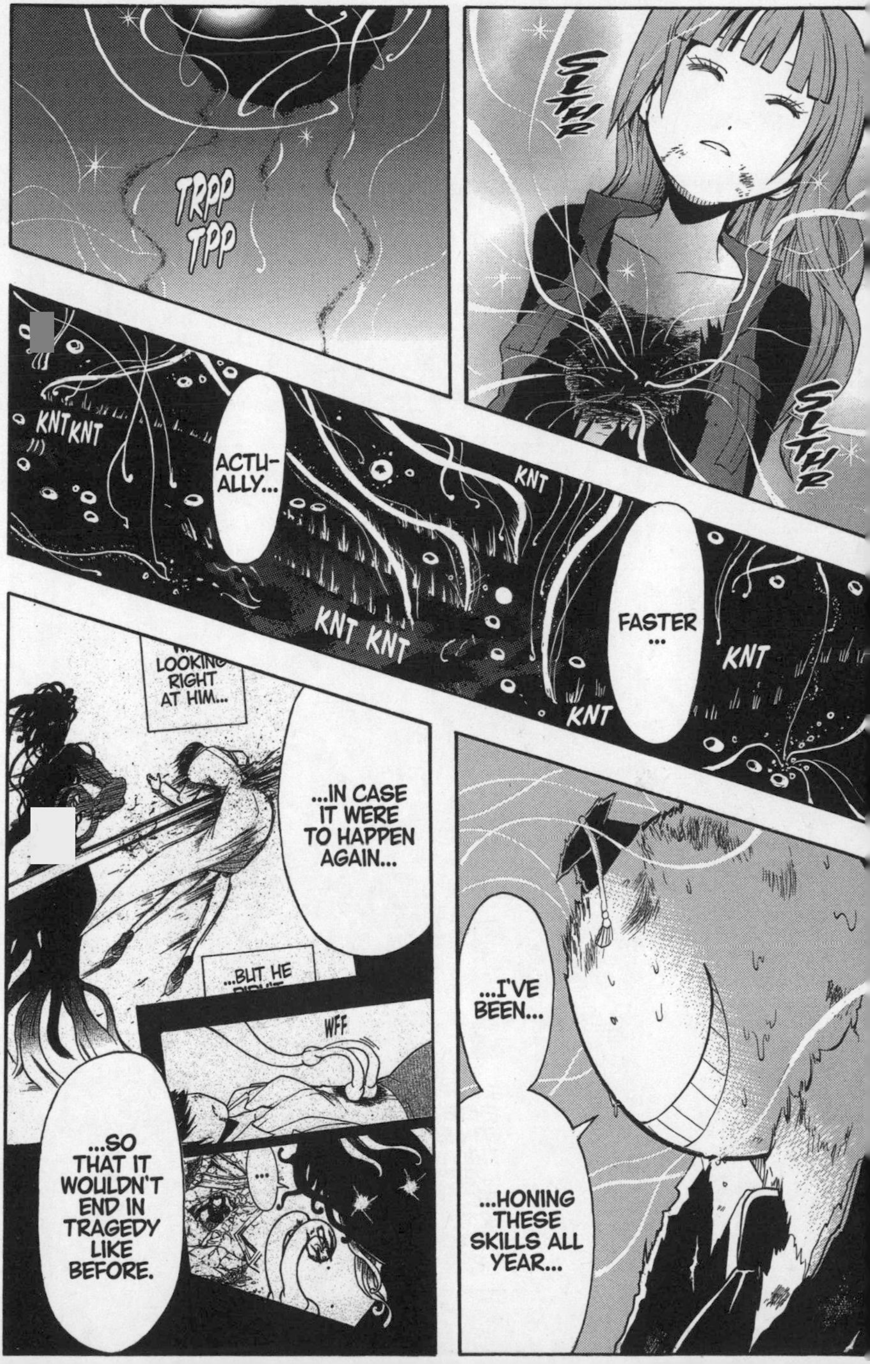
SLTHR
SLTHR
TRPP TPP
FASTER...
KNT
KNT
KNT KNT
KNT
ACTU-ALLY...
KNT KNT
...I'VE BEEN...
...HONING THESE SKILLS ALL YEAR...
...IN CASE IT WERE TO HAPPEN AGAIN...
LOOKING RIGHT AT HIM...
...BUT HE
WFF
...
...SO THAT IT WOULDN'T END IN TRAGEDY LIKE BEFORE.

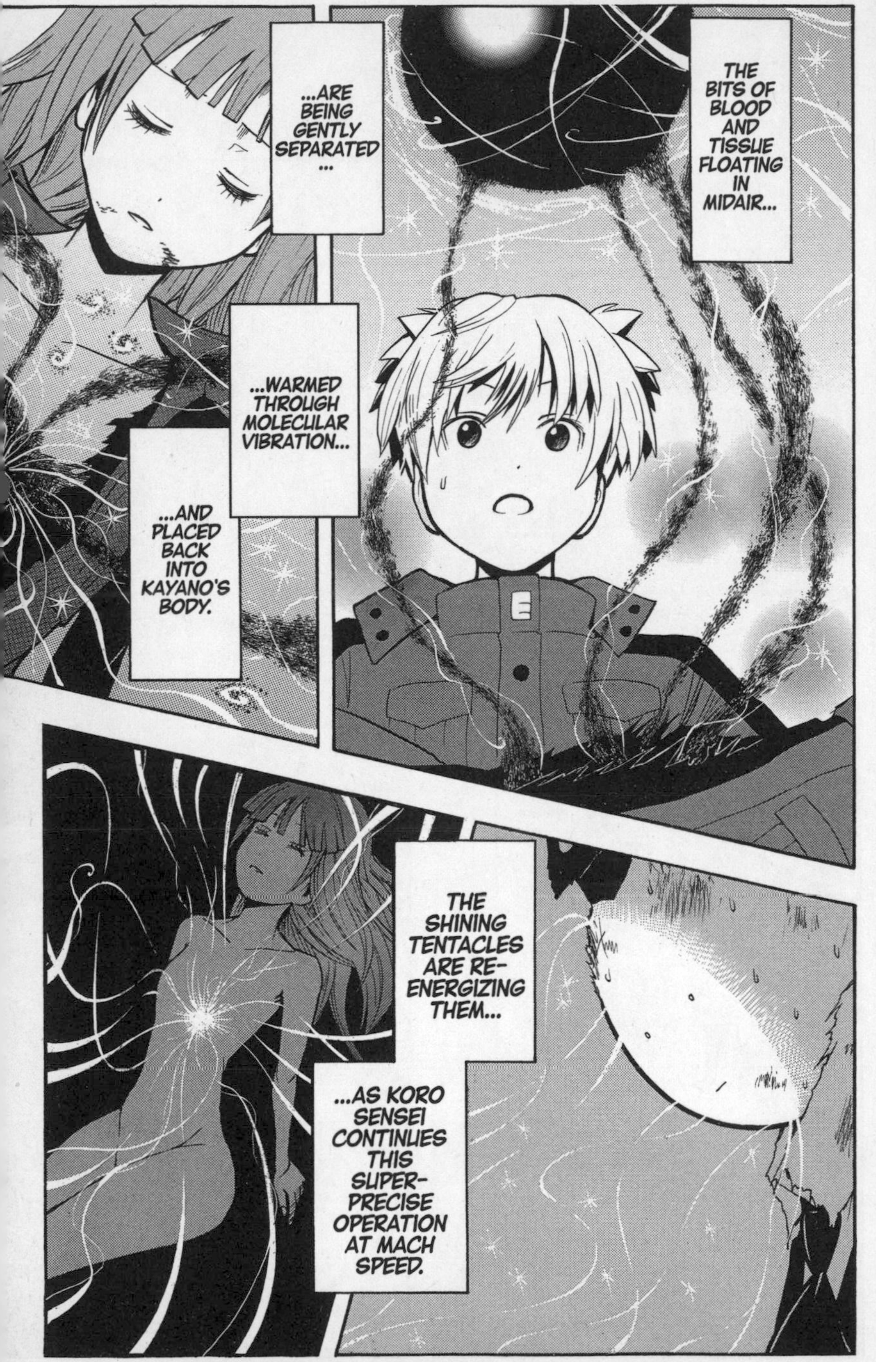
THE BITS OF BLOOD AND TISSUE FLOATING IN MIDAIR...
...ARE BEING GENTLY SEPARATED...
...WARMED THROUGH MOLECULAR VIBRATION...
...AND PLACED BACK INTO KAYANO'S BODY.
THE SHINING TENTACLES ARE RE-ENERGIZING THEM...
...AS KORO SENSEI CONTINUES THIS SUPER-PRECISE OPERATION AT MACH SPEED.

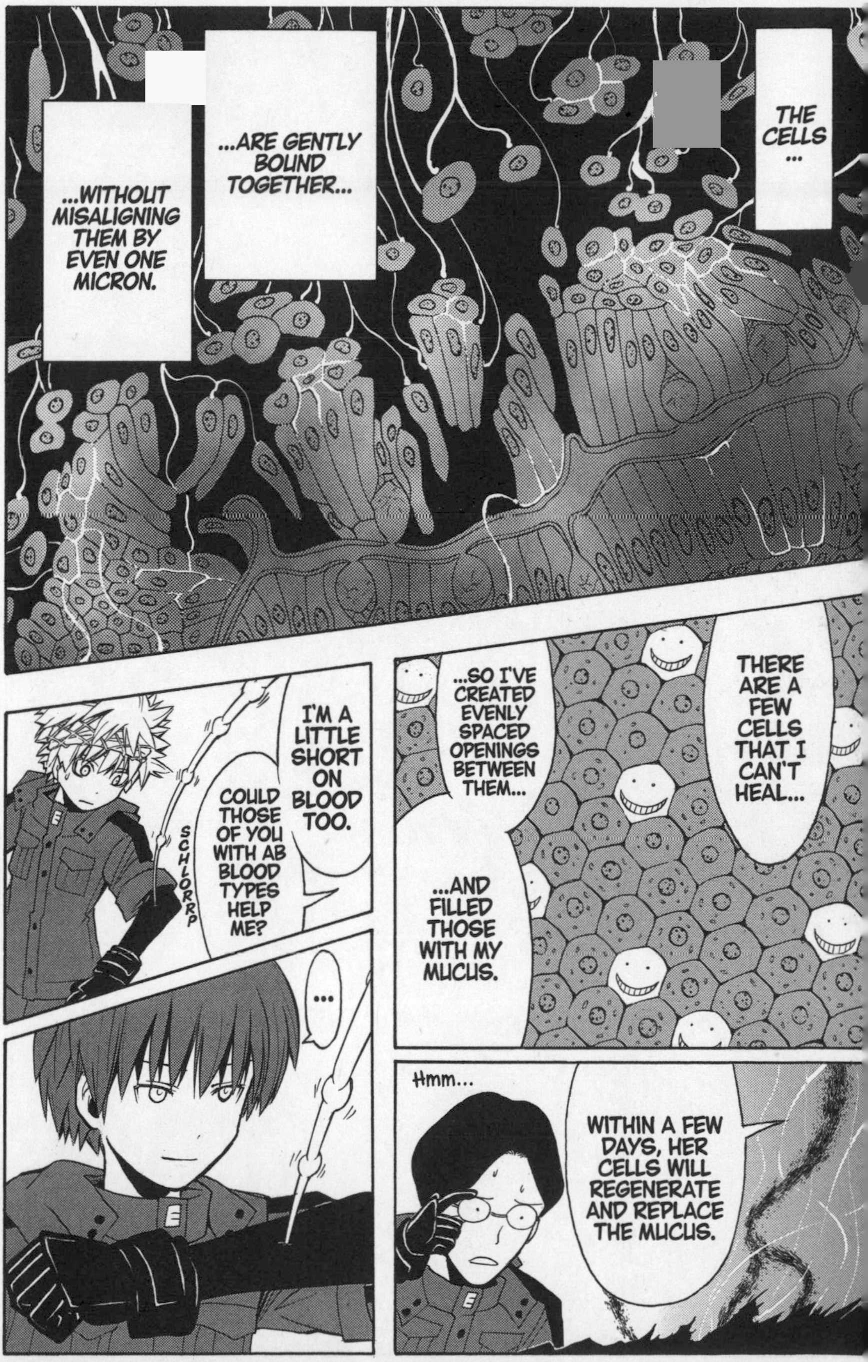
THE CELLS...
...ARE GENTLY BOUND TOGETHER...
...WITHOUT MISALIGNING THEM BY EVEN ONE MICRON.
THERE ARE A FEW CELLS THAT I CAN'T HEAL...
...SO I'VE CREATED EVENLY SPACED OPENINGS BETWEEN THEM...
...AND FILLED THOSE WITH MY MUCUS.
I'M A LITTLE SHORT ON BLOOD TOO.
COULD THOSE OF YOU WITH AB BLOOD TYPES HELP ME?
SCHLORRP
Hmm...
WITHIN A FEW DAYS, HER CELLS WILL REGENERATE AND REPLACE THE MUCUS.
...

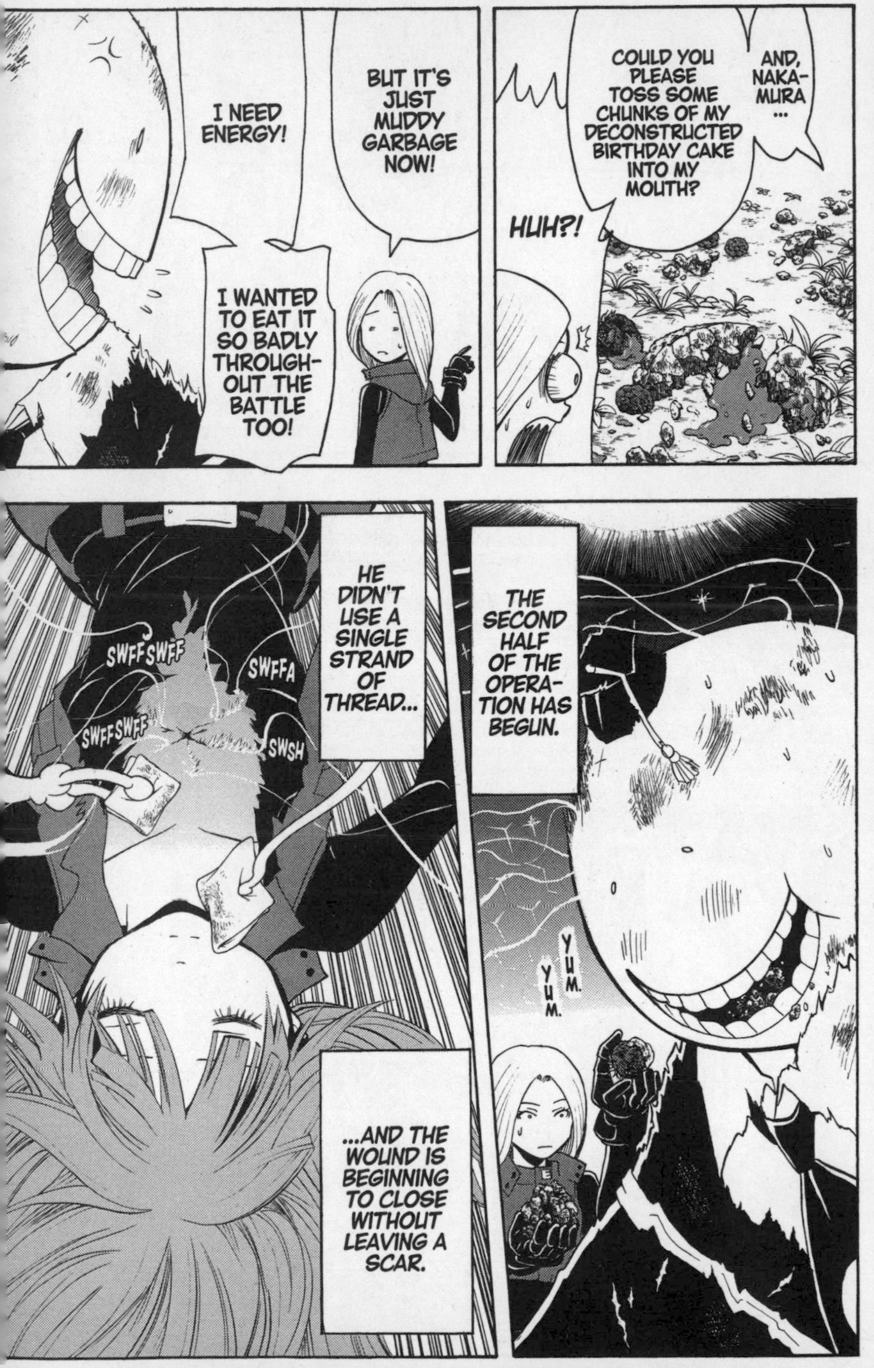
AND, NAKAMURA...
COULD YOU PLEASE TOSS SOME CHUNKS OF MY DECONSTRUCTED BIRTHDAY CAKE INTO MY MOUTH?
HUH?!
BUT IT'S JUST MUDDY GARBAGE NOW!
I NEED ENERGY!
I WANTED TO EAT IT SO BADLY THROUGHOUT THE BATTLE TOO!
THE SECOND HALF OF THE OPERATION HAS BEGUN.
YUM.
YUM.
HE DIDN'T USE A SINGLE STRAND OF THREAD...
SWFF SWFF
SWFFA
SWFF SWFF
SWSH
...AND THE WOUND IS BEGINNING TO CLOSE WITHOUT LEAVING A SCAR.

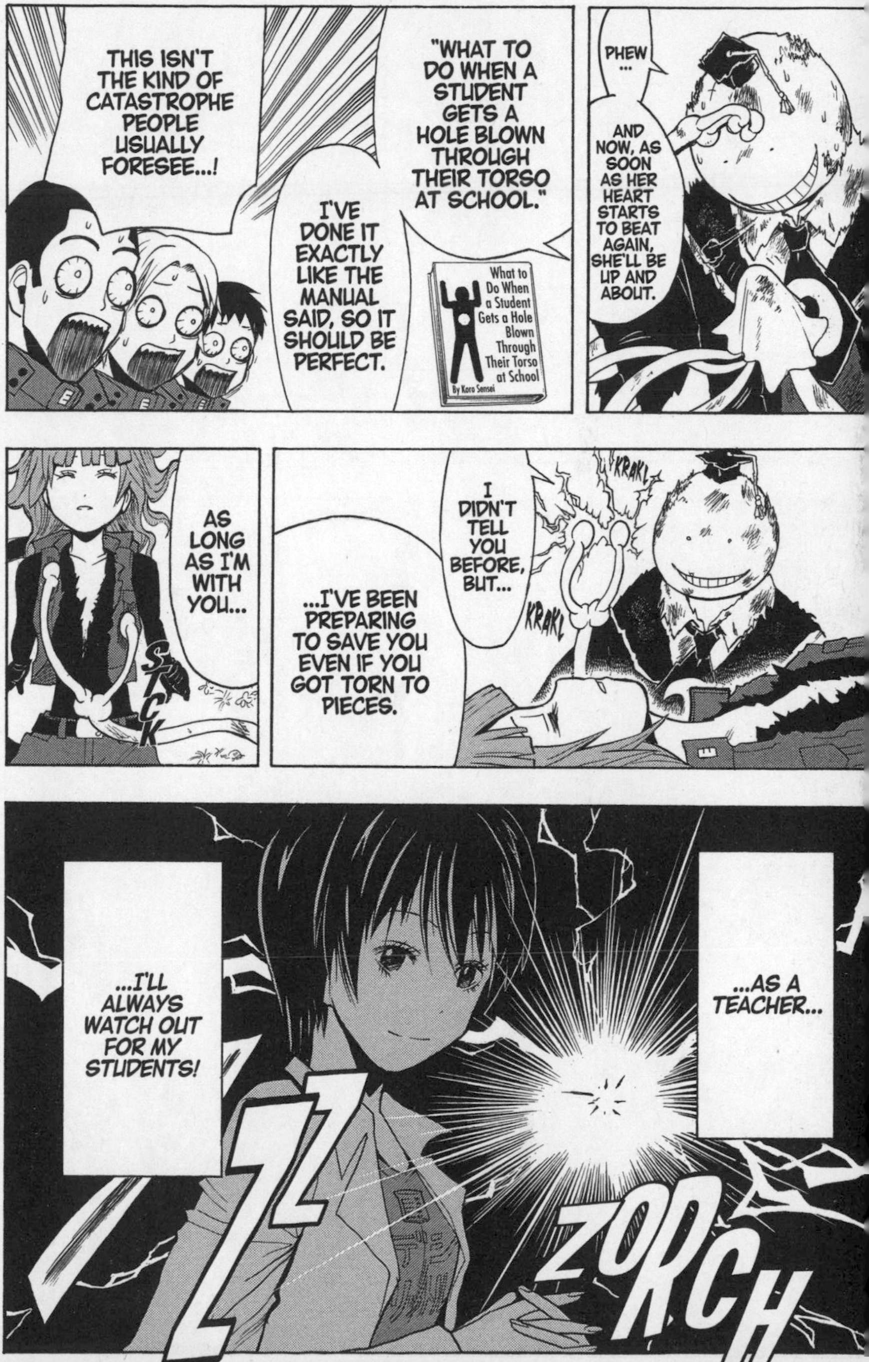
PHEW ...
AND NOW, AS SOON AS HER HEART STARTS TO BEAT AGAIN, SHE'LL BE UP AND ABOUT.
"WHAT TO DO WHEN A STUDENT GETS A HOLE BLOWN THROUGH THEIR TORSO AT SCHOOL."
I'VE DONE IT EXACTLY LIKE THE MANUAL SAID, SO IT SHOULD BE PERFECT.
What to Do When a Student Gets a Hole Blown Through Their Torso at School
By Koro Sensei
THIS ISN'T THE KIND OF CATASTROPHE PEOPLE USUALLY FORESEE...!
KRAKL
I DIDN'T TELL YOU BEFORE, BUT...
KRAKL
...I'VE BEEN PREPARING TO SAVE YOU EVEN IF YOU GOT TORN TO PIECES.
AS LONG AS I'M WITH YOU...
STICK
...AS A TEACHER...
...I'LL ALWAYS WATCH OUT FOR MY STUDENTS!
ZZZ
ZORCH

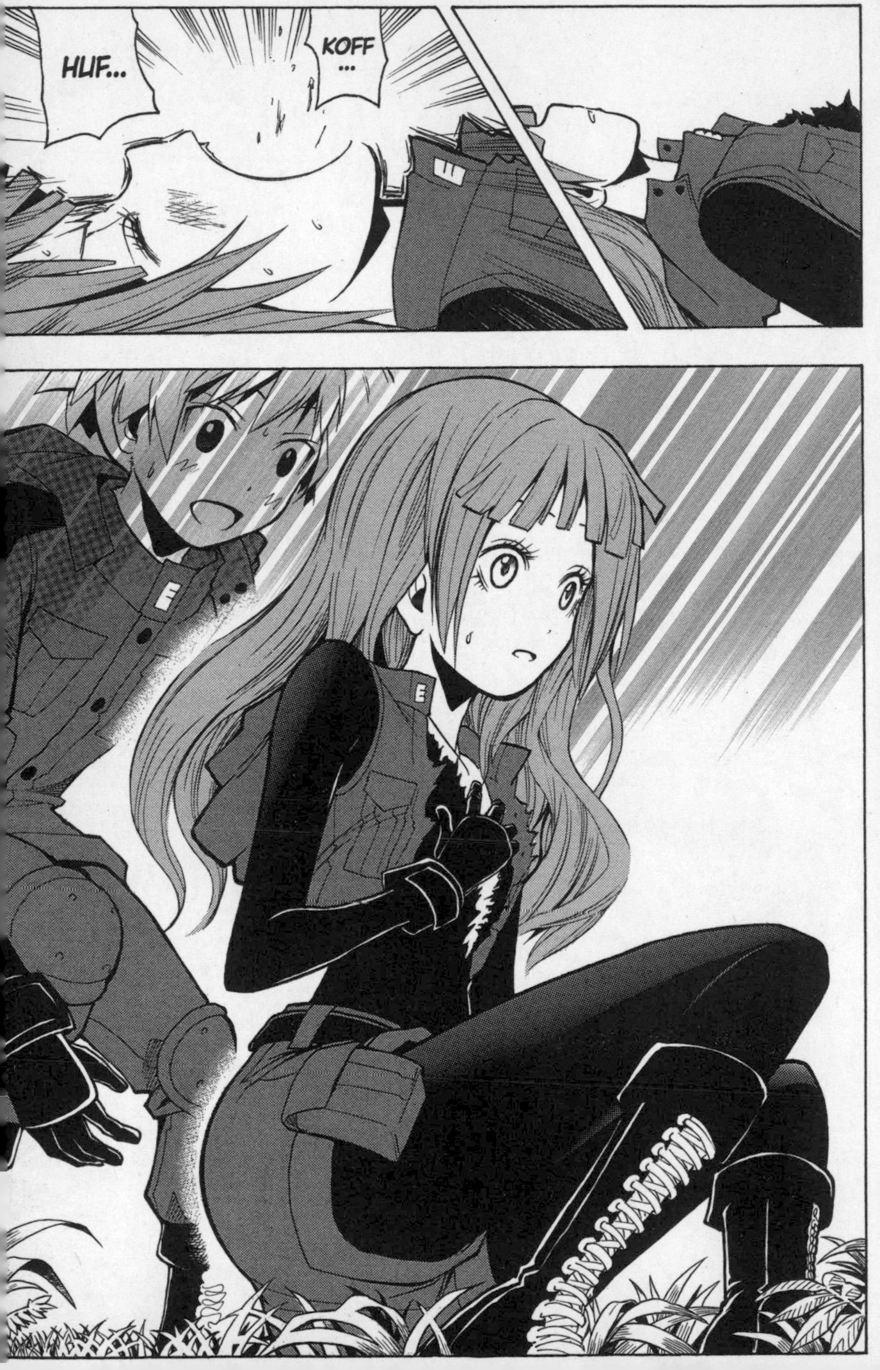
KOFF
...
HUF...

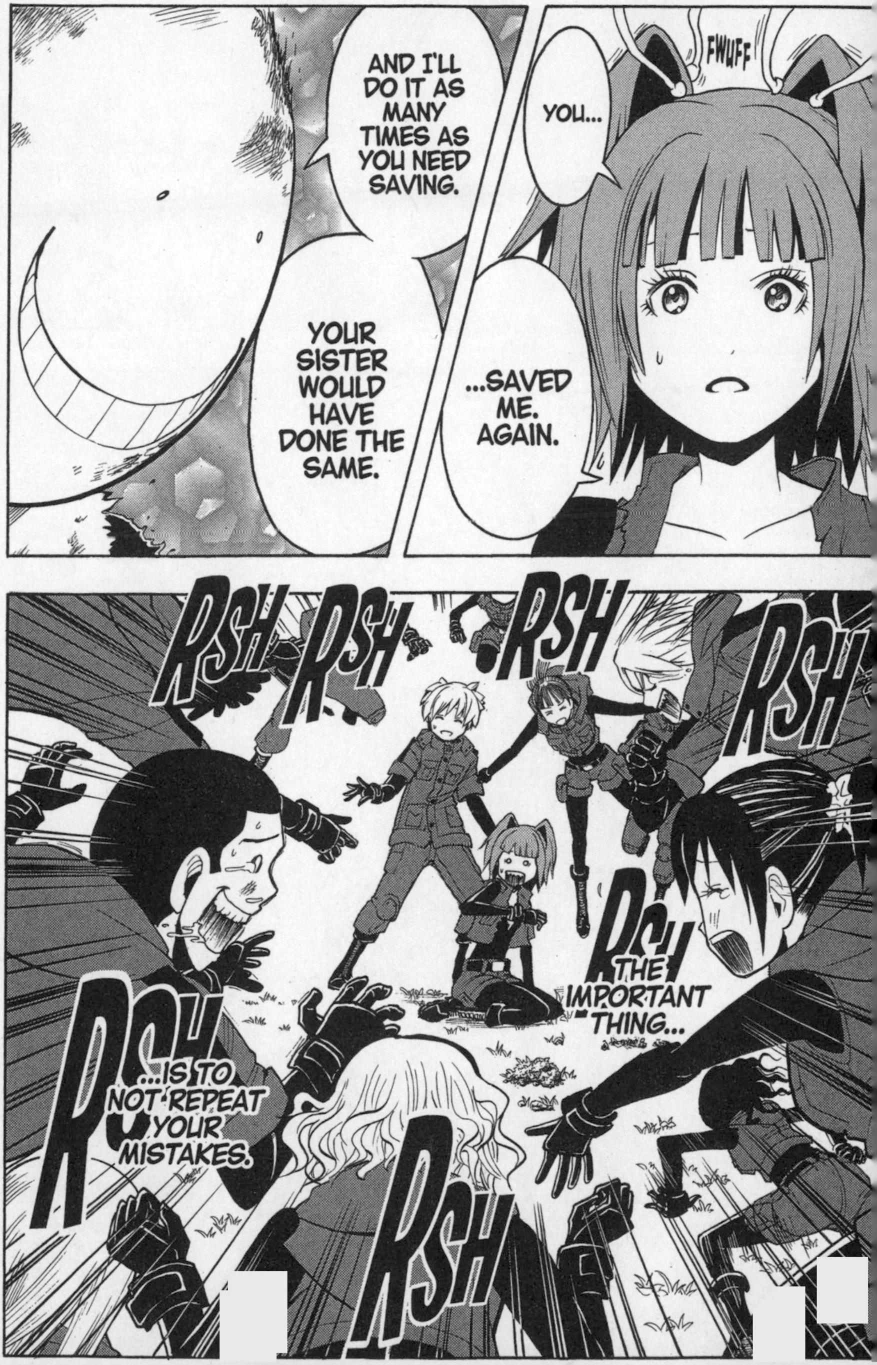
FWUFF
YOU...
...SAVED ME. AGAIN.
AND I'LL DO IT AS MANY TIMES AS YOU NEED SAVING.
YOUR SISTER WOULD HAVE DONE THE SAME.
RSH RSH RSH RSH
RSH
THE IMPORTANT THING...
RSH
...IS TO NOT REPEAT YOUR MISTAKES.
RSH

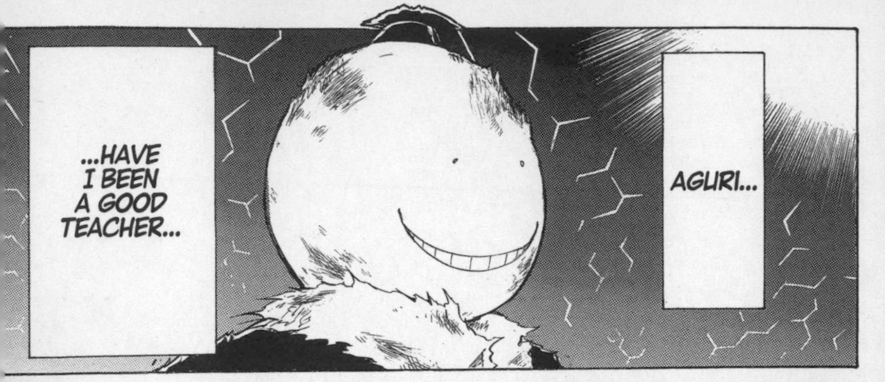
AGURI...
...HAVE I BEEN A GOOD TEACHER...

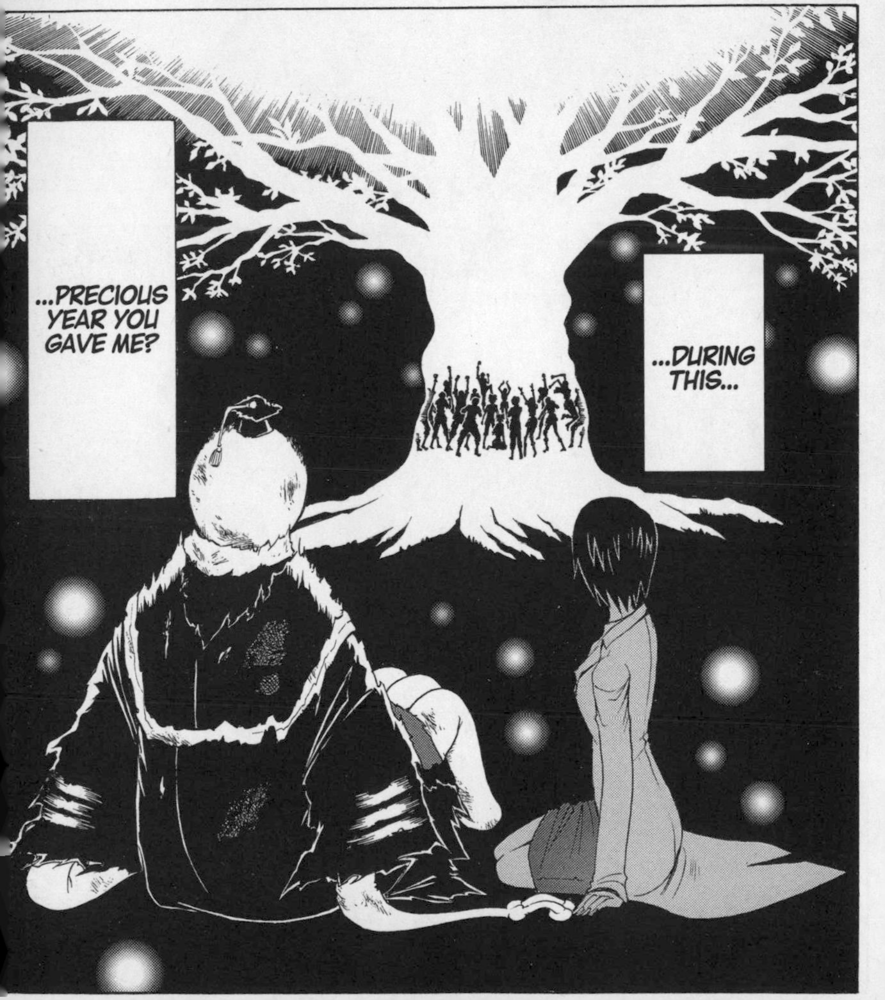
...DURING THIS...
...PRECIOUS YEAR YOU GAVE ME?

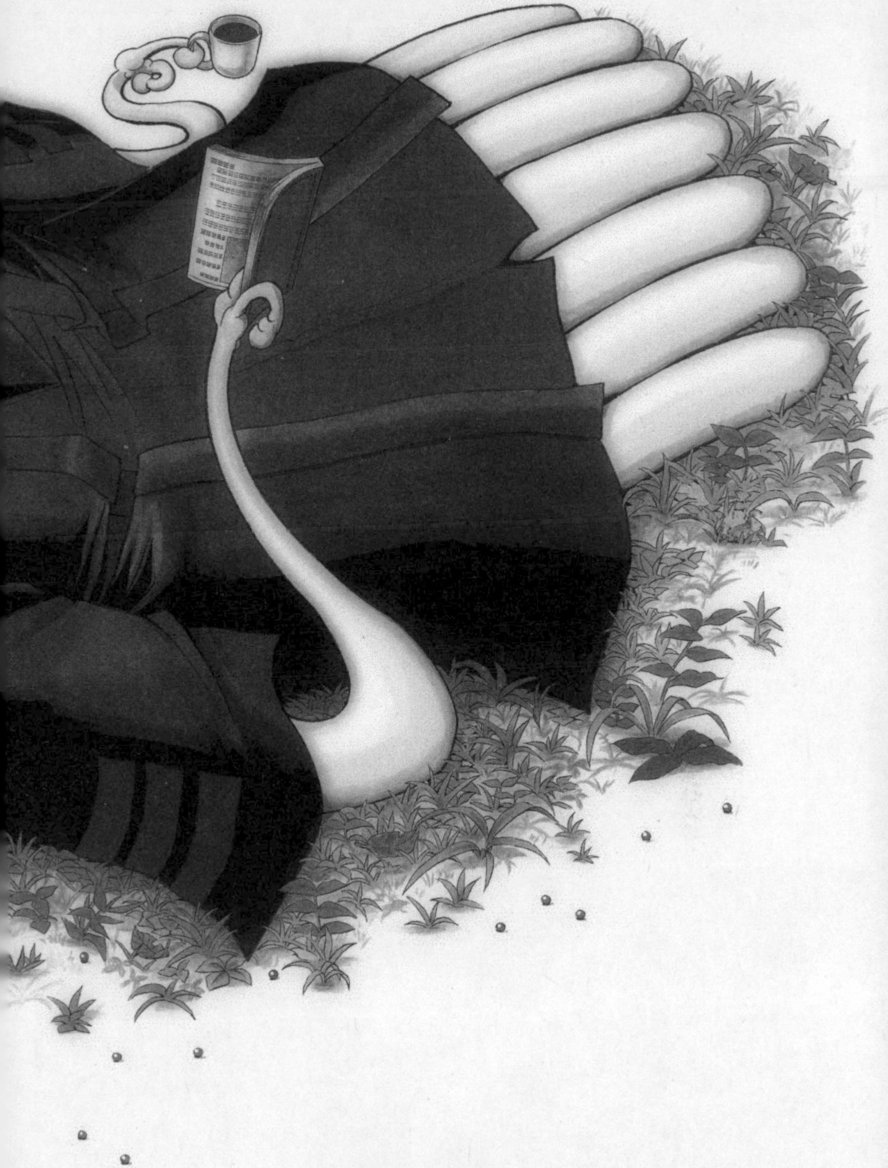

CLASS 176 THE TIME HAS COME

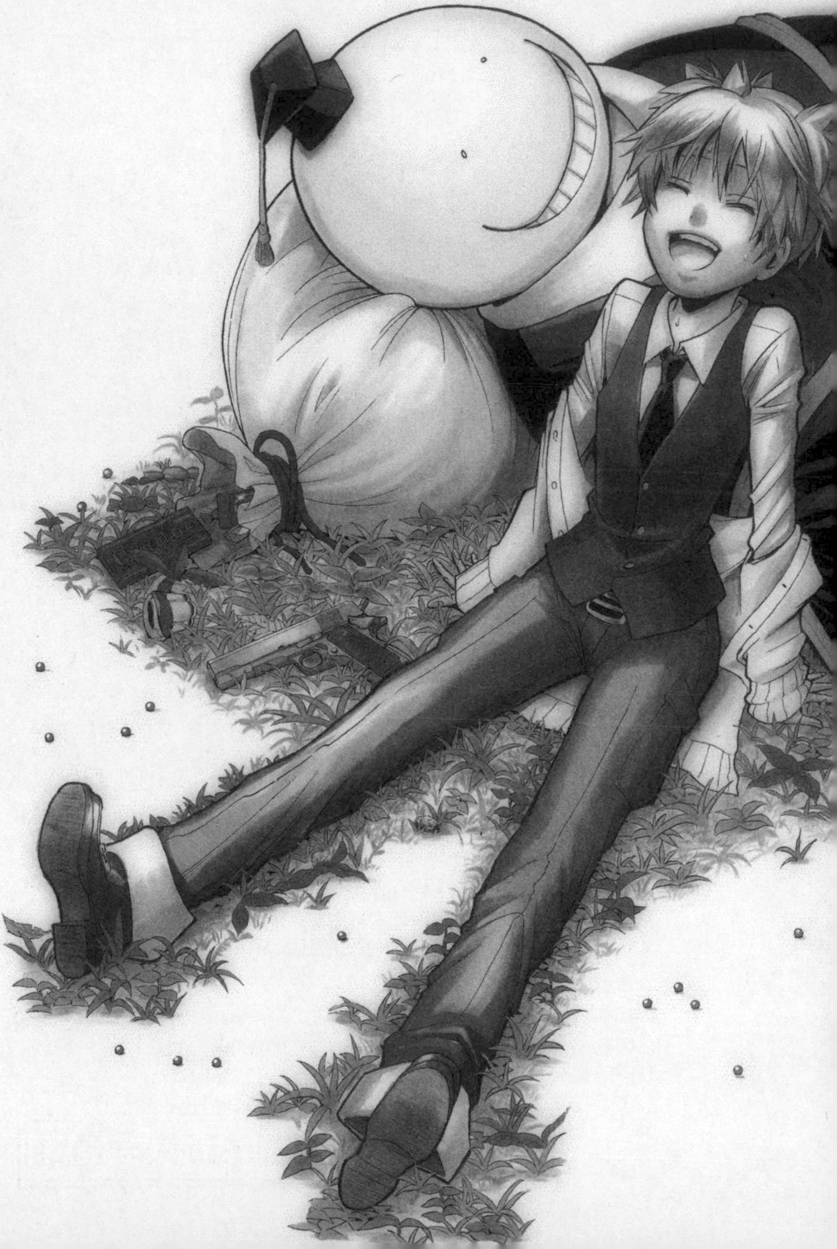

KORO SENSEI

- DATE OF BIRTH: UNKNOWN
- HEIGHT: AROUND TEN FEET IF HE STRETCHES
- WEIGHT: LIGHTER THAN HE LOOKS
- CAREER HISTORY: AGENT OF DESTRUCTION/ TEACHER OF CLASS E
- HOBBY/SKILL: EDUCATION
- TEACHER SKILLS HE HAS ACQUIRED IN THE PAST YEAR: ROUGHLY THREE TIMES THE AMOUNT OF TEACHING AND MEDICAL SKILLS VERSUS ASSASSINATION SKILLS
- MOST USEFUL SKILL: MEMORIZATION OF EVERY STUDY GUIDE IN THE WORLD
- MOST USELESS SKILL: HOW TO SAVE A STUDENT BEFORE THEY FALL INTO THE CENTER OF THE EARTH IF THE CLASSROOM WERE TO SUDDENLY CAVE IN CREATING A HOLE THAT REACHES ALL THE WAY TO BRAZIL

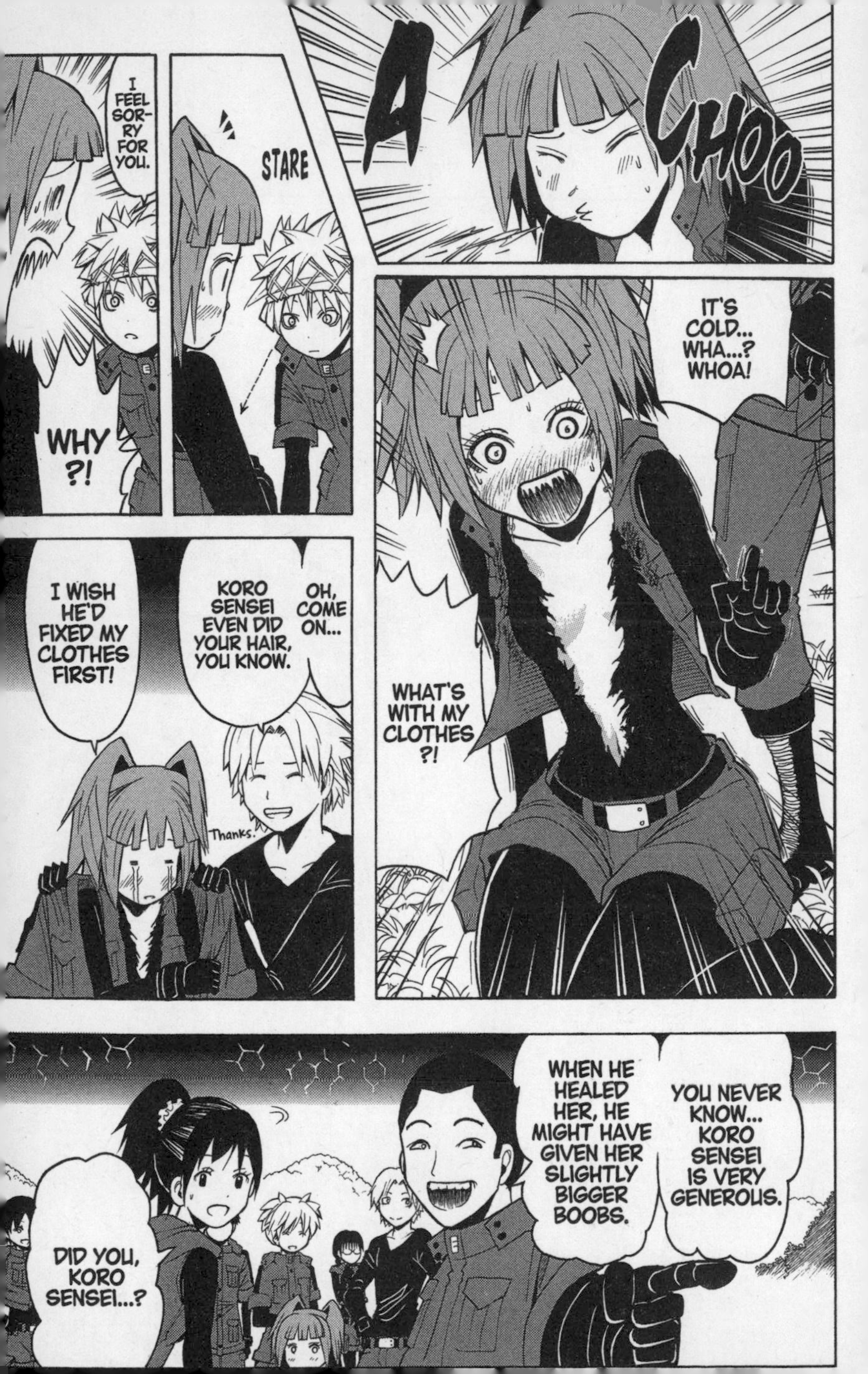
A CHOO
IT'S COLD... WHA...? WHOA!
WHAT'S WITH MY CLOTHES?!
STARE
I FEEL SORRY FOR YOU.
WHY?!
OH, COME ON...
KORO SENSEI EVEN DID YOUR HAIR, YOU KNOW.
I WISH HE'D FIXED MY CLOTHES FIRST!
Thanks.
YOU NEVER KNOW... KORO SENSEI IS VERY GENEROUS.
WHEN HE HEALED HER, HE MIGHT HAVE GIVEN HER SLIGHTLY BIGGER BOOBS.
DID YOU, KORO SENSEI...?

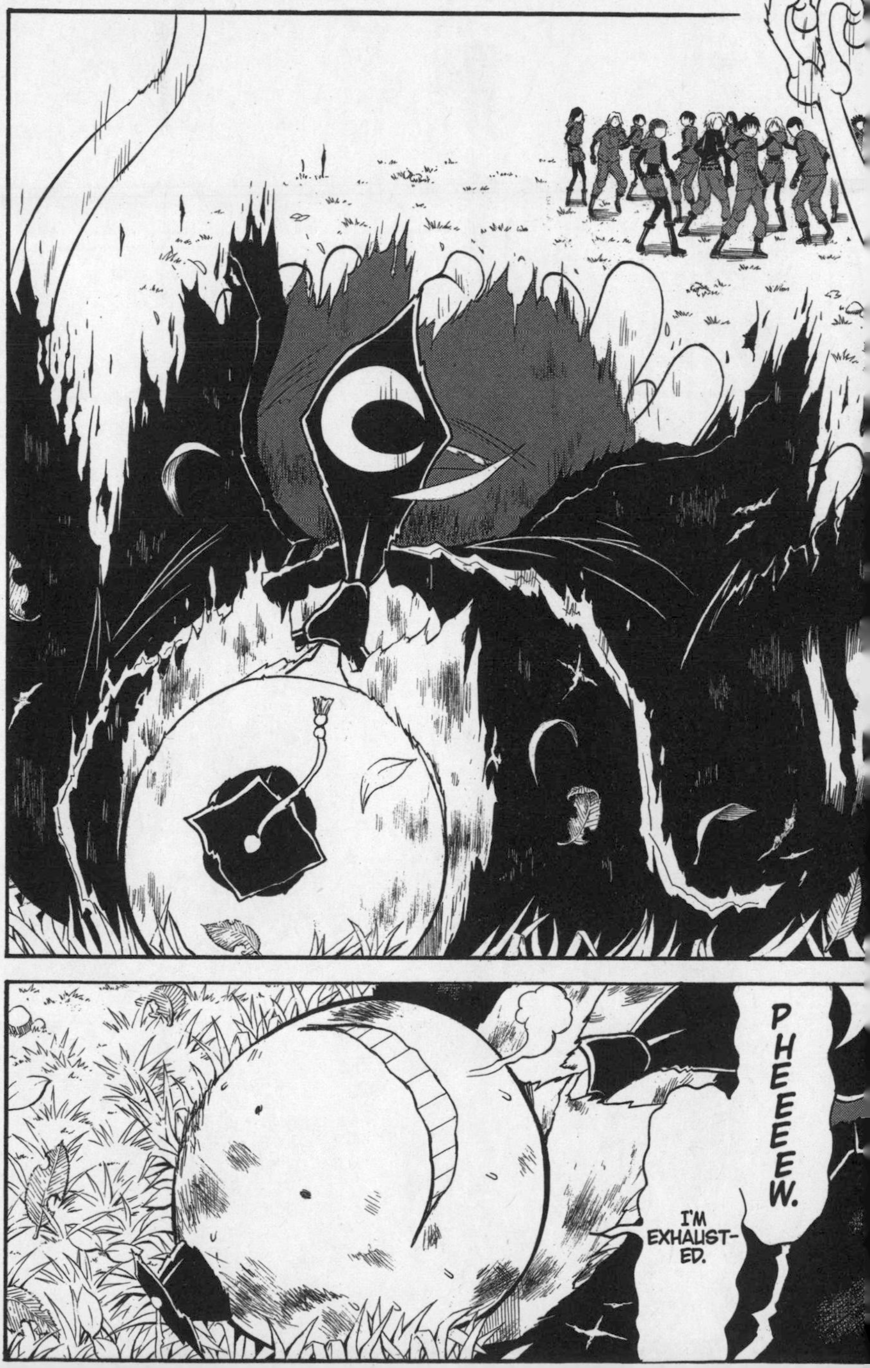
PHEEEEW.
I'M EXHAUST-ED.

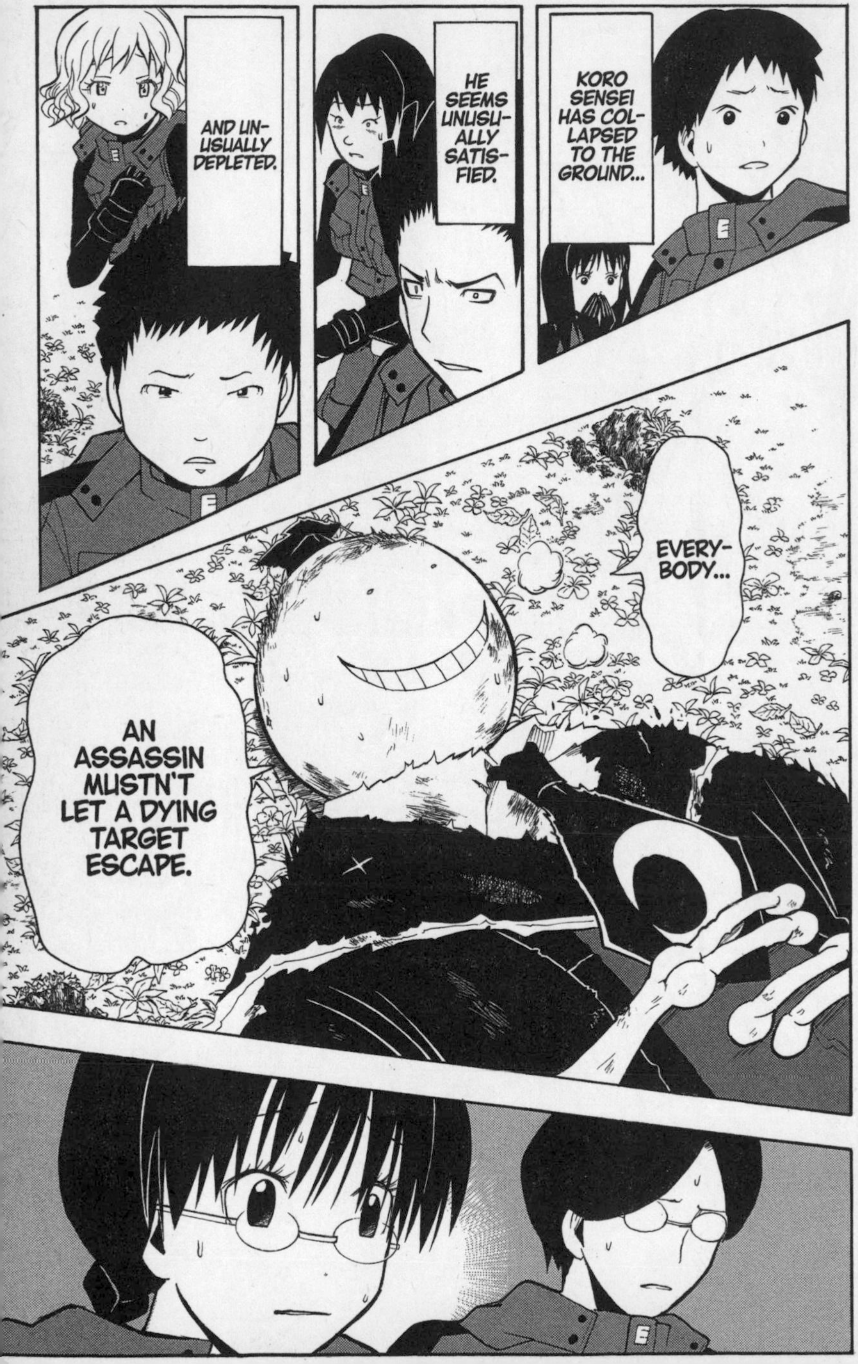
KORO SENSEI HAS COL-LAPSED TO THE GROUND...
HE SEEMS UNUSU-ALLY SATIS-FIED.
AND UN-USUALLY DEPLETED.
EVERY-BODY...
AN ASSASSIN MUSTN'T LET A DYING TARGET ESCAPE.

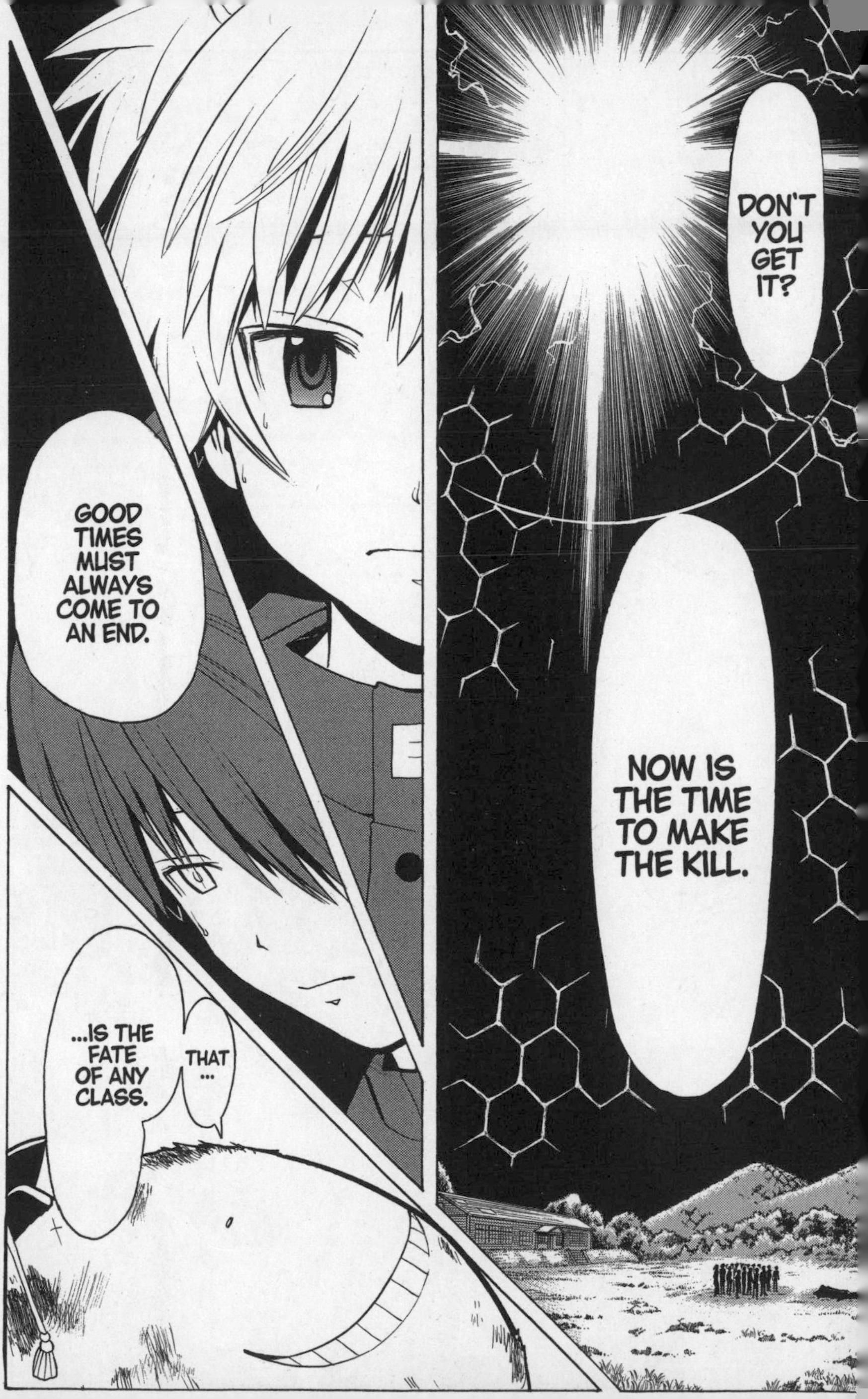
DON'T YOU GET IT?
NOW IS THE TIME TO MAKE THE KILL.
GOOD TIMES MUST ALWAYS COME TO AN END.
THAT...
...IS THE FATE OF ANY CLASS.

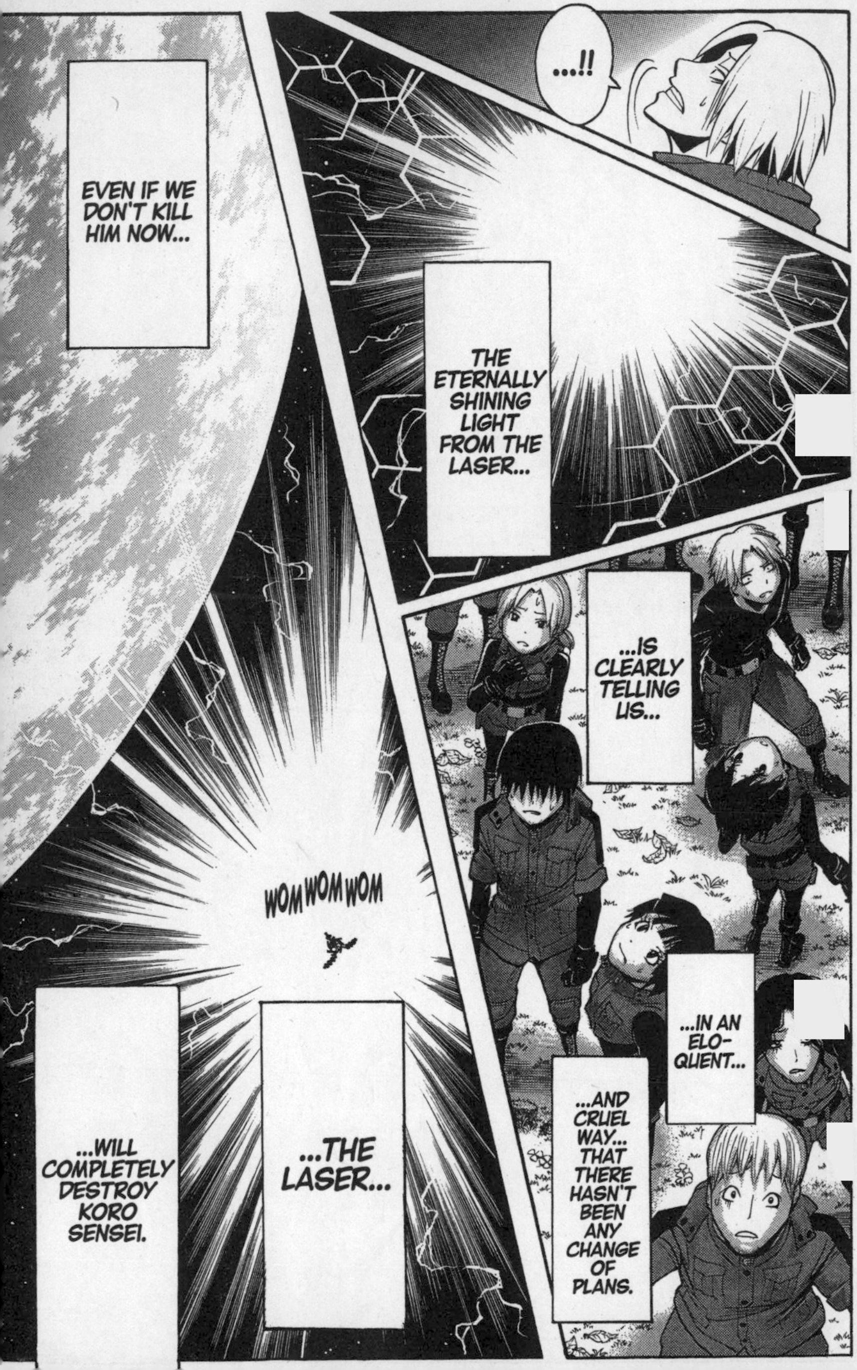
...!!
THE ETERNALLY SHINING LIGHT FROM THE LASER...
...IS CLEARLY TELLING US...
...IN AN ELO-QUENT...
...AND CRUEL WAY... THAT THERE HASN'T BEEN ANY CHANGE OF PLANS.
EVEN IF WE DON'T KILL HIM NOW...
WOM WOM WOM
...THE LASER...
...WILL COMPLETELY DESTROY KORO SENSEI.

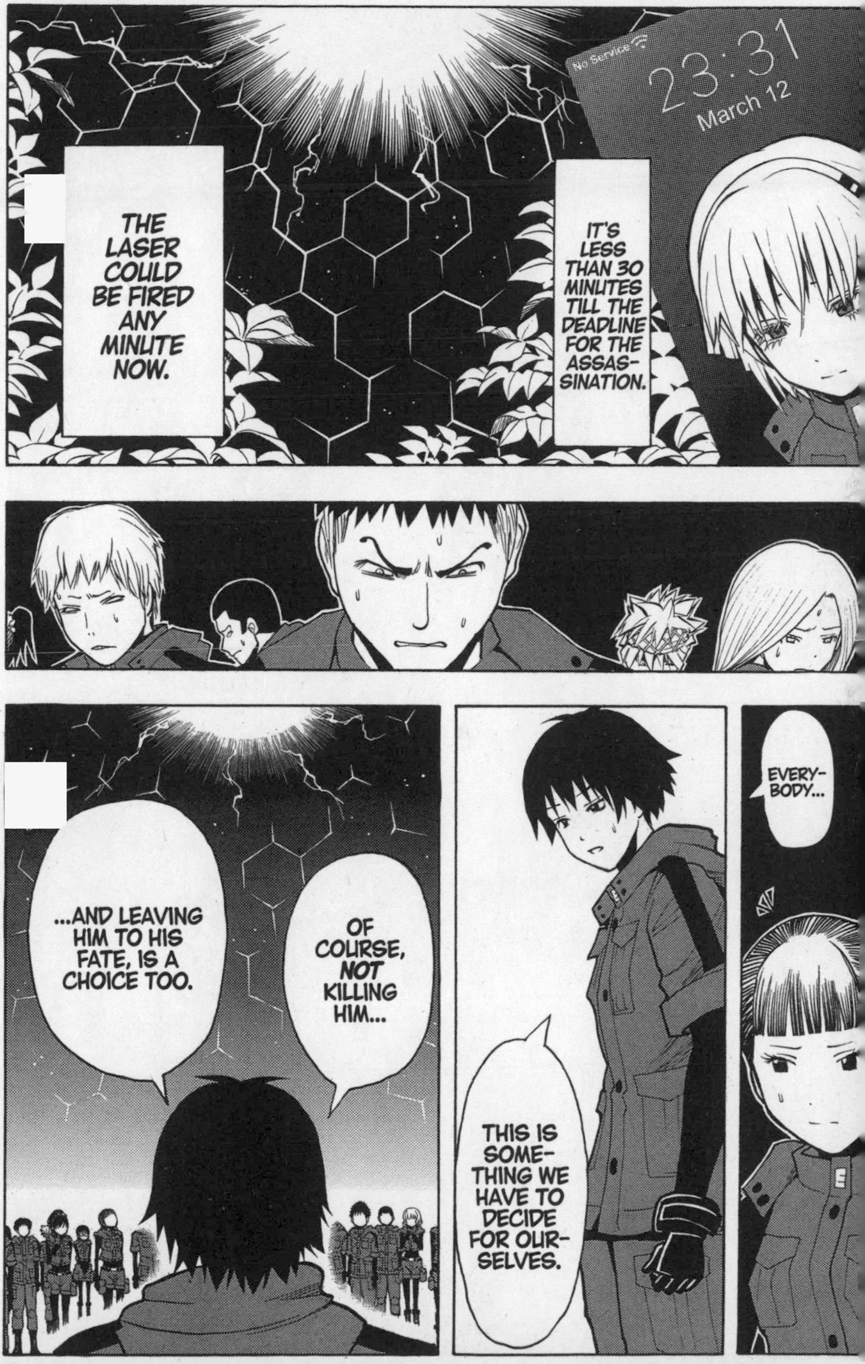
No Service
23:31
March 12
IT'S LESS THAN 30 MINUTES TILL THE DEADLINE FOR THE ASSAS-SINATION.
THE LASER COULD BE FIRED ANY MINUTE NOW.
EVERY-BODY...
THIS IS SOME-THING WE HAVE TO DECIDE FOR OUR-SELVES.
OF COURSE, *NOT* KILLING HIM...
...AND LEAVING HIM TO HIS FATE, IS A CHOICE TOO.

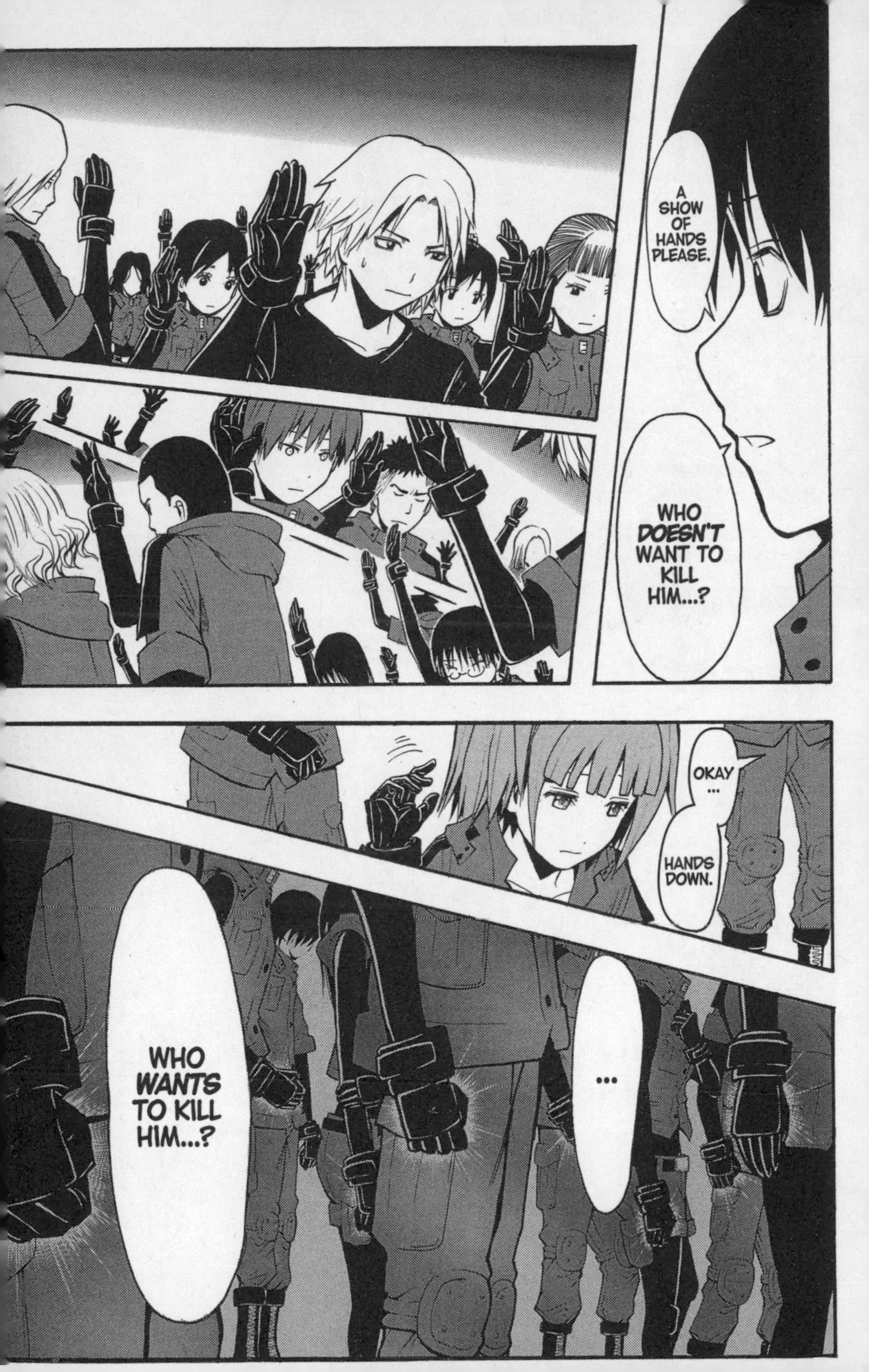
A SHOW OF HANDS PLEASE.
WHO DOESN'T WANT TO KILL HIM...?
OKAY ...
HANDS DOWN.
...
WHO WANTS TO KILL HIM...?

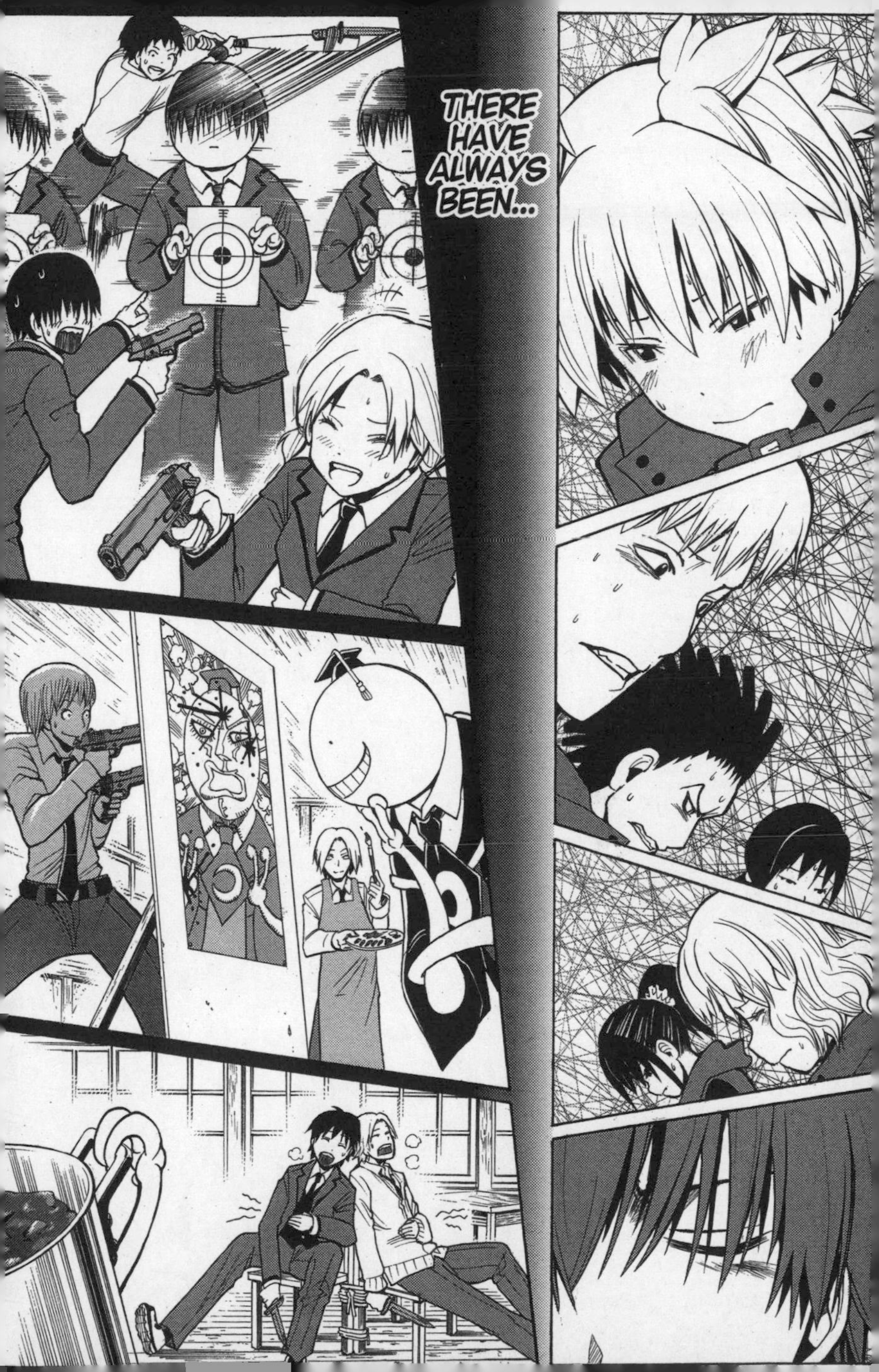
THERE HAVE ALWAYS BEEN...

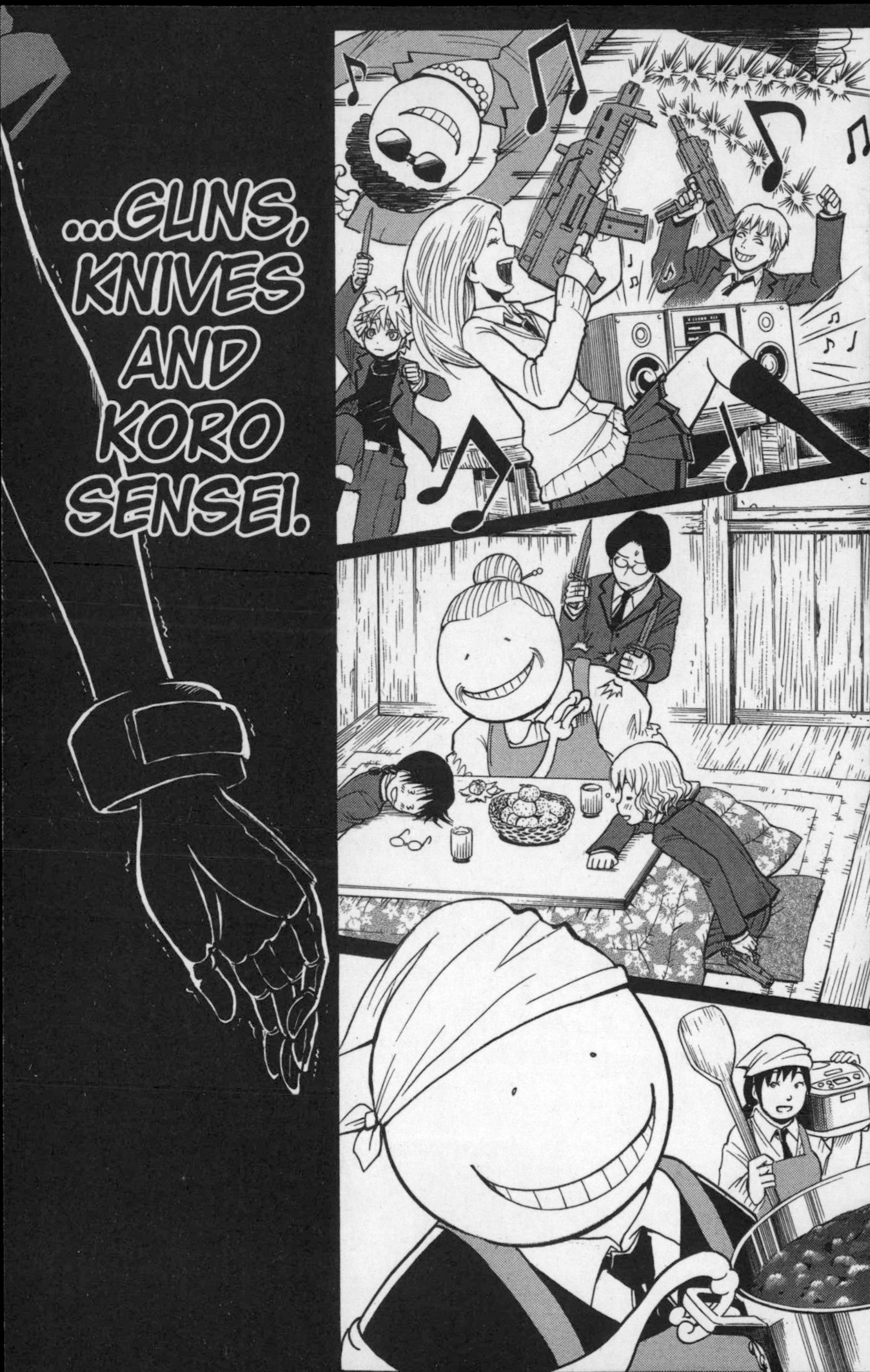
...GUNS, KNIVES AND KORO SENSEI.

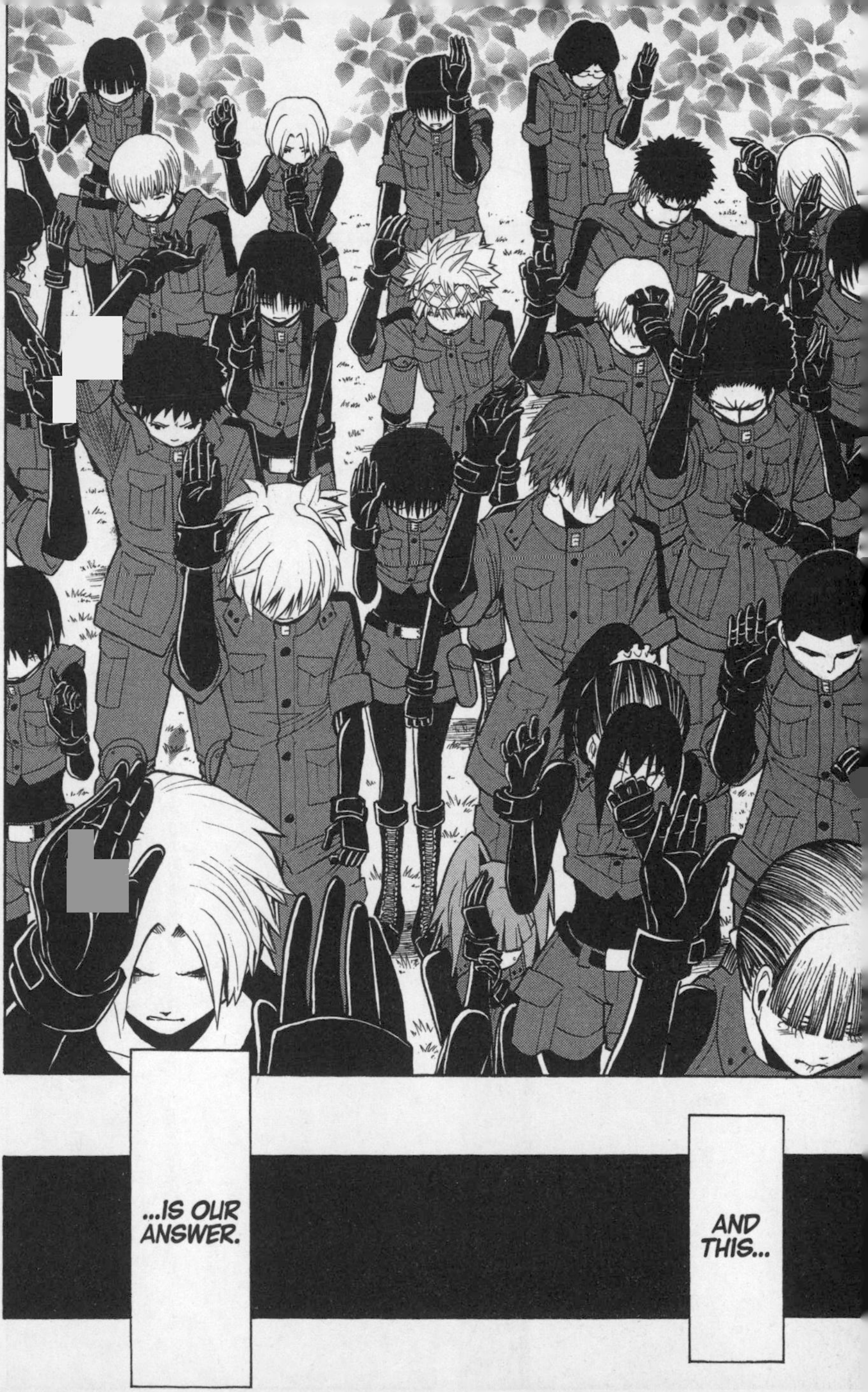
AND THIS...
...IS OUR ANSWER.

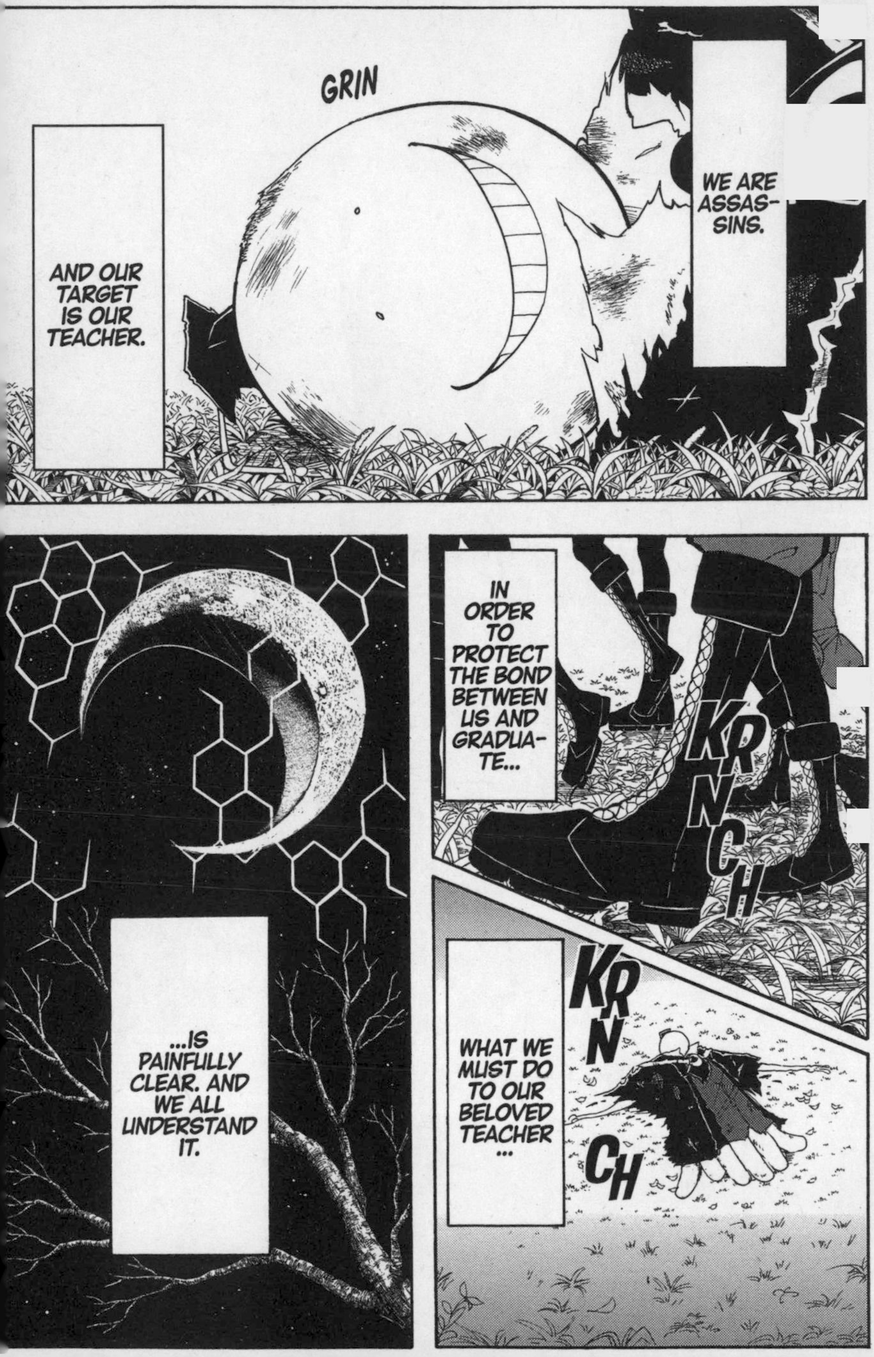
WE ARE ASSAS-SINS.
GRIN
AND OUR TARGET IS OUR TEACHER.
IN ORDER TO PROTECT THE BOND BETWEEN US AND GRADUA-TE...
KRNCH
WHAT WE MUST DO TO OUR BELOVED TEACHER ...
KRNCH
...IS PAINFULLY CLEAR. AND WE ALL UNDERSTAND IT.

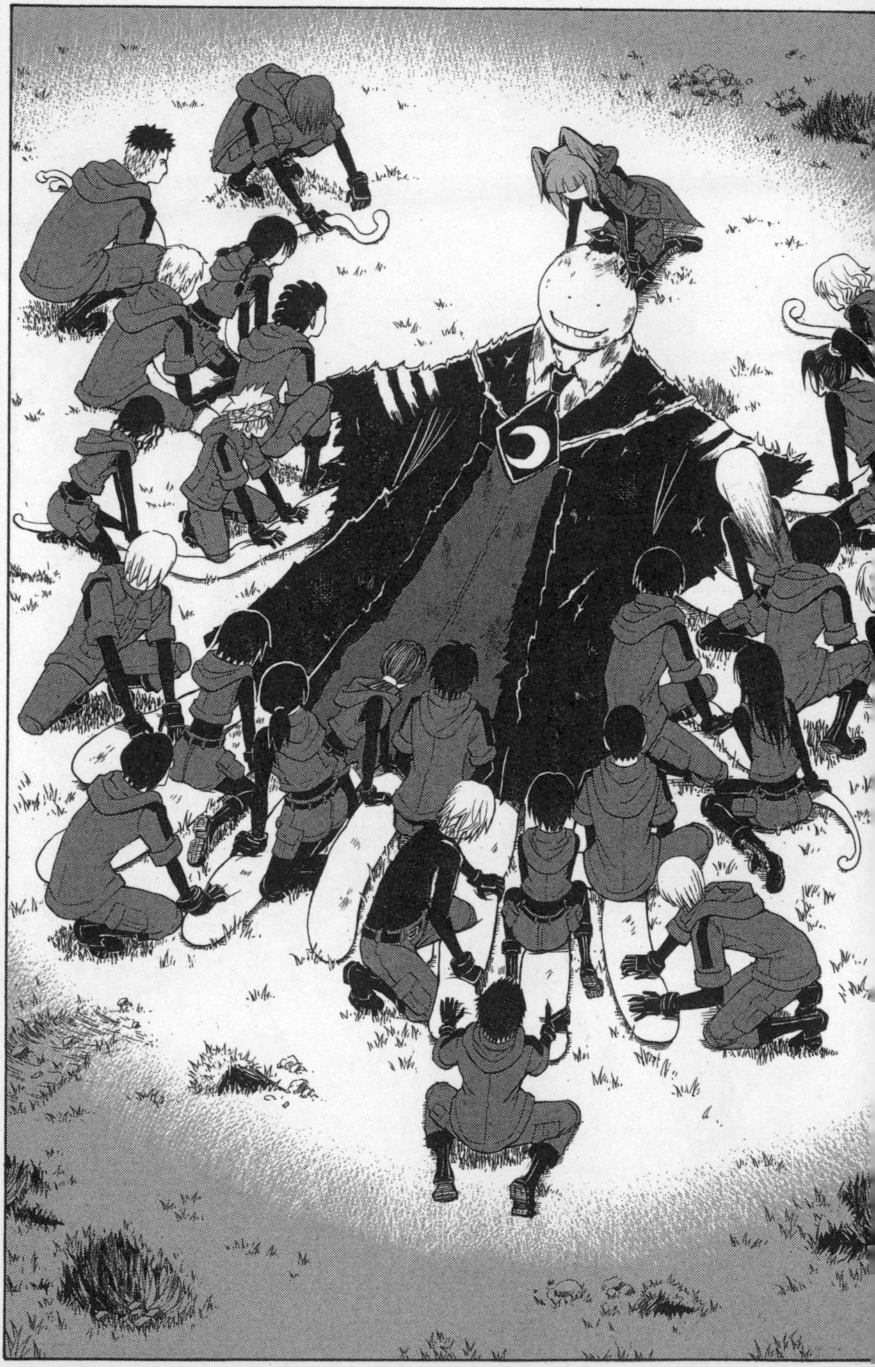

Koro Sensei's Weakness 37
We can catch him if we all hold him down at once.

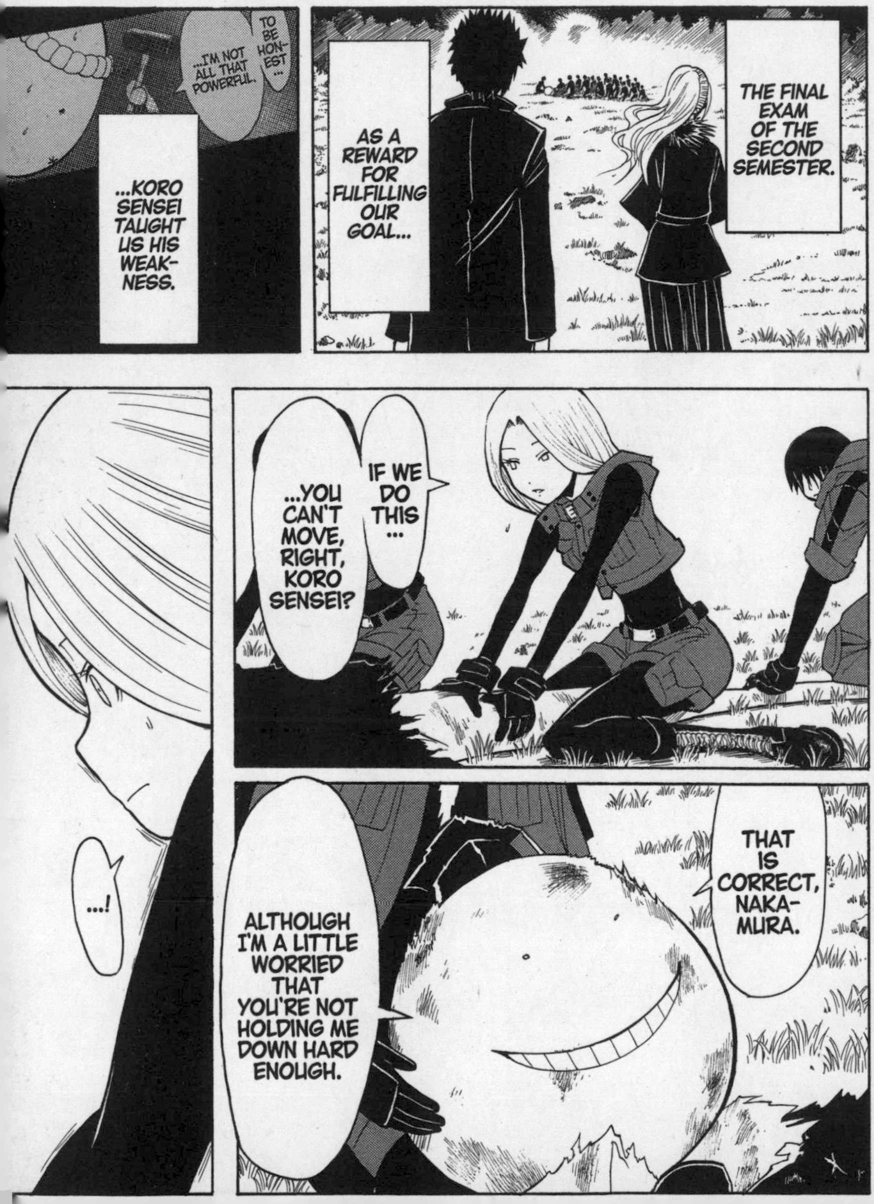
THE FINAL EXAM OF THE SECOND SEMESTER.
AS A REWARD FOR FULFILLING OUR GOAL...
TO BE HON-EST...
...I'M NOT ALL THAT POWERFUL.
...KORO SENSEI TAUGHT US HIS WEAK-NESS.
IF WE DO THIS...
...YOU CAN'T MOVE, RIGHT, KORO SENSEI?
THAT IS CORRECT, NAKA-MURA.
ALTHOUGH I'M A LITTLE WORRIED THAT YOU'RE NOT HOLDING ME DOWN HARD ENOUGH.
...!

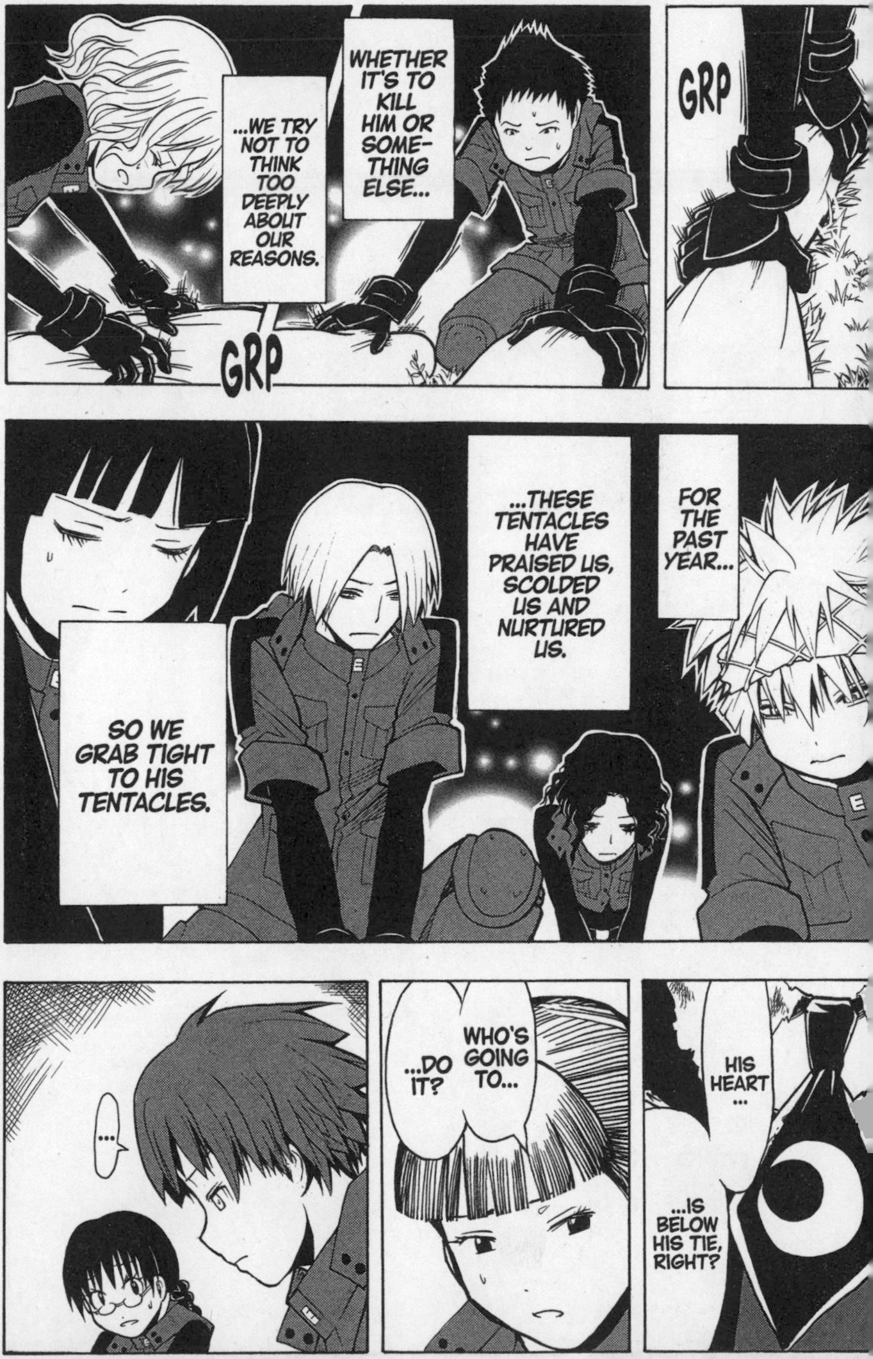
GRP
WHETHER IT'S TO KILL HIM OR SOME-THING ELSE...
...WE TRY NOT TO THINK TOO DEEPLY ABOUT OUR REASONS.
GRP
FOR THE PAST YEAR...
...THESE TENTACLES HAVE PRAISED US, SCOLDED US AND NURTURED US.
SO WE GRAB TIGHT TO HIS TENTACLES.
HIS HEART...
...IS BELOW HIS TIE, RIGHT?
WHO'S GOING TO...
...DO IT?
...

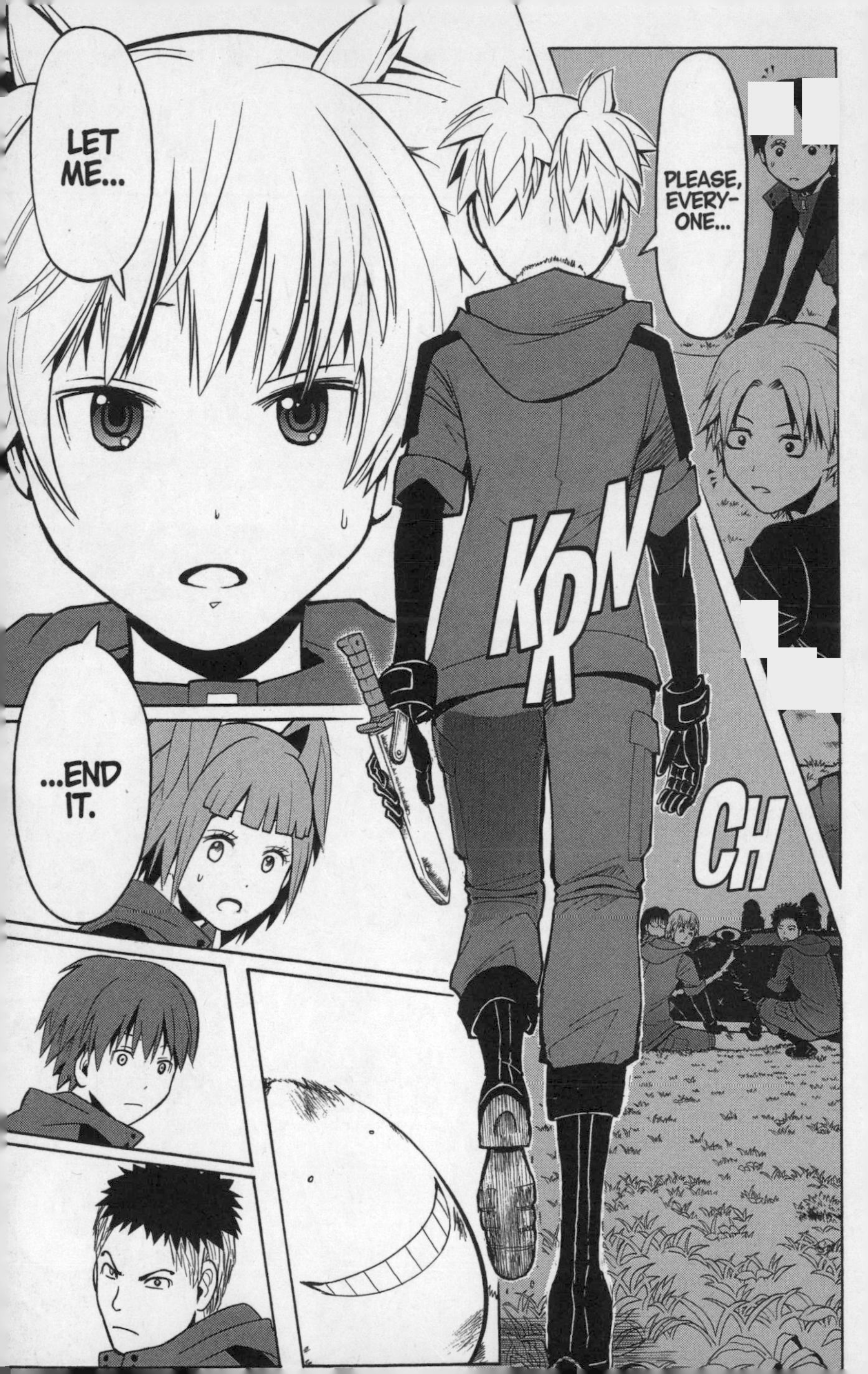
PLEASE, EVERY-ONE...
LET ME...
KRN
CH
...END IT.

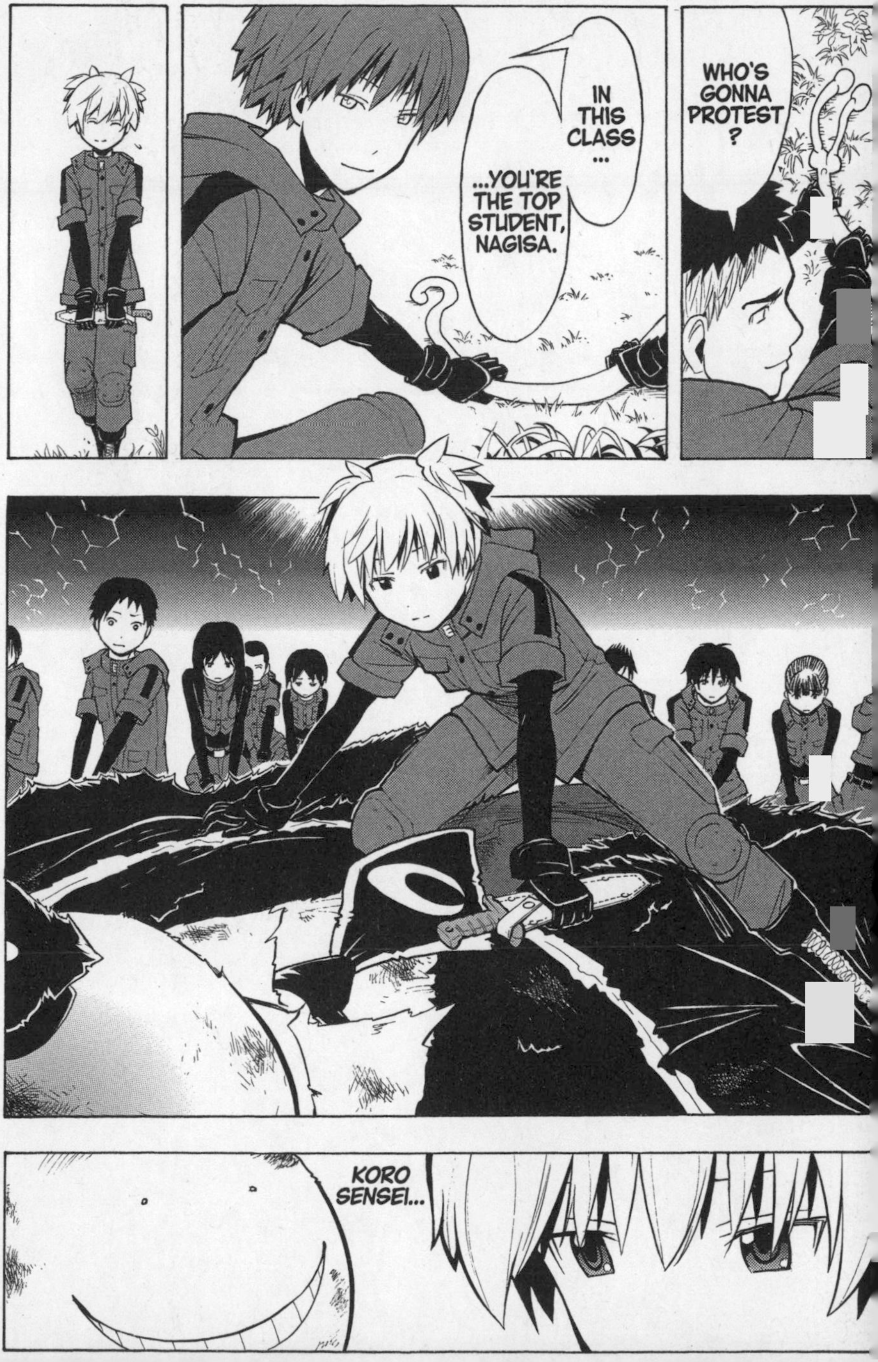
WHO'S GONNA PROTEST?
IN THIS CLASS...
...YOU'RE THE TOP STUDENT, NAGISA.
KORO SENSEI...

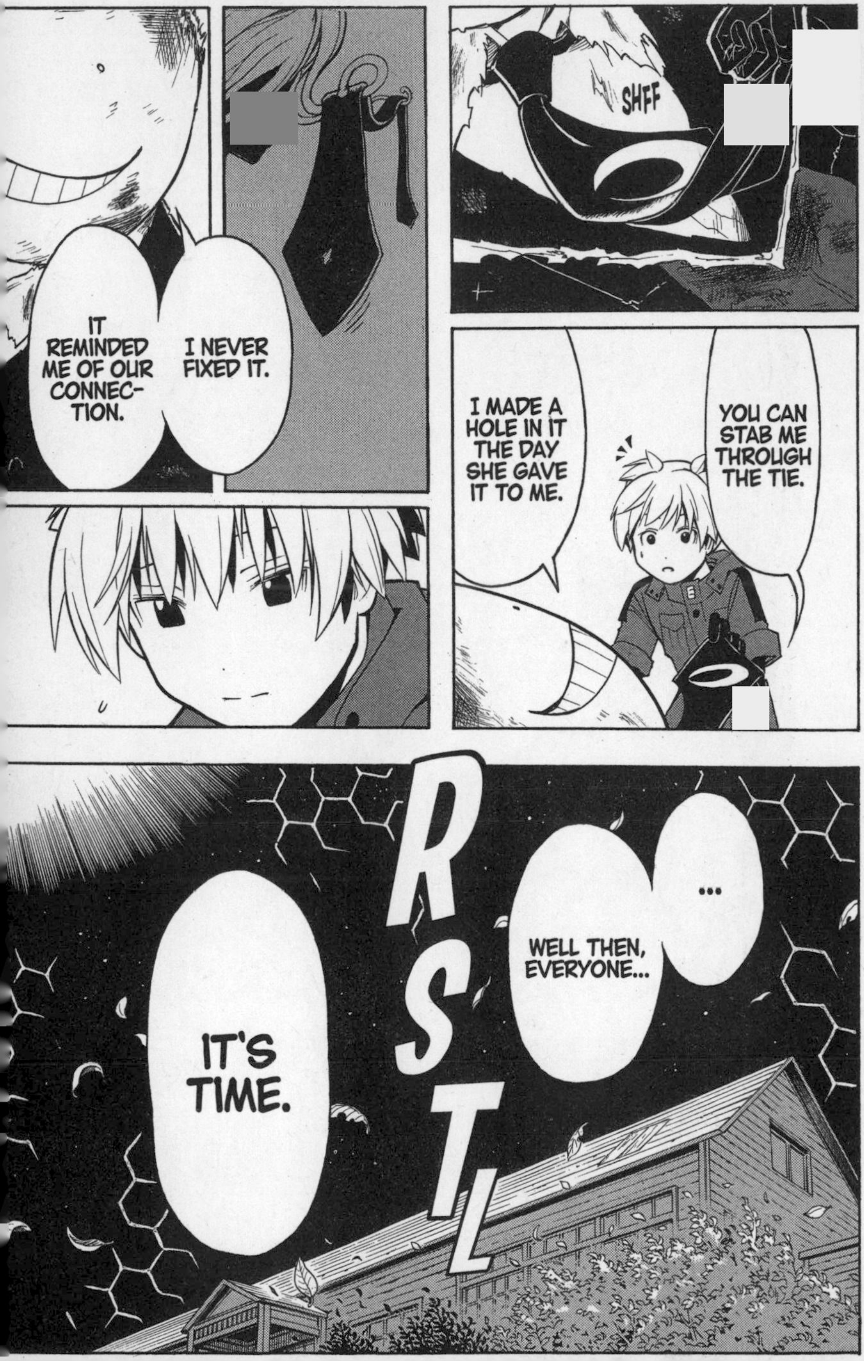
SHFF
I NEVER FIXED IT.
IT REMINDED ME OF OUR CONNECTION.
YOU CAN STAB ME THROUGH THE TIE.
I MADE A HOLE IN IT THE DAY SHE GAVE IT TO ME.
...
WELL THEN, EVERYONE...
IT'S TIME.
RSTL

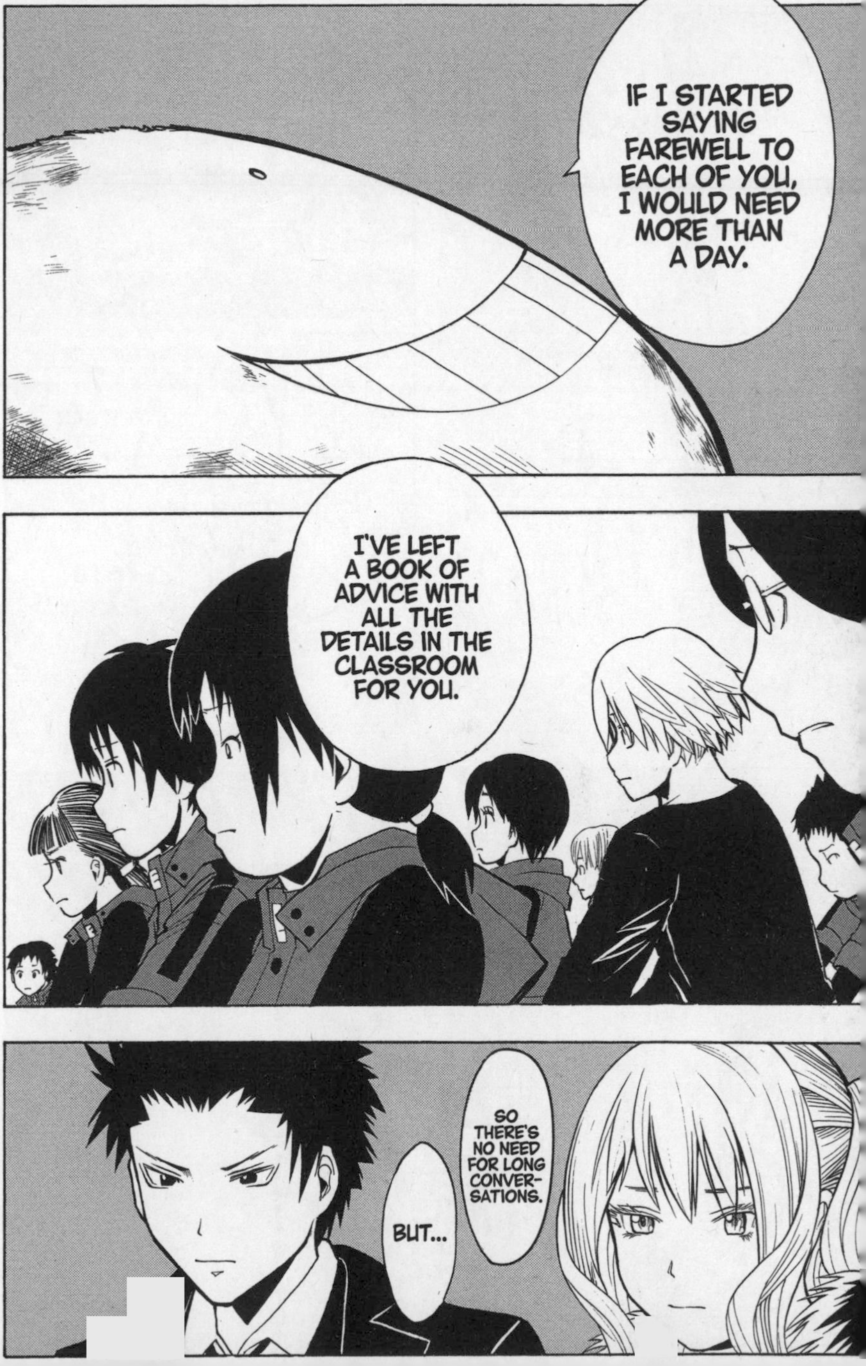
IF I STARTED SAYING FAREWELL TO EACH OF YOU, I WOULD NEED MORE THAN A DAY.
I'VE LEFT A BOOK OF ADVICE WITH ALL THE DETAILS IN THE CLASSROOM FOR YOU.
SO THERE'S NO NEED FOR LONG CONVER-SATIONS.
BUT...

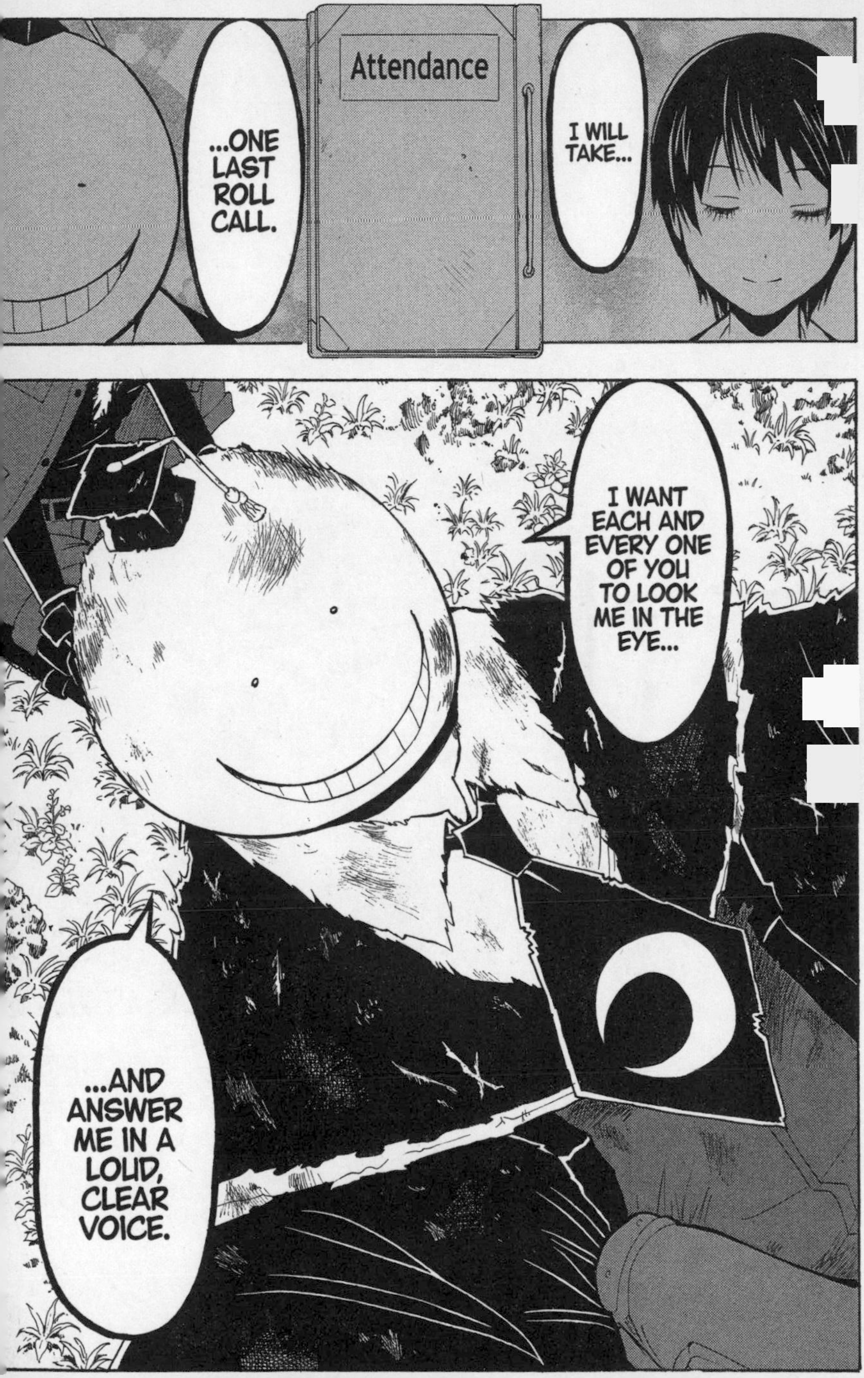
I WILL TAKE...
Attendance
...ONE LAST ROLL CALL.
I WANT EACH AND EVERY ONE OF YOU TO LOOK ME IN THE EYE...
...AND ANSWER ME IN A LOUD, CLEAR VOICE.

Class 177 Time to Graduate

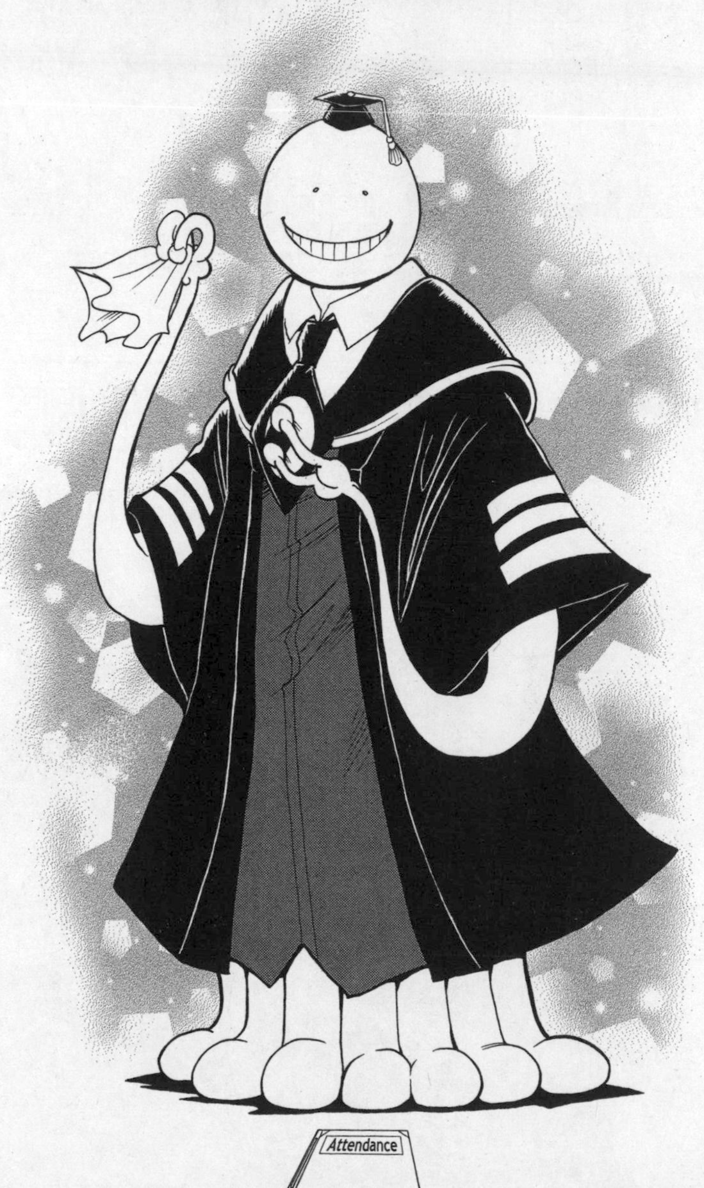
Attendance

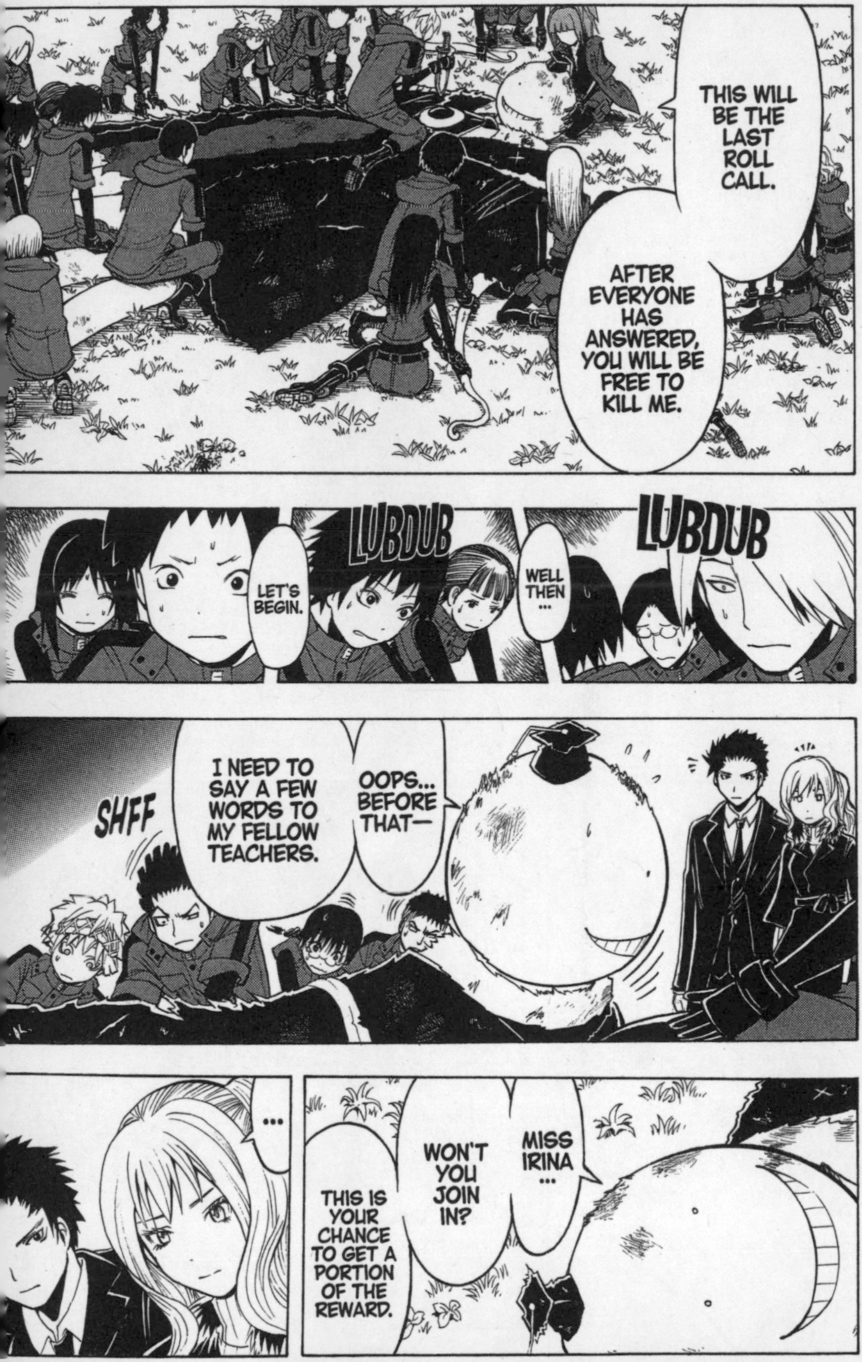
THIS WILL BE THE LAST ROLL CALL.
AFTER EVERYONE HAS ANSWERED, YOU WILL BE FREE TO KILL ME.
LUBDUB
WELL THEN...
LUBDUB
LET'S BEGIN.
OOPS... BEFORE THAT—
I NEED TO SAY A FEW WORDS TO MY FELLOW TEACHERS.
SHFF
MISS IRINA...
WON'T YOU JOIN IN?
THIS IS YOUR CHANCE TO GET A PORTION OF THE REWARD.
...

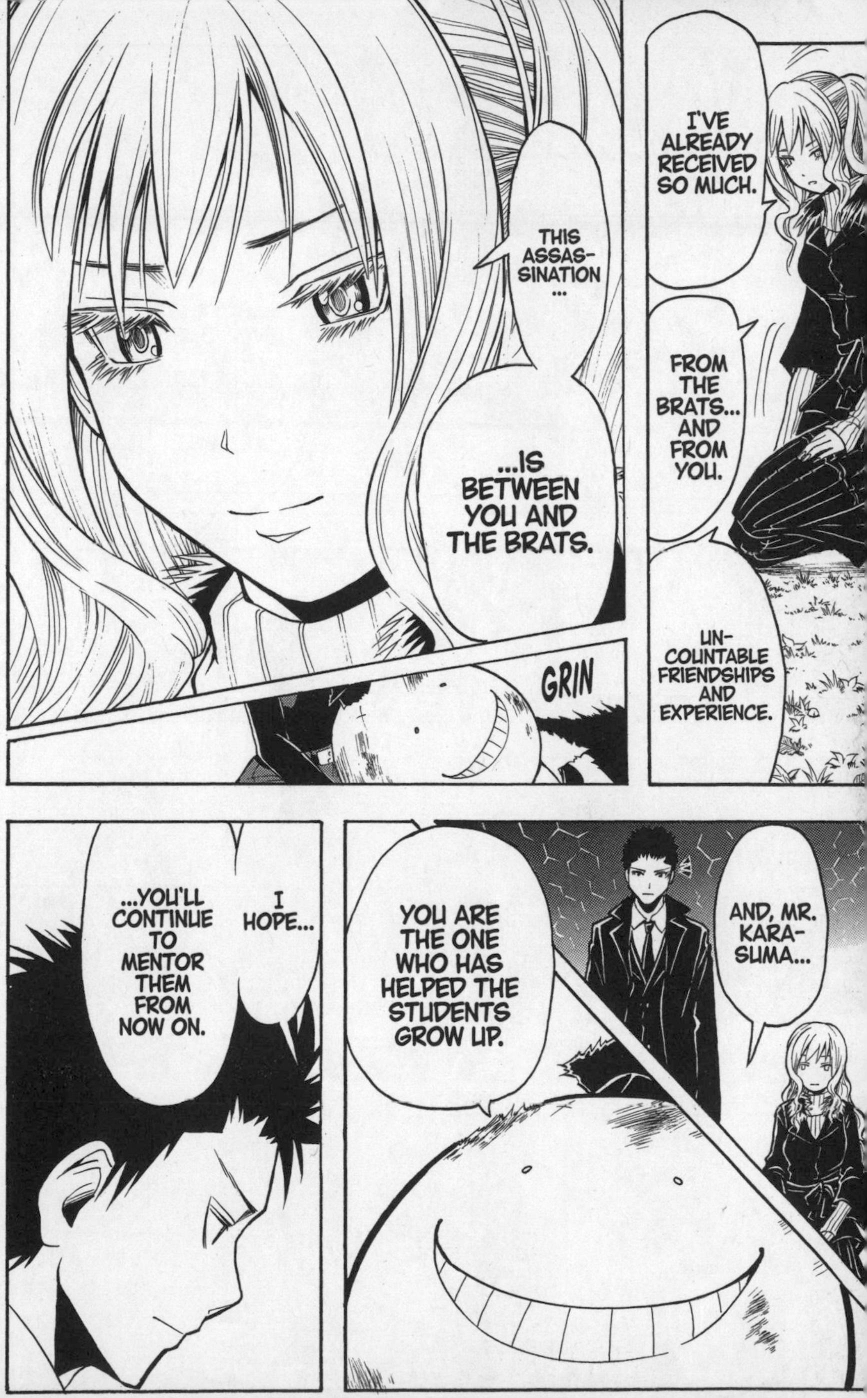
I'VE ALREADY RECEIVED SO MUCH.
FROM THE BRATS... AND FROM YOU.
UN-COUNTABLE FRIENDSHIPS AND EXPERIENCE.
THIS ASSAS-SINATION...
...IS BETWEEN YOU AND THE BRATS.
GRIN
AND, MR. KARA-SUMA...
YOU ARE THE ONE WHO HAS HELPED THE STUDENTS GROW UP.
I HOPE...
...YOU'LL CONTINUE TO MENTOR THEM FROM NOW ON.

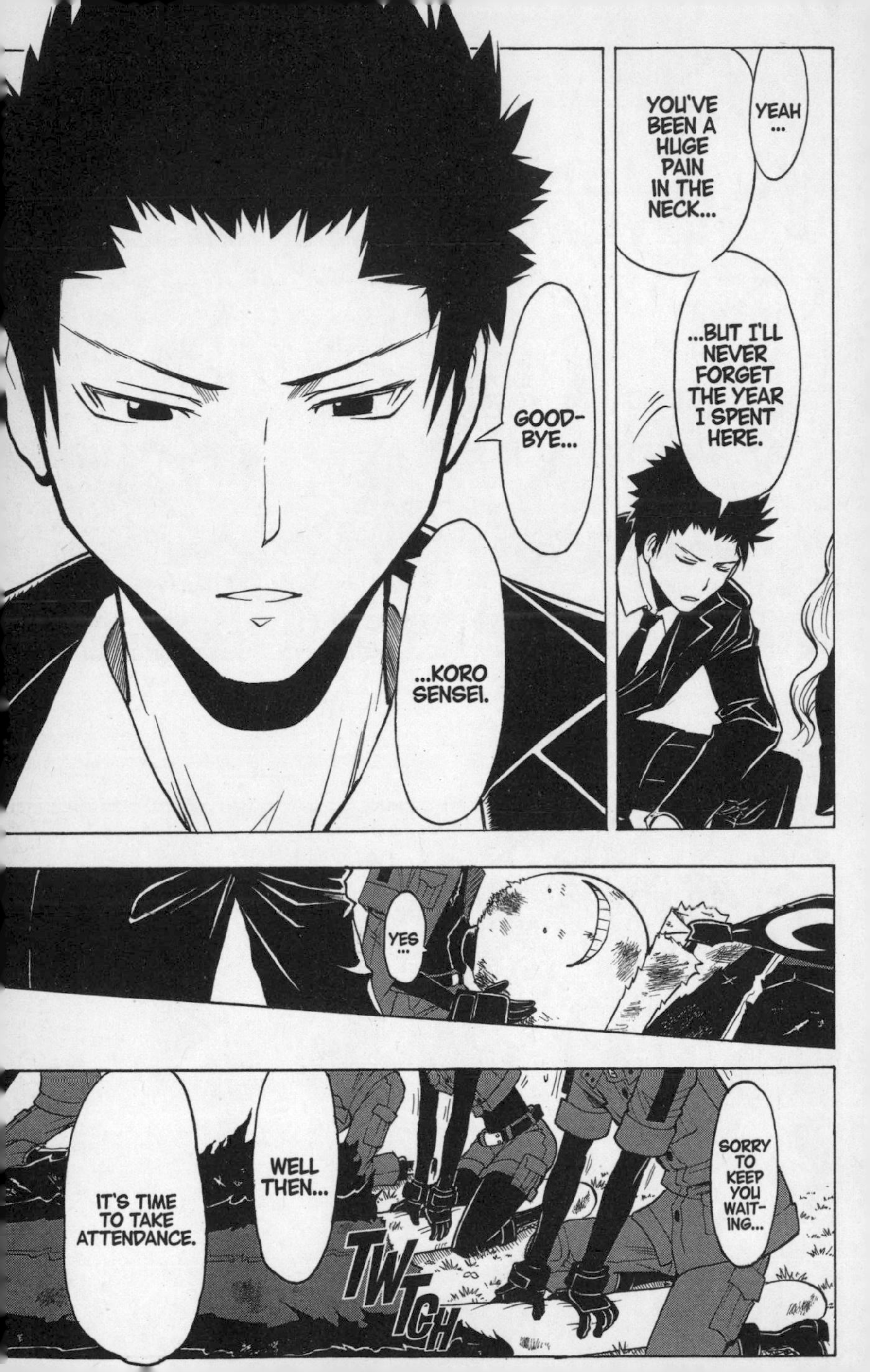
YEAH...
YOU'VE BEEN A HUGE PAIN IN THE NECK...
...BUT I'LL NEVER FORGET THE YEAR I SPENT HERE.
GOOD-BYE...
...KORO SENSEI.
YES...
SORRY TO KEEP YOU WAITING...
WELL THEN...
IT'S TIME TO TAKE ATTENDANCE.
TWITCH

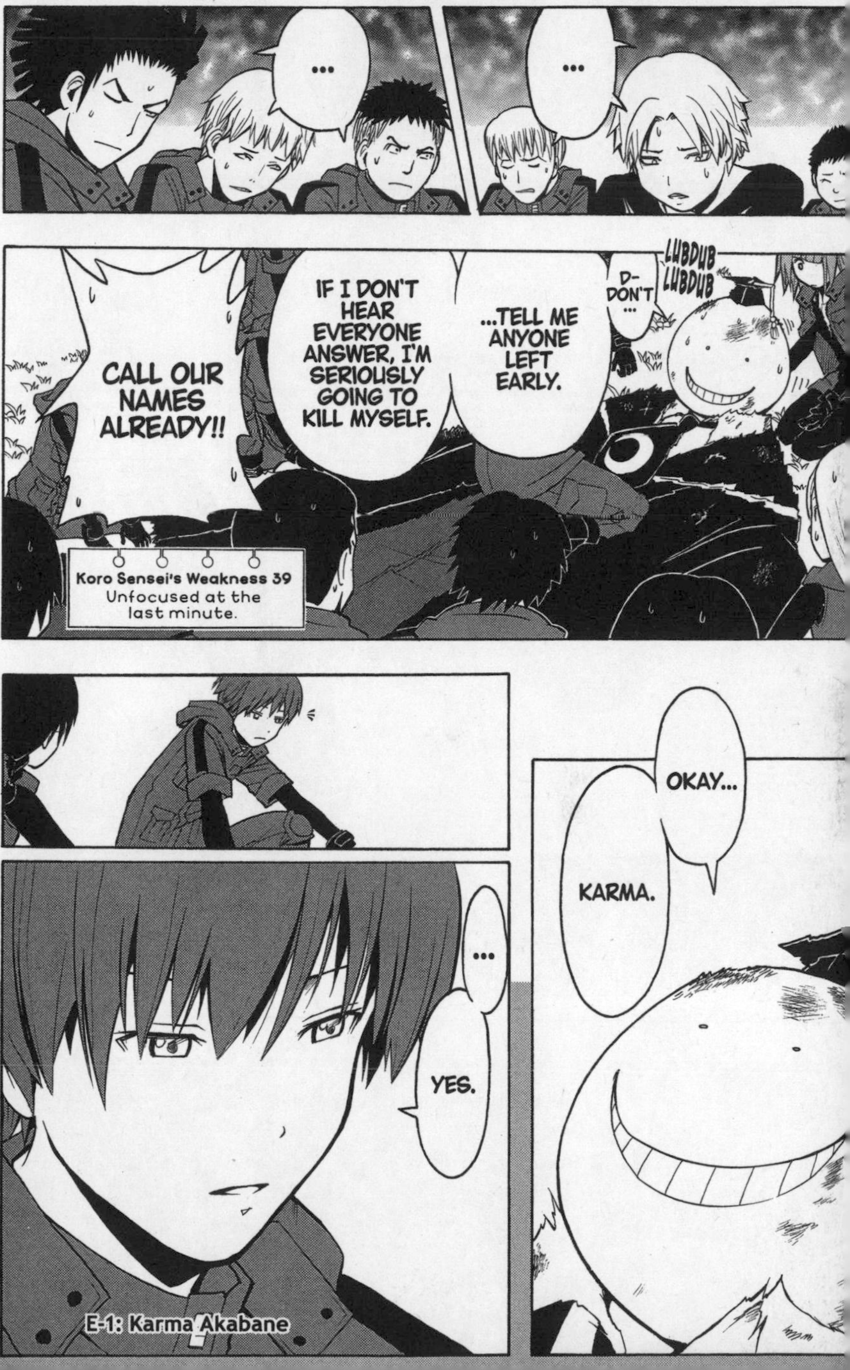
...
...
LUBDUB LUBDUB
D-DON'T ...
...TELL ME ANYONE LEFT EARLY.
IF I DON'T HEAR EVERYONE ANSWER, I'M SERIOUSLY GOING TO KILL MYSELF.
CALL OUR NAMES ALREADY!!
Koro Sensei's Weakness 39
Unfocused at the last minute.
OKAY...
KARMA.
...
YES.
E-1: Karma Akabane

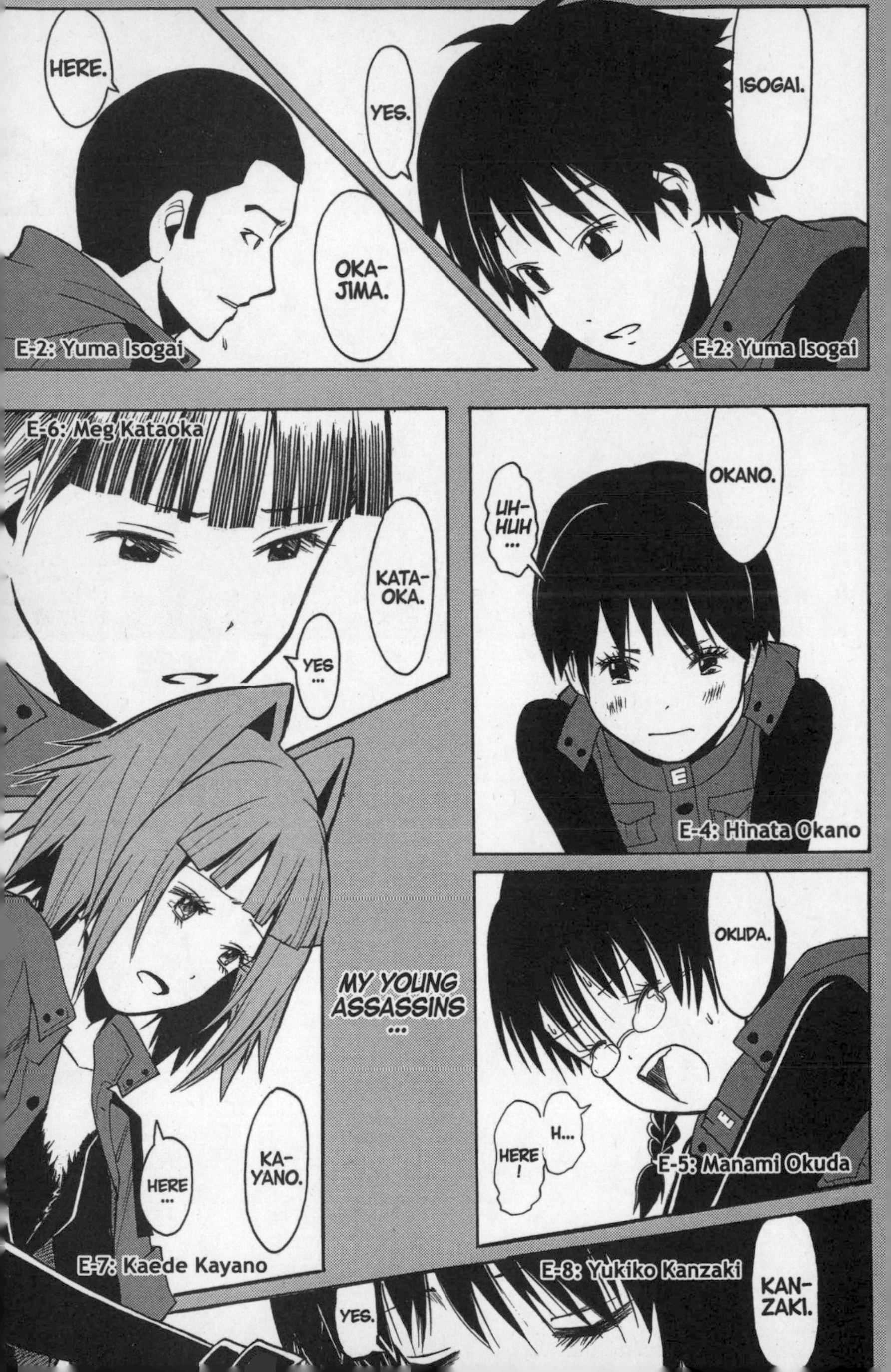
ISOGAI.
YES.
E-2: Yuma Isogai
OKA-JIMA.
HERE.
E-2: Yuma Isogai
OKANO.
UH-HUH...
E-4: Hinata Okano
KATA-OKA.
YES...
E-6: Meg Kataoka
OKUDA.
H...
HERE!
E-5: Manami Okuda
MY YOUNG ASSASSINS...
KA-YANO.
HERE...
E-7: Kaede Kayano
KAN-ZAKI.
YES.
E-8: Yukiko Kanzaki

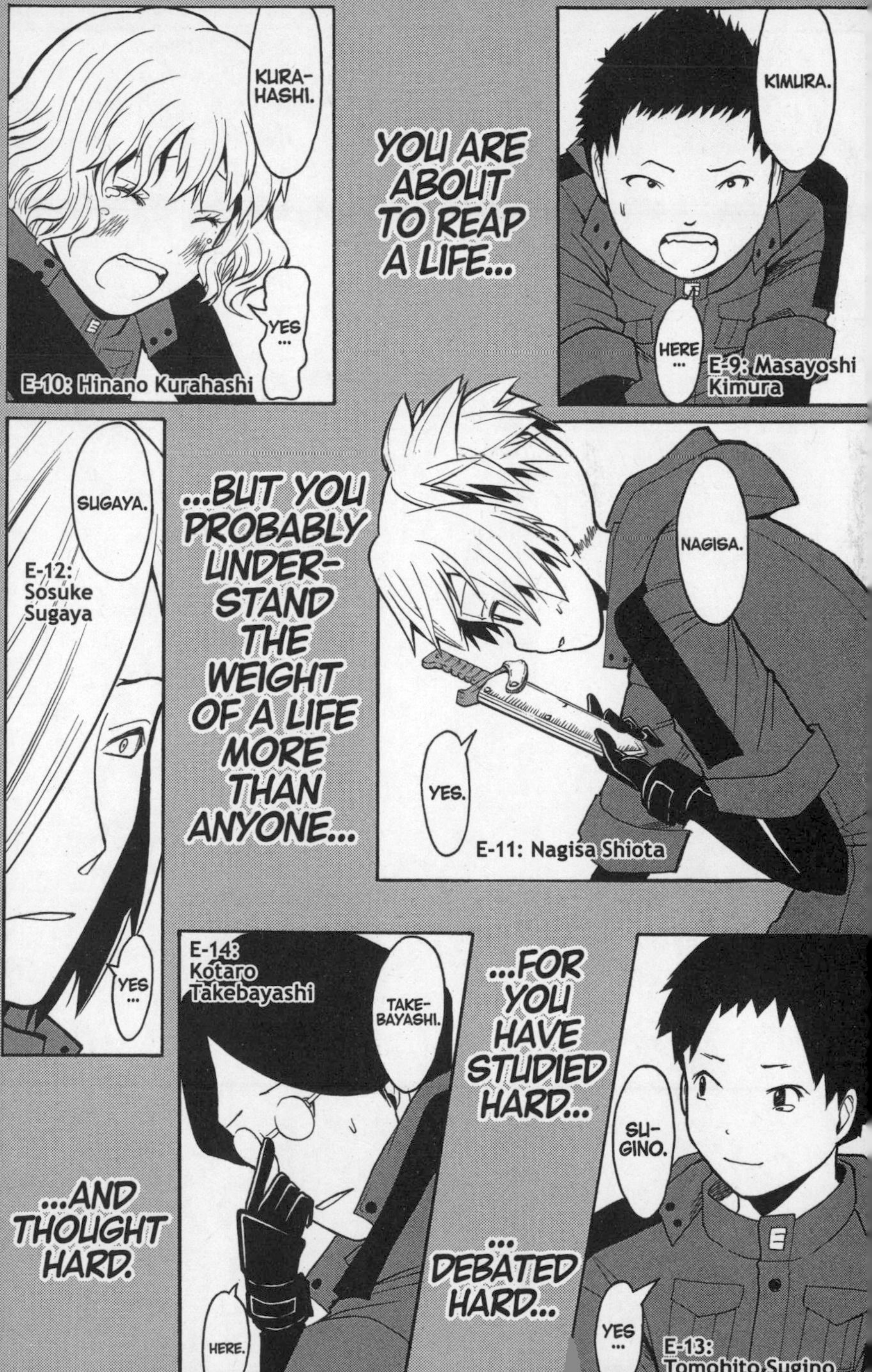
KIMURA.
HERE...
E-9: Masayoshi Kimura
YOU ARE ABOUT TO REAP A LIFE...
KURA-HASHI.
YES...
E-10: Hinano Kurahashi
NAGISA.
YES.
E-11: Nagisa Shiota
...BUT YOU PROBABLY UNDER-STAND THE WEIGHT OF A LIFE MORE THAN ANYONE...
SUGAYA.
E-12: Sosuke Sugaya
YES...
...FOR YOU HAVE STUDIED HARD...
SU-GINO.
...DEBATED HARD...
YES...
E-13: Tomohito Sugino
E-14: Kotaro Takebayashi
TAKE-BAYASHI.
HERE.
...AND THOUGHT HARD.

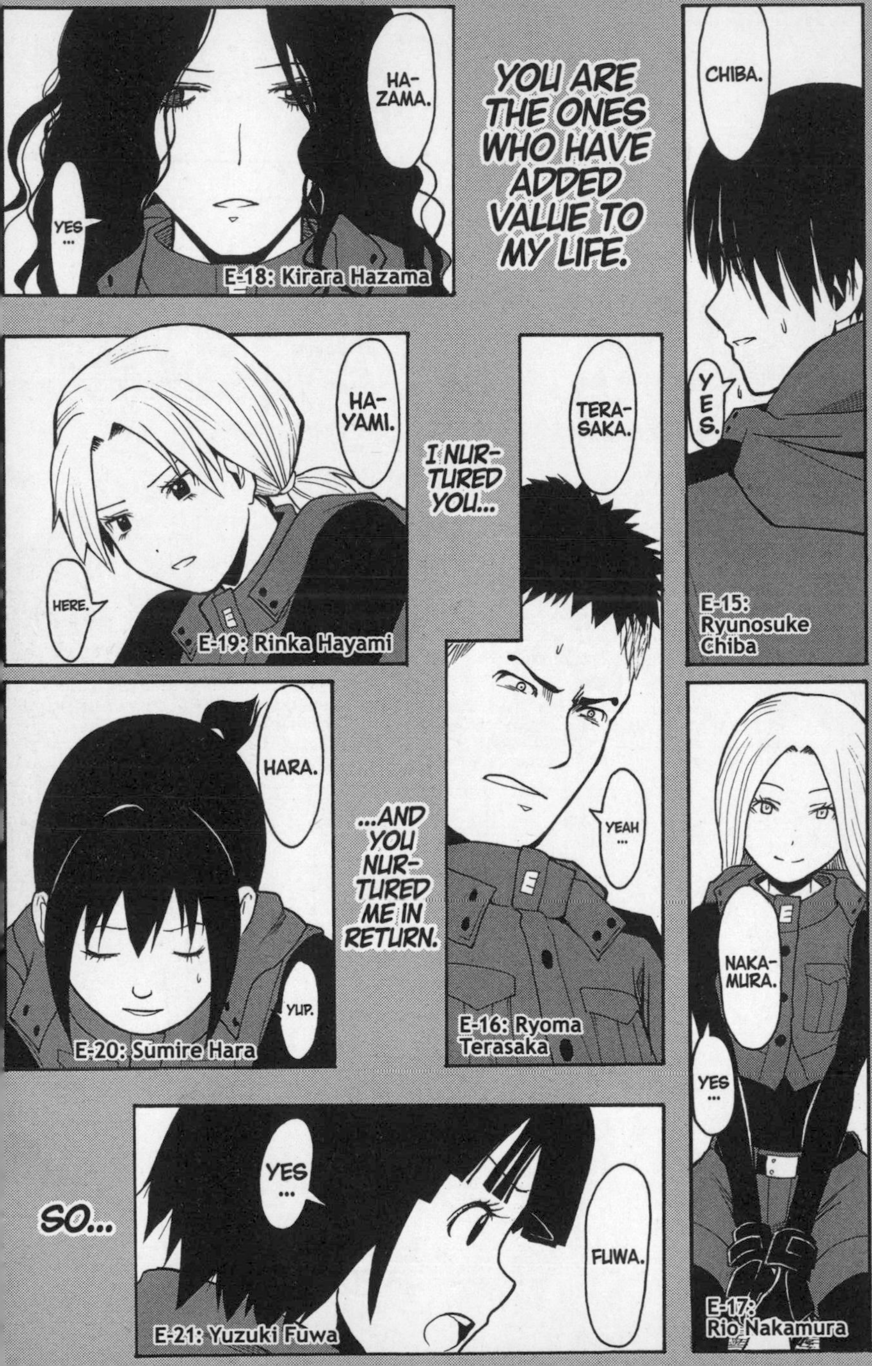
CHIBA.
YES.
E-15: Ryunosuke Chiba
YOU ARE THE ONES WHO HAVE ADDED VALUE TO MY LIFE.
HAZAMA.
YES...
E-18: Kirara Hazama
TERASAKA.
YEAH...
E-16: Ryoma Terasaka
I NURTURED YOU...
HAYAMI.
HERE.
E-19: Rinka Hayami
NAKAMURA.
YES...
E-17: Rio Nakamura
...AND YOU NURTURED ME IN RETURN.
HARA.
YUP.
E-20: Sumire Hara
FUWA.
YES...
E-21: Yuzuki Fuwa
SO...

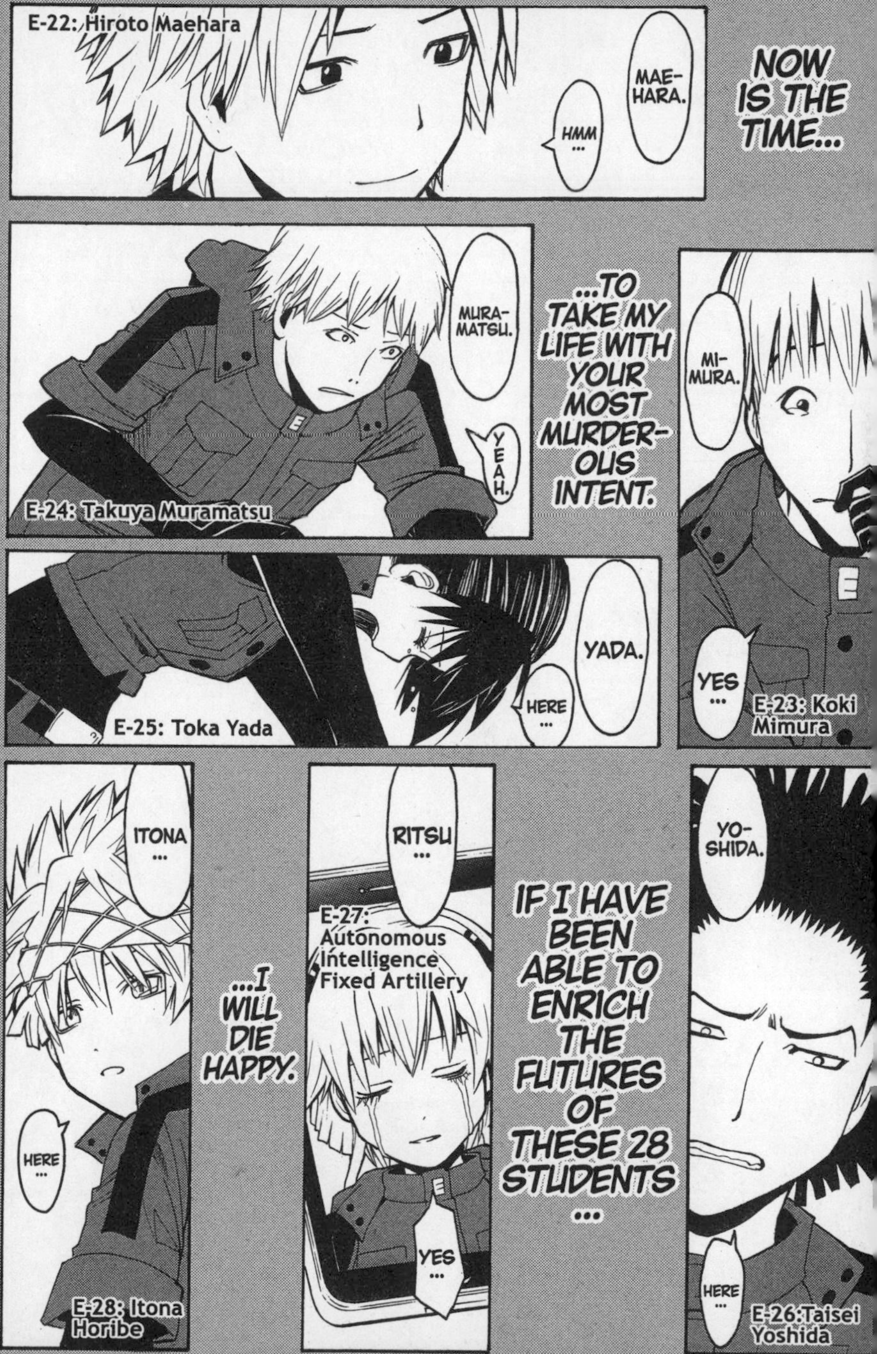
NOW IS THE TIME...
MAE-HARA.
HMM...
E-22: Hiroto Maehara
MI-MURA.
YES...
E-23: Koki Mimura
...TO TAKE MY LIFE WITH YOUR MOST MURDER-OUS INTENT.
MURA-MATSU.
YEAH.
E-24: Takuya Muramatsu
YADA.
HERE...
E-25: Toka Yada
YO-SHIDA.
HERE...
E-26:Taisei Yoshida
IF I HAVE BEEN ABLE TO ENRICH THE FUTURES OF THESE 28 STUDENTS...
RITSU...
E-27: Autonomous Intelligence Fixed Artillery
YES...
...I WILL DIE HAPPY.
ITONA...
HERE...
E-28: Itona Horibe

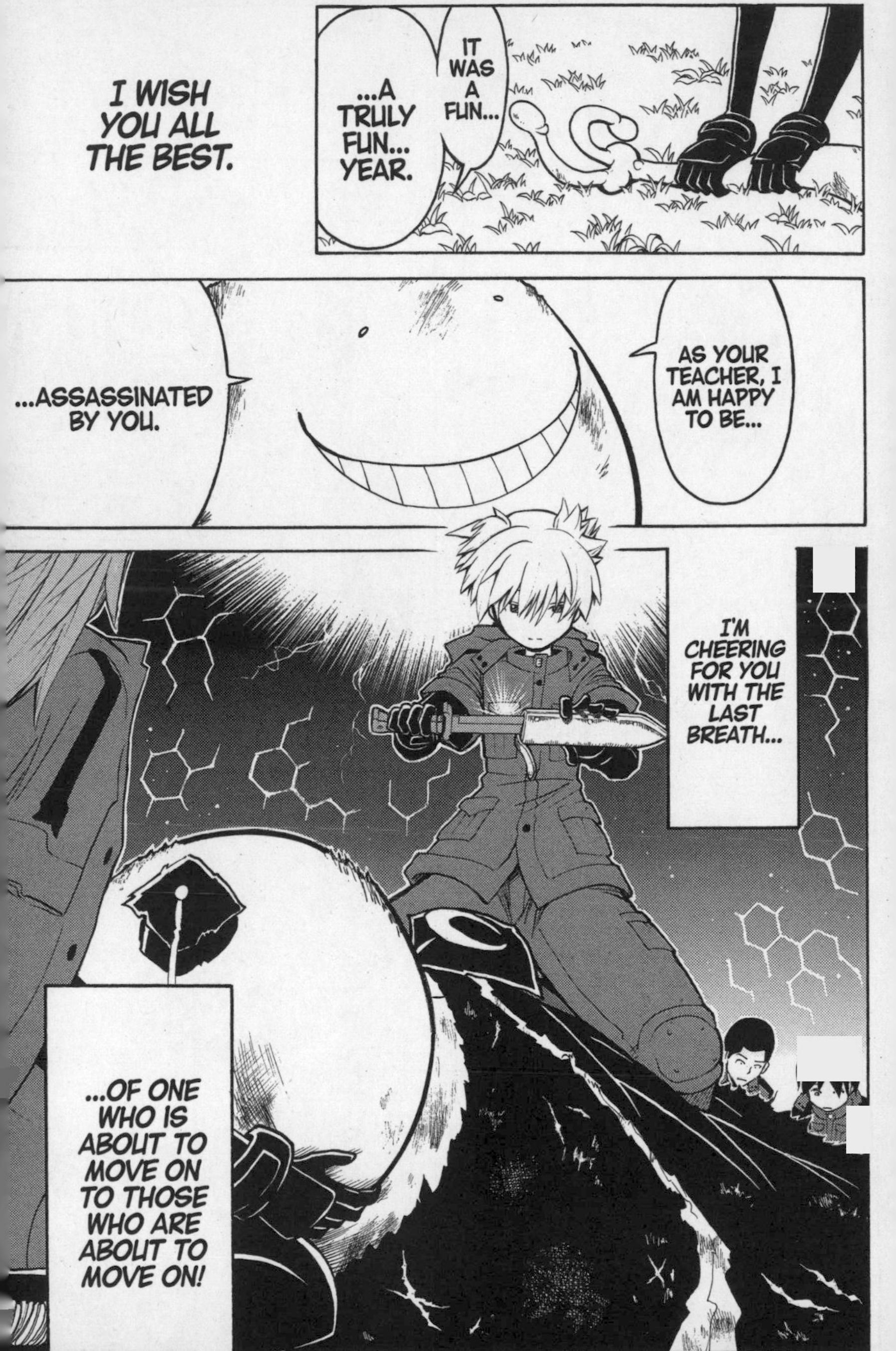
IT WAS A FUN...
...A TRULY FUN... YEAR.
I WISH YOU ALL THE BEST.
AS YOUR TEACHER, I AM HAPPY TO BE...
...ASSASSINATED BY YOU.
I'M CHEERING FOR YOU WITH THE LAST BREATH...
...OF ONE WHO IS ABOUT TO MOVE ON TO THOSE WHO ARE ABOUT TO MOVE ON!

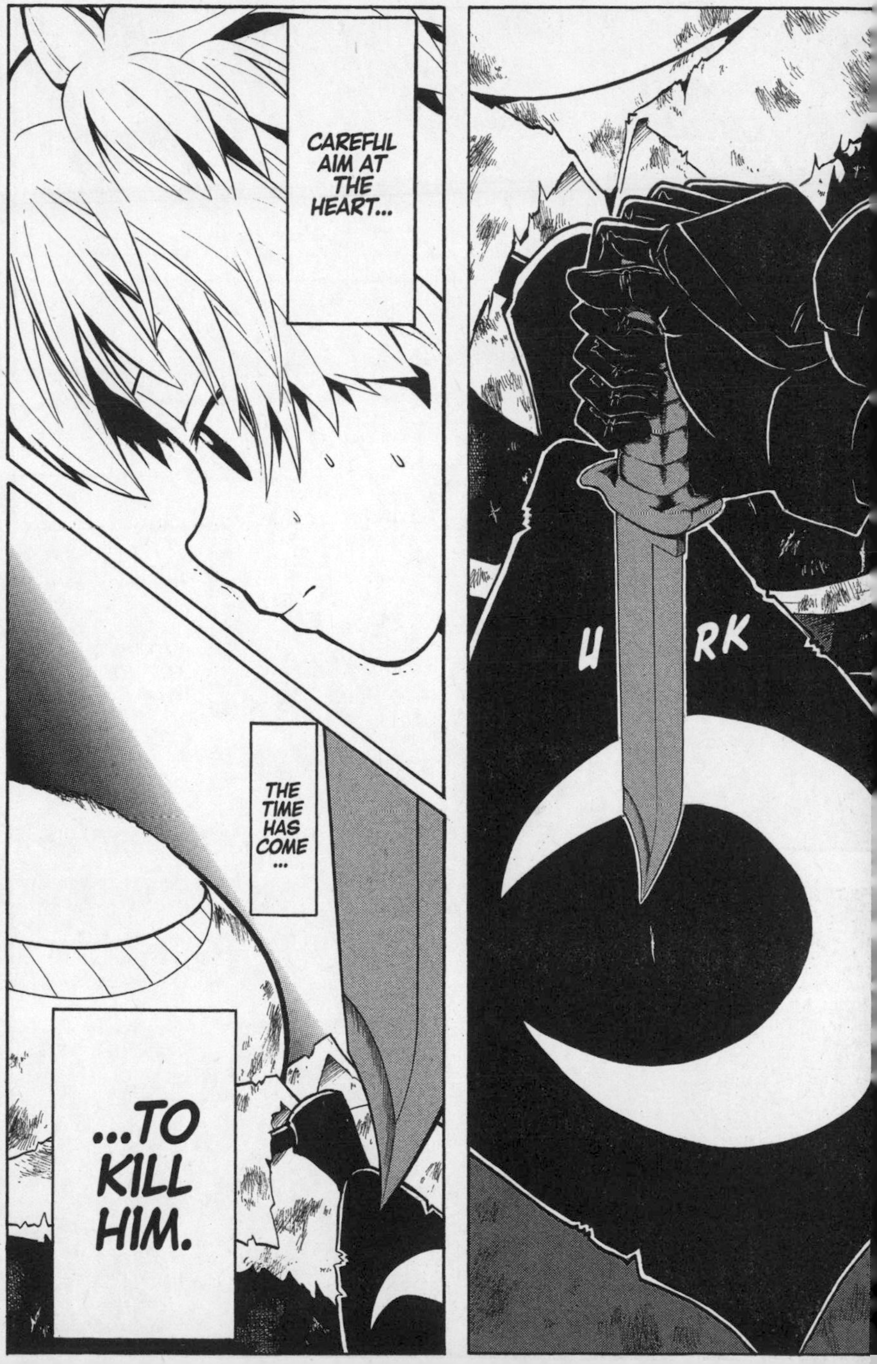
U RK
CAREFUL AIM AT THE HEART...
THE TIME HAS COME ...
...TO KILL HIM.

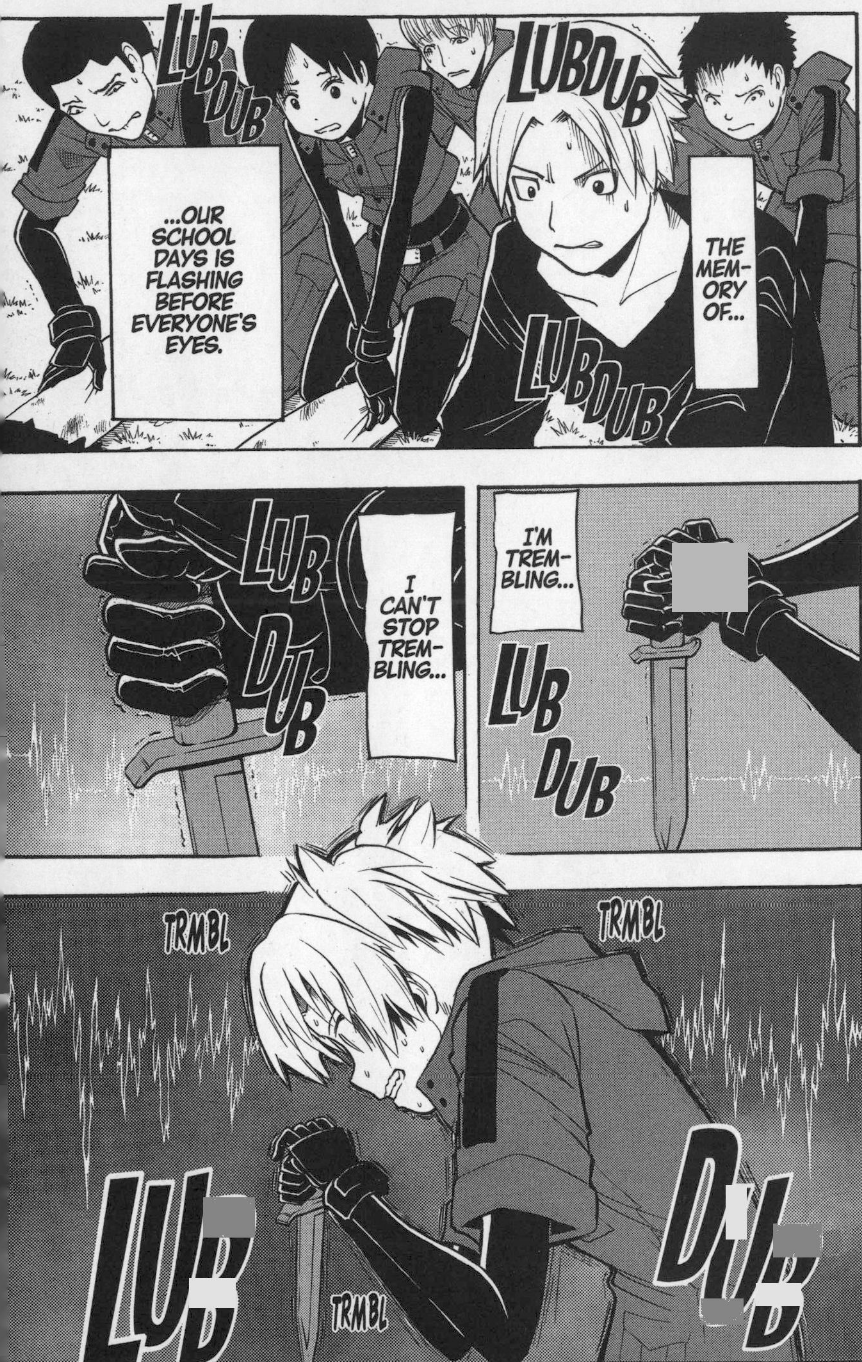
THE MEM-ORY OF...
LUBDUB
LUBDUB
LUBDUB
...OUR SCHOOL DAYS IS FLASHING BEFORE EVERYONE'S EYES.
I'M TREM-BLING...
LUB DUB
I CAN'T STOP TREM-BLING...
LUB DUB
TRMBL
TRMBL
TRMBL

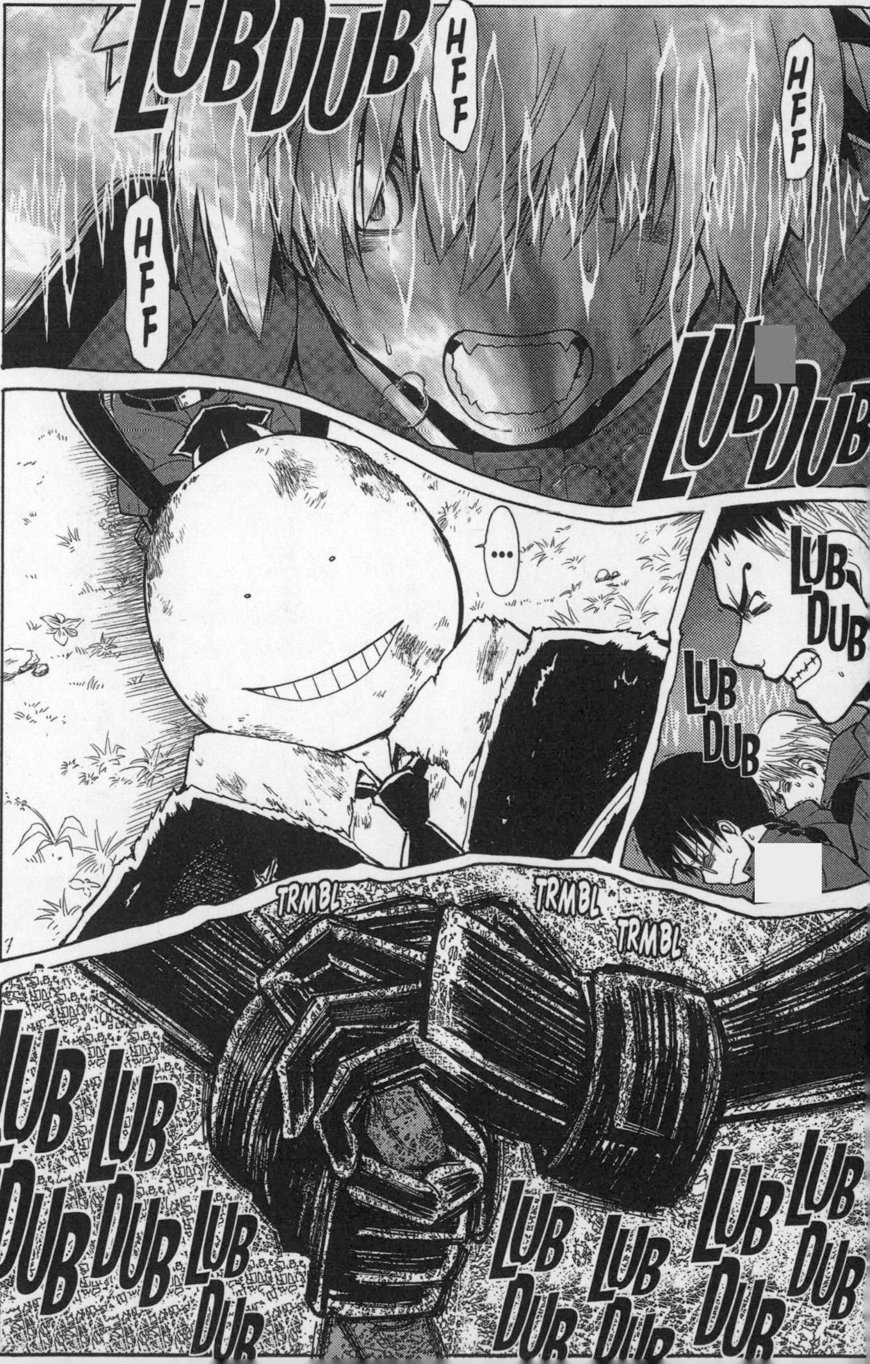
HFF
LUBDUB
HFF
LUBDUB
HFF
LUB-DUB
LUB DUB
...
TRMBL
TRMBL
TRMBL
LUB DUB LUB DUB LUB DUB LUB DUB LUB DUB LUB DUB LUB DUB

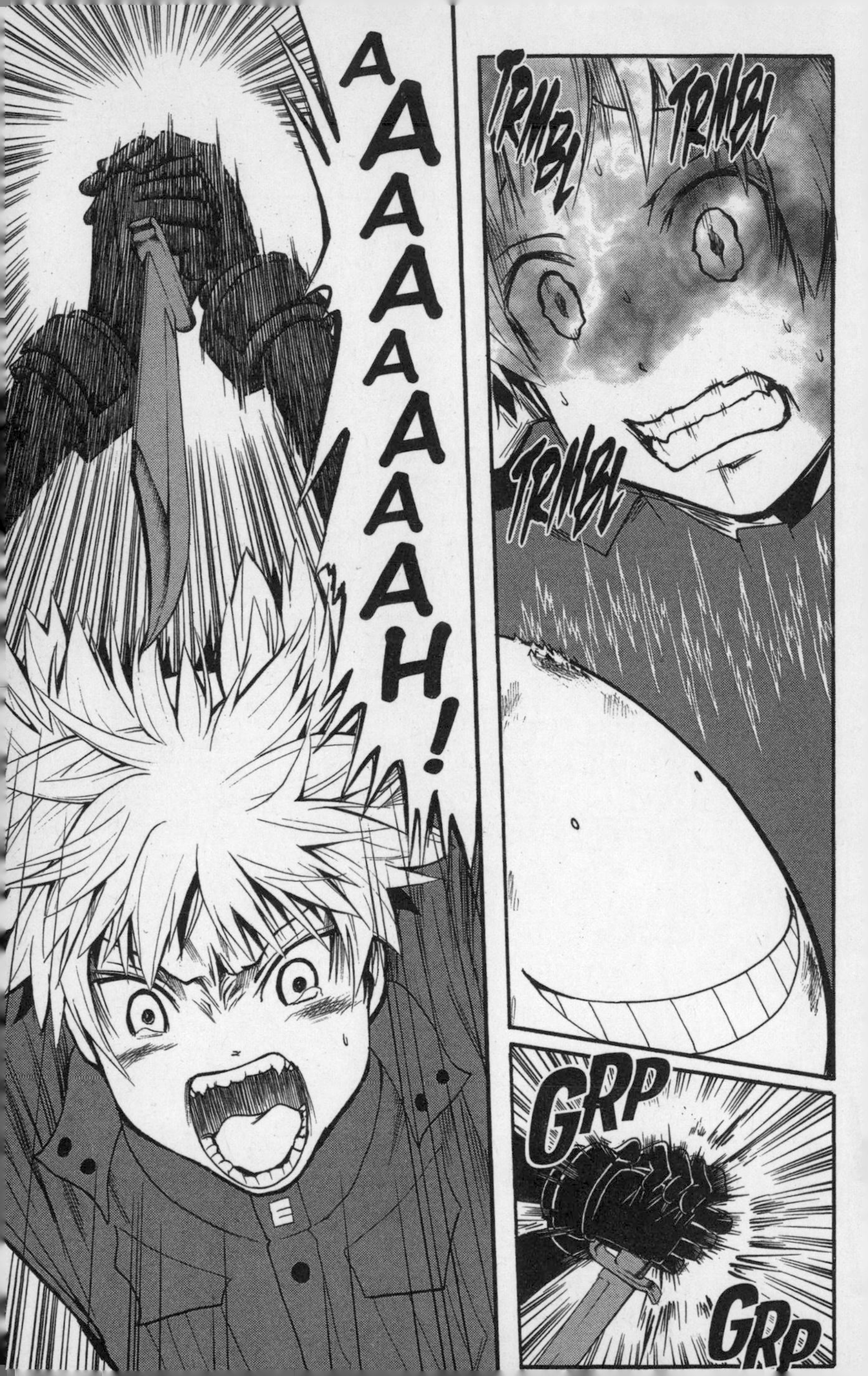
TRMBL
TRMBL
TRMBL
GRP
GRP
AAAAAAAAH!

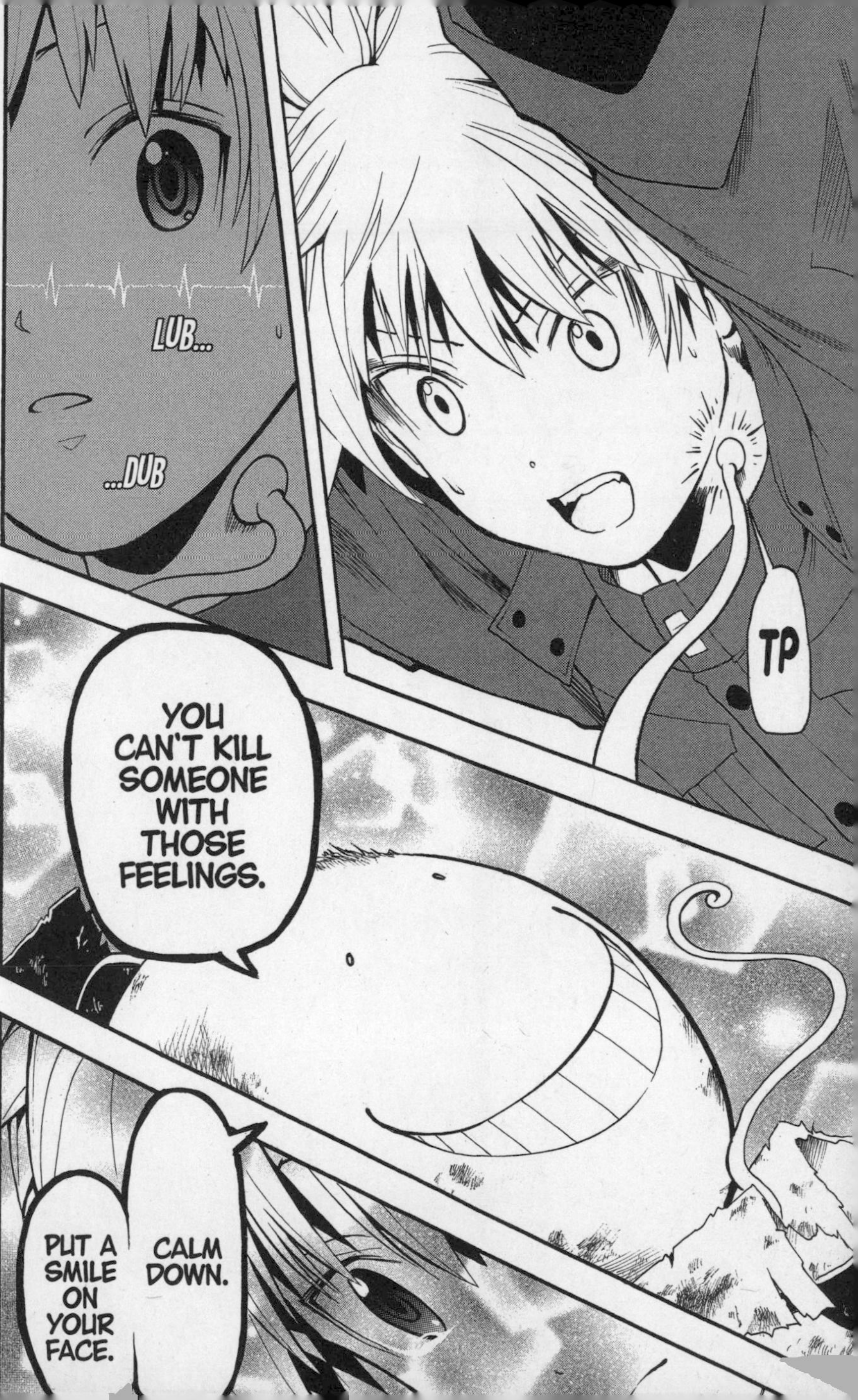
TP
LUB...
...DUB
YOU CAN'T KILL SOMEONE WITH THOSE FEELINGS.
CALM DOWN.
PUT A SMILE ON YOUR FACE.

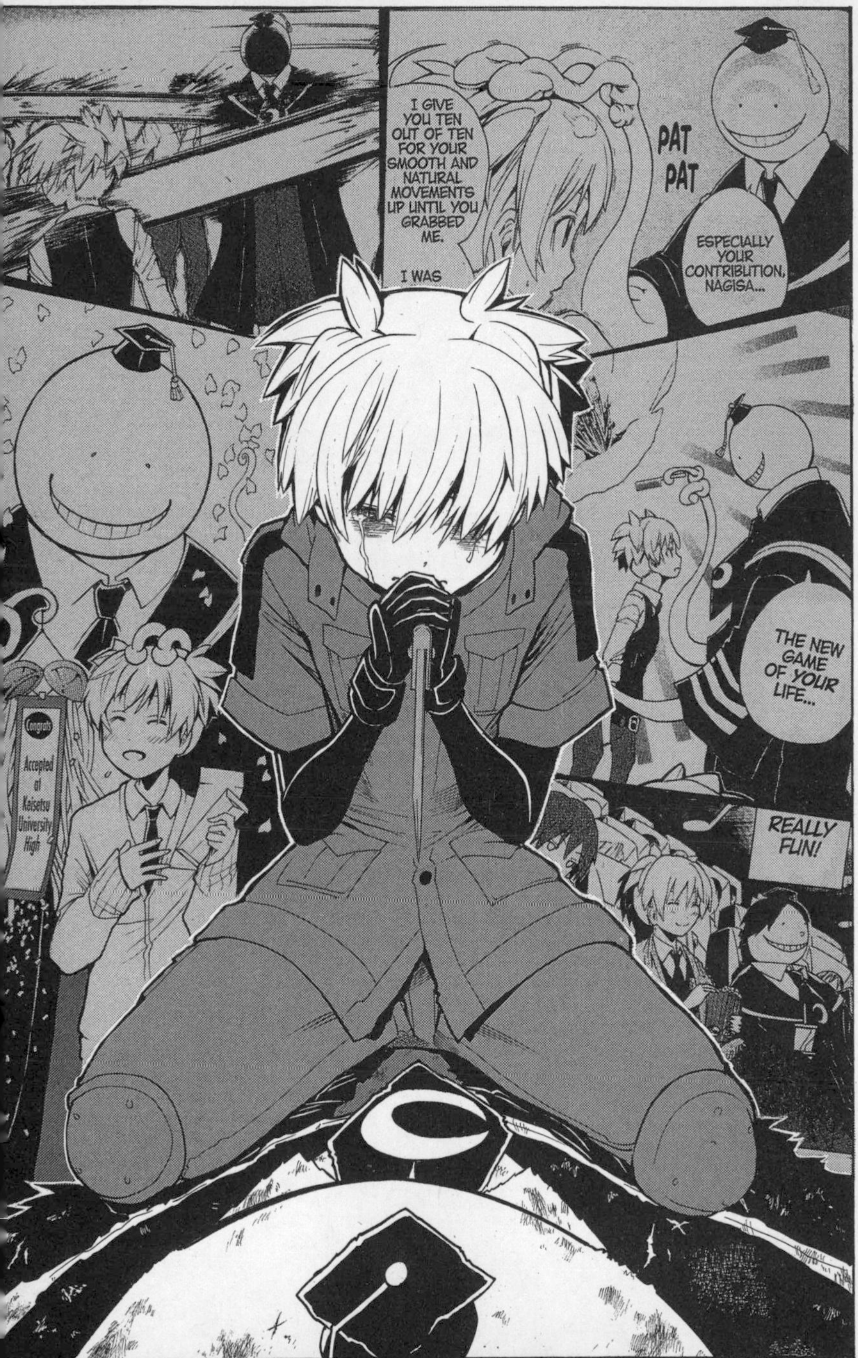
PAT PAT
I GIVE YOU TEN OUT OF TEN FOR YOUR SMOOTH AND NATURAL MOVEMENTS UP UNTIL YOU GRABBED ME.
ESPECIALLY YOUR CONTRIBUTION, NAGISA...
I WAS
THE NEW GAME OF YOUR LIFE...
REALLY FUN!
Congrats
Accepted at Kaisetsu University High

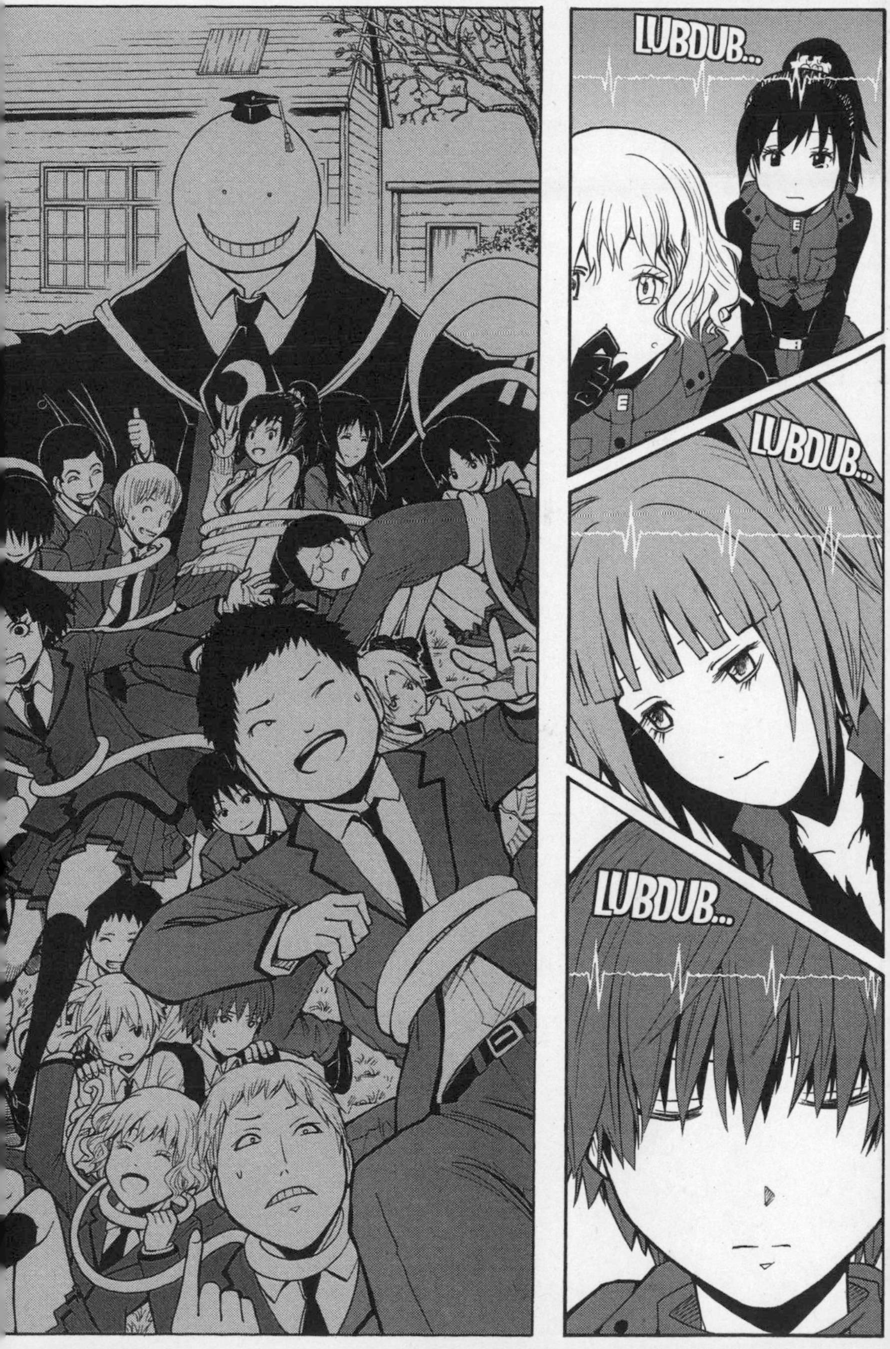
LUBDUB...
LUBDUB...
LUBDUB...

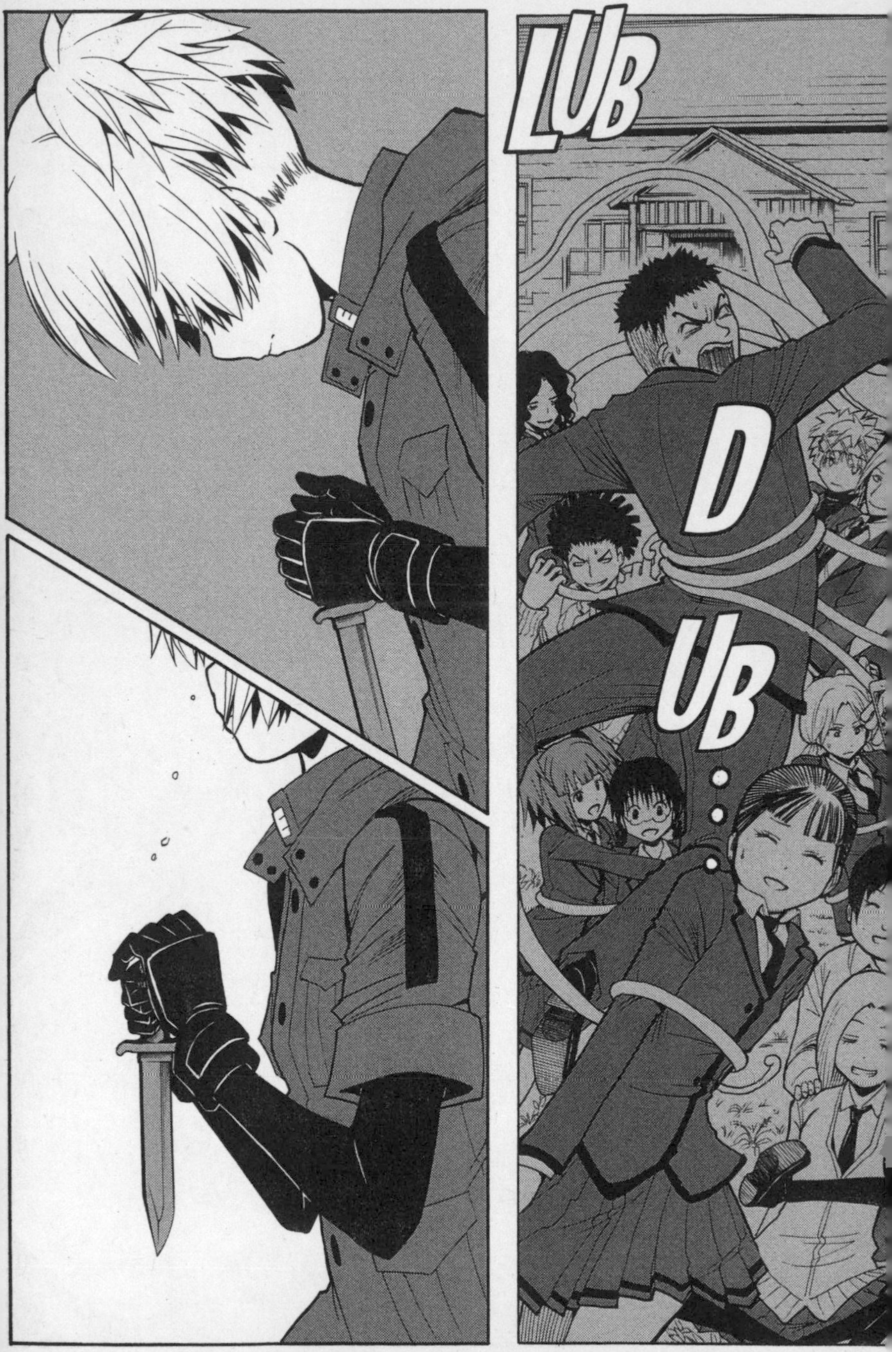
LUB
D
UB

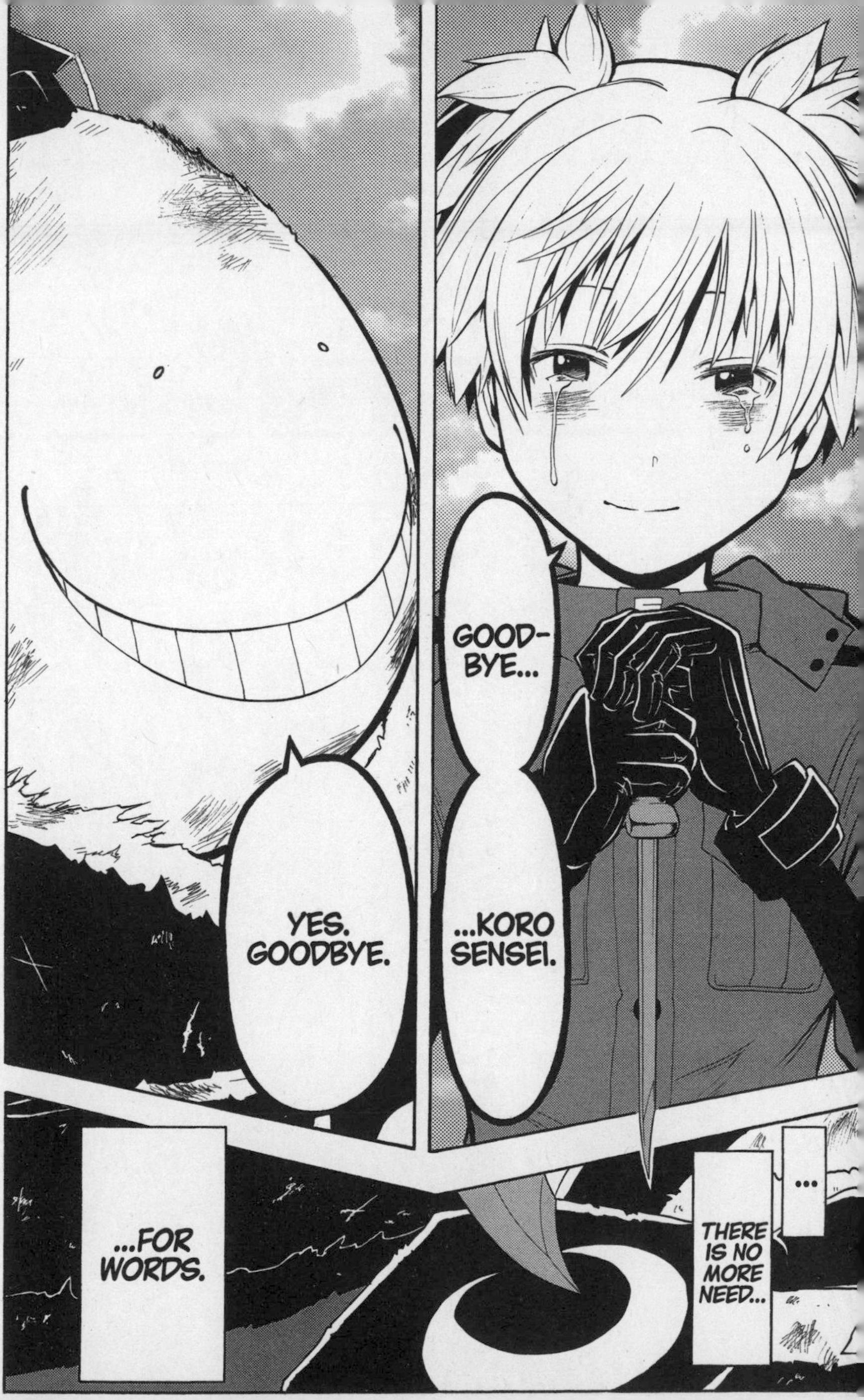
GOOD-BYE...
...KORO SENSEI.
YES. GOODBYE.
...
THERE IS NO MORE NEED...
...FOR WORDS.

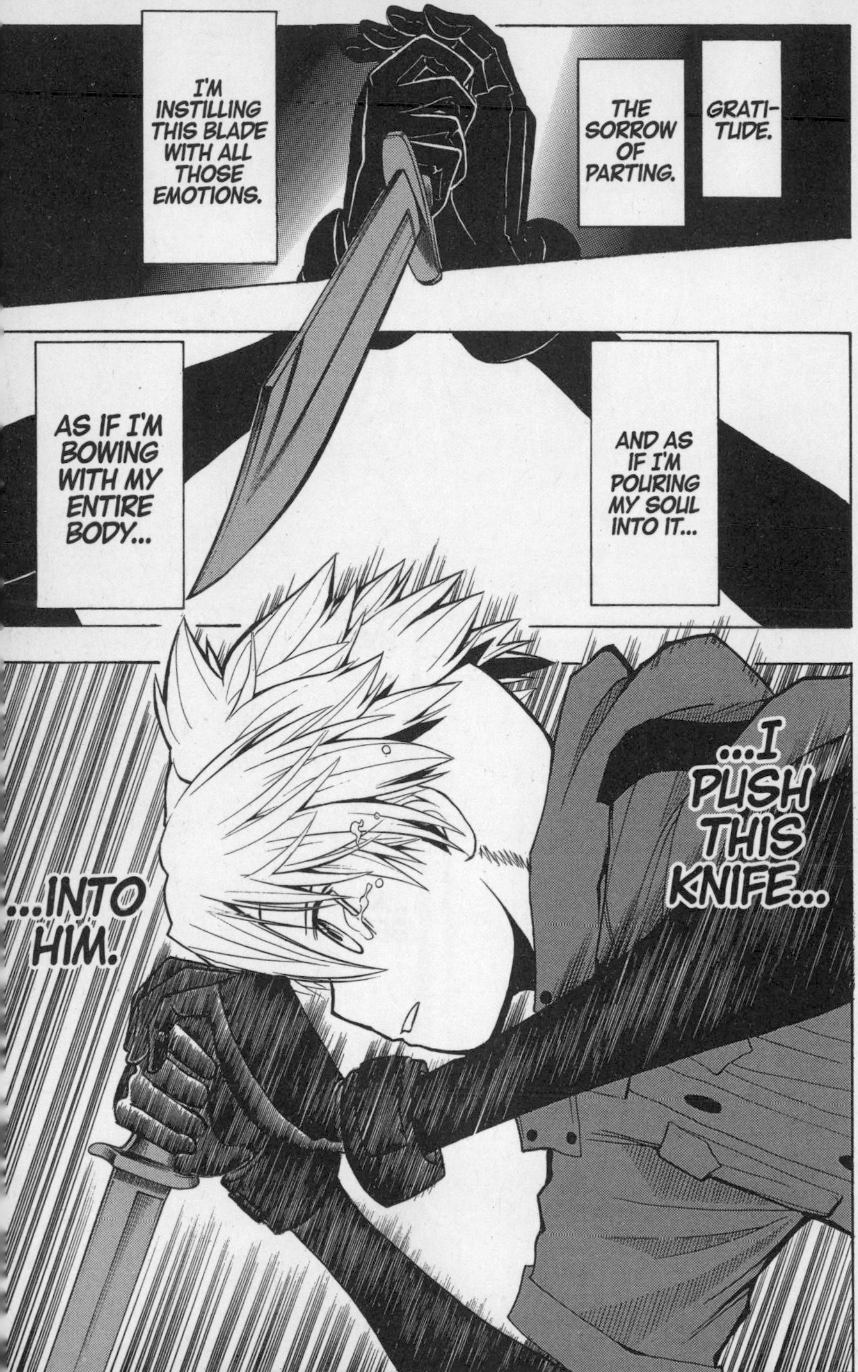
GRATI-
TUDE.
THE SORROW OF PARTING.
I'M INSTILLING THIS BLADE WITH ALL THOSE EMOTIONS.
AND AS IF I'M POURING MY SOUL INTO IT...
AS IF I'M BOWING WITH MY ENTIRE BODY...
...I PUSH THIS KNIFE...
...INTO HIM.

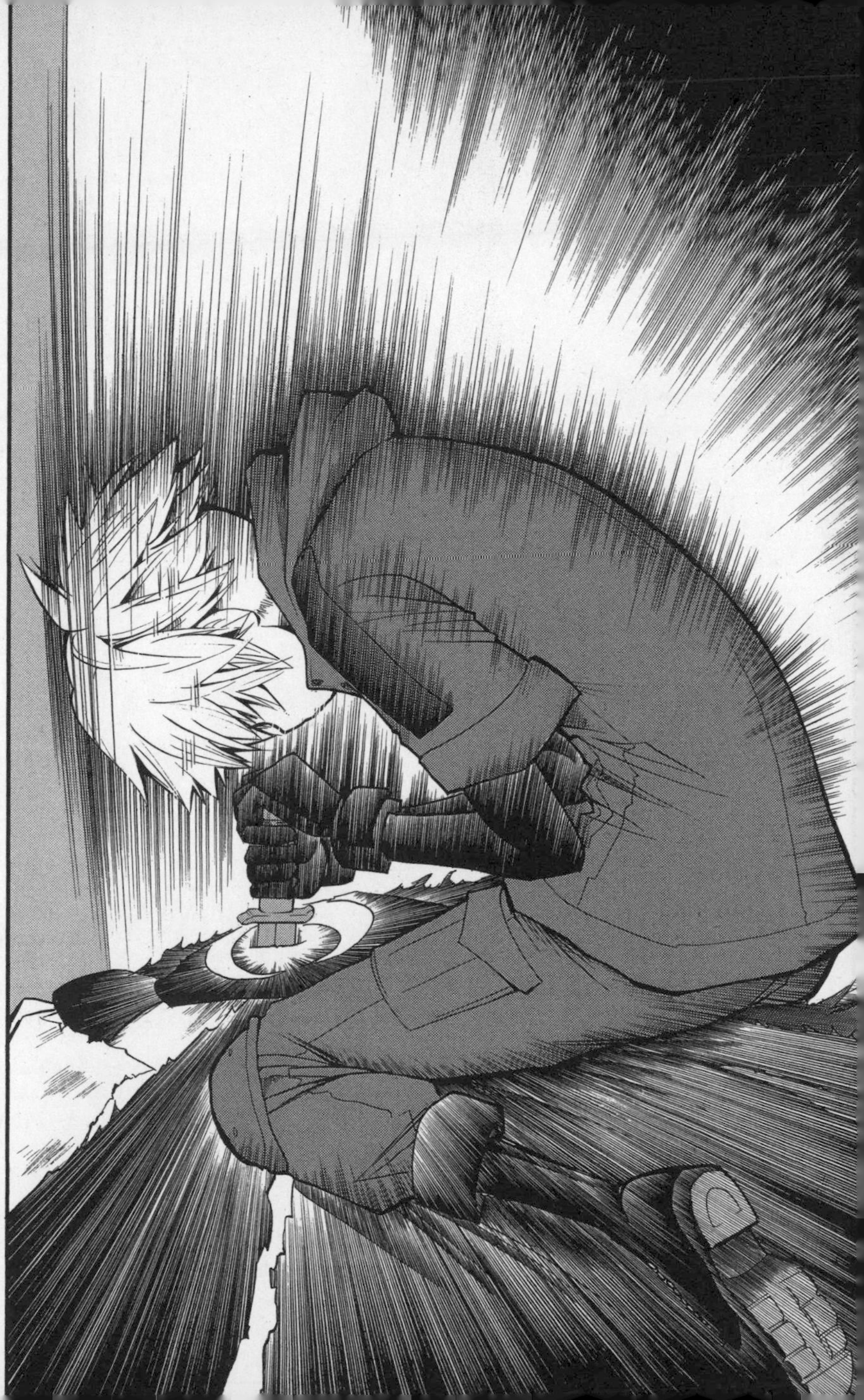

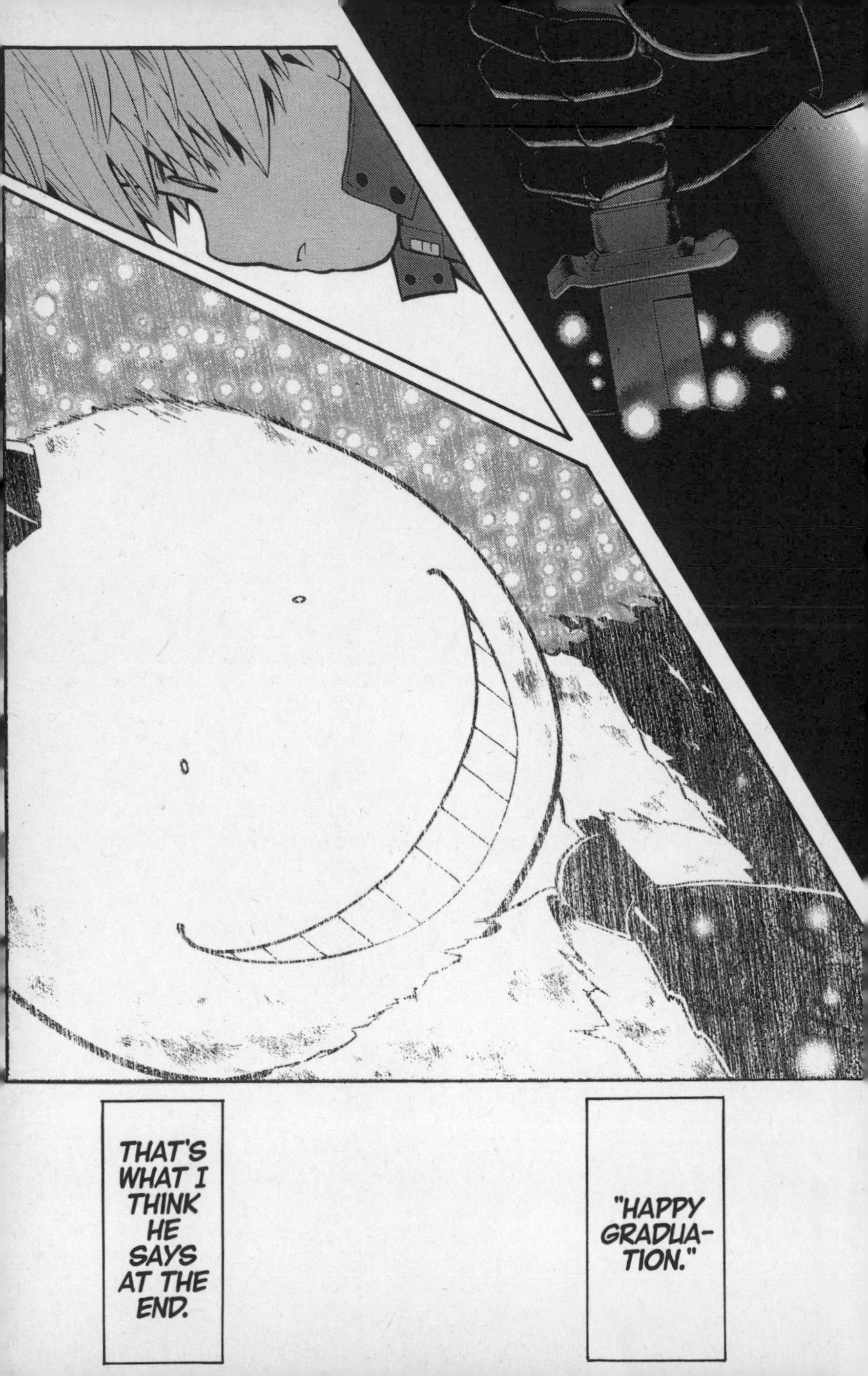
"HAPPY GRADUATION."
THAT'S WHAT I THINK HE SAYS AT THE END.

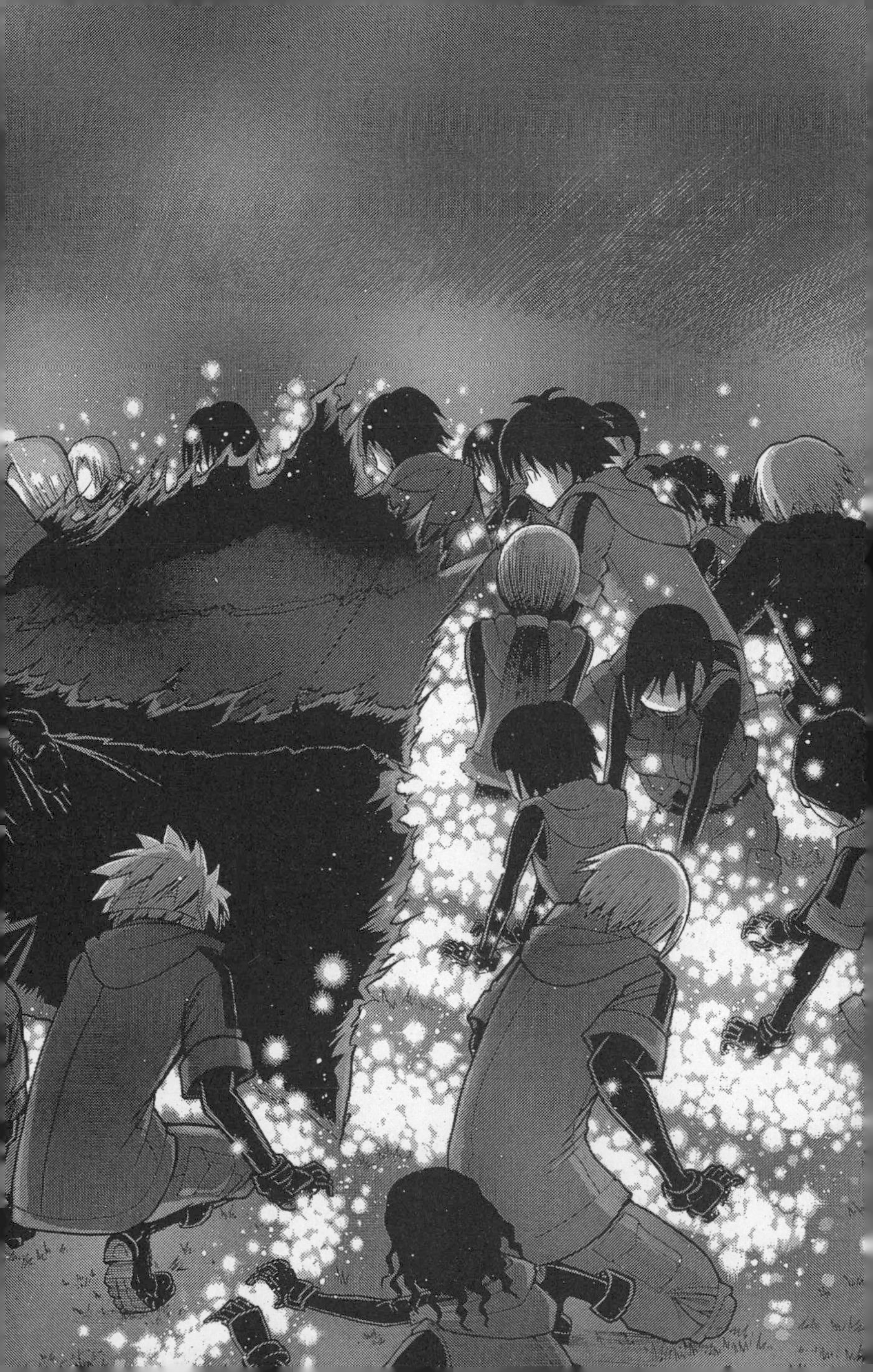

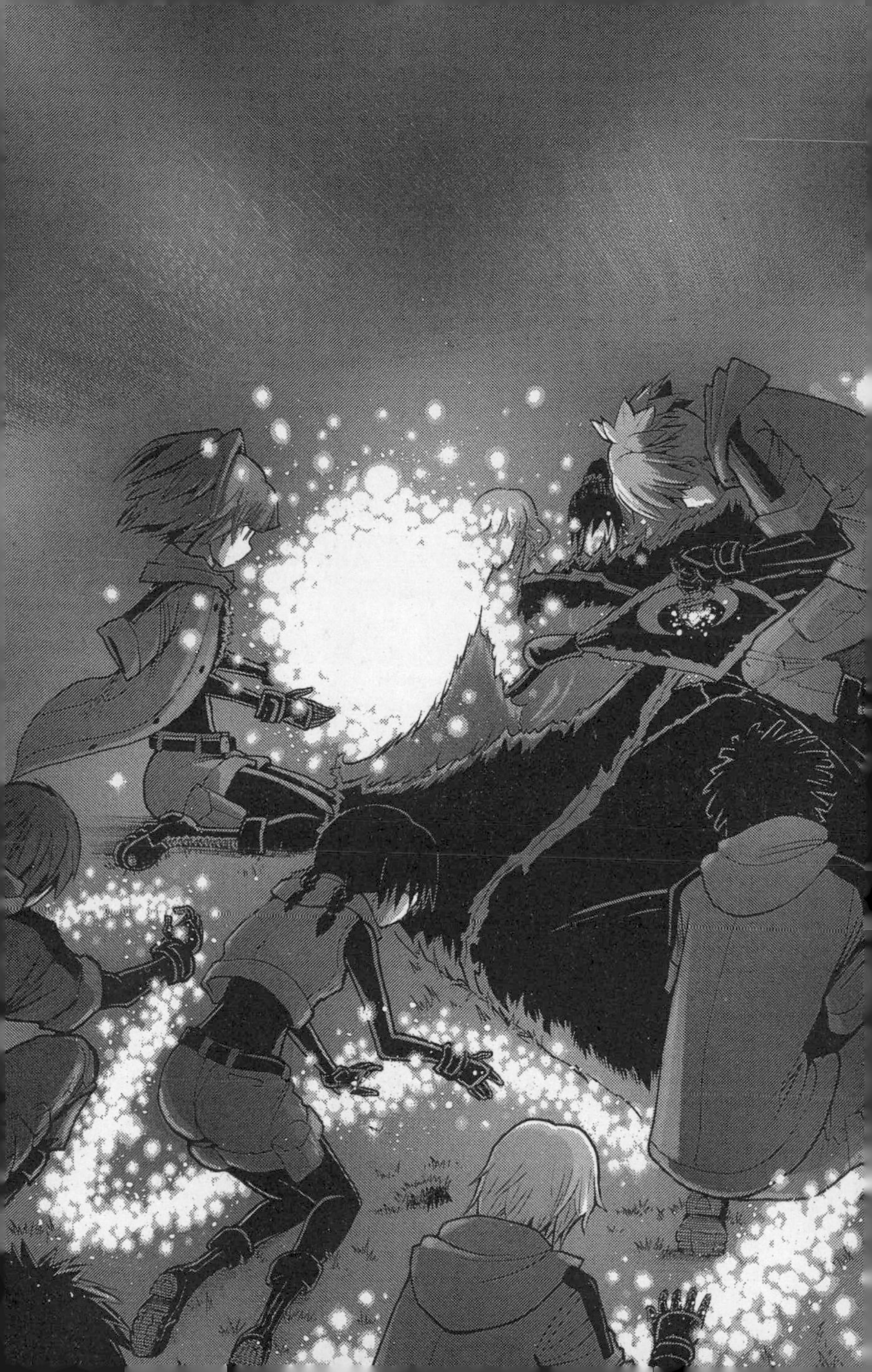

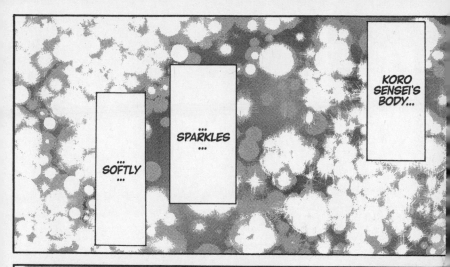

KORO SENSEI'S BODY...

SPARKLES ...

SOFTLY ...

...AND BURSTS INTO PARTICLES OF LIGHT.

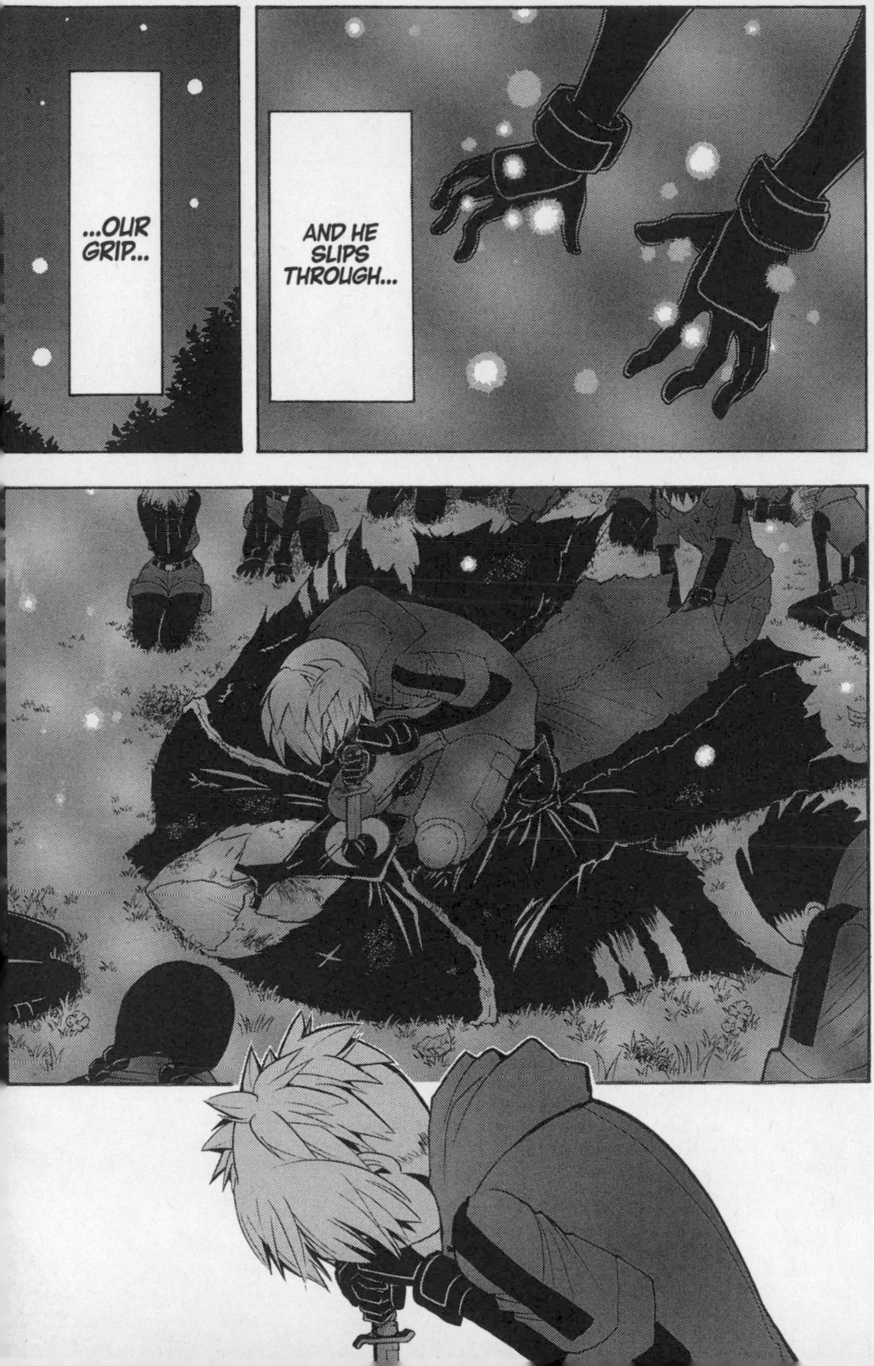
AND HE SLIPS THROUGH...
...OUR GRIP...

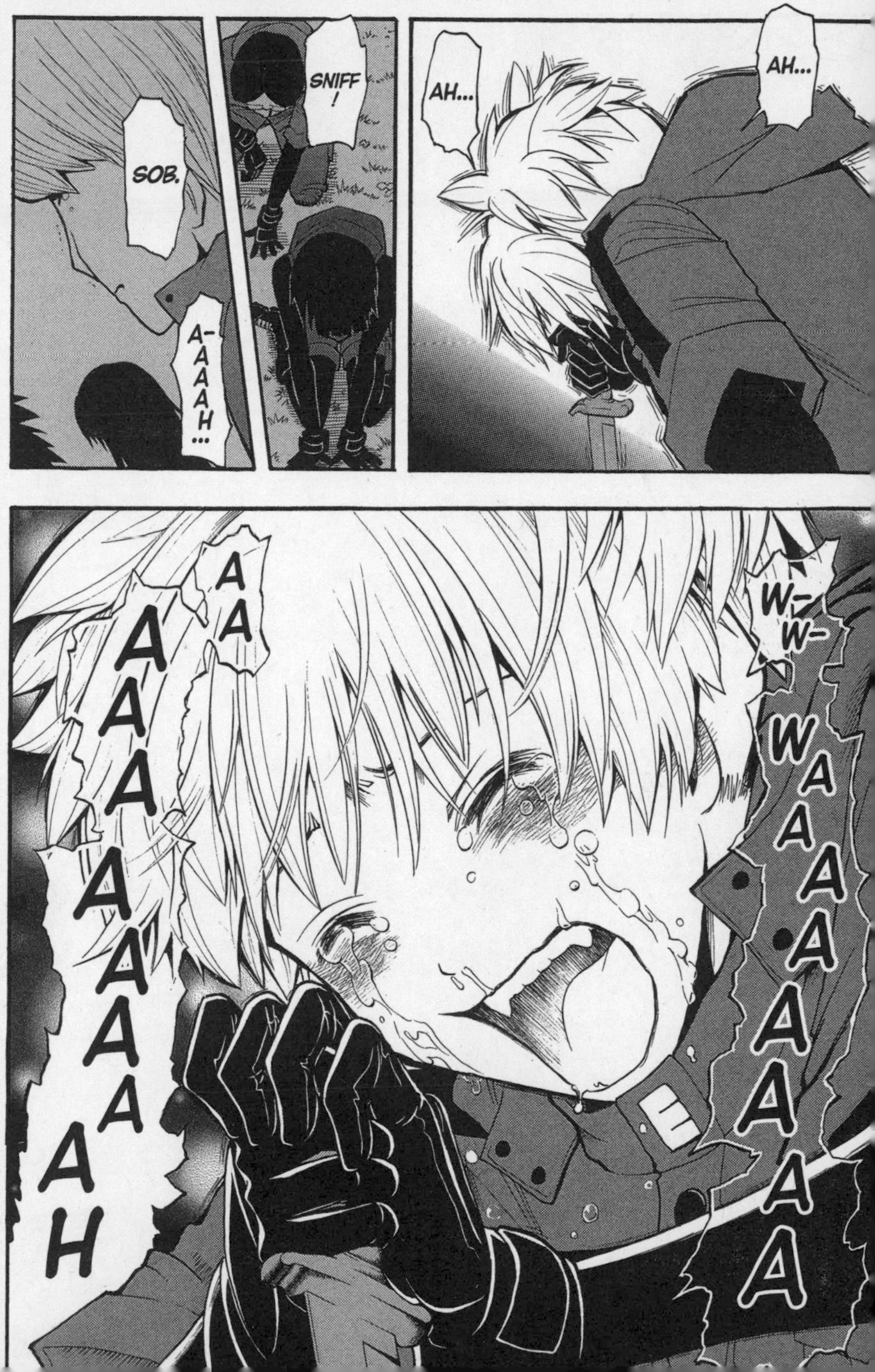
AH...
AH...
SNIFF!
SOB.
A-AAAAH...
W-W-WAAAAAAAAAAA
AA
AAAAAAAAAH

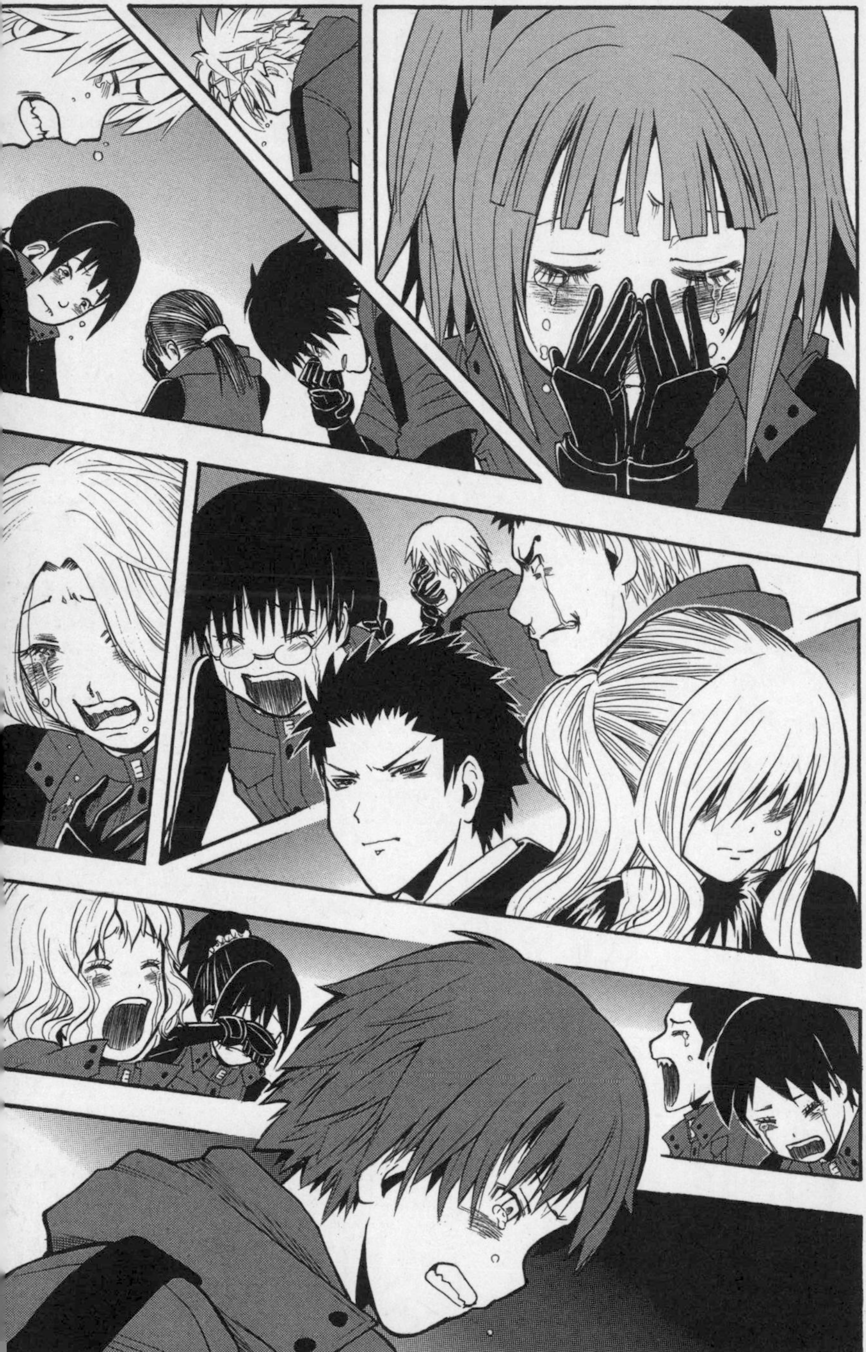

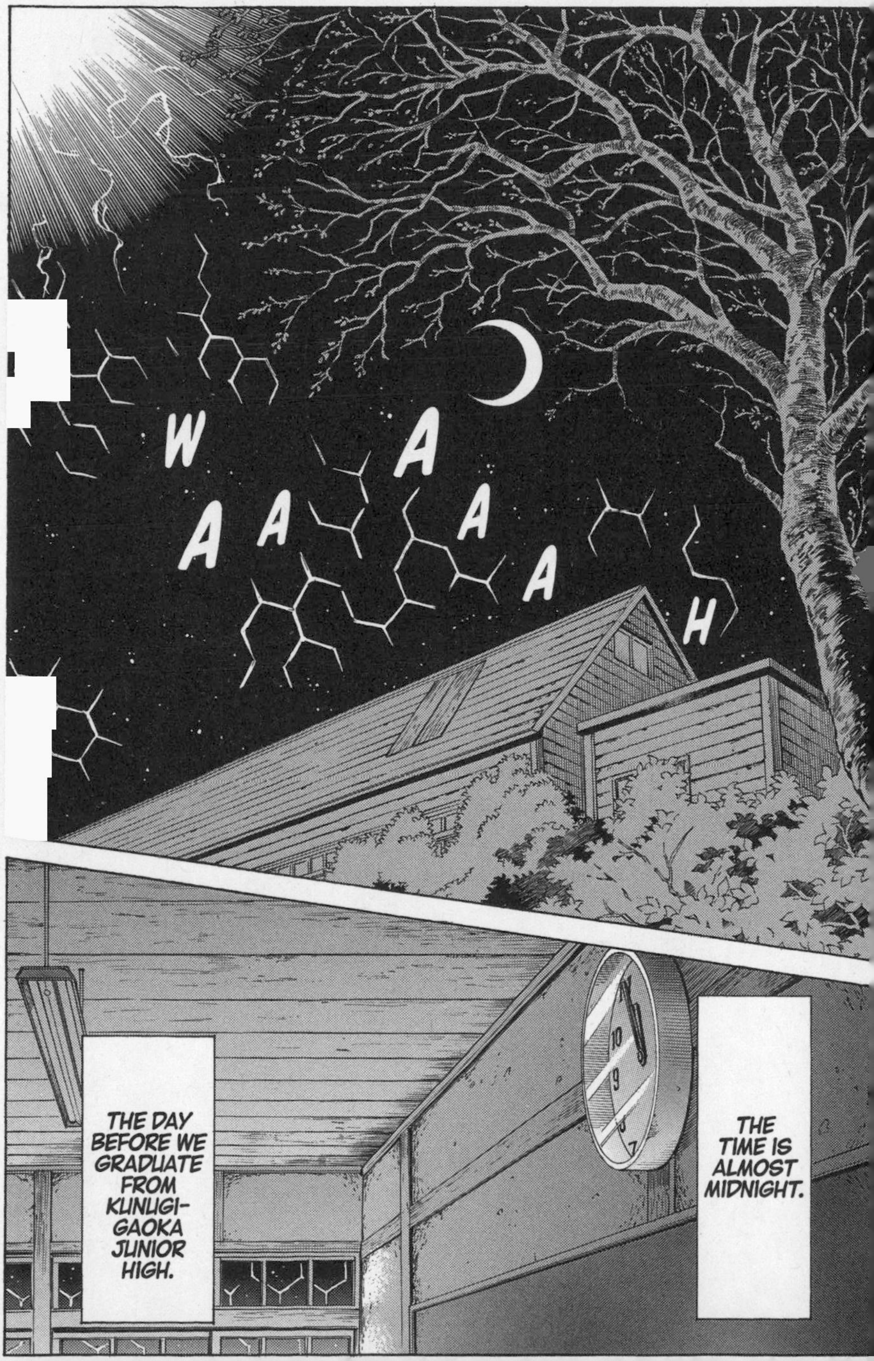
WAAAAAH
THE TIME IS ALMOST MIDNIGHT.
THE DAY BEFORE WE GRADUATE FROM KUNUGIGAOKA JUNIOR HIGH.

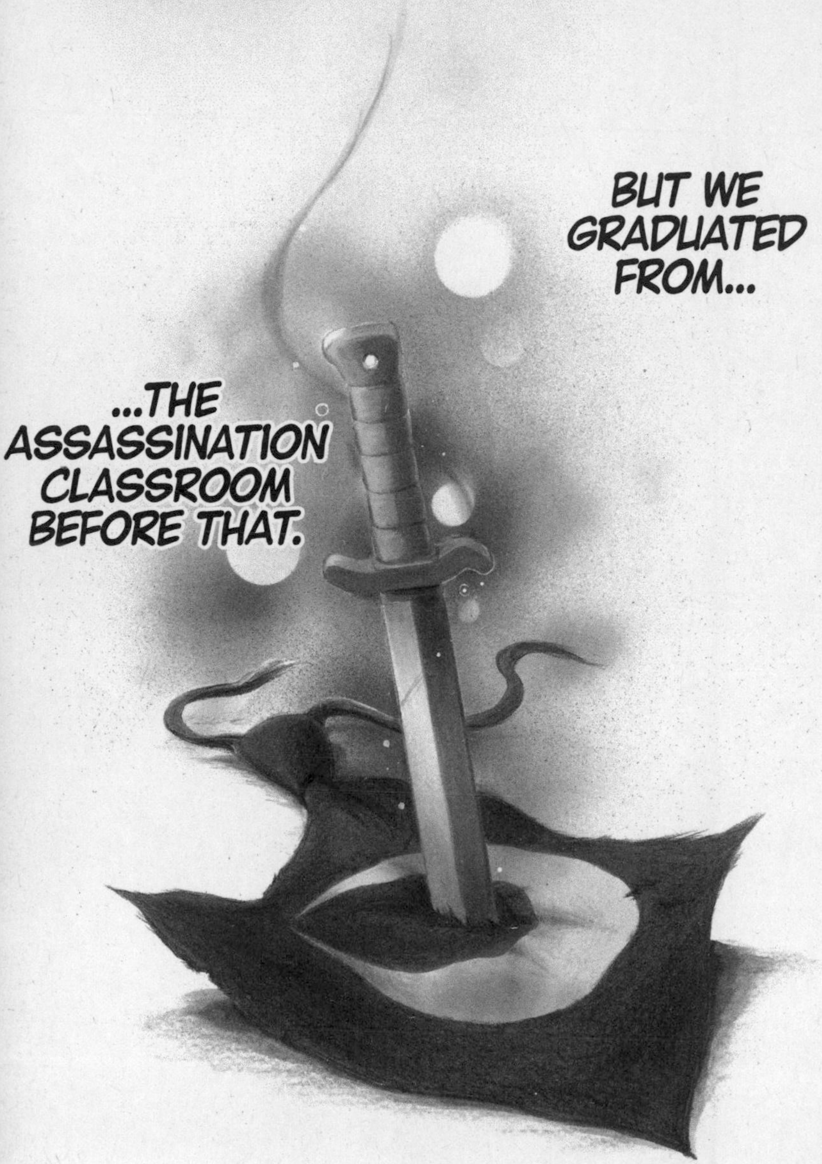
BUT WE GRADUATED FROM...
...THE ASSASSINATION CLASSROOM BEFORE THAT.

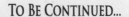

TO BE CONTINUED...

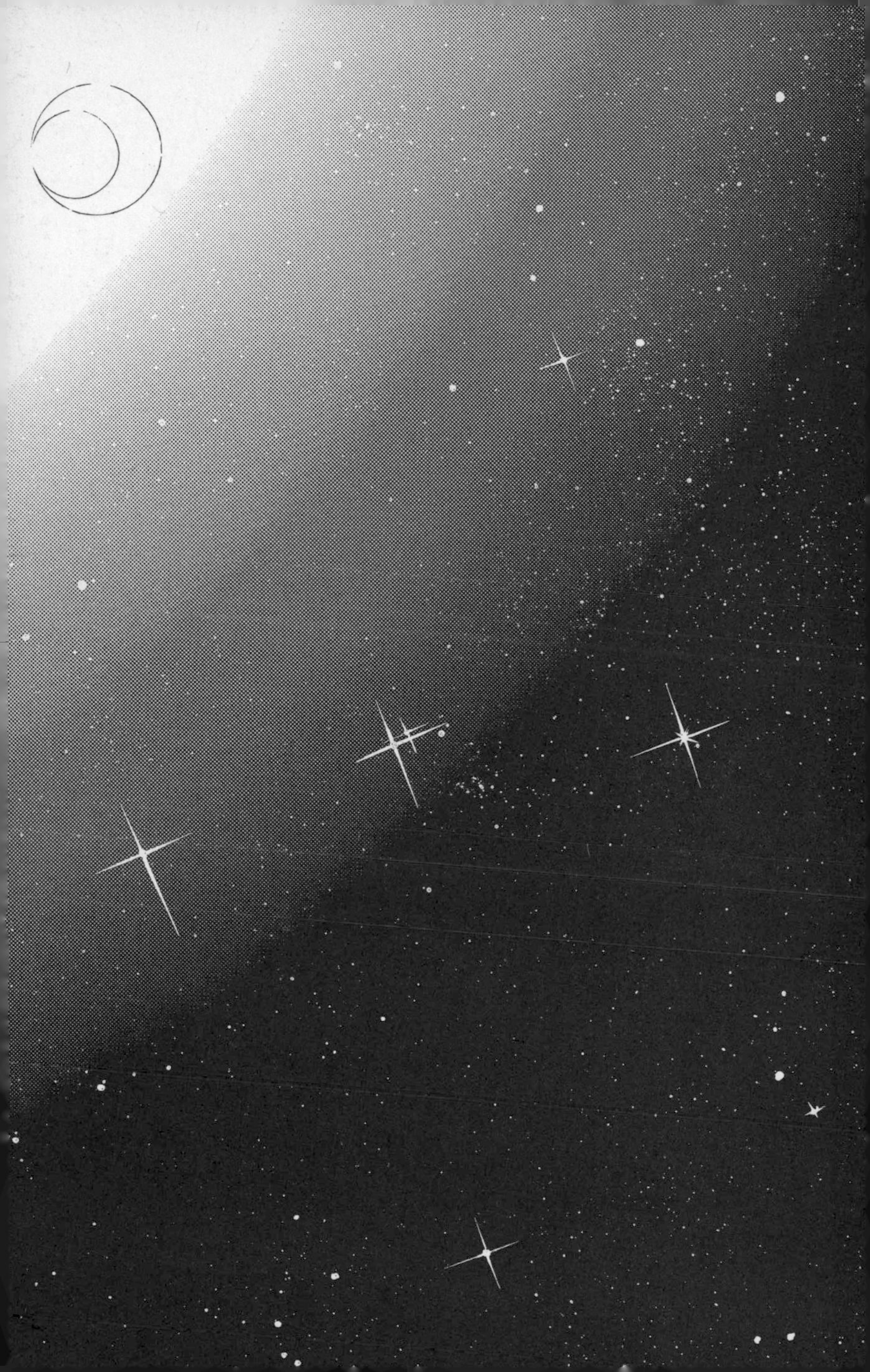

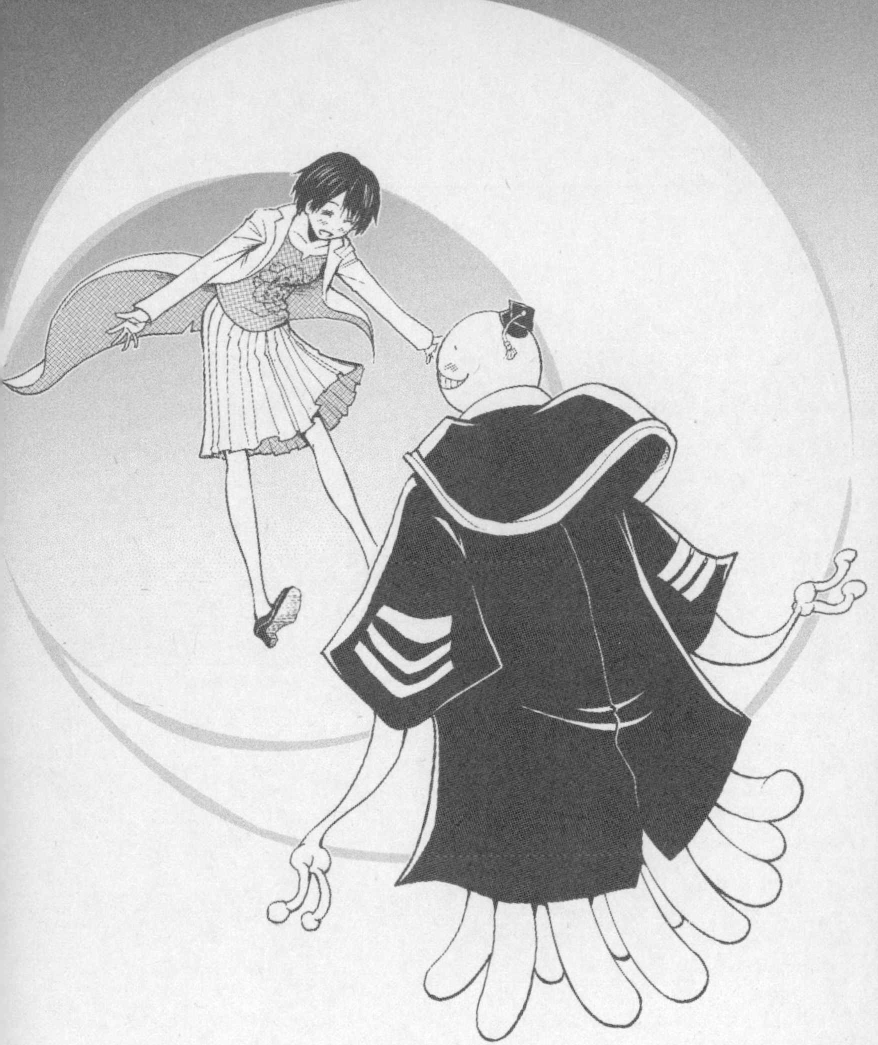

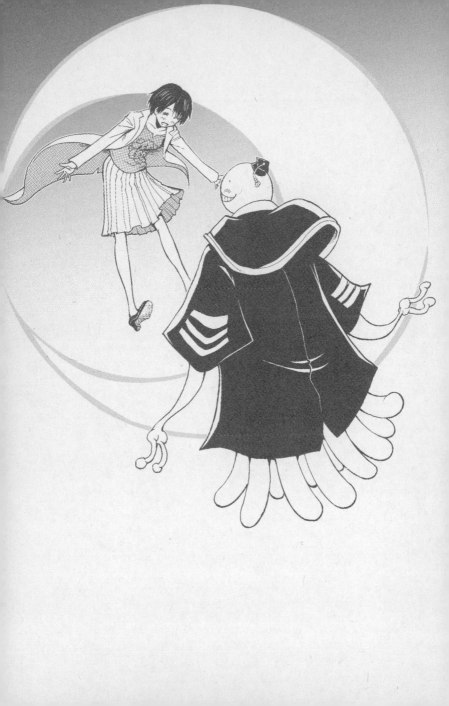

Ever since I started this series, I've had a clear image of the last scene of this volume.

I always believed that the success or failure of the story of Assassination Classroom would depend upon how well I did chapter 177.

Volume 20 and the following volume 21 bring the series to an end.

I apologize for having to end on this chapter, due to page limitations, just before the conclusion of the series.

But the final volume will be filled with all kinds of stories to make up for that!

I hope you will support the series all the way through to the very end!!

—Yusei Matsui

Yusei Matsui was born on the last day of January in Saitama Prefecture, Japan. He has been drawing manga since elementary school. Some of his favorite manga series are *Bobobo-bo Bo-bobo*, *JoJo's Bizarre Adventure* and *Ultimate Muscle*. Matsui learned his trade working as an assistant to manga artist Yoshio Sawai, creator of *Bobobo-bo Bo-bobo*. In 2005, Matsui debuted his original manga *Neuro: Supernatural Detective* in *Weekly Shonen Jump*. In 2007, *Neuro* was adapted into an anime. In 2012, *Assassination Classroom* began serialization in *Weekly Shonen Jump*.

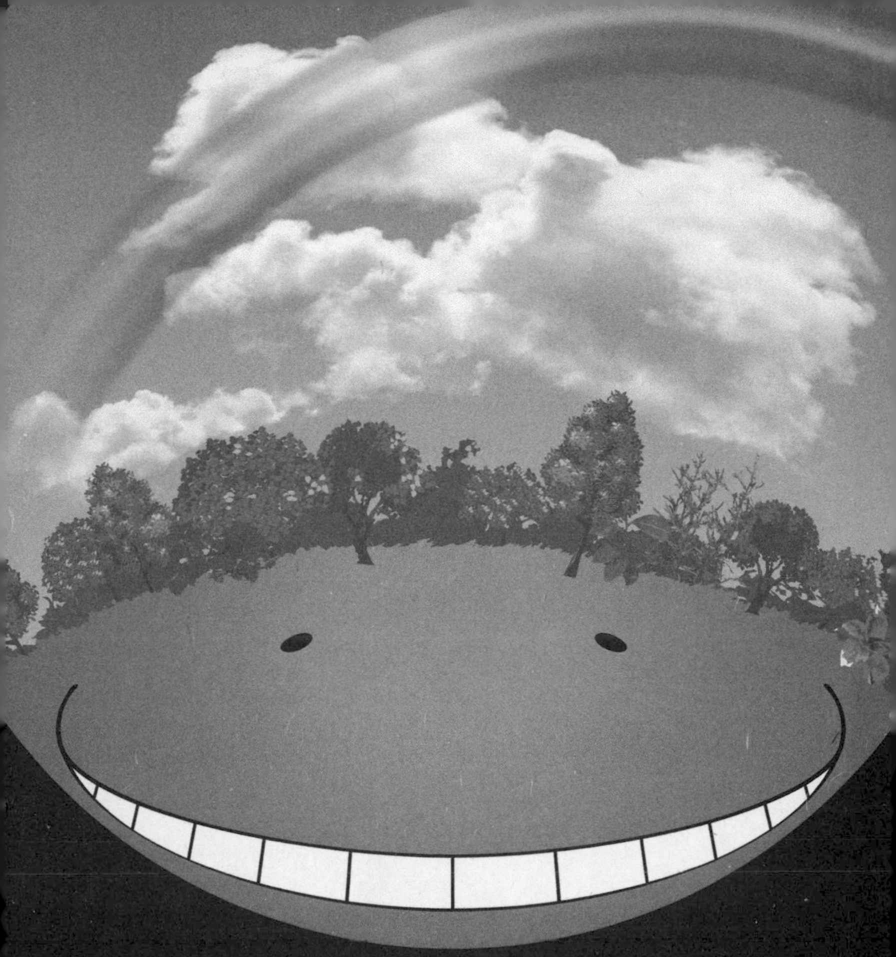

Koro Sensei has become a mountain.
Flowers bloom, thick stands of trees form, fruits and berries grow.
Even when the weather is cold, we feel warm when we're all together.
That is Octopus Mountain.

ASSASSINATION CLASSROOM

YUSEI MATSUI

20

TIME FOR GRADUATION

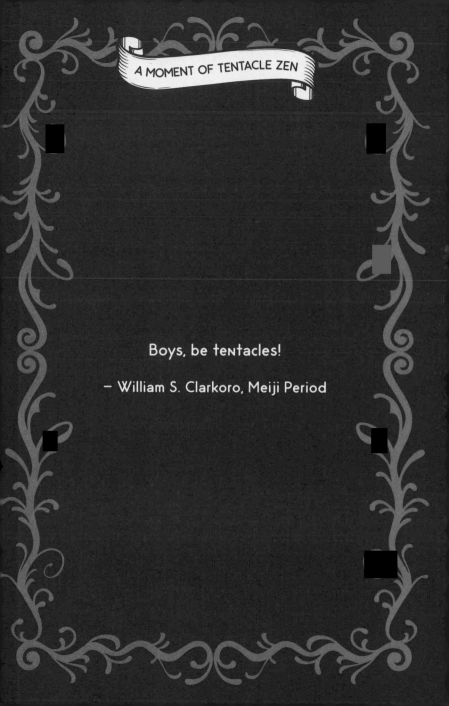

A MOMENT OF TENTACLE ZEN

Boys, be tentacles!

— William S. Clarkoro, Meiji Period

ASSASSINATION CLASSROOM

Volume 20
SHONEN JUMP ADVANCED Manga Edition

Story and Art by YUSEI MATSUI

Translation/Tetsuichiro Miyaki
English Adaptation/Bryant Turnage
Touch-up Art & Lettering/Stephen Dutro
Cover & Interior Design/Sam Elzway
Editor/Annette Roman

Printed in the U.S.A.

Published by VIZ Media, LLC
P.O. Box 77010
San Francisco, CA 94107

10 9 8 7 6 5 4 3 2 1
First printing, February 2018

www.viz.com

www.shonenjump.com

RATED T+ FOR OLDER TEEN

PARENTAL ADVISORY
ASSASSINATION CLASSROOM is rated T+ for Older Teen and is recommended for ages 16 and up. It contains realistic violence and suggestive situations.

ratings.viz.com

Syllabus for
Assassination Classroom, Vol. 21

In the aftermath of tragedy, the students of 3–E nevertheless march proudly in their graduation ceremony. Will their futures still unfold as planned? And what will they do with their reward money...? Then, enjoy a long side story revealing what Koro Sensei was *really* up to over winter break! Can Koro Sensei truly make a friend and ally out of *anyone*...?! Plus, a bonus short story with all-new characters, set in a dystopian future.

Available April 2018!